The Ultimate Solut

Microsoft Exchange Server 5.5 On Site

Just like a real roadmap, these seven maps will help you solve problems using *Microsoft Exchange Server 5.5 On Site* as you work through important tasks on Exchange Server. Each map corresponds to a major task covered in the book, from planning and installing your Exchange Server system to publishing information and integrating Exchange Server with the Internet.

The major task is divided into three or four smaller tasks that you should finish along the way to task completion. Each smaller task is further broken down into more detailed steps. This shows you at a glance exactly what steps are required to complete each major task. To learn how to complete a step, simply turn to the page numbers indicated. Using these roadmaps, you will get where you want to go with Exchange Server quickly and easily—saving time, energy, and money!

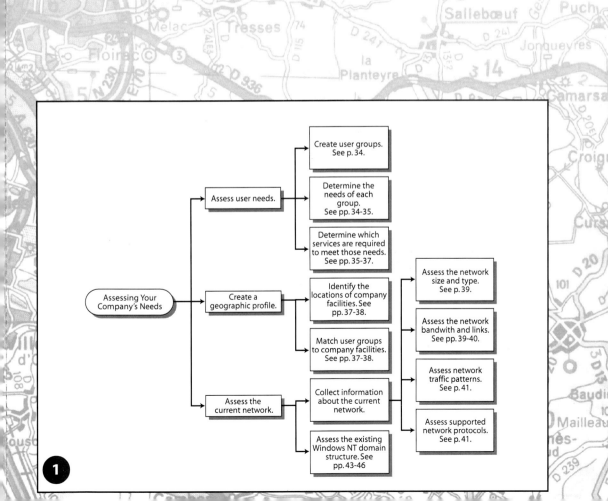

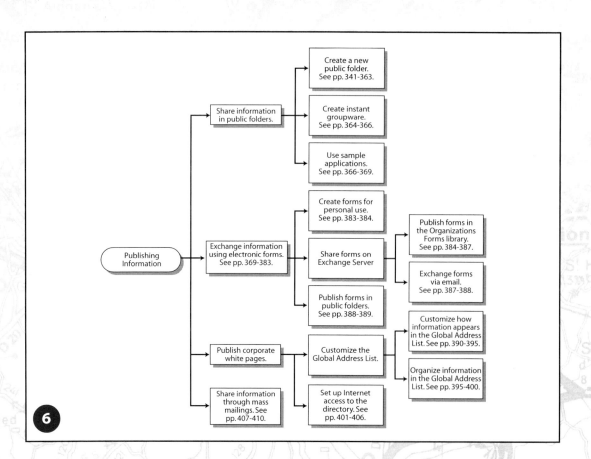

Publishing Information

Share information in public folders.
- Create a new public folder. See pp. 341-363.
- Create instant groupware. See pp. 364-366.
- Use sample applications. See pp. 366-369.

Exchange information using electronic forms. See pp. 369-383.
- Create forms for personal use. See pp. 383-384.
- Share forms on Exchange Server.
  - Publish forms in the Organizations Forms library. See pp. 384-387.
  - Exchange forms via email. See pp. 387-388.
- Publish forms in public folders. See pp. 388-389.

Publish corporate white pages.
- Customize the Global Address List.
  - Customize how information appears in the Global Address List. See pp. 390-395.
  - Organize information in the Global Address List. See pp. 395-400.

Share information through mass mailings. See pp. 407-410.
- Set up Internet access to the directory. See pp. 401-406.

6

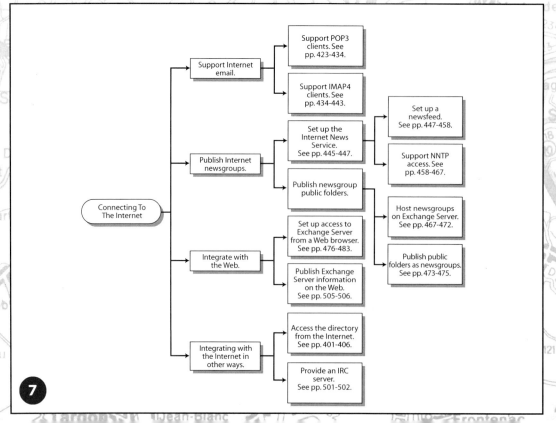

Connecting To The Internet

Support Internet email.
- Support POP3 clients. See pp. 423-434.
- Support IMAP4 clients. See pp. 434-443.

Publish Internet newsgroups.
- Set up the Internet News Service. See pp. 445-447.
  - Set up a newsfeed. See pp. 447-458.
  - Support NNTP access. See pp. 458-467.
- Publish newsgroup public folders.
  - Host newsgroups on Exchange Server. See pp. 467-472.
  - Publish public folders as newsgroups. See pp. 473-475.

Integrate with the Web.
- Set up access to Exchange Server from a Web browser. See pp. 476-483.
- Publish Exchange Server information on the Web. See pp. 505-506.

Integrating with the Internet in other ways.
- Access the directory from the Internet. See pp. 401-406.
- Provide an IRC server. See pp. 501-502.

7

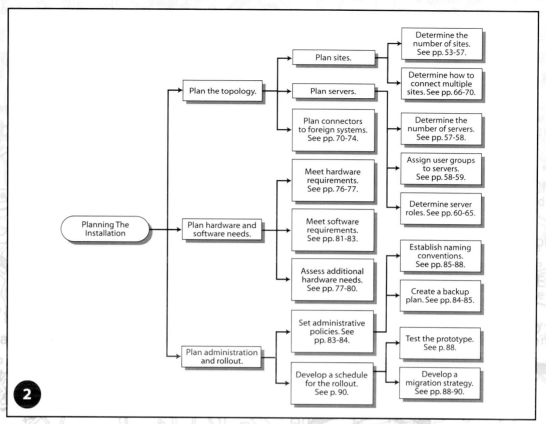

2

Planning The Installation → Plan the topology.

Plan the topology. → Plan sites.

Plan sites. → Determine the number of sites. See pp. 53-57.

→ Determine how to connect multiple sites. See pp. 66-70.

Plan the topology. → Plan servers.

Plan servers. → Determine the number of servers. See pp. 57-58.

→ Assign user groups to servers. See pp. 58-59.

→ Determine server roles. See pp. 60-65.

Plan the topology. → Plan connectors to foreign systems. See pp. 70-74.

Planning The Installation → Plan hardware and software needs.

Plan hardware and software needs. → Meet hardware requirements. See pp. 76-77.

→ Meet software requirements. See pp. 81-83.

→ Assess additional hardware needs. See pp. 77-80.

→ Establish naming conventions. See pp. 85-88.

→ Create a backup plan. See pp. 84-85.

Planning The Installation → Plan administration and rollout.

Plan administration and rollout. → Set administrative policies. See pp. 83-84.

→ Develop a schedule for the rollout. See p. 90.

→ Test the prototype. See p. 88.

→ Develop a migration strategy. See pp. 88-90.

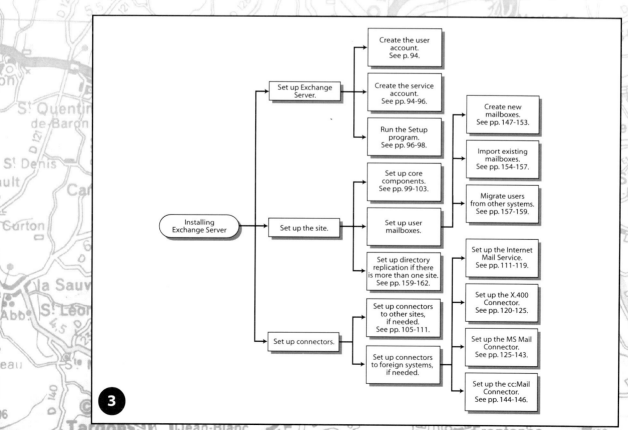

3

Installing Exchange Server → Set up Exchange Server.

Set up Exchange Server. → Create the user account. See p. 94.

→ Create the service account. See pp. 94-96.

→ Run the Setup program. See pp. 96-98.

Installing Exchange Server → Set up the site.

Set up the site. → Set up core components. See pp. 99-103.

→ Set up user mailboxes.

Set up user mailboxes. → Create new mailboxes. See pp. 147-153.

→ Import existing mailboxes. See pp. 154-157.

→ Migrate users from other systems. See pp. 157-159.

→ Set up directory replication if there is more than one site. See pp. 159-162.

Installing Exchange Server → Set up connectors.

Set up connectors. → Set up connectors to other sites, if needed. See pp. 105-111.

→ Set up connectors to foreign systems, if needed.

Set up connectors to other sites → Set up the Internet Mail Service. See pp. 111-119.

→ Set up the X.400 Connector. See pp. 120-125.

→ Set up the MS Mail Connector. See pp. 125-143.

→ Set up the cc:Mail Connector. See pp. 144-146.

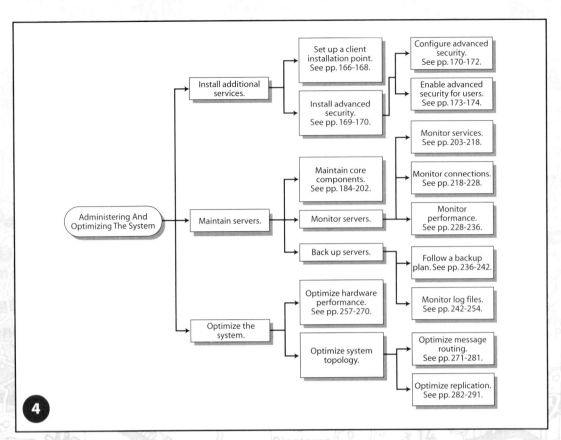

Administering And Optimizing The System

- **Install additional services.**
  - Set up a client installation point. See pp. 166-168.
    - Configure advanced security. See pp. 170-172.
    - Enable advanced security for users. See pp. 173-174.
  - Install advanced security. See pp. 169-170.
- **Maintain servers.**
  - Maintain core components. See pp. 184-202.
  - Monitor servers.
    - Monitor services. See pp. 203-218.
    - Monitor connections. See pp. 218-228.
    - Monitor performance. See pp. 228-236.
  - Back up servers.
    - Follow a backup plan. See pp. 236-242.
    - Monitor log files. See pp. 242-254.
- **Optimize the system.**
  - Optimize hardware performance. See pp. 257-270.
  - Optimize system topology.
    - Optimize message routing. See pp. 271-281.
    - Optimize replication. See pp. 282-291.

4

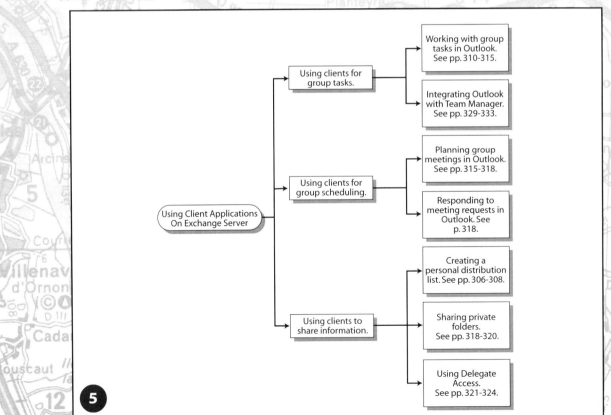

Using Client Applications On Exchange Server

- **Using clients for group tasks.**
  - Working with group tasks in Outlook. See pp. 310-315.
  - Integrating Outlook with Team Manager. See pp. 329-333.
- **Using clients for group scheduling.**
  - Planning group meetings in Outlook. See pp. 315-318.
  - Responding to meeting requests in Outlook. See p. 318.
- **Using clients to share information.**
  - Creating a personal distribution list. See pp. 306-308.
  - Sharing private folders. See pp. 318-320.
  - Using Delegate Access. See pp. 321-324.

5

Here's praise for Certification Insider Press's best-selling Exam Cram series. These comments come to us via craminfo@coriolis.com. We look forward to hearing from you, too.

I just finished writing and passing my Networking Essentials exam (70-058). I really couldn't have done it without the aid of the Exam Cram Networking Essentials book. I actually failed my first attempt at this exam about ten days ago, and based on the area where I did poorly (Implementation), I studied this area in the book. Not only did I pass that part of the test on the second exam, I got 100%!!!!! I studied two other manuals (from cover to cover) that are approved Study Guides for the MCSE, and the Exam Cram was really the one that did the trick. It let me know the key points to know cold and gave excellent reference material if I wanted to know more. Also, the thing that was key, between the other two manuals and the exam cram book, all the standards and terminology, etc., were completely up to date, so you weren't second guessing yourself when it came to the exam. I will definitely be purchasing the whole line of books for my future MCSE exams.

— Ken Campbell
   Consultant

My boss came to me and told me that I needed to pass my NT Server 4 test within a month. Although I had been planning to take the test, I was only studying when I had extra time. Suddenly, I needed to pass it NOW! I bought the Exam Cram and really focused on what I needed to study. In less than a week, I took the test and PASSED. This was the first time I passed a Microsoft test on my first try! I'm ready to cram for the NT Server in the Enterprise with another Exam Cram!

— Catherine Bostic

Yes, this was the best book I have ever purchased. That is the NT Server in the Enterprise. I self-studied the materials for that test and found the test to be very difficult. I scored 675—not enough to pass. After going through your manual from cover to cover and reviewing some material, I took the test again with a score of 895. Thanks—your study guide helped very much and saved me many hours of study time!!!!

— Darrel Corazalla

I bought the 4-pack at a reasonable rate and am very happy with the information I am getting. I have definitely gotten much more information than I expected or paid for.

— Shams Mohammad
   LAN Administrator

These are very good books, and I have ordered several of the other books in the series based on what I have read so far. I haven't finished the book yet, but it has a lot of information and explanations that are missing from my other study guides.

—Michael Towers
   Systems Administrator

What a great idea—Cliffs Notes for NT. As a study tool, to better focus on the exam strategy, I think it's great. I especially like your approach of asking the question, answering the question, and most importantly explaining how the other choices were wrong, totally made-up, or not as completely correct. I feel that this is where your books have it over any of the others. Keep up the GREAT work.

— Jerry Nagano
   Systems Administrator

Let Us Help You Jumpstart Your Career

I remember the first job I had right out of college. Armed with a computer science degree and too much confidence for my own good, I was ready to take on the world. Unfortunately, my lack of real-world experience and day-to-day problem-solving abilities got me into more trouble than I like to admit. But one thing I learned quickly was that teaming up with other people who knew how to quickly detect and solve tricky problems was a surefire way to greater success. (It also makes people think you're really smart!)

In developing our new *On Site* guides, we started with one simple goal—to create a book and software set that could help you solve problems like a seasoned pro. Let's face it, implementing technologies like Exchange Server or Proxy Server across an enterprise network can turn into a complicated mess, especially if you haven't done it before. In each *On Site* guide, you'll find hundreds of pages of useful tips and techniques for planning, deploying, configuring, and troubleshooting network technology.

We've incorporated a number of unique features throughout each *On Site* guide to help you become an "in-demand" expert. Inside the front cover we start with a tear-out visual problem-solving card to help you get your bearings. If you are having difficulty solving a problem, simply look up your problem and the card will direct you to solutions inside the book. Later in the book, you'll find useful visual decision trees and checklists to help you solve complex problems, step-by-step. You'll also find numerous time-saving tips that are designed to keep you from wasting your valuable time.

I hope that you find each *On Site* guide up to the standards of our bestselling *Exam Cram* and *Exam Prep* books. Whether you are an MCSE Certified Professional, planning to get certified, or just implementing Microsoft network technology, we want you to be able to count on getting the expert advice you need from our On Site guides.

To help us continue to provide the very best problem-solving and certification guides, we'd like to hear from you. Write or email us at **craminfo@coriolis.com** and let us know how our *On Site* guides have helped you in your work, or tell us about new features you'd like us to add. If you send us a story about how an *On Site* guide has helped you and we use it in one of our guides, we'll send you an official *Certification Insider Press* shirt for your efforts.

Keith Weiskamp
Publisher, Certification Insider Press

ON SITE™

Microsoft
EXCHANGE
SERVER 5.5

PLANNING
DEPLOYMENT
CONFIGURATION
TROUBLESHOOTING

Shannon R. Turlington
and Kevin Schuler

The Coriolis Group, Inc.
An International Thomson Publishing Company
14455 N. Hayden Road, Suite 220
Scottsdale, Arizona 85260

602/483-0192
FAX 602/483-0193
http://www.coriolis.com

Library of Congress Cataloging-in-Publication Data
Turlington, Shannon R.
    Microsoft Exchange Server 5.5 on site/by Shannon R. Turlington and Kevin Schuler.
        p.   cm.
    Includes index.
    ISBN 1-57610-258-0
    1. Microsoft Exchange.   2. Client/server computing.
I. Schuler, Kevin.   II. Title.
QA76.9.C55T86   1998
005.7'13769—DC21

98-14506
CIP

Printed in the United States of America
10 9 8 7 6 5 4 3 2 1

an International Thomson Publishing company

Albany, NY • Belmont, CA • Bonn • Boston • Cincinnati • Detroit • Johannesburg • London • Madrid
Melbourne • Mexico City • New York • Paris • Singapore • Tokyo • Toronto • Washington

Publisher
Keith Weiskamp

Acquisitions
Shari Jo Hehr

Project Editor
Ann Waggoner Aken

Production Coordinator
Kim Eoff

Cover Design
Anthony Stock

Layout Design
April Nielsen

CD-ROM Development
Robert Clarfield

Marketing Specialist
Josh Mills

I would like to dedicate this book to the memory of Buffy, one of my oldest and dearest friends.
—*Shannon R. Turlington*

I dedicate this book to author and researcher Starr Roxanne Hiltz. It is her publication of Online Communities *(Ablex, 1984) that first roused my interest in computer communications as a collaborative process. Her seminal work demonstrated the importance of understanding societal issues as a crucial element in the development of online communications. In 1984, understanding that online communities were a "new kind of social system" was a controversial, and even revolutionary concept. Today, the influence of online communications in the establishment of a new world order is abundantly clear. This monumental change, brought about through the worldwide availability of the Internet and empowered by technologies such as Microsoft Exchange Server, is truly creating a "new kind of social system." I thank Starr Roxanne Hiltz for her insight and scientific direction.*
—*Kevin Schuler*

About The Authors

Shannon R. Turlington is a writer and World Wide Web publisher. She authored *Exploring ActiveX, Walking the World Wide Web* (now in its second edition), and *Official Netscape Plug-in Book* (also in its second edition), all published by Ventana Press. She also edited and was a contributing author to *EarthLink Total WebSite Solution* (Ventana) and a contributing author to *Internet Roadside Attractions* (Ventana). She maintains a literature and writing resource archive and publishes the Voodoo Information Pages on the Web at http://www.arcana.com/shannon/shannon.html. She lives in Chapel Hill, North Carolina, with her two dogs and three ferrets.

Kevin Schuler is President of InDepth Technology, Inc. a technical consulting firm dedicated to delivering to its clients an in-depth understanding of Microsoft's emerging technologies. Additionally, Kevin serves as a Microsoft Regional Director. Kevin is also a member of the Microsoft TechEd advisory board, assisting with the creation of content for Microsoft's largest channel event. Kevin also serves as a consultant to Microsoft for its MCSD (Microsoft Certified Solutions Developer) program. Before establishing InDepth Technology, Inc., Kevin worked from 1988 to 1997 as Executive Vice President and General Manager for Babbage-Simmel, a technology consulting and training firm. Kevin is also the author of *Microsoft Proxy Server 2.0 On Site* published by The Coriolis Group.

Acknowledgments

I would first like to thank my co-author, Kevin Schuler. For our first time working together, we easily created a cooperative and supportive partnership, and I greatly appreciate all of his efforts and patience. I would also like to thank my local Exchange Server expert, Dykki Settle, for lending me equipment and advice. Finally, thanks go out to my agent, Martha Kaufman, and everyone at my publisher's who made this book possible—particularly Julia Higdon, Chris Grams, Michelle Nichols, Shari Jo Hehr, Ann Waggoner Aken, Kim Eoff, Robert Clarfield, Josh Mills, and Tony Stock.
—Shannon R. Turlington

First, I thank my co-author, Shannon Turlington, for her wonderful writing, bountiful technical skills, and unwavering professionalism. Her efforts continually went beyond what was called for. Moreover, her steady encouragement bolstered my efforts not only in this project, but another simultaneously occurring book project. Shannon is always a delight to work with. I thank Microsoft Corporation for its contribution to this project. Special thanks to: Peggy Seymour, the Product Manager for the Exchange Group; Michael Werner, Developers Relations Group; Bob Curtis and Brad Rosen, Microsoft Field Representatives; Kostos Malios, Community Marketing; and all the Microsoft Regional Directors throughout the world for their continued support, insight, and encouragement. I appreciate the continued support and technical insights provided by the local Microsoft Windows NT user group COUNT (Central Ohio Users NT). In particular: Brian Keller, Vice President; Jeff Schmidt, Executive Board Member; Ty Wait, Executive Board Member; and Ed Zirkle, President. Thanks to Kathy Schuler for her help with the CD-ROM. Finally, my appreciation goes out to everyone at my publisher for their continued support and encouragement. Specific thanks to: Ann Waggoner Aken, Kim Eoff, Robert Clarfield, Josh Mills, Tony Stock, Chris Grams, Amy Moyers, Michelle Nickles, and Ginny Phelps.
—Kevin Schuler

Table Of Contents

Part II   Planning And Installing Microsoft Exchange Server

Part III   Administering And Optimizing Microsoft Exchange Server

Introduction

In today's fast-paced business environment, your organization needs more from its internal messaging system than just the ability to exchange email. Ideally, a messaging system should integrate an entire suite of useful capabilities, such as scheduling, task planning, information management, and online discussion. The system should improve productivity by enabling employees to work together across the network in virtual teams. It should provide choices for the publishing and dissemination of important information throughout the enterprise. It should foster communication with customers and partners through integration with other messaging systems and, most importantly, with the Internet. And the system must be easy to administer, scalable to organizations of any size, and able to grow as your company grows.

Welcome to the world of Microsoft Exchange Server, the first messaging system that does all of this and more. Exchange Server is the ideal messaging infrastructure for organizations of any size, simply because it is so adaptable and customizable that it can be tailored to provide solutions to almost any business's needs. And despite its wide range of features, Exchange Server can be easily implemented and administered by anyone, from the full-time system administrator of a large enterprise to the non-techie employee or owner of a small business or home-based office.

This book will show you everything that Exchange Server has to offer and provide a practical, easy-to-use guide to implementing the features that meet the needs of your organization. From planning and deploying your Exchange Server system to creating collaboration and groupware applications and integrating with the Internet—this book tells you how to do it all, in a no-nonsense way that will help you get your Exchange Server system doing more for your organization than you ever thought possible.

What's Inside

This book is organized and written in a user-friendly, practical format to help anyone get Exchange Server 5.5 up and running as their organization's messaging and information management infrastructure, whether they're installing Exchange Server in the home office, on a small network, or on a large enterprise. Decision trees, worksheets, and checklists help plan the implementation of Exchange Server and make sure that deployment goes smoothly. Step-by-step instructions and screen shots illustrate every step, making it easy to install and configure Exchange Server and to implement Exchange Server's wide range of features. And practical examples, tips, and tricks help put Exchange Server to work to meet an organization's unique needs.

The book is organized into several broad sections, with each section covering a different aspect of deploying and using Exchange Server. Part I, "Microsoft Exchange Server And Your Organization," introduces you to the benefits and features of Exchange Server and helps you plan how Exchange Server can meet your organization's needs. Part II, "Planning And Installing Microsoft Exchange Server," provides a complete tutorial for planning your organization's implementation of Exchange Server and installing the system according to your plans. Part III, "Administering And Optimizing Microsoft Exchange Server," covers everything that the Exchange Server administrator needs to know to keep the system running smoothly. Part IV, "Communication And Collaboration With Microsoft Exchange Server," guides you in using Exchange Server's many features for communicating with others and working in groups. Finally, the glossary, the appendices and CD-ROM provide additional information and software that will aid you in using Exchange Server and help you extend Exchange Server's features even further.

Each broad section of the book is further broken down into chapters that address a narrower topic, as follows:

➤ Chapter 1, "What Is Microsoft Exchange Server?," gives a broad overview of Exchange Server 5.5 and introduces you to the Exchange Server features that will benefit your business.

➤ Chapter 2, "Needs Assessment," uses worksheets and examples to help you assess your organization's needs and how Exchange Server can meet them.

➤ Chapter 3, "Installation Planning," provides decision trees, worksheets, and checklists for planning every aspect of your Exchange Server system, including system topology, hardware and software needs, and company policies.

➤ Chapter 4, "Installing Exchange Server," takes you step by step through the installation and configuration of the Exchange Server system and components in accordance with your deployment plans.

➤ Chapter 5, "Administering Exchange Server," describes the tasks involved in managing the Exchange Server system, including installing clients and security features, maintaining system components, monitoring the system for problems, backing up the system, and managing log files.

➤ Chapter 6, "Optimizing Exchange Server," helps you optimize your Exchange Server configuration as your system grows and evolves, with tips and tricks for improving server, hardware, and network performance.

➤ Chapter 7, "Using Microsoft Client Applications," shows how the Outlook and Team Manager 97 clients work with the Exchange Server system to accomplish workgroup and collaboration tasks.

➤ Chapter 8, "Publishing Information With Exchange Server," describes how to use Exchange Server's public folder, electronic form, distribution list, and directory features to publish information on the system and build collaboration applications.

➤ Chapter 9, "Building An Online Community," shows how to integrate your internal messaging infrastructure with the Internet and start building virtual communities using email, USENET newsgroups, and the World Wide Web.

➤ Chapter 10, "Extending Exchange Server," provides an overview of third-party and Microsoft products that work with Exchange Server to extend the system's administration, information publishing and management, communication, and collaboration capabilities.

➤ Appendix A, "Troubleshooting Tips And Tricks," gives no-nonsense advice for troubleshooting problems with your Exchange Server implementation.

➤ Appendix B, "Related Internet Resources," points you toward World Wide Web, USENET, and email resources where you can further extend your knowledge of Exchange Server.

➤ A glossary provides definitions of Exchange Server terms used throughout the book.

Finally, the CD-ROM provides many valuable software utilities, add-ins, and sample applications that you can use with Exchange Server to make working with the system easier and add additional capabilities. Many of these tools are described in Chapter 10, along with practical examples for how they can be put to work in your implementation of Exchange Server.

What You Need

This book is written to be used with Microsoft Exchange Server 5.5. The client application used with Exchange Server 5.5 in this book is Microsoft Outlook 97.

You can download an evaluation version of Exchange Server 5.5 and Outlook 97 8.03 from the Exchange Server Web site at **http://www.microsoft.com/exchange/**. The evaluation version includes everything you need to run Exchange Server 5.5 on one server computer and to run Outlook 8.03 on one client computer.

To build a full Exchange Server messaging system that runs on a single server or across a network of multiple servers, you will need to license Exchange Server from Microsoft. The licensed version includes all the software needed to implement Exchange Server across your organization, the optional components described in this book, and the Outlook client application. You can get more information about licensing Exchange Server 5.5 from the same Web site.

The hardware, software, and network requirements for Exchange Server vary considerably depending on the size and geographic disbursement of your organization, the needs of your users, and the Exchange Server functions you intend to implement. Chapter 3 provides a complete overview of the required software and hardware for running the basic Exchange Server system and for running any additional components you intend to implement, such as connectors to other systems or security features. It is essential that you consult the information in Chapter 3 when planning your organization's customized implementation of the Exchange Server system.

At the very least, you will need to install Exchange Server 5.5 on a computer running Microsoft Windows NT Server, version 4.0 or later; Internet Information Server, version 3.0 or later; and Service Pack 3 or later. The computer running Exchange Server should have an Intel Pentium 60 or faster processor, at least 24MB memory, and at least 250MB hard disk space. Consult Chapter 3 for additional hardware requirements needed to fully optimize your Exchange Server system.

Moving On

You're ready to start learning everything that Exchange Server 5.5 can do for your business. Chapter 1, "What Is Microsoft Exchange Server?," provides an overview of the beneficial features of Exchange Server, so you can begin planning how Exchange Server will meet your organization's unique needs. This chapter describes Exchange Server's centralized administration, client/server architecture, and extensibility and scalability features, all of which make Exchange Server the perfect solution for organizations of any size. It also goes over the diverse capabilities of Exchange Server for increasing productivity and for enabling users to work together across the enterprise by using client applications, such as Outlook. Finally, this chapter describes the Exchange Server features not offered by any other messaging system, including its wide range of choices for publishing and sharing information, its support of all Internet standards, and its integration with the World Wide Web. You might not be aware of how much Exchange Server 5.5 can do, so turn the page and find out.

PART   I

Microsoft Exchange Server And Your Organization

What Is Microsoft Exchange Server?

With the advent of the personal computer, the corporate intranet, and the worldwide Internet, businesses have discovered that information is their most valuable commodity. Many of the new networking systems have been aimed at helping corporate users gather information, so that the volume of information that must be processed has become unwieldy, and everyday business activities have become more complex. The critical needs for accessing that information quickly and communicating and collaborating with trading partners, customers, and employees using Internet technologies are not being met. Without reliable, secure, and easy-to-use tools to help organize, manage, share, and analyze information, there really is no effective way to put the information to work for your business.

Microsoft Exchange Server 5.5 was designed to offer solutions for the changing needs of business users. (From now on, we will refer to Microsoft Exchange Server 5.5 as Exchange Server.) Rather than simply providing your business with a new way to gather information, Exchange Server extends complete solutions for managing, sharing, and analyzing information so that it becomes useful, rather than overwhelming.

Exchange Server is the first client/server messaging system designed for corporate use to integrate electronic mail, group scheduling, electronic forms, and groupware into a single system with centralized management capabilities. Exchange Server has tools that provide easy ways to sort and organize all types of information. It gives everyone in your organization a single access point to critical business information and to exchanging information with anyone, both on the company's internal network and outside it.

Using Exchange Server, you can create virtual teams within your business and virtual communities that include your customers and business partners all over the world. Built on existing Internet and email standards, Exchange Server simplifies the process of accessing information and communicating with members of your organization and with business partners and customers, even on different messaging systems. Exchange Server enables you to exchange information securely with users in other sites, organizations, and systems through email, public folders, electronic forms, discussions, shared databases, reference libraries, and more. With Exchange Server, collaboration becomes easy, even over geographical distances, with capabilities for scheduling appointments, planning group meetings, and tracking team tasks.

Exchange Server is both customizable and powerful, so that its capabilities can extend to businesses of all sizes, from the home office to the departmental workgroup to the enterprise, or adapt to the needs of your growing business. To make it easy to take advantage of these capabilities, Exchange Server includes all the tools required to move users from existing systems and makes it easy to exchange messages and share information with users on other systems.

This chapter provides a complete introduction to Exchange Server. It includes a general overview of Exchange Server's key features and how they can benefit your organization, a description of Exchange Server's architecture, an introduction to Active Server Components, and an introduction to Microsoft Outlook. Although all these topics are covered in greater detail in later chapters of this book, this chapter provides the grounding in Exchange Server basics that you'll need before moving on to those later chapters.

Features And Benefits

Exchange Server's many features encompass a complete, Windows NT-based messaging and groupware infrastructure that is scalable for organizations of all sizes, built on existing standards, and easy to administer. Using Exchange Server, you can build powerful client/server solutions for gathering, organizing, sharing, and publishing information in any way that fulfills your business's needs. Key features of Exchange Server include centralized administration, fulfillment of a wide variety of productivity tasks, fulfillment of a wide variety of group tasks, publishing information in a multitude of ways, support for all Internet standards, and extensibility and customization capabilities.

Centralized Administration

As corporate operations become more decentralized, system administrators are faced with the overwhelming task of managing a growing number of applications developed at the workgroup level. Centralized storage and security for these applications and for information, as well as a way to integrate the applications into the overall environment, have become critical. One of the key features of Exchange Server is the ability to administer all the server's applications, information storage, and security from one centralized location, regardless of whether your company is confined to a home office or spread across a large geographical region. This means that the administrator of the server can manage the entire Exchange Server environment from a single location, using standard management tools, such as the Administrator tool included with Exchange Server.

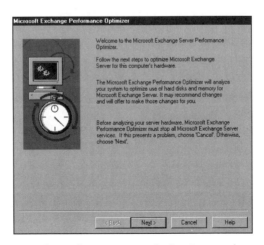

Exchange Server is integrated with the Microsoft Windows NT Server network operating system to make administering the entire server environment from a single location possible. Exchange Server is also compatible with the Windows NT Server administration tools, including the *Performance Monitor, Backup program,* and *Event Viewer.* By taking advantage of the built-in Remote Access Services (RAS) in Windows NT Server, Exchange Server provides a consistent method for dialing into the network, so that administrators have the same functionality when operating remotely as they do when in their offices.

Key functions of Exchange Server's centralized administration include server monitoring, link monitoring, and performance optimization. Through server monitoring, administrators can oversee key services, such as the directory service or the information store, on any server in the system. Administrators receive information on the status of key servers immediately and can set up an automatic escalation process if a service stops. Link-monitoring functions enable administrators to monitor the status of intersite connections, even to sites without Microsoft messaging systems. Administrators know that all connections are available, and they are quickly alerted to problems so that action can be taken. You can also use Exchange Server's built-in performance optimization tool to improve system memory and hard disk configurations quickly and easily (see Figure 1.1).

The centralized nature of Exchange Server ensures that email, scheduling, groupware, and collaboration tools are located in one place and are designed to work with each other, making accessing and sharing information among a network of users quick and easy. For example, a network user can develop an application for use on the desktop and then have the administrator install it on Exchange Server. Once the application is on the server, the administrator can set access permissions and replication properties for the application, so that it is secure and replicated across the enterprise. It also gives all users a single logon

Figure 1.1 Exchange Server's performance optimization tool.

access to both the network and their messaging and collaboration applications. Exchange Server's industrial-strength engine is designed to provide the scalability, connectivity, and security features required for a centralized messaging and collaboration system.

The Administrator Application

Administrating your Exchange Server is made easy with Exchange Server's Administrator application (see Figure 1.2). The *Administrator program* is a graphical user interface that enables system administrators to manage and configure all objects of the Exchange Server, including server computers, server components, and users. The Administrator program can be run on the Windows NT Server or Windows NT Workstation.

The Administrator program lets you view and manipulate the structure of your organization and perform administrative tasks from a centralized location. It provides paths to the tasks involved in setting up and maintaining Exchange Server. Using a graphical view of all users and resources in the organization, you can move through the various branches of the structure to view a complete layout of the organization. Thus, the Administrator program makes it easy to manage all components, users, gateways, connectors, and servers across the organization from one location.

Administrator supports all the following key features:

➤ 24-hour-a-day, 7-day-a-week availability to messages and data.

➤ Integration with Windows NT Server administration tools.

➤ Data recovery in the event of a server failure.

Figure 1.2 The Exchange Server Administrator program.

➤ Automatic notification and escalation of system problems.

➤ Intelligent tracking and routing of messages.

➤ Batch creation of users.

➤ *Global Address List* containing the recipients for the organization.

➤ *Directory* storage of all information about the organization's resources and users automatically replicated to all servers in the site.

➤ *Single instance message storage* and quota limits for maximizing disk space.

➤ Built-in gateways and connectors for migrating data from other networks and providing message transfer and translation to and from other messaging systems.

➤ Advanced security features.

With its centralized nature and graphical interface, Administrator takes the headaches out of managing Exchange Server and allows you to do more with your server to meet the needs of your organization.

Scalability

Because Exchange Server is built on Windows NT Server, it scales to virtually any level of performance, allowing your server's growth to consistently match the growth of your business. Exchange Server's scalable platform is designed to be higher performing and more reliable than competing products, such as Netscape Mail Server. Exchange Server can scale to fit the higher volume corporate usage profile for sending and receiving email, yet remains a viable solution for the lower volume usage of smaller businesses and even home offices. For example, Exchange Server installed on a mid-level server platform running Windows NT can support more than 2,500 active email users, each sending and receiving more than 22 messages in a typical day. Yet, Exchange Server can support a high message throughput of more than one million messages per day, can support up to 22,000 users on a single server, and can run on systems from a 64MB 90MHz Pentium up to an 8-processor Alpha or Pentium Pro server. In this way, Exchange Server is adaptable to the messaging needs and number of users of almost any organization, and your business won't outgrow it—protecting your investment.

Connectivity

Exchange Server's support of a wide range of protocols and systems allows the server to connect with many different systems outside the enterprise, facilitating electronic communication with your organization's employees, partners, vendors, distributors, and customers. Exchange Server includes both connectors and gateways, important assets for migrating from other systems to Exchange Server and for coexistence with other systems. *Connectors* are components included with Exchange Server that allow the server to connect to other messaging systems. *Gateways* connect networks that use different protocols so that those networks can exchange data. Through Exchange Server's connectors and gateways, users on dissimilar systems can exchange information seamlessly, as if they were all using the same system.

For example, the *Microsoft Mail Connector* supports connectivity between Microsoft Mail gateways and Exchange Server. The *Microsoft Exchange Connector for Lotus cc:Mail* enables seamless email exchange and directory synchronization between Lotus cc:Mail and Exchange Server. The *X.400 Connector* can be configured to connect sites within an organization or to route messages to foreign X.400 messaging systems, converting Exchange Server messages to native X.400 messages. An Internet connector enables users to exchange messages across the Internet. Exchange Server's gateways connect to additional email systems, including IBM PROFS/OfficeVision and SNADS. Built-in utilities make it possible to migrate data from Microsoft Mail for PC Networks and AppleTalk Networks, Netscape Collabra, Novell GroupWise, DEC All-In-1, Verimation MEMO, UNIX SendMail, and other systems. This integration makes it easier for administrators to monitor systems, manage directories, and track messages, even across disparate systems.

Security

Tight security features are provided both through Exchange Server's core features and through its integration with Windows NT Server's security tools and standards, protecting your organization's data and sent messages from unauthorized access. The security capabilities are designed to give administrators a high degree of control over access to Exchange Server resources, such as files, printers, and more.

The Windows NT Server security model provides for *secure logons,* which help prevent access by unauthorized users. Secure logons require users to identify themselves by entering a unique logon ID and password before they are allowed access to the system. Support for *discretionary access control* allows the owner of a resource, such as a folder or service, to determine who can access the resource and how much access they have. Auditing support provides the ability to detect and record important security events or any attempts to create, access, or delete system resources. *Memory protection* prevents anyone from reading information directly from memory after a data structure has been released back to the operating system. Using logging, administrators get a record of application, security, and system events, which are displayed in the graphical Windows NT Event Viewer.

To ensure the security of information during transmission across the network and even over the Internet, Exchange Server utilizes *advanced security* features like digital signatures and public and private key encryption. *Digital signatures* allow users to verify the source of information they receive or send and to verify that the contents of a sent message have not been modified during transmission. *Encryption* is the process of encoding information so that only parties who understand the code can read that information.

Data remains encrypted as it resides on disk and as it travels over the network connection. Keys are used to digitally sign and encrypt data. Each mailbox has two key pairs; one key pair is used for signing and verifying operations, while the other pair is used for encrypting and decrypting operations. Each key pair consists of a *public key,* which is made publicly known and is used to sign or encrypt data, and a *private key,* which is known only to the key's owner and is used to verify or decrypt data.

Productivity Tasks

Using Exchange Server and its client applications, each user works with a single, consistent user interface to perform a variety of productivity tasks. For instance, users can employ Exchange Server to send and receive email messages, manage tasks, organize calendars, review and organize information, and much more in one convenient location. Instead of having to look in several places for the information they need, users can go to one application on their desktops every time. Sending and accessing information from a single interface makes it easy for users to communicate with anyone, regardless of where they are located or even if they are on the road.

The interface works across all popular computing platforms, including MS-DOS, Windows, Windows NT Server, and Macintosh, as well as across different networks, including *Transport Control Protocol/Internet Protocol (TCP/IP),* NetWare, AppleTalk, and others. Users can also access information on the Exchange Server with their preferred client applications, including the *Exchange Client,* Microsoft Outlook, popular Web browsers, Internet email clients, Internet newsreaders, and LDAP clients. By seamlessly integrating with existing messaging systems, networks, and applications running on the desktop, users can work with tools that they are already familiar with or that require little learning time. This means that users can get productive faster. And your business can take advantage of its existing investments in software and hardware to migrate smoothly to Exchange Server.

Group Tasks

As well as performing individual tasks with Exchange Server and its client applications, users can perform a wide variety of group tasks using Exchange Server's tools and functionality. Group tasks supported by the server include *group scheduling,* managing meetings, assigning tasks, and other communication and collaboration activities. Using the group scheduling and planning tools of Exchange Server, you can create virtual teams of your employees whose tasks, resources, and schedules are tightly managed and coordinated and that involve experts from all over the world who can be called on at any time.

For example, a virtual team can use Exchange Server client applications, such as Outlook or *Schedule+,* to schedule meetings across the organization and reserve resources like a conference room for the meeting. The team leader can assign and manage tasks among team members, regardless of their geographical locations, using Outlook, *Team*

Manager 97, or Project. Internet newsgroups, discussion groups, and knowledge bases accessible to anyone on the team can be set up for easy sharing of important information. Instant groupware can also be created and deployed to team members using Outlook, or intranet-based and Web-based collaboration applications can be developed through integration with the Microsoft BackOffice family of products or the Active Server Platform framework. By supporting a wide range of group tasks, Exchange Server streamlines the process of collaborating with a workgroup.

Publishing Information

Exchange Server makes it possible to publish important information in a variety of ways for access by your employees within the organization, your business partners, and even your customers through the Internet. Instead of being limited to publishing information in the same way every time, Exchange Server expands your options for organizing and publishing information so that it can be used more effectively. For example, Exchange Server supports publishing information on the *World Wide Web* and the creation of mailing lists, knowledge bases, corporate white pages, and more.

Web Publishing

Using Microsoft's Active Server Platform technology, which is supported by Exchange Server, you can create dynamic Web pages in HTML format by publishing the information on your Exchange Server directly to a Web server. Exchange Server information then becomes available over the Internet to employees and customers using Web browsers to access the standard HTML content. Dynamic Web pages are customized for each user, based upon their actions or requests while viewing the page. For example, different Web pages might be displayed to different kinds of visitors to the Web site, or pages in an online catalog might query a database so that they always reflect the most current pricing and availability information. The dynamic nature of the Web pages ensures that changes you make to your Exchange Server information, and thus to your Web site information, will be reflected immediately, making for more efficient information sharing.

Mailing Lists, Knowledge Bases, And White Pages

With Exchange Server, you can easily create and manage mailing lists of customers numbering into the millions. You can then use Exchange Server to automate mass mailings to your customers. This provides an alternative venue for sharing important information and building an ongoing relationship with your customers.

Using Exchange Server's tools, you can set up knowledge bases that are easily accessible to your employees, business partners, and customers. *Knowledge bases* are comprehensive collections of articles that provide a way to share important information on a specific subject from one single location.

Exchange Server also makes it easy to publish a corporate white pages listing of names, email addresses, and phone numbers of members of your organization. Centrally accessible white pages make collaboration between your organization's employees and business partners more efficient. Since corporate white pages are published on Exchange Server, they can be viewed by anyone using a variety of clients.

Internet Standards Support

Exchange Server is the only server to embrace all Internet standards, as well as existing messaging and groupware standards, and it will continue to support new Internet protocols. This support for Internet standards enables businesses to use Exchange Server as a corporate intranet or worldwide Internet messaging and collaboration solution. Using Exchange Server, employees can communicate and collaborate both over the corporate intranet and over the Internet, extending virtual teams to include business partners and customers who do not have access to the internal network.

Natively, Exchange Server supports all the following standards:

➤ *Simple Mail Transfer Protocol (SMTP)* for sending and receiving email over the Internet.

➤ *Post Office Protocol 3 (POP3)* for reading and sending email and accessing the mailbox on Exchange Server with any POP3 client.

➤ *Internet Message Access Protocol 4 (IMAP4)* for reading and sending email and participating in online discussions on the Exchange Server system with any IMAP4 client.

➤ *Network News Transport Protocol (NNTP)* for hosting and access of Internet discussion groups, knowledge bases, and list servers by any Internet newsreader.

➤ *Lightweight Directory Access Protocol (LDAP)* for access to the Exchange Server directory with any LDAP client.

➤ *HyperText Transfer Protocol (HTTP)* for access to all Exchange Server information through a Web browser.

➤ *HyperText Markup Language (HTML)* for rendering native hypertext content through a Web browser.

➤ *Multipurpose Internet Mail Extensions (MIME)* for attachments to email messages of multimedia objects, word processing documents, PostScript files, graphics, voice messages, and more.

➤ *Secure Sockets Layer (SSL)* for secure communication between POP3 email readers, NNTP newsreaders, LDAP clients, Web browsers, and the Exchange Server.

➤ *Remote Access Service (RAS)* for integrated remote connectivity.

➤ *Universal Inbox* for access to information sources through Messaging Application Programming Interface (MAPI) and Point-to-Point Protocol (PPP).

Internet Email

Exchange Server's support of the POP3 and IMAP4 protocols means that users can employ any email client that supports the POP3 or IMAP4 standard for reading and sending electronic mail, including Microsoft Internet Explorer Mail, Netscape Navigator Mail, and Eudora (see Figure 1.3). Exchange Server's Internet email feature also provides a standard SMTP server for any POP3 or IMAP4 client to submit email messages. POP3 and IMAP4 administration is fully integrated with administration of the server through a single interface and can be monitored through tools like *message tracking*, the Event Viewer, and the Performance Monitor.

Support for POP3 and IMAP4 opens up Exchange Server to the wider world of Internet email, extending messaging capabilities. Users can even switch between an Exchange Server email client and an Internet email client as their needs dictate. Since Exchange Server also supports the HTML and MIME standards, rich content can be included in email messages, including hyperlinks and multimedia. Messages can be formatted with different fonts and colors. Formatting and attachments are configurable by mailbox, server, and site to adapt to users with different clients that might not support all the formatting and multimedia included in a particular message. Finally, Exchange Server's support for the SSL and S/MIME protocols can be used as part of a security solution for encrypting data sent and received by Internet email clients.

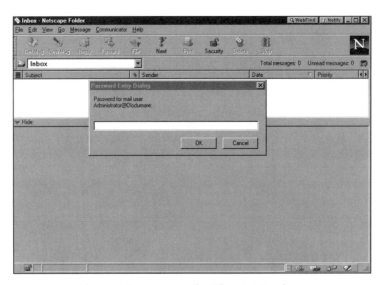

Figure 1.3   Accessing Exchange Server email with a POP3 client.

MAPI

Messaging Application Programming Interface (MAPI) is a common interface that clients on Exchange Server use to access data from the server components. Messaging applications and information services that comply with MAPI can be plugged into Exchange Server to provide additional functionality.

Internet Newsgroups

Exchange Server's support of the NNTP protocol enables your server to host Internet discussion groups, knowledge bases, and list servers and replicate them throughout the enterprise. *USENET newsgroups,* knowledge bases, and list servers can be accessed by any Internet newsreader, the Exchange Client, Outlook, or a Web browser (see Figure 1.4). Any Exchange Server public folder can be published as an Internet newsgroup that can then be accessed by an NNTP client or replicated with other NNTP servers, allowing you to set up content-specific discussion groups that can be accessed by your employees, business partners, and customers, thus extending your virtual community. Like any other public folder, newsgroups in Exchange Server support categorized views, content indexing, threaded discussion, cross-folder searching, and offline folder synchronization. Existing USENET discussion groups can also be pulled into Exchange Server and then replicated and viewed throughout the enterprise.

Since the NNTP protocol is fully integrated with Exchange Server, there is a single administrative interface for email, newsgroups, and public folders. With its additional support for the HTML and MIME standards, the content of newsgroups can be enhanced by text formatting, such as different fonts and colors; HTML formatting, such as clickable

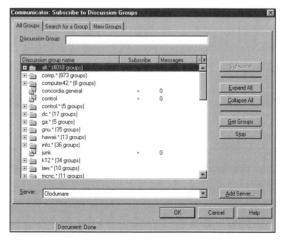

Figure 1.4   Accessing an Internet newsgroup on Exchange Server.

links; and other types of files, including multimedia. Using Exchange Server's security features, you can provide anonymous access or secure logon access to newsgroups, as well as data encryption through the SSL protocol.

Exchange Directory Service

The LDAP standard is a way for clients to access the information held in Exchange Server's global directory. Using an LDAP client, users can browse or search the directory for specific entries. LDAP support also enables your company to publish the directory or portions of it to outside users, choosing which directory information to make available. This allows your company to share basic employee information with the public and with business partners.

Extensibility And Customization

Exchange Server is not just a static set of tools. Rather, it is an extensible and customizable foundation built on an industrial-strength engine so that it can better meet the growing needs of your organization. By extending Exchange Server's client, extending existing applications, and even writing new applications using widely available development tools, you can put Exchange Server to work for your business in a variety of ways.

Exchange Server supports all the following extensibility capabilities:

➤ Extensibility of the client through electronic form-based applications.

➤ Extensibility through the Active Server Platform framework for building and deploying Web-based, groupware solutions.

➤ Extensibility through Visual Basic to add functionality to the client or to add communication and collaboration capabilities to existing applications.

Exchange Server includes many built-in tools for extending server capabilities and customizing collaboration applications. The *Microsoft Exchange Scripting Agent* supports server-side scripting of event-driven agents, which are used to create automated applications. *Visual InterDev,* a visual development tool, can be used to create HTML forms and collaborative Active Server Pages applications within the Outlook client.

Developers can utilize programming languages like C++, MAPI, VBScript, or JavaScript to write new communication and collaboration applications for customizing the functions of Exchange Server. Exchange Server is also integrated with the Microsoft BackOffice family of products, enabling developers to build powerful intranet solutions by combining different servers. For example, the Exchange Server system can host real-time, online discussion through integration with the *Microsoft Exchange Chat Service.*

Electronic Forms

Electronic forms provide a structure for posting and viewing specific types of information. Examples of electronic forms include *send forms,* which are used to exchange information with other users and include purchase requisitions and expense reports, and *post forms,* which are used to post and view information in a public folder. By using the *Forms Designer* tool, you can customize electronic forms to fit the needs of your organization.

Architecture

Exchange Server employs a client/server architecture, a system in which each process on the network is either a client or a server. The *client* is a software program that can access services on the network. The software that provides the services is called the *server.* The server manages the network's resources, and clients depend on the server for resources, such as files and devices. The client connects to the server and, according to a protocol, makes requests for information or services. The server then carries out the instructions or obtains the requested information and sends it back to the client. Clients hide many of the networking details from the user, including computer names, ports, and commands, making the system easier to use and more intuitive. This model allows clients and servers to be placed independently on nodes in a network, such as on different hardware or operating systems appropriate to their function.

To provide further flexibility, Exchange Server employs a modular architecture and a manageable messaging infrastructure that enable the server to grow as your organization grows, to perform reliably, and to adapt to the changing needs of your users.

Modular Architecture

Exchange Server is composed of separate components, called *modules,* that can be connected together, giving it a *modular architecture.* Using a modular architecture, you can replace or add any one component without affecting the rest of the system.

As mentioned earlier in this chapter, Exchange Server supports all the standard *Internet protocols,* including POP3, IMAP4, SMTP, NNTP, LDAP, HTTP, and HTML. Exchange Server's modular architecture makes it possible for all these protocols to be implemented natively. When using any of these protocols, Exchange Server requires no protocol translation or overhead, so that it remains scalable and retains its high performance, no matter what protocol is being used to access the data on the server.

For example, when implementing the LDAP protocol on Exchange Server, the Exchange client can access the directory information simultaneously as portions of the directory are made available to LDAP clients. Since protocol mapping or translation is not required, performance and scalability are not impacted. The LDAP clients simply make their requests of the directory natively against the Exchange Server.

All other supported Internet protocols are implemented in the same way. Exchange Server's modular and flexible architecture ensures that as new protocols become important, the server will also support them natively. Users will continue to be able to access data on your Exchange Server in the future, no matter what protocols become important or which tools users choose to employ.

Manageable Infrastructure

To build reliable applications using the Internet protocols supported by Exchange Server, there must be a solid foundation. As the applications become used by all members of the company network, the Exchange Server supporting those applications becomes more important. To ensure that all group applications function reliably every time, Exchange Server's architecture includes a manageable messaging infrastructure. Exchange Server's infrastructure supports the following key features:

➤ **Available 24 hours a day.** Exchange Server is always operating, even during backups and normal system maintenance, so users have continuous access to messages and data.

➤ **Centralized administration.** An easy-to-use, unified administration program gives administrators a view into every aspect of Exchange Server's environment.

➤ **Data recovery.** In the event of a server failure, Exchange Server's transaction log allows rollback recovery to the last transaction.

➤ **Security.** Since Exchange Server is integrated with Windows NT Server security standards, your business's information is protected.

➤ **Message tracking.** You can easily locate individual messages anywhere in the system.

➤ **Efficient message storage.** Storage of single copies of messages reduces the amount of disk space required for storage.

➤ **Quota limits.** Per-server and per-user quotas allow you to develop and implement organization-wide policies that contain online storage requirements.

Active Server Components

Many businesses are adapting Internet technology, such as the Web, to foster wider communication internally among employees and externally among trading partners and customers. Microsoft, recognizing this trend, included support of existing and new Web technologies in Exchange Server, so that Exchange Server can become a key component of your business's intranet or Internet messaging solution.

Exchange Server supports the *Active Server Platform,* a development platform designed to give developers an easy way to build applications by combining Internet and PC technologies. As part of the Active Server Platform, Exchange Server includes support for *Active Server Components,* the technology for integrating Exchange Server functionality with Web applications. Active Server Components make it possible to combine HTML and core Exchange Server technologies, such as messaging, calendaring, public folders, and groupware, to create a host of new business applications for the Web. Since Active Server Components integrate with the entire Active Server Platform, developers can leverage all the services of Exchange Server and other Microsoft and third-party services on the Web.

Using Active Server Components, it becomes possible to access email boxes, threaded discussion groups, customer mailings, databases, form processing, files, dynamic billboards, scheduling data, public folders, calendars, and the directory on the Exchange Server using any Web browser. Active Server Components give users live access to dynamic Exchange Server information, translating the information to HTML format on-the-fly for viewing with a Web browser. The browser also provides limited read-and-write access to Exchange Server data. This gives users a seamless browsing experience, regardless of the operating system they are using. Exchange Server features can be included on any public Web site as well, creating dynamic, interactive, Web-based applications.

Accessing Email

Developers can use Active Server Components to build custom applications and user interfaces that allow the users of the Exchange Server to read and manage email with a *Web browser.* A completed Active Server application that uses this technology, *Outlook Web Access,* is included with Exchange Server. Using Outlook Web Access, users can read their email and access their private mailboxes with any Web browser that has frames and Java support, such as Microsoft Internet Explorer or Netscape Navigator (see Figure 1.5). With full read-and-write access, users can create, send, and reply to messages and organize their mailbox from within the Web browser. Outlook Web Access also allows users to access public folder discussions, scheduling data, and the Exchange Server directory from within the browser.

By enabling access to mailboxes and other Exchange Server information sources through a Web browser, Exchange Server opens its resources to all computing platforms, including UNIX and OS/2. In this way, Active Server Components extend Exchange Server's benefits to every computing platform used by members of your organization. Also, if a user is on the road or working from home, he or she can still securely access email from any location with Internet connectivity, including public terminals at conventions, hotels, and airports. Thus, Active Server Components make Exchange Server more flexible and easily accessible by all of your company's users, no matter what platform they are using or where they are connecting.

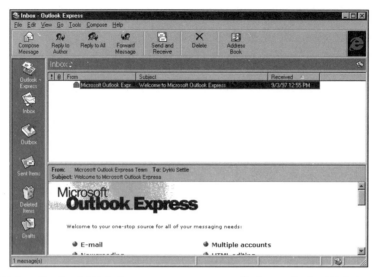

Figure 1.5 Using Outlook Web Access to access email through the Web browser.

Developing Web Applications

Most Web sites today are relatively simple because they use the storage facilities afforded by the computer's file system. Data is stored in individual files that are not cross-referenced, and pages are generally static and offer little in the way of interactivity. However, Web site users are demanding more complexity and functionality from corporate Web sites, such as full-featured applications that perform useful functions directly on the Web.

Building these Web-based applications requires a combination of different storage features. For example, an application that tracks contacts would benefit from a relational data store, such as SQL Server, and would use Exchange Server to provide messaging and collaboration capabilities. By using Microsoft's Active Server Platform as the environment for developing Web-based applications, the server is unified, providing a means for building groupware applications by combining the features of Exchange Server.

Developers can employ Exchange Server's Active Server Components to quickly and easily build interactive applications for deployment on the Web, taking advantage of Exchange Server's data storage, directory, messaging, and collaboration capabilities. Web applications constructed with Active Server Components can utilize Exchange Server to deliver specific aspects of the application's functionality. By incorporating Active Server Components applications into ordinary Web pages, HTML content becomes more interactive and compelling with the addition of interactive elements, such as threaded discussion groups, email responses, customer mailings, and more.

Active Server Components leverage the Web design tools and skills in which your organization's developers have already invested, making it a simple task to build Web-based applications with them. The applications are based on *Active Server Pages (ASP)* technology. ASP files combine HTML and ActiveX scripting to call specific Active Server Components, so that applications can be designed and modified easily. An ASP application is a set of Active Server Pages that uses Active Server Components. When writing ASP applications, developers are not limited to a unique scripting language or authoring tool, but can employ languages and tools with which they are already familiar, making the most of your company's existing investments. The resulting applications are compatible with any Web browser running on any operating system.

Using the power of Active Server Components enables developers to create applications that combine Exchange Server's functionality and the Web, extending the value of your business's investment in Exchange Server. Existing Exchange Server applications can also be extended to all operating systems that support Web browsers, and existing Web sites can be easily enhanced by higher levels of interactivity and functionality.

Microsoft Outlook 97

A powerful client tool, *Microsoft Outlook 97,* is included with Exchange Server. Outlook is a centralized application that provides your users with a complete workgroup and individual desktop information management solution. Outlook takes an integrated approach to organizing desktop information and communicating and sharing information with others, using email as the central thread of communications.

Outlook operates from one window, integrating all tasks into an easy-to-use interface. With Outlook, users can manage all their desktop activities, including email, tasks, documents, and scheduling, from a single graphical tool, giving users more control over their daily activities. Personal, public, and online information is organized in one location, so that information can be found easily and viewed in a variety of ways. Outlook's features let users choose how to organize their information so it makes the most sense for them, either by Outlook's standard views or customized views. Outlook includes many convenience features to save users from unnecessary manual data entry, including drag-and-drop between Outlook modules, automatic conversion of one item to another, and more. Outlook also aids communication and collaboration through email, phone support, and group scheduling. Finally, through integration with Exchange Server, any applications developed with Outlook can take advantage of the centralized administration, replication, and security capabilities of the entire server.

Outlook enables your users to perform many fundamental computing activities on Exchange Server, including the following tasks:

➤ Management and sending of email.

➤ Group and individual scheduling.

➤ Task assignment and management.

➤ Contact management.

➤ Access and sharing of information through public folders, electronic forms, and the Internet.

➤ Creation and deployment of instant groupware.

➤ Integration with Microsoft Office applications.

Outlook And Email

Outlook is Microsoft's premier email client. As a full MAPI client, Outlook can work with any email system that supports MAPI, including Exchange Server. Outlook's email functionality makes organizing and managing messages easier than ever before. Combining Exchange Server with Outlook's email module, called the Universal Inbox, enables users to customize and automate many important email tasks (see Figure 1.6). For example, users can create *rules* to help process and organize messages in the Universal Inbox, such as a rule that forwards all messages from a coworker to the rest of the team.

The Universal Inbox includes many unique features to aid your employees with using email to advantage. The *AutoPreview* feature displays the first three lines of each message, so users can scan through messages and prioritize them. A *Message Flag* feature enables marking up of messages with due dates or follow-up actions. *Voting* and *message tracking* capabilities let a virtual team gather and tally members' opinions on different issues, aiding collaboration. *Message Recall* enables sent messages to be recalled by the user who sent them, as long as they haven't been opened; sent messages can even by replaced by new messages. These are just a few of Outlook's unique features that make managing large volumes of email a snap.

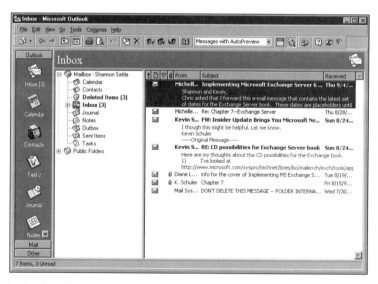

Figure 1.6   Outlook's Universal Inbox.

Figure 1.7 Outlook's Calendar module.

Outlook And Scheduling

Outlook's Calendar module helps users organize, schedule, and otherwise manage their time from the desktop (see Figure 1.7). The Calendar module's Date Navigator intuitively displays appointments, meetings, and events in a daily, weekly, or monthly schedule. The *TaskPad* displays the day's tasks so that time to work on them can be scheduled in the Calendar. Other unique tools of the Calendar module are also designed to help users become more productive by more efficiently scheduling and managing their time.

The Calendar module provides tools for enabling group scheduling across the server. One of Microsoft's goals for Outlook was to create a tool that addresses the need for virtual teams of users to work together across the network. Outlook addresses this need with features for group collaboration, including the ability to schedule group meetings using email and the Calendar module's *Meeting Planner* feature. Users can invite attendees to group meetings and coordinate available times for meetings. The Meeting Planner also allows for reserving resources, such as a conference room or audio-visual equipment, for meetings. And when permission is granted, Outlook can delegate access to other members of the team to read or modify users' personal Calendars for task assignment and other scheduling needs.

Outlook And Task Management

Outlook's Tasks module makes it easy for your organization's employees to keep on top of their tasks and assignments. The Tasks module is a business and personal to do list in which tasks can be prioritized, organized, tracked, and even assigned to others (see Figure 1.8). The Tasks module fosters both individual and group productivity by allowing

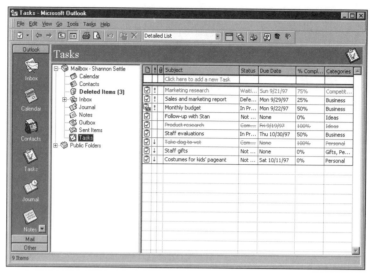

Figure 1.8   Outlook's Tasks module.

task assignments and progress to be made and tracked across a virtual team of employees, with unique features like automatic sending of status reports when a task is completed.

The Journal module adds more task management functionality by making it possible to maintain an itemized log of activities, track activities over time, and track phone calls (see Figure 1.9). Using the Journal module, users can automatically track and record all activities related to a particular contact or task, including email messages sent, phone calls made, and meetings attended. Users can also find documents and email messages based on when they were last modified, rather than searching for elusive file names or locations.

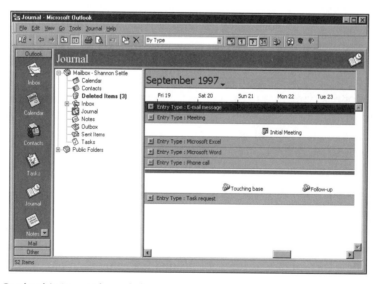

Figure 1.9   Outlook's Journal module.

On Site

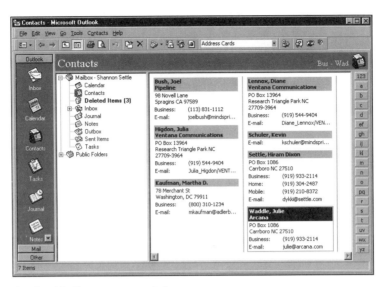

Figure 1.10 Outlook's Contacts module.

Outlook And Contact Management

Using Outlook's powerful contact management tool, the Contacts module, users can store and organize extensive information about their personal and business contacts (see Figure 1.10). Multiple phone numbers, mailing addresses, email addresses, Web pages, and additional information about a contact can be organized, sorted, filtered, and grouped any way the user chooses. Furthermore, the Contacts module enables users to dial a phone and keep a record of the call, send email, request a meeting, assign a task, send a fax, or go to a Web site associated with a stored contact. As with the Tasks module, the Journal module integrates with the Contacts module to display recorded activities for contacts, such as notes on phone calls or meetings with that particular contact.

Outlook And Information Sharing

With Outlook, information can be accessed and shared in a number of ways, including through folders, electronic forms, and even the Web. For example, users can share information with the group by posting that information to an Exchange Server public folder, a *shared private folder,* or an Internet site, making the information continuously accessible to anyone on the virtual team who needs it. The team may choose to share schedules, contact lists, or task lists in a public folder, increasing communication among the group (see Figure 1.11).

Outlook's *Delegate Access* feature allows some users, such as managers and supervisors, to manage email messages, tasks, appointments, or folders in another person's Outlook modules. Outlook's integration with the Web enables users to store, manage, and navigate to Web files through an integrated Web browser. Outlook also supports electronic forms built by the Forms Designer.

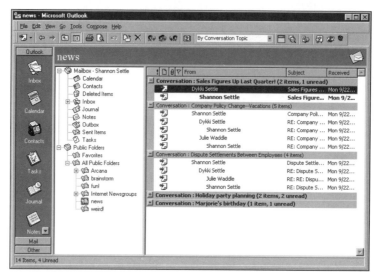

Figure 1.11   Viewing information in a public folder with Outlook.

Outlook And Instant Groupware

Using Outlook, users can build and deploy "instant" groupware that fits the specific needs of an organization or a virtual team. Instant groupware takes advantage of Outlook's built-in productivity modules, such as the Calendar, Tasks, Journal, and Contacts modules, which can all be easily customized. By locating a module in a public folder on the Exchange Server, workgroups can share calendars, schedules, task lists, or contact information across the enterprise, instantly creating groupware. Because the groupware application takes advantage of the existing forms and behavior of the Outlook module, programming custom codes and designing custom forms are not necessary. Using instant groupware, teams of employees can work the built-in modules harder to schedule group events, manage a project through group tasks, and maintain the workgroup's customer contact list.

By customizing modules without the need for programming, the groupware can be adapted to the needs of the workgroup. For example, adding custom views to a generic public folder containing the built-in Calendar module enables the module to be used

Public Folders

On Exchange Server, *public folders* hold information that can be shared by several users. Public folders reside in the public information store on the server and can be copied to additional Exchange Servers. When a change is made to the information in a public folder, that change is then updated in every replica of the folder throughout the organization, making public folders an efficient information sharing and collaboration tool.

specifically for entering and viewing the schedule of the workgroup, such as training classes or group meetings. In this way, virtual teams can create customer status reports, contact lists, expense reports, or survey forms that can be accessed and used by anyone on the Exchange Server, regardless of geographical location or client.

Outlook And Microsoft Office

Outlook is fully integrated with all Microsoft Office 97 applications so that information is communicated seamlessly across all applications on the desktop and among other users in the organization. Office 97 files can thus be opened, viewed, and shared from within Outlook. Office files, including Access, Excel, Word, or Schedule+ data, can be attached to any Outlook item, such as appointments, tasks, contacts, or email messages. For example, Outlook email supports all the features of WordMail and formatting of Microsoft Word 97. Using Word, Excel, or PowerPoint, users can create tasks for Outlook's Tasks module. Outlook's Journal tool can be used to find an Office file and automatically notes when an Office file is worked on. Drag-and-drop between Outlook items and Office applications is also supported. Even consistent title bars, command bars, pull-down menus, shortcut menus, dialog boxes, toolbars, icons, and right-mouse clicks can be shared among all Office applications and Outlook.

Moving On

In this chapter, you've learned about the many features and benefits of Exchange Server, including its key functions, its flexible architecture, and its useful tools like Active Server Components and the Outlook client. In later chapters, you will be putting all this information to use through practical applications of Exchange Server's features and tools. The following chapter, "Needs Assessment," will help you get started by providing worksheets for assessing the needs Exchange Server will meet for your organization before you begin installing and implementing the server.

Needs Assessment

Before beginning your installation and implementation of Exchange Server, you should carefully plan how your company will use Exchange Server, how your Exchange Server system will be organized, and your company's transition from your current system to Exchange Server. The extent of planning that you need to do depends on a number of factors, including the size of your company, your company's requirements for a messaging system, and your company's existing resources. Smaller companies, for example, will find the planning process to be less complex than larger ones. However, every business—both large and small—should do this crucial step. Thorough planning will make your rollout of Exchange Server proceed more efficiently, causing fewer disruptions for your company during the transition and fewer problems with your Exchange Server installation after it is up and running.

The first step in planning the Exchange Server installation is a thorough assessment of your users' needs and your existing resources. In this chapter, you will learn the steps required in completely assessing your company's needs and resources. First, you should become familiar with how an Exchange Server system is organized and the components of the server, so you know what elements you will be considering when planning your company's Exchange Server system. Then, you will need to assess your company's needs and existing resources. You will use the information you gather during the assessment process to implement a rollout plan, as described in Chapter 3.

How Exchange Server Works

Before beginning to assess how your company can best put Exchange Server to work, you should understand how Exchange Server works. This includes knowledge of the server and client components that make up Exchange Server, the services that Exchange Server provides, and the way Exchange Server networks are organized. Knowledge of how Exchange Server works will be an invaluable help when you plan how to set up your own company's Exchange Server system.

two

The Exchange Server Site And Organization

Exchange Server's scalable system is based on the concept of sites and organizations. Arranging the Exchange Server system into sites and organizations makes it easier to manage multiple servers and clients from a centralized location.

An *Exchange Server site* is made up of one or more computers running Exchange Server that are connected by a high-bandwidth, permanent network and establish synchronous *Remote Procedure Call (RPC)* connections to communicate with each other. By connecting through RPCs, Exchange Server computers can communicate efficiently, regardless of the network type. The servers in one site share the same directory information, and directory changes are updated and replicated automatically throughout the site.

The *Exchange Server organization* consists of one or more sites that can be connected to each other in a number of ways. Generally, your company will have only one Exchange Server organization, which will vary in size from one or two sites for a small company to several sites for a large company. The organization is fundamentally scalable and grows as your company grows. For example, you can add additional servers to existing sites and add additional sites to an existing organization as your needs dictate. You can also add advanced functionality as needs arise, such as security features or connections to the Internet. You can fully administer the entire Exchange Server organization and view all the sites in the organization from one location using the Administrator program.

The Exchange Server

Each Exchange Server in a site is hosted on a computer running *Windows NT Server*, version 4.0 or later. As you learned in the previous chapter, Exchange Server works on the *client/server model*. The Exchange client applications work together with the server computer to accomplish tasks across the company's network. The *clients* make requests of the *server* to perform certain actions, such as looking up names, sending email messages, and storing information in folders. For example, you would use a client application to compose and send an email message. The Exchange Server then acts as a central post office to route the message to its destination. The recipient of the message also uses a client application to contact the server and download the message.

Server Components

Each Exchange Server consists of core and optional components, which are all implemented as Windows NT Server services. The core components must be running at all times and reside on the same Windows NT Server computer. They provide the main messaging and directory services, including message transfer, delivery, and storage. The optional components support connectivity and information exchange with other systems, and they support advanced security features.

Each Exchange Server consists of the following core server components:

➤ **Directory.** The *directory* functions like an address book to maintain information about all *objects* in the Exchange Server infrastructure, including users, servers, public folders, and distribution lists. Other server components use the directory to map addresses and route messages. Users can also use client applications to look up information in the directory about other Exchange Server users, such as their email addresses. The information stored in the directory is automatically replicated to all Exchange Servers in a site.

➤ **Information store.** The *information store* provides server-based storage of Exchange Server information. It is divided into two databases: the private information store and the public information store. The *private information store* has all the contents of users' mailboxes. The *public information store* contains information that is shared with all Exchange Server users and is organized into *public folders*. The information store is also responsible for enforcing security, replicating public folders, enforcing storage limits, and delivering messages to users on the same server.

➤ **Message Transfer Agent (MTA).** The *Message Transfer Agent* acts as the Exchange Server post office, delivering email messages to their intended destinations by moving them from one server to another. It submits, routes, and delivers email messages to other MTAs, information stores, connectors, and third-party gateways.

➤ **System attendant.** The *system attendant* is a maintenance service that runs as a background process to ensure that the system is functioning smoothly and that email is routed correctly. It assists the server with such tasks as generating email addresses and running monitoring tools. As part of its monitoring functions, the system attendant gathers information about the services running on each Exchange Server computer, checks messaging connections, checks replication of the directory and corrects inconsistencies, provides tracking of messages, builds *routing tables,* generates *email addresses,* and enables and disables security features for users' mailboxes. It must be running for other Exchange Server components to function.

Client Components

Exchange Server client applications are used to connect to and perform activities on Exchange Server. You can provide any of these client applications for your users to install on their client computers, depending on which activities your users need to perform on the server.

The following client components are included with Exchange Server:

➤ **Exchange Client.** The *Exchange Client* is a basic information management tool that enables users to access, organize, and share information on the Exchange Server.

For example, users can employ Exchange Client to manage email, private folders, and documents. Exchange Client can also be used to access and create public folders and to look up information in the directory. The Exchange Client is typically used with earlier versions of Exchange Server than version 5.5 and is valuable for less powerful client workstations.

➤ **Microsoft Schedule+.** *Schedule+* helps users manage their calendars, organize tasks into to do lists, and work more effectively with others across the Exchange Server organization. Using this client, users can maintain a personal calendar of appointments and keep track of tasks, as well as schedule and plan group meetings with other Exchange Server users. Although less full-featured than the Calendar module in Outlook, Schedule+ works well on less powerful workstations or where hard disk space is at a premium. Schedule+ is typically used in conjunction with the Exchange Client.

➤ **Microsoft Outlook 97.** Providing an alternative to the Exchange Client, *Outlook* is a full-fledged desktop information manager. With Outlook, users can perform all of the following fundamental tasks: email management; personal calendaring; *group scheduling;* contacts management; organizing, assigning, and tracking tasks; journaling; browsing and sharing of documents; management and sharing of private folders; public folder and custom groupware design and access; electronic forms design; and accessing of information in the directory. Also, Outlook is extensible; with minimal effort, you can create valuable Outlook applications for your organization. Outlook is the primary client used with Exchange Server 5.5.

➤ **Forms Designer.** Using *Forms Designer,* users can create custom *electronic forms* that automate and streamline common processes, such as purchase requisitions or expense reports. Forms Designer is a visual, non-programming way to define the layout and operation of full-fledged electronic forms that make workgroups more productive.

Exchange Server's flexibility allows users to employ other clients than these. For example, through support of *Internet protocols,* users can choose a *Post Office Protocol version 3 (POP3)* client to access email or an *Internet Message Access Protocol version 4 (IMAP4)* client to access email and information in public and private folders.

When assessing users' needs and how they will be using Exchange Server, you should also determine which clients would best fulfill their needs. For example, you should install the more robust Outlook client where there is a need for advanced email, scheduling, and groupware client features or a need for integration with Office 97 programs, which are not supported by the basic Exchange Client.

Exchange Server Services

It will be easier for you to assess users' needs for the Exchange Server system if you are already familiar with the types of services Exchange Server provides. Later, when you are determining what functions your users will have to perform on Exchange Server and what problems Exchange Server will solve for your company, you can map specific services to the general solutions for each problem. Then, you will have a better idea of how to lay out your Exchange Server organization, how to use different Exchange Server computers in each site, and which server components need to be installed during setup.

Exchange Server supports all of the following services:

➤ **Advanced security.** *Advanced security* features provide the ability to protect and verify email messages during transmission through such security measures as *digital signatures* and *encryption.*

➤ **Chat Service.** The *Microsoft Exchange Chat Service* provides an *Internet Relay Chat (IRC)* server for real-time discussion in chat groups across the Internet.

➤ **Collaboration Data Objects and Visual InterDev.** *Collaboration Data Objects* are programming objects and *Visual InterDev* is a programming tool that enable *HyperText Markup Language (HTML)* to be combined with core Exchange Server components to create dynamic, interactive applications for the *World Wide Web.*

➤ **Connectivity to other systems.** Using the Exchange Server *connector* components, messages can be routed between Exchange Server sites and a variety of other mail systems, including Microsoft Mail, Lotus cc:Mail, and X.400 systems.

➤ **Delegate Access.** Users can grant *Delegate Access* to private folders and delegate tasks to others, such as sending email and managing schedules, through client tools like Outlook.

➤ **Distribution lists.** Using the ability to address a *distribution list* of recipients with a single email address, you can create mailing lists of customers, employees, and business partners numbering into the thousands and easily available from the Exchange Server directory.

➤ **Electronic forms.** Customized forms are used in place of paper forms to automate and streamline common operations, such as posting information in a folder or submitting an expense report.

➤ **Group scheduling.** Using client tools like Outlook and Schedule+, users can share schedule information and plan group meetings across the Exchange Server organization.

➤ **Group task management.** Using client tools like Outlook and *Team Manager 97,* users can assign tasks to others, track the progress made on assigned tasks, and share task lists among members of a team.

➤ **IMAP4 support.** Users with IMAP4 clients can access email in their Exchange Server mailboxes, access information in their private folders stored on the server, and access public folders stored on the server.

➤ **Instant groupware.** By combining Outlook and public folders, users can easily create full-fledged applications called *instant groupware,* such as group calendars, to do lists, contact lists, and *electronic bulletin boards.*

➤ **Internet Mail Service.** The *Internet Mail Service* connector routes email messages between Exchange Server and *Simple Mail Transfer Protocol (SMTP)* servers, enabling Exchange Server users to send mail across the Internet.

➤ **Internet News Service.** The *Internet News Service* enables hosting of *USENET newsgroups* on Exchange Server and access to newsgroups by Exchange clients and third-party *Network News Transfer Protocol (NNTP)* clients.

➤ **LDAP support.** With support for the *Lightweight Directory Access Protocol (LDAP),* third-party clients and anonymous users can access and search the Exchange Server directory.

➤ **Messaging infrastructure.** Exchange Server's most basic function is the storage and routing of email messages between users of the Exchange Server system on the same Exchange Server, between servers, and across sites.

➤ **Outlook Web Access.** The *Outlook Web Access* component uses the *Active Server Platform* function of the Internet Information Server (IIS) to provide access to Exchange Server information in public folders, the directory, and private mailboxes and calendars through a *Web browser.*

➤ **POP3 support.** Users with POP3 clients can access email in their Exchange Server mailboxes and send email using Exchange Server.

➤ **Public folders.** Folders stored in the public information store contain such information as email messages, documents, graphics, and multimedia that can be accessed, edited, and updated by a group of Exchange Server users.

➤ **Remote access.** Because remote networking is built into all Exchange clients, users can download, compose, and otherwise manage email and directory information offline, providing *remote access* to Exchange Server functions while on the road or at home.

➤ **Sample applications.** Full-fledged public folder and electronic form applications can be used as-is to provide solutions to common problems, such as contact tracking, helpdesk, and interpersonal forms applications; *sample applications* can also be modified, often without programming, to suit the needs of your workgroup or company.

➤ **Scripting Agent and Event Service.** The *Microsoft Exchange Scripting Agent* and the *Microsoft Exchange Event Service* enable the design of customized, automated, *workflow* applications.

The Assessment Process

As you plan the installation of your company's Exchange Server organization, you will need to decide how to organize the servers into sites and how to organize the sites into an organization. You will also need to decide where to install the server components that provide the services your company needs. By conducting a thorough assessment of your company's needs and resources before installing Exchange Server, you can streamline the installation process and make sure that your Exchange Server organization works efficiently and solves all of your company's demands for a messaging infrastructure. You can also ensure that your Exchange Server organization can grow and adapt to your company's changing needs over time.

The first and most important step in planning your Exchange Server organization is to assess your existing needs and resources. This will give you a clear idea of how your company will use Exchange Server before you start the installation, so you can implement Exchange Server as efficiently as possible. During the assessment stage, you should perform the following tasks:

1. Determine the needs your users have and which Exchange Server services and applications are required to meet those needs.

2. Create a company geographic profile.

3. Collect information about your current underlying network topology.

4. Determine your Windows NT Server domain structure.

Assessing User Needs

During this step, you will decide how user needs are met by the Exchange Server system. Assessing user needs is a two-part process. First, you should find out how employees of your company use the existing system and how that functionality will be replaced with Exchange Server services. Second, you should identify the problems your users have that are not solved by the current system and how you can meet those needs with Exchange Server.

When assessing user needs, you will determine which specific Exchange Server services your users will require. For example, will your users require public folders and, if so, how many will they need, what types of public folders will they use, who will be accessing them, and how heavily will they be used? Or will your users need to send messages to other types of systems; if so, what types of connectors and gateways must you install to support those connections?

two

You also need to identify which Exchange client applications your users will require to perform these activities. For example, users who need to coordinate and track group tasks might require the Outlook and Team Manager 97 clients, whereas users who need to perform group-scheduling activities might require either Outlook or a combination of the Exchange Client and Schedule+ applications.

This process will help you more effectively organize your Exchange Server organization for the most efficient traffic flow and determine what Exchange Server services and applications you need to install. Assessing user needs will also help you determine software, hardware, server disk space, and training needs. For example, if you expect users to use public folders heavily, you might decide to dedicate a specific Exchange Server to act as a *public folder server*, making it easier to manage and back up public folder resources while providing better server performance to users who are accessing the email facilities only.

Creating User Groups

Before you analyze user needs, it helps to make descriptions of the people who will be using the Exchange Server system. You should break down users into small groups in a way that makes sense to you, such as by organization, by network location, or with the data they work with. Try to keep each group a similar size, placing users into groups that provide flexibility for planning servers. Then, analyze each group to learn about the kind of information they generate, how they exchange information, and their storage and performance needs. Once you have identified groups of users, describe them in a way that helps you design a server installation that meets each group's unique needs. Later, this information will simplify performance, load balancing, and budget decisions, and help you organize users onto different servers.

Analyzing The Needs Of Each Group

When assessing user needs, ask the following questions about each group of users:

➤ How many users will use the Exchange Server system and how many users are in each group?

➤ What functions does each group of users perform on the current system?

➤ What new services does each group of users require that are not being met by the current system (such as email, calendaring, public folders, or a connection to the Internet)?

Answering these questions should result in a list of general services and features your users require. Associate these needs with specific services or clients available with Exchange Server, and determine how many users will be making use of each Exchange Server feature and how heavily they will be using them. Use this data to categorize users and determine the software, hardware, amount of server disk space, predicted amount of traffic, and training each category of user will require. You can then plan your Exchange Server servers around these categories of users.

User needs assessment worksheet.

User Group	Number of Users in the Group	Most Important Needs	Exchange Server Services

Use the user needs assessment worksheet designed for grouping users and determining their Exchange Server needs.

In this worksheet, note a short description of each group of users in the "User Group" column. Enter the number of users in each group in the second column. All groups should be close to the same size to make it easier when assigning user groups to different servers, as you will want to keep the number of users housed on each server approximately the same. If some groups are much larger than others, then break down the larger groups even if they have similar functions, so that all groups are approximately the same size. In the "Most Important Needs" column, write down one or more of that group's needs for Exchange Server; this column should include functions that each group uses now and requirements that the group has that are not being met by your current system. In the "Exchange Server Services" column, enter a corresponding Exchange Server feature or service for each item in the "Most Important Needs" column.

Tip

You might want to include an "All" group in your worksheet to classify which Exchange Server services all of your users will be using; for example, all of your users might be using Exchange Server to exchange email or to access company-wide information in public folders. Then, you will have a good idea of which services need to be supported by all Exchange Servers in the organization.

User Needs Assessment Example

You are the network administrator of a small real estate firm. You originally purchased Exchange Server to deal with the following needs and problems that your company was experiencing:

➤ The firm needed a company-wide messaging infrastructure that could connect to other types of systems.

➤ The firm needed a way to share continuously updated information, such as listings and financial information, quickly and easily among employees.

➤ The firm wanted to take its listings to the Internet, providing continuously updated, dynamic information to customers in an exciting way.

All of these problems address user needs. Besides finding Exchange Server solutions to these problems and assigning them to the groups they most impact, you also need to assess how employees are using the current messaging system and how those uses can be fulfilled by Exchange Server. Finally, you should determine if any employees of the firm have additional needs that are not being met by the current system but that can be addressed by Exchange Server's services.

You determine that the logical way to break down employees is by function. You then identify the most important needs for each of these smaller groups and determine the solutions to those needs. For each need, you identify one or more Exchange Server services that will solve that user group's particular problems. This completed worksheet shows how the user groups were broken down and how the needs for each group were assessed.

Completed user needs assessment worksheet.

User Group	Number of Users in the Group	Most Important Needs	Exchange Server Services
Sales Team 1	7	Access to email while on the road.	Remote email connectivity.
		Sharing of updated listings information.	Public folders; sample applications.
		Ability to schedule group meetings.	Group scheduling through Outlook.
Sales Team 2	7	Same as Sales Team 1.	Same as Sales Team 1.
Administrative Assistants	5	Ability to manage email and calendars for salespeople.	Delegate access.
		Management of company contact list.	Public folders; instant groupware.
Financial Team	8	Connectivity to other locations through X.400.	X.400 Connector.
		Ability to share continuously updated financial information.	Public folders; electronic forms.
		Secure messaging.	Advanced security.
Listings Design Team	6	Ability to work together on group tasks.	Group tasks capability through Outlook and Team Manager 97.

Continued

Completed user needs assessment worksheet (Continued).			
User Group	**Number of Users in the Group**	**Most Important Needs**	**Exchange Server Services**
Web Design Team	5	Ability to publish listings information as dynamic Web pages.	Collaboration Data Objects; Visual InterDev.
		Email connectivity to the Internet for communication with customers.	POP3 and IMAP4 support; Internet Mail Service.
All	38	Internal email.	Exchange Server messaging infrastructure.
		Sharing of company-wide information.	Public folders.
		Same tools and functionality on different operating systems.	Common interface through the Outlook client.

Creating A Geographic Profile

The purpose of creating a *geographic profile* for your company is to identify where your company's offices and other facilities are located. The geographic profile can represent a small area, such as an office building, or a much larger area, such as a nationwide company. The profile helps you understand how your company's facilities are laid out physically, so you can incorporate that information into your overall layout of the Exchange Server organization. For example, the physical locations of company facilities might determine the placement and size of Exchange Server sites.

Analyzing The Geographic Profile

When you create a geographic profile for your company, you should identify your company's physical locations by city and country. The profile should include all locations where your company has a facility, whether those facilities are clustered in a small region or dispersed over a large area. For example, are your company's offices located in one city, in one country, or worldwide? You should also identify which user groups are located at each facility. By determining the types of users and how many users are located at each facility, you can better estimate the amount of network traffic traveling between facilities.

Create a geographic profile worksheet to help organize the information you collected about your company's geographic profile. Later, you can use the geographic profile to help plan the locations and placement of the different sites of your Exchange Server organization.

Geographic profile worksheet.

Facility Location   **User Groups Located at the Facility**

In the "Facility Location" column, note the city, state, and country location of each of your company's facilities. If your company has more than one facility in a city, you might find it helpful to further break down facilities by building and even office numbers in this column. Under "User Groups Located at the Facility," list the user groups that you previously defined during the user needs assessment stage that are located at each facility; note that a single user group should not span more than one facility. You might also find it useful to make notes about the number of users at each facility.

Tip

When creating your company's geographic profile, you might find it helpful to use a map or diagram to lay out the profile and make notes about user groups, locations of facilities, and types of facilities directly on the map or diagram.

Geographic Profile Example

Returning to our real estate company, you note that the firm has two facilities: the main office and a branch office located in a neighboring city. Therefore, the completed geographic profile worksheet for the firm looks like this.

Completed geographic profile worksheet.

Facility Location	User Groups Located at the Facility
San Francisco, California	Sales Team 1 Administrative Assistants Listings Design Team Financial Design Team (26 users total)
Palo Alto, California	Sales Team 2 Web Design Team (12 users total)

Assessing Current Network Resources

After creating a geographic profile, you should thoroughly analyze the network topology currently in use by all of your company's facilities. The underlying network is one of the most important factors affecting the Exchange Server topology and its configuration, so it is important that you understand all aspects of it. When planning your Exchange Server organization, you will find that site boundaries, site connectors, message routing, directory replication, and system administration will all be affected by the underlying network. Key network elements that you should analyze include the network size, type, bandwidth, links, traffic patterns, and protocols.

Network Size And Type

The Exchange Server organization can easily span networks of different sizes and types. Your company network's size and type affect many other decisions you have to make, including the layout of the organization, the number of sites in the organization, the services provided to different segments of the network, and the methods for moving data over network links. You must make different considerations when working with networks of different sizes. For example, a small Local Area Network (LAN) might require only one site or a few sites, whereas a large network will require multiple sites, considerations for how to move data over Wide Area Network (WAN) links, and decisions about configuring the organization to provide needed information and servers at the LAN level, where users create and receive information. You should also consider the reliability of your network. For example, a satellite network might have very high bandwidth but might not be as reliable as a TCP/IP network that has lower bandwidth.

Network Bandwidth And Links

Network performance is largely affected by network bandwidth, which influences many decisions when organizing your Exchange Server layout. *Network bandwidth* is the data transmission capacity of your network links. The term *bandwidth* refers literally to the difference between the highest and the lowest frequencies that are carried over a communication channel—the higher the bandwidth, the more information can be carried. The amount of available bandwidth depends on the data transfer rate across the network and the physical characteristics of the communications line. Both the *total available bandwidth*—the bandwidth provided by a network connection—and the *net available bandwidth*—the bandwidth available after consumption by other applications—are important in planning your Exchange Server layout and installation.

The total available bandwidth affects all of the following Exchange Server installation decisions: appropriate site links, directory and public folder replication schedules, costs, and sharing of public folders across multiple sites. Bandwidth is an important consideration when deciding on server locations; for instance, servers in the same site require faster and higher bandwidth connections than servers on different sites. A small Exchange

two

Server organization that has low message traffic and light public folder usage does not require as much bandwidth as a more heavily trafficked, larger organization that has frequent mail and public folder usage.

The bandwidth of your servers also affects the applications that can coexist with Exchange Server on the same network, because performance decreases as network traffic increases and applications compete for bandwidth, so you should be aware of the bandwidth consumed by each application. You should ensure that the net available bandwidth between servers is sufficient to support the Exchange Server services you plan to provide. For example, if you plan to run a database application with Exchange Server, you should take into consideration how much of the total available bandwidth the database application consumes when it transfers data.

The net available bandwidth on a network link between servers also determines whether servers can be placed in the same site. As well as ensuring that links between servers have enough bandwidth to handle the common load due to message traffic, bursts in traffic, and public folder and directory replication traffic, you should consider the bandwidth consumed by Exchange clients if users routinely send email messages with large audio, video, and image file attachments.

Another important consideration is network bandwidth costs, which are affected by the ways data is transmitted across the organization. For example, both Point-to-Point Protocol (PPP) dial-up lines and dedicated PPP lines might provide the same bandwidth, but dedicated PPP lines are more expensive because they are available 24 hours a day.

The higher the traffic volume between servers, the more bandwidth is needed. Generally, you should design your Exchange Server sites so that the synchronous RPC connections between servers are in the medium-to-high or very high bandwidth range. However, you might be able to use low-to-medium bandwidth ranges for server connections that have low message volume or little public folder use.

Remember that Exchange Server's client/server architecture maximizes the efficient use of bandwidth because all client requests are processed on the server and only the results are transmitted to the client, minimizing overhead. Nevertheless, you should consider additional ways to minimize network traffic when using Exchange Server. For example, if you configure traffic-intensive processes, such as public folder replication, to occur after business hours, you will minimize bandwidth consumption during the hours when email and other network traffic is highest.

Tip

You will find many helpful suggestions throughout this book for minimizing network traffic and optimizing network resources—look for them!

Network Traffic Patterns

Network traffic is a generic term used to describe the amount of data traveling over a network backbone at a given period in time. You should analyze current network *traffic patterns,* the predictable trends of data flow through a link over a period of time. Knowing network traffic patterns helps you determine whether the total available bandwidth is enough to sustain bursts of traffic during heavy use of the network. For example, if your network traffic exceeds the available network bandwidth, then client/server response becomes unpredictable. To monitor network traffic, you could use Windows NT Performance Monitor on a small network, or a packet sniffer, Microsoft System Management Server, or other dedicated network-monitoring products. Specifically, you will want to measure the *network bandwidth utilization,* or how close a network link is to full capacity, and the *total packets per second,* or how close bridges and routers are to reaching full capacity.

Network Protocols

Determine what type of network protocols you have so you can configure links between sites appropriately when designing the topology of the Exchange Server organization. You need to make sure there is basic network connectivity between servers and clients, because network connectivity must be established before the Exchange client can connect to the Exchange Server computer. Clients and servers must use the same *network protocols,* or the rules that govern the behavior or method of operation that enable computers to communicate over a network.

To integrate clients on other networks, you must choose one or more of the protocols supported by Windows NT Server. Windows NT Server supports the following built-in protocols, which Exchange Server can use:

➤ Transport Control Protocol/Internet Protocol (TCP/IP).

➤ Internetwork Packet Exchange/Sequenced Packet Exchange (IPX/SPX [NWLink]).

➤ NetBIOS Extended User Interface (NetBEUI).

Collecting Information About The Underlying Network

Create a network assessment worksheet to make notes about your current network. By organizing this information into one place, you can get an overall picture of your current network that will come in handy when planning the topology of your Exchange Server organization.

Tip

Again, a map or diagram showing the underlying network topology connecting different facilities might be helpful.

Network assessment worksheet.		
Network Size:		
Network Type:		
Network Bandwidth	Total Available Bandwidth:	
	Net Available Bandwidth:	
	Network Links:	
	Notes:	
Network Traffic Patterns	Network Bandwidth Utilization:	
	Total Packets Per Second:	
	Notes:	
Network Protocols:		

Network Assessment Example

When analyzing the existing network resources for the fictional real estate firm, we combined notes about the network connecting the two facilities into one worksheet (the branch office is referred to as "Office 2" in the worksheet). You might also find it helpful to adapt and complete separate worksheets for each facility, particularly if your company has several facilities, and then complete another worksheet that shows how the network connecting the separate facilities is configured.

Completed network assessment worksheet.		
Network Size:	3 cascaded 10 port hubs with ISDN WAN link to Office 2	
Network Type:	10baseT Ethernet	
Network Bandwidth	**Total Available Bandwidth:**	10MB/sec
	Net Available Bandwidth:	6MB/sec
	Network Links:	1 bridge with 128MB/sec throughput (ISDN WAN link)
	Notes:	Plan to upgrade to 100baseT in Q2 '98
Network Traffic Patterns	**Network Bandwidth Utilization:**	75%
	Total Packets Per Second:	500
	Notes:	Why are there large bandwidth bursts after 3:00 p.m. on Fridays? Internet movies?
Network Protocols:	TCP/IP, IPX	

Determining Your Windows NT Domain Structure

Exchange Server relies on Windows NT domains to provide security, such as *authentication* of user logons and Exchange Server services. A *domain* is a group of servers that share common security policies and user account databases. A domain can contain a single Windows NT Server computer or multiple Windows NT Server computers, as well as other types of servers and clients.

A *domain model* is a group of one or more domains arranged for best management of users and resources. There are four Windows NT domain models: single domain model, master domain model, multiple master domain model, and complete trust model.

It is important to choose the Windows NT domain model for your network carefully or study the existing one thoroughly, because it will be difficult to change the domain structure once it is implemented. Knowing how your Windows NT Server domains are arranged will be invaluable when you lay out your Exchange Server sites and organization. You need to locate user accounts and Exchange Server services in the same domain as your Exchange Server computers or in a trusted domain, or users and services cannot be properly validated across the site. Site boundaries also depend on the domain structure already in place.

The domain model that best fits your company's needs depends on your administrative resources and the size of your network. If there is already a domain model in place, you should determine which one it is, how it is structured, how trust relationships are set up, why that model was chosen, and where *domain controllers* are located. You should also be aware of how user accounts and global groups from one domain can be used in another domain, if at all. All of this information will be incorporated into your plan for the Exchange Server organization.

Trust Relationships

A *trust relationship* is a link between domains that enables a user with an account on one domain to access resources on the linked domain. Establishing trust relationships between domains simplifies account management and makes domain models more flexible and extensible. For example, using trust relationships, you can distribute the management of users and domains among departments, rather than having a centralized management. This allows each department to manage its own domain and define its own users and global accounts, while enabling users and global accounts to be used on all domains.

two

Tip

Be careful about making Exchange Server function as a Backup Domain Controller (BDC). A BDC places significant background task load on a server. Unless you have a small site, it's best for your Exchange Server computer to function in a dedicated mode.

Single Domain Model

The *single domain model* is the simplest and the easiest to administer, having only one domain in which all Windows NT users are created and requiring no trust relationships. It works best for smaller organizations that have fewer than 40,000 users that require a centralized management, in which trust among the organizational groups is not an issue. However, this domain model might not be flexible enough if you are anticipating growth in your organization, because it does not allowing grouping of users into departments or grouping of resources. It could also exhibit poor performance if the domain acquires too many users, groups, or servers.

Master Domain Model

The *master domain model* works well for companies that have fewer than 10,000 users where the network must be split into multiple domains for organizational purposes while maintaining a centralized administration. User accounts and global groups are defined only in the master, or first-tier, domain. Each organizational group manages its own resources on separate resource, or second-tier, domains. Each resource domain establishes a one-way trust relationship with the master domain, so that users with accounts in the master domain can access resources in all second-tier domains. The entire network, including users and resources, is managed through the master domain.

This model is much more flexible than the single domain model and allows you to consolidate the administration of user accounts and global groups into one domain, instead of creating a separate user account database for each domain. At the same time, resources are grouped logically and can be managed by departmental administrators. However, this model might exhibit poor performance if the master domain acquires too many users and global groups, and local groups must be redefined in each domain where they are to be used.

Multiple Master Domain Model

The *multiple master domain model* is organized into two tiers. The first tier contains two or more single master domains connected by a two-way trust relationship. These domains serve as the account domains; every user account is created and maintained on one of the master domains. The second tier serves as resource domains, providing resources like shared file servers and printers. Each second-tier, resource domain establishes a one-way trust relationship with all master domains. Resource domains can also trust each other, but this is not required.

This model works well for companies that have more than 10,000 users organized by groups, departments, or locations that maintain a centralized administration. As it is the most scalable model, it is also good for companies that anticipate substantial growth. This domain model has some disadvantages, though: Administrative requirements can be considerably greater than for other models; local and global groups might have to be defined several times, because not all accounts are located in one domain; and there are several trust relationships to manage.

Complete Trust Model

In the *complete trust model,* every domain on the network trusts every other domain. Each domain has full control over its own user accounts and resources. The complete trust model is a good model for companies that have less than 30,000 users that want to distribute management of users and domains among different departments, working well for organizations lacking centralized management. It is also scalable to networks with any number of users, providing for growth in the future. However, it is more difficult to establish the integrity of global groups that other domains might use within this model. Another downside is the potential for a very large number of trust relationships to manage.

Assessing The Existing Domain Model

Create a domain model assessment worksheet to record notes about your existing Windows NT Server domain model. This information will be used when you begin planning your Exchange Server organization's layout.

Domain Model Assessment Example

Returning to our real estate firm example, you need to assess the domain model already in place. You find that the firm implemented a master domain model with the following characteristics (as with the network assessment worksheet, the two facilities are designated as Office 1 and Office 2 in this worksheet).

Domain model assessment worksheet.

Domain Model Type:
Domain Model Structure:
Types of Trust Relationships:
Reason for Choosing This Domain Model:
Domain Controller Locations:

Completed domain model assessment worksheet.	
Domain Model Type:	Master domain model.
Domain Model Structure:	First-tier domain where user groups are located. Second-tier domain at Office 1 for shared resources. Second-tier domain at Office 2 for shared resources.
Types of Trust Relationships:	One-way trust relationship from the second-tier domain at Office 1 to the first-tier domain. One-way trust relationship from the second-tier domain at Office 2 to the first-tier domain.
Reason for Choosing This Domain Model:	Because there are so few users, all users are defined on the first-tier domain, enabling centralized management of user accounts. Because there are two separate facilities, distributed management of network resources at the office level makes more sense. Users can connect to resources in all trusted domains as the result of pass-through authentication.
Domain Controller Locations:	1 Primary Domain Controller (Office 1). 1 Backup Domain Controller (Office 1). 1 Backup Domain Controller (Office 2).

Moving On

After going through this chapter, you should have a complete assessment of your users' needs and your company's existing network resources. You should have made notes on the following: the different user groups that will be residing on the Exchange Server system; the Exchange Server services each user group will require; the geographic locations of your company's facilities; your company's existing network resources; and your company's existing Windows NT Server domain model. All of this information will be required when planning the layout and installation of your Exchange Server, which you will do in the next chapter.

PART II

Installation Planning

Now that you have thoroughly assessed your user needs and existing resources, you are ready to plan the installation of your Exchange Server organization. You should not skip the planning process. Whether your organization is small, with only a few servers, or large, with multiple sites spanning a large region, planning will make the deployment of the Exchange Server system go more smoothly and will ensure fewer problems after Exchange Server is installed.

The installation planning process incorporates the following broad steps:

1. Design a prototype topology for the Exchange Server organization.

2. Determine your hardware needs.

3. Determine your software needs.

4. Put administrative policies and naming conventions into place.

5. Schedule the rollout of the Exchange Server system.

Because every company is different, no set planning process will fit every company's needs. However, the steps outlined in this chapter apply to almost every Exchange Server system, and you can omit the steps that are not required to meet your needs. Keep in mind that your implementation of Exchange Server will require fine-tuning as your organization grows and changes and as your needs for Exchange Server expand.

Organization Planning Worksheet

As you move through the steps in this chapter, make notes about your plans for your Exchange Server organization using a worksheet similar to the Exchange Server organization planning worksheet presented here.

Exchange Server organization planning worksheet.

Exchange Server Organization

Organization Name:

Windows NT Domain Name:

Site Naming Convention:

Server Naming Convention:

Mailbox Naming Convention:

Number of Sites:

Administrator(s):

Information Storage Policy:

Backup Policy and Schedule:

Rollout Schedule:

Exchange Server Site

Complete a separate worksheet for each site. Attach the site layout, showing how the site corresponds to the physical network, the placement and descriptions of user groups, and the placement and descriptions of servers.

Site Name:

Number of Servers in the Site:

Number of Users on the Site:

Service Account Name:

MS Mail Address:

X.400 Address:

SMTP Address:

Schedule+ Public Folder Location:

Administrator(s):

Client Installation Plan

Client Installation Point Location:

Network Share Location:

Hardware Needed for Client Computers:

Clients to Support:	◯ Roving	◯ Remote
Connect via:	◯ Shiva ◯ RAS	◯ Other Remote Access Software

Continued

Exchange Server organization planning worksheet (Continued).

Connectors To Other Sites

Messaging Bridgehead Server(s):

Method of Site Connection: ○ Site Connector ○ Dynamic RAS Connector
 ○ X.400 Connector ○ Internet Mail Service

Connectors To Foreign Systems

Check all the connectors to be installed and identify where they will be installed by server name.

❏ X.400 Connector:

❏ MS Mail (PC) Connector:

❏ MS Mail (AppleTalk) Connector:

❏ Lotus cc:Mail Connector:

❏ Internet Mail Service:

Exchange Server

Complete a separate worksheet for each server.

Server Name:

Site Location:

Number of User Mailboxes:

Administrator(s):

Server Use (Check All That Apply):

❏ Schedule+ Public Folder ❏ Client Installation Point ❏ Connector
❏ Key Management Server ❏ Public Folder Storage ❏ Administrator Program
❏ Primary Domain Controller ❏ Backup Domain Controller ❏ Remote Access Service

❏ Other:

Hardware Requirements

Hardware Needed to Support Exchange Server 5.5:

CPU Upgrade:

RAM Upgrade:

Disk Upgrade:

Network Adapter Upgrade:

Hardware Needed to Support Remote Users:

Hardware Needed to Support Connectors:

Software Requirements

Software Needed to Support Exchange Server 5.5:

Software Needed to Support Additional Exchange Server Services:

Topology Checklist

Planning the Exchange Server topology is essentially the process of designing and laying out your *Exchange Server organization*. Designing the topology involves the following tasks:

1. Plan your Exchange Server sites:

   Determine the number of sites to include in the organization.

   Decide on the size for each site, or site boundaries.

   Create a site layout for each site in the organization.

2. Plan your Exchange Server servers:

   Decide how many servers to locate in the site.

   Determine which user groups will be located on each server.

   Assign the services each server will provide.

3. Determine how to connect multiple Exchange Server sites, if there are any.

4. Determine how to connect the Exchange Server system to foreign systems, if necessary.

Planning your Exchange Server organization builds directly on the work you did during the needs and resource assessment process in Chapter 2. Consult the notes you made during the assessment process while laying out the Exchange Server topology, taking all of the following into account:

➤ Your Exchange Server organization should meet users' current and future needs.

➤ Your Exchange Server organization should conform to the user groups and company facilities already in place.

➤ Your Exchange Server organization should minimize impact on your existing network and should take advantage of existing network resources.

➤ Your Exchange Server organization should stay within your budget.

With those factors in mind, you can make a detailed plan of exactly how your Exchange Server organization will be laid out, starting with sites and site boundaries.

Planning Sites

The needs of different organizations can vary widely: Your company might require only one simple site, or you might find you need multiple sites if your organization has many servers or if your company facilities are spread across a wide geographic area. Your site plans should be based on the information that you gathered during the resource assessment stage: network bandwidth, network traffic, cost, performance, and the Windows NT Server *domain model*.

Determining The Number Of Sites And Site Boundaries

Plan the number of sites and site boundaries carefully. Although it is a relatively simple matter to add or subtract individual servers from existing Exchange Server sites, it is difficult to split existing sites or join other sites to them once the sites have been created. If you change site boundaries after setting up sites, you might have to reinstall and reconfigure all the affected servers.

Several factors affect where to draw site boundaries. Some are conditions that all Exchange Server computers must satisfy so that they can be placed in the same site. Others, while not mandatory, should also be taken into consideration, including administration, cost, security, and performance.

To help you determine how many Exchange Server sites you'll need, see Decision Tree 3.1.

Tip

To simplify configuration and administration of your Exchange Server organization, keep the number of sites to a minimum and draw sites as large as possible.

Required Site Conditions. The following conditions must be met to place servers together in the same site:

➤ **Synchronous *Remote Procedure Call (RPC)* connectivity.** Site boundaries cannot span a connection that does not support synchronous RPC connections between all Exchange Server computers. For example, you define one site to include all of your company's North American facilities. But if synchronous RPC connections between the North and South American facilities are not supported, you must define a second site to encompass the South American facilities—you cannot put the North American and South American facilities in the same site.

➤ **Permanent connections.** Permanent connections, rather than periodic connections, must be supported between all Exchange Server servers in a site. Permanent connections include Local Area Networks (LANs), leased lines, and some types of Wide Area Network (WAN) links. Periodic connections encompass any connections that are not available at all times, such as dial-up connections through a modem.

➤ **Adequate *network bandwidth*.** All Exchange Servers within a site should be connected with network links that support relatively high bandwidth. The available bandwidth must be able to handle the volume of data transferred between servers, including message volume, *directory replication*, and *public folder replication*. However, if you expect message traffic between servers to be low and public folder use to be light, bandwidth requirements can be adjusted accordingly.

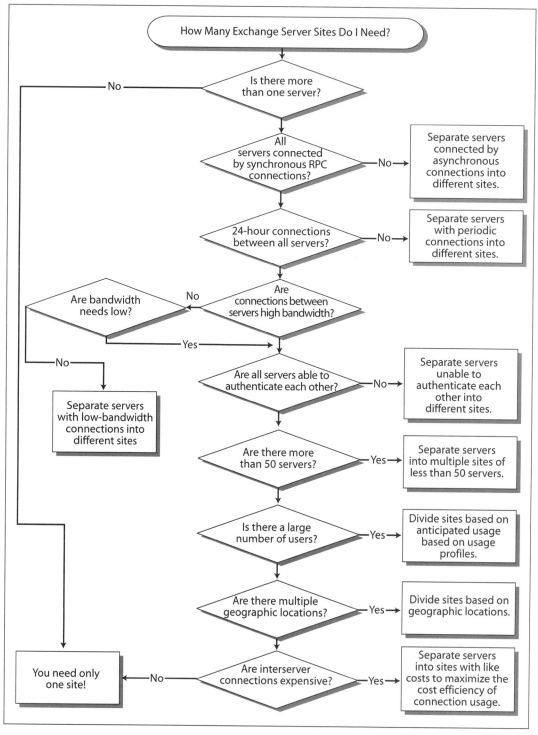

Decision Tree 3.1   How many Exchange Server sites do I need?

Mapping Sites To Windows NT Domains

Your Exchange Server sites can map to your Windows NT Server *domains* in many different ways, and no special rules apply. For example, you can map sites to domains on a one-to-one basis, or a site can span several domains (as long as the domains trust each other). You also do not need to map all existing domains to your sites, as long as the domains containing the Exchange Server computers can authenticate Exchange Server users and services. For example, if you have set up a complete trust model, you could place all Exchange Servers in one domain or spread them among all domains. In the master and multiple domain models, you could place all Exchange Servers in a single second-tier domain, in a single first-tier domain, or spread across several first-tier domains.

The choice of how to map your Exchange Server sites to your domains depends largely on how you want to structure administration of the domains and the Exchange Server computers that reside in them. You might find it easiest to map the Exchange Server sites to the Windows NT domain topology that is already established or to span multiple trusted Windows NT domains that already exist. Therefore, it is important for you to have a complete understanding of your Windows NT domain topology before you lay out the Exchange Server organization.

➤ **Security.** All Exchange Server servers within a site must be able to authenticate each other, because all Exchange Server services within the site must be run under the same security context and use the same *service account,* the Windows NT *user account* used to run Exchange Server services. Therefore, Windows NT user accounts and service accounts must be in the same domains as the servers or in trusted domains.

Other Factors To Consider. Although the following conditions do not have to be met to place servers together on one site, they should be taken into consideration, as they will also affect the size of your sites:

➤ **Number of users at each location and their usage profiles.** It often makes sense to group users who habitually work together in the same site. This improves the overall performance of the system by reducing network traffic and resource utilization. For example, if members of the same workgroup are located on different sites, you have to replicate public folder information between the two sites frequently; however, if the workgroup members are all located on a single server, you eliminate the need for public folder replication.

three

➤ **Administration.** Many Exchange Server administrative services are configured automatically within a site, making it easier to administer the servers grouped within the site. You should configure sites to include as many servers as possible so that you can administer those servers collectively. Keeping the number of sites low also reduces administrative duties. However, sites should have no more than 50 servers to keep administrative duties from getting out of hand.

➤ **Geographic profile.** It is not necessary to have a one-to-one correspondence between the number of sites and the geographic locations of your company facilities, but it can simplify site administration and placement. For example, if your organization is distributed across a wide area, you should consider dividing the organization into multiple sites based on geographic regions.

➤ **Connection costs.** The cost of transferring information between two servers is determined by the cost of maintaining the link between the servers and the cost of sending data over the link. In a site, all Exchange Server computers replicate directory information automatically, and many of them replicate public folder information as well. Place on a separate site any Exchange Server computer that is connected to another Exchange Server computer over a line with charges based on the amount of data sent. Then, you can control when information is replicated between the two sites and minimize the costs of using the link.

➤ **Performance.** The same considerations for information replication apply when considering performance. For example, if two Exchange Server computers are connected by a slow link, try to place the servers in different sites. Then, you can configure information replication between the two sites so that the slow link is used less often. Remember that the number of servers in a site also affects performance.

Creating A Site Layout

After you determine the number of sites in your organization and the boundaries for each site, you should create a *site layout,* which shows different views of each site and collects your notes about all the factors that affect the site design. The physical network already in place is the groundwork on which to lay the foundation of your site, so start the site layout with a drawing of the physical network. Laying the site on top of the physical network minimizes the effect Exchange Server has on the network.

Add information to the drawing about the location of each segment of the network. Each part of the network that connects into a router or bridge is a *network segment,* which corresponds to a physical location. For instance, a network segment could serve an entire building or just a floor in the building. The layout of network segments helps you understand where different user groups are located.

After diagramming the physical network underlying the site, add users to the site layout, grouping them according to their usage patterns and needs. Include the name of the

3

group, an estimate of the group's size, and a description of the group (you should have already gathered this information during the user needs assessment process). Later, you can use this information to determine the placement of servers and assign user groups to their *home servers*, or the servers that contain the users' mailboxes.

Planning Servers

Use the site layout to begin deciding how many servers to locate on each site and the services those servers will provide. Knowing where user groups are located and the needs that each group has will help you make these decisions. Show the placement of the servers on the physical network and match user groups with each server on the site layout. You can then use this information to assess what hardware and software are needed to fulfill the functions of each server.

Determining The Number Of Servers In The Site

The number of servers you should place in a site depends mostly on the number of users, public folders, and connectors needed. The site layout shows how many users are located in the site and the general needs they have for Exchange Server services. You can begin determining how many servers to place on the site by locating servers along the site layout to fulfill the needs of different user groups in the site.

Tip

To keep administration of the Exchange Server site as efficient as possible, no site should have more than 50 servers.

When deciding on the number of servers, you will want to keep performance at a maximum while keeping costs at a minimum. Based on your desired cost-to-performance ratio, you might decide to implement a greater number of less powerful servers or a smaller number of more powerful servers. If your site has a mixture of large and small workgroups, a similar mixture of large and small servers might best fit your needs.

Table 3.1 outlines some of the advantages and disadvantages to using a larger number of less powerful servers.

Table 3.2 outlines some of the advantages and disadvantages to using a smaller number of more powerful servers.

Assigning User Groups To Servers

Locating user groups and servers along the site layout should show you which user groups to house on each server. Housing users on a server entails configuring those users' mailboxes on the server and storing messages to those users in the server's private information store (the *mailbox* is the delivery location for incoming mail messages to an Exchange Server user).

Table 3.1   Advantages and disadvantages to having a greater number of less powerful servers in a site.

Advantages	Disadvantages
Fewer users impacted by a single-server failure.	Increases in users or load require more hardware.
Servers can be customized to the user group they serve.	Customized hardware often requires increased support costs.
Adding incremental increases in capacity is generally less expensive.	More hardware to maintain.
More choices in off-the-shelf small hardware available.	Greater network overhead and storage space required for replicated data.
Each server can be physically close to its user groups, reducing network traffic for client/server interactions.	Bottlenecks due to information replication increase with fewer users per server.

Table 3.2   Advantages and disadvantages to using a smaller number of more powerful servers.

Advantages	Disadvantages
Easier upgradability of processors and disk arrays.	Fewer vendors from which to choose.
More likely that message recipients are located on the same server.	You might not be able to use the hardware of the existing mail system.
More users per server reduces network traffic.	Larger information store takes longer to back up and restore
Fewer servers for directory replication results in less network traffic.	Network adapter card must be able to handle a high volume of user traffic to each server.
Overall disk storage requirements lower due to single-instance store architecture.	Increased vulnerability to a single point of failure.
More powerful hardware ensures better fault-tolerant designs and error correction.	
Fewer servers reduces administration requirements.	

It is generally more efficient to place together on one server those user groups that have similar functions and are from the same network segment, because those users will most often be sending messages to each other. Messages sent between users on the same server are transferred by *local delivery* rather than the *Message Transfer Agent (MTA)*, reducing disk and CPU load. Messages sent to a group of people on the same server are stored as single copies in the information store, conserving disk space. If data does not have to flow outside a network segment, traffic across bridges and routers is reduced. However, you might determine that one user group is too large for a single server and will require two servers.

3

There is no explicit limit to the number of users you can configure for a server. The number of users a server can support is primarily a function of server performance and the load each user places on the server. Each organization uses email in different ways and has different hardware resources. Different users vary in how they employ the scheduling, messaging, and workgroup functions of Exchange Server. Even a company's culture and location can affect how users make use of the messaging system.

Direct user interactions with the server are the most significant load factor. The load created by these *user actions* is proportional to the number of users actively interacting with the server and the actions they perform. The number of users a server can support also depends on what the company considers to be acceptable response times and what kind of trade-offs can be made between server load and client response times.

Servers also perform *background actions,* such as delivering messages, making routing decisions, replicating public folder and directory information, executing rules, and monitoring storage quotas. The load caused by background actions is also generally proportional to the number of users on the server, but other factors, such as whether the server is connected to other sites or systems, can significantly impact load.

To determine how many users to place on a server, you should estimate how many actions a user in a particular user group performs over time and how many background actions the server performs on the user's behalf over the same amount of time. Assess the load these actions place on the server, and make rough performance predictions based on the "average" user in the user group. Using these averages, you can classify different user groups by low, medium, and heavy usage and determine which user groups each server can support.

There are practical limits to the number of users that can comfortably be housed on one server, as well. For instance, the public and private information stores are each limited to 16GB, which could limit the number of users on large servers, depending on the amount of storage space each user needs. There can also be limitations dictated by the time it takes to back up a large server.

The Load Simulator

The Exchange Server *Load Simulator* tool shows a realistic load on an Exchange Server computer by simulating the behavior of users on Outlook clients. This helps you assess the level of performance that is acceptable for your company's users and how many users your Exchange Servers can support.

● ● ● *Tip* ● ● ●

When determining which users to place on your servers, you should consider distributing administrators' mailboxes, important public folders, and connectors among different servers, so that the failure of a single server does not stop business.

Determining Server Roles

After deciding how many servers to place in your site and which users will be located on those servers, you can assign roles to the Exchange Servers to provide needed services. You might even choose to add additional servers to the site to fulfill certain roles. As you decide on server roles, make notes on the site layout so that you can see at a glance if any one server is performing too many functions or is being underutilized. To help you decide how services should be distributed among the servers in the site, see Decision Tree 3.2.

While all Exchange Servers that are members of the same site perform identical core functions—directory services, mail transfer, and mail storage—any Exchange Server can provide specialized services or contain additional software. For example, you might designate some Exchange Servers to include the Administrator program software, provide connections to other sites, or function as client installation points. Other servers could be configured as *gateway* servers, public folder servers, *Post Office Protocol 3 (POP3)* servers, *Network News Transport Protocol (NNTP)* servers, or advanced security servers. The Windows NT Server hosting the Exchange Server can also perform tasks not related to the Exchange Server, including acting as a domain controller, Remote Access Service (RAS), Structured Query Language (SQL) server, or Microsoft Systems Management Server (SMS).

Performance can be greatly affected by additional applications running on the server, so try dedicating your Exchange Server computers to Exchange Server services whenever possible. Exchange Server is a CPU, hard disk, and RAM intensive network application, so combining it with SQL Server, which also places great demands on the server, typically does not make good economic sense. Adding a second server computer would be more cost effective than increasing the performance of a single server computer to the level required to run both applications together for even a moderate size workgroup. However, simultaneously providing services that are not resource intensive, such as domain controllers, will not greatly impact performance.

In addition to hosting user mailboxes, Exchange Servers can have the following roles:

➤ Schedule+ Free Busy Information public folder.

➤ Client installation point or network share.

➤ Connectivity to other sites, foreign systems, or the Internet.

➤ Key Management server for advanced security.

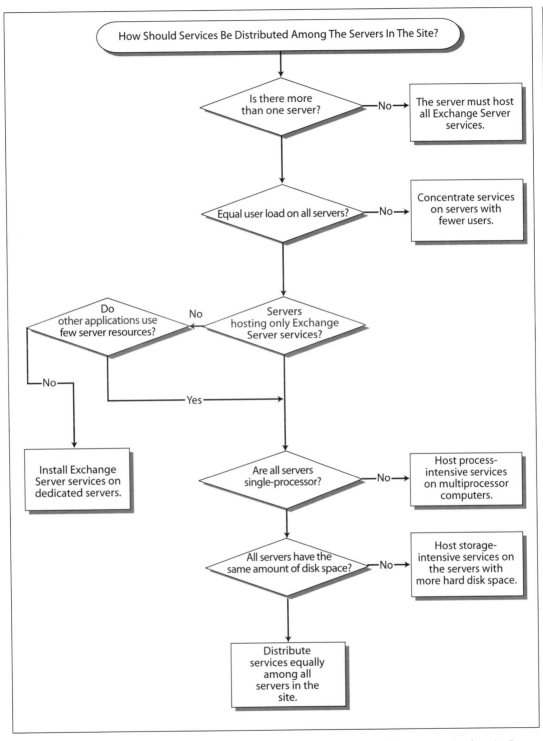

Decision Tree 3.2 How should services be distributed among the servers in the site?

➤ Public folder storage.

➤ Primary and backup domain controllers.

➤ Remote Access Service.

If all the servers in the site use a standardized configuration and have an equal user load, you can distribute Exchange Server services evenly among them. If all servers in the site except one are single-processor computers that have an equal user load, the multiprocessor computer is the best choice for processor-intensive services. If one server has more available hard disk space than others in the site, it becomes a good choice for a public folder storage server. You should carefully decide which roles all your Exchange Server computers will play to fulfill the needs of your users, because these roles will impact server load, performance, and hardware requirements. To help you determine what types of servers are required in the site, use Decision Tree 3.3.

Schedule+ Free Busy Information Public Folder. The first server in the site always contains a *hidden public folder* that stores the free and busy information for every Schedule+ and Outlook user in the Exchange Server organization. When a user is scheduling a group meeting, Schedule+ or Outlook reads the free and busy information from this *Schedule+ Free Busy Information public folder* for each invitee not located on the home server. The load on this public folder depends on the use of Schedule+ or Outlook to plan meetings with resources and people outside the home server. Be sure to install first the server where you want this public folder to reside.

Client Installation Point Or Network Share. If users need to run an Exchange client application from their local disks, you must set up a *client installation point* on an Exchange Server computer or on a file server. If users need to run an Exchange client application from a network server, you need to set up a *network share* on an Exchange Server computer or on a file server; the network share must be installed on a server that has enough network, memory, processor, and disk input/output (I/O) capacity to handle the increased load and traffic.

Table 3.3 outlines the advantages and disadvantages of running the client application from a network share.

Connectivity Server. The appropriate *connectors* must be installed on an Exchange Server computer to enable communication with other sites in the organization, foreign systems, or the Internet. Any Exchange Server can run the connectors, and a single server can run multiple connectors of different types. Connectors do increase the load on the server, so you might consider putting connectors on a server that has no user mailboxes.

Key Management Server. If you plan to use the advanced security features of Exchange Server, you must configure one server in the organization to store and manage the

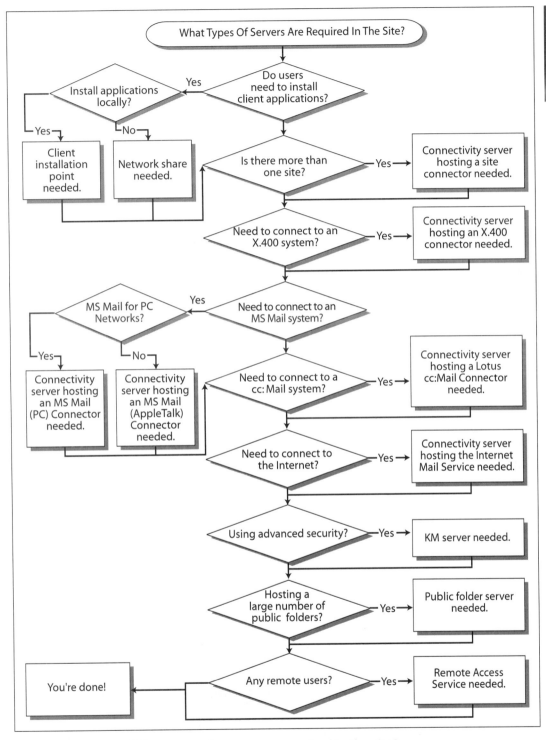

Decision Tree 3.3   What types of servers are required in the site?

three

Table 3.3 Advantages and disadvantages to configuring clients on a network share.	
Advantages	**Disadvantages**
Less disk space is required on client computers.	Remote users cannot use the network share.
User's system configurations are managed from a centralized location.	Server providing the network share is used more and might require more capacity.
Upgrading clients is easier.	Client performance is slower than running it from the local disk.
Backing up client files is easier.	Increased network traffic.
Faster client installation.	
If other applications are run from the network, a consistent policy within the organization is maintained.	

advanced security database. This server is called the *Key Management (KM) server.* The load on the KM server is negligible, because the server is primarily used to generate keys for digitally signing and encrypting data, which is done infrequently.

The KM server must fulfill the following requirements:

➤ Located in the domain where you plan to centralize administration.

➤ Physically secure.

➤ Backed up on a regular basis.

➤ Uses the Windows NT Server File System (NTFS) format.

➤ Have Microsoft Certificate Server and Internet Information Server (IIS), version 4.0 or later, installed.

● ● *Tip* ● ● ● ●

If you have the extra hardware and maximum security is critical to your organization, consider making the KM server a dedicated server in a separate site.

Public Folder Server. Every Exchange Server can maintain public folders, but you might choose to dedicate one or more servers for storing all public folders for the site (these servers are called *public folder servers*). Devoting a server to public folder storage has the following advantages:

➤ One or more servers can use the same public folder server.

➤ The memory, CPU, and disk requirements are reduced for the servers that maintain user mailboxes.

➤ Planning and administration of servers are simplified.

➤ Mail delivery performance is improved.

➤ Backing up public folders is made easier.

If you dedicate one server to public folder storage, you should take into account the server's disk type, disk space, and expandability. The public information store should be located on a fas-ks, providing both high capacity and high performance). Also consider increasing the RAM and CPU power of the public folder server, particularly if you expect public folders to be large, frequently searched and sorted, or replicated to other servers.

Domain Controllers. Domain controllers in the Windows NT Server domain authenticate usernames and passwords during logon requests. There is one Primary Domain Controller (PDC) per domain, which maintains the security database of all user account information in the domain. A domain can also have any number of Backup Domain Controllers (BDCs) to provide load balancing and fault tolerance, store copies of the domain's security database, and authenticate user logons when the PDC is unavailable.

Deciding whether to host Exchange Servers on the established domain controllers is based on the type and number of Windows NT Servers available in the site. If Exchange Server computers are the only Windows NT Server computers in your network, you must designate one of them as the PDC. Other Exchange Server computers can either function as BDCs or as servers without domain control responsibilities. Only designate an Exchange Server computer as a domain controller if it has the capacity both to perform Exchange Server functions and to authenticate logon requests.

Tip

The PDC in a large domain can be kept very busy validating Windows NT user accounts as users log on. If this activity is overloading an Exchange Server computer, consider installing another Windows NT Server computer to act as the PDC instead.

Remote Access Service. If users plan to connect to the Exchange Server system using remote access, a Remote Access Service (RAS) is required. Users can either connect to the Exchange Server via a dedicated RAS server, or they can connect directly to a computer that provides both Exchange Server and RAS connectivity. Installing Exchange Server on a RAS server might require additional hardware to compensate for the increased load. Generally, you should increase the processor speed and the amount of memory for every expected simultaneous connection.

three

Planning Site Connectors

Deciding how to connect multiple sites affects both site and server planning. You will need to configure connectivity servers between the sites in your organization to enable messages, directory information, and public folder information to be exchanged across sites. Site connectors also enable *pass-through traffic,* which originates in one site and is destined for a third site, increasing the load on the servers it passes through.

At least one Exchange Server computer in each site, called the *messaging bridgehead server,* must host the site connector and establish communications between sites. You will need to decide how many messaging bridgehead servers to configure for each site. If you have several sites, you can balance the load by choosing a different messaging bridgehead server for each remote site. You can also design multiple messaging bridgehead servers to take advantage of high available bandwidth. However, if the bandwidth is low, you should configure a single messaging bridgehead server in order to control network traffic between the sites. Make sure that the connection is reliable and can be carefully monitored.

 **Tip**

You can add additional messaging bridgehead servers as new sites are added to your Exchange Server organization.

To connect Exchange Server sites, you can choose from the following connectors:

➤ Site Connector.

➤ Dynamic RAS Connector.

➤ X.400 Connector.

➤ Internet Mail Service.

To help you decide what type of site connector to use, see Decision Tree 3.4.

Message Routing

Message routing is the process of transferring and delivering messages. You can create a routing strategy for load balancing and least-cost routing by configuring redundant connectors on different servers in one site. Assign costs to each connector, weighting them to the cheapest, fastest, or most reliable connections. The connectors intelligently transmit information over the route with the lowest cost. If one route goes down, messages are sent through an alternate connector. Connectors are also able to load balance routing over the remaining connections.

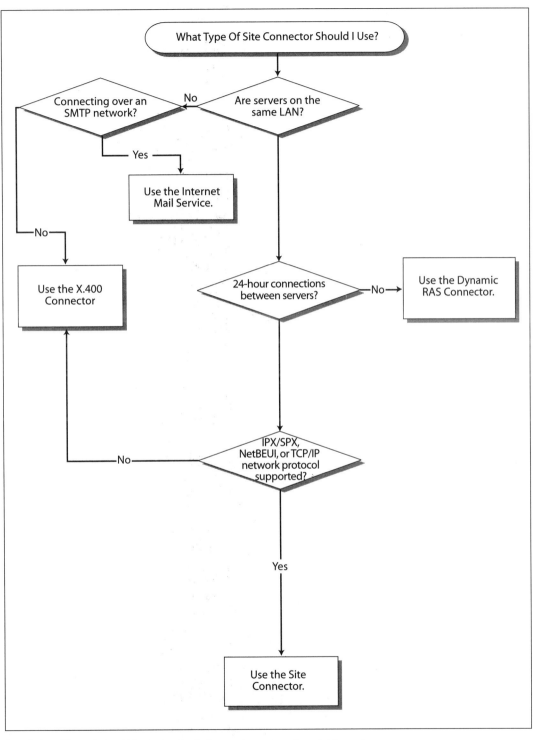

Decision Tree 3.4   What type of site connector should I use?

three

Site Connector

The *Site Connector* is the easiest and most efficient way to connect two Exchange Server sites. It uses RPCs to enable any server in one site to deliver a message to any server in another site on the same LAN. Using RPCs makes the Site Connector easy to set up, because no network transport needs to be configured.

Table 3.4 outlines the advantages and disadvantages of using the Site Connector to connect Exchange Server sites.

To use the Site Connector, you must have permanent, high bandwidth, LAN connectivity between the sites and a protocol capable of using RPCs, such as *Internetwork Packet Exchange/Sequenced Packet Exchange (IPX/SPX)* through Microsoft NWLink, *NetBIOS Extended User Interface (NetBEUI)*, or *Transport Control Protocol/Internet Protocol (TCP/IP)*. You also must have administrative permissions on both Exchange Servers where you want to configure the Site Connector.

Dynamic RAS Connector

The *Dynamic RAS Connector* uses Windows NT RAS-asynchronous connections instead of permanent connections to connect sites on the same LAN. This enables you to configure when the connections should be made and to connect sites even when you do not have a permanent network connection.

Table 3.5 outlines the advantages and disadvantages to using the Dynamic RAS Connector.

Table 3.4   Advantages and disadvantages to using the Site Connector.

Advantages	Disadvantages
Minimized message routing steps.	Connections cannot be scheduled.
Connections in the local and remote site configured at the same time.	Network connections can be saturated when multiple are servers attempt to connect at the same time.
Automatic load balancing and fault tolerance.	

Table 3.5   Advantages and disadvantages to using the Dynamic RAS Connector.

Advantages	Disadvantages
Control when connections are made.	Data transfer depends on the speed of the modem or ISDN adapter.
Supports asynchronous, nonpermanent connections.	Bottlenecks may occur because all message traffic must pass through one bridgehead server on each site (unless you configure multiple bridgehead servers for the site).
Supports ISDN connectivity.	Public folder hierarchy replication can consume significant network bandwidth.

X.400 Connector

You might want to choose the *X.400 Connector* if you are connecting Exchange Server sites across slower network connections or across private or public packet networks. The X.400 Connector can also be used to take advantage of an existing X.400 backbone to connect sites.

Table 3.6 outlines the advantages and disadvantages to using the X.400 Connector to connect Exchange Server sites.

An X.400 transport stack—either Transport Class 4 (TP4), X.25, or TCP/IP—must be configured on the messaging bridgehead server. The *X.400 transport stack* is the networking software required to support X.400 server-to-server message transport.

Internet Mail Service

The *Internet Mail Service* connects Exchange Server sites over an existing *Simple Mail Transport Protocol (SMTP)* network. Table 3.7 outlines the advantages and disadvantages of using the Internet Mail Service to connect sites.

Table 3.6   Advantages and disadvantages to using the X.400 Connector.

Advantages	Disadvantages
You can schedule connections.	Bottlenecks may occur due to all message traffic passing through one bridgehead server on each site (unless you configure multiple bridgehead servers for the site).
You can control message size.	Existing bridges and routers must support the specific network protocols used with the X.400 Connector.
Messages pass in a native, or highly efficient, format.	

Table 3.7   Advantages and disadvantages to using the Internet Mail Service.

Advantages	Disadvantages
Message sizes can be controlled.	Connections cannot be scheduled.
Internet Mail Service can be configured to receive messages, send messages, or both.	Required message format conversion.
	Because all message traffic must go through one bridgehead server at each site, bottlenecks may occur (unless you configure multiple bridgehead servers for the site).

Planning Connectors To Other Systems

An important feature of Exchange Server is its capability for establishing communications between the Exchange Server system and a wide number of foreign messaging systems, enabling your users to send messages to recipients in outside systems. While planning your Exchange Server organization, consider whether you need to provide connectivity to *foreign systems* to satisfy user needs. If a connection to an outside system is needed, you must decide which connectivity components to use and how to set up connectors.

Message routing to foreign systems is affected by factors like the amount of data being transferred, the effect of pass-through traffic on servers, and routing costs. Taking all these factors into account, decide whether to use one connector for the entire organization or whether to configure one or more connectors for each site.

It might be more cost effective to route all messages to a foreign system from one site. For example, if you are using a fax gateway, long-distance charges might be lower from one site than from another. If you use one connector to link your entire organization to the foreign system, messages then have to pass through your other sites to reach the site that has the connector. This pass-through traffic can greatly increase network traffic between site connectors.

To minimize pass-through traffic, you might choose to route messages through multiple connectors in different sites. Configuring connectors to foreign systems in more than one site might also be more economical. For example, if you are using a fax gateway, you could install a connector in every site to ensure that each site pays for its own long-distance fax charges.

The connectors you choose to install are determined by the message transfer protocols used by the systems to which you want to connect. Exchange Server natively supports five connectivity components:

➤ X.400 Connector.

➤ Microsoft Mail Connector for PC Networks.

➤ Microsoft Mail Connector for AppleTalk Networks.

Network Considerations

When deciding where to install connectors to foreign systems, keep in mind that LAN and WAN connections typically provide the highest throughput, but other connection types can also be used. When you use a LAN or WAN connection, a common network protocol must be configured on the connected systems, and the systems must be able to communicate with each other over the network.

➤ Microsoft Exchange Connector for Lotus cc:Mail.

➤ Internet Mail Service.

X.400 Connector

The *X.400 Connector* routes messages to foreign X.400 systems. Keep in mind that each X.400 Connector you install increases the number of tasks that the MTA on the Exchange Server must perform. Each X.400 Connector also increases the load on the Exchange Server computer that is running the transport software and maintaining the connection; this load varies with the amount of message traffic sent over the connection.

You also need to take into consideration the hardware and software required to support the X.400 connection. The X.400 Connector supports connections using the TP0/X.25, TP4, and TCP/IP protocols.

To use the TP0/X.25 connection, you must install the following on the Exchange Server computer with the X.400 Connector:

➤ Eicon X.25 port adapter and a direct or dial-up connection to the X.400 system.

➤ Eicon WAN services for Windows NT Server software, version 3, Release 3 or later (which also provides X.25 services).

➤ Exchange Server X.400 MTA transport stack for X.25, including TP0 software for use with X.25 (provided with the X.400 Connector software).

To use the TP4 connection, the Exchange Server computer with the X.400 Connector must have the following:

➤ Network adapter and connection that support TP4.

➤ Windows NT Server TP4 network services.

➤ Exchange Server X.400 MTA transport stack for TP4, including Connectionless Network Protocol (CLNP) software for use with TP4 (included with Exchange Server).

To use a TCP/IP connection, the Exchange Server computer with the X.400 Connector must have the following:

➤ Network adapter and connection that support TCP/IP.

➤ Windows NT Server TCP/IP network services (included with Windows NT Server).

➤ Exchange Server X.400 MTA transport stack for TCP/IP, including Request for Comments (RFC) 1006 software that supports X.400 connections over a TCP/IP network.

After selecting the type of *MTA transport stack* you need, you should install and configure the network software and hardware required to support the connection first. For example, if you are connecting to the X.400 system over TCP/IP, install and configure the TCP/IP network software for Windows NT Server before configuring the X.400 transport stack and X.400 Connector.

Microsoft Mail Connector For PC Networks

The *MS Mail (PC) Connector* connects the Exchange Server and one or more MS Mail (PC) systems over LAN, asynchronous, or X.25 connections. This connector also provides connectivity to MS Mail (PC) 3.x gateways, including AT&T Mail, Fax, IBM Professional Office System (PROFS)/OfficeVision, MCI MAIL, NetWare MHS, and SNADS (these components must be purchased separately).

You can install as many MS Mail (PC) Connectors as you want in a site. The number of connectors you choose to install is determined by message volume. For example, you can centralize traffic between the Exchange Server site and an MS Mail (PC) system on the same LAN. This configuration uses Exchange Server as a backbone for MS Mail (PC) postoffices in your organization and requires an MS Mail (PC) Connector in every site.

You might also choose to connect the MS Mail (PC) Connector to an MS Mail (PC) postoffice that has been set up as a hub for message transfer. This enables you to route mail to every MS Mail (PC) postoffice directly connected to the hub. If you are using a LAN connection, you can upload routing information for these MS Mail (PC) postoffices from the hub to the connector. The hub provides an indirect connection between the single MS Mail (PC) Connector and all the MS Mail (PC) postoffices.

Microsoft Mail Connector For AppleTalk Networks

The *MS Mail (AppleTalk) Connector* connects the Exchange Server and one or more Microsoft Mail for AppleTalk Networks systems or QuarterDeck Mail systems over a LAN. The number of MS Mail (AppleTalk) Connectors you need to configure is usually determined by your network topology. For example, if you want to connect to multiple MS Mail (AppleTalk) servers that are geographically dispersed across multiple LANs, you might require one MS Mail (AppleTalk) Connector on each LAN.

You should also take into consideration the number of MS Mail (AppleTalk) servers that will indirectly connect to the MS Mail (AppleTalk) Connector through access components. The performance of the connector depends on message traffic. Therefore, a single MS Mail (AppleTalk) Connector connecting to one MS Mail (AppleTalk) server and servicing the remaining MS Mail (AppleTalk) servers on the same LAN through access components is not advisable. In that case, you should use more than one MS Mail (AppleTalk) Connectors to connect your site to multiple MS Mail (AppleTalk) servers on the same LAN.

You can configure only one instance of the MS Mail (AppleTalk) Connector per Exchange Server computer. Also, you cannot configure multiple connections from a single site to a single MS Mail (AppleTalk) server. The Windows NT Server running Exchange Server must have the following hardware and software to support the MS Mail (AppleTalk) Connector:

➤ Windows NT Server Services for Macintosh.

➤ Exchange Server installed on the NTFS partition (required to support Windows NT Server Services for Macintosh).

➤ Sufficient hard disk space to store incoming and outgoing messages until they are transferred to the MS Mail (AppleTalk) server.

You must also be able to support the Microsoft Exchange Connection, a gateway for the MS Mail (AppleTalk) server that works with the MS Mail (AppleTalk) Connector MTA to transfer messages between the connector postoffice and the server. To support the Microsoft Exchange Connection, the connected MS Mail (AppleTalk) server must have the following:

➤ Macintosh computer with the basic RAM requirements for an MS Mail (AppleTalk) server and an extra 2MB RAM.

➤ Sufficient hard disk space to store incoming and outgoing messages until they are transferred to the MS Mail (AppleTalk) Connector postoffice.

➤ MS Mail (AppleTalk), version 3.1c or later.

➤ System 7.1 or later.

Microsoft Exchange Connector For Lotus cc:Mail

Use the *Microsoft Exchange Connector for Lotus cc:Mail* to connect the Exchange Server system and one or more cc:Mail systems in order to transfer messages and synchronize directories. You might choose to connect a cc:Mail network to your Exchange Server organization using one connector or multiple connectors, depending upon your messaging requirements. For example, if there are multiple cc:Mail post offices in your organization or if they are spread over a large area, you can set up multiple cc:Mail Connectors to service all cc:Mail and Exchange Server users.

Each Exchange Server computer in the organization can run one instance of the cc:Mail Connector, directly servicing one connection to a cc:Mail post office. However, you cannot service more than one cc:Mail post office from one connector. To use the cc:Mail Connector, the following software must be installed on the cc:Mail post office that is directly connected to the Exchange Server computer with the connector:

➤ Lotus cc:Mail Post Office Database, version 6, with Lotus cc:Mail Import, version 5.15, and Lotus cc:Mail Export, version 5.14.

or

➤ Lotus cc:Mail Post Office Database, version 8, with Lotus cc:Mail Import, version 6.0, and Lotus cc:Mail Export, version 6.0.

Internet Mail Service

The *Internet Mail Service* lets you exchange information with foreign systems that use SMTP. You most often use this connector to connect to the Internet or to an SMTP backbone. If any of your users need to exchange messages with others on the Internet or if you plan to include POP3 or *Internet Message Access Protocol 4 (IMAP4)* support on your Exchange Server system, you must configure the Internet Mail Service.

Each Internet Mail Service you configure can accept multiple incoming connections and initiate multiple outbound connections. To control heavy message traffic, consider using multiple Internet Mail Services in your organization or even in each site. You might also choose to configure different Internet Mail Services to only accept messages, only send messages, both receive and send messages, forward all mail to relay hosts for final delivery, or send mail to final destinations using DNS to better control traffic.

You must install TCP/IP network services on the Exchange Server computer where you want to run the Internet Mail Service. Consider using a higher speed network connection if you expect a high level of message traffic over the connection.

Internet Mail Service And SMTP Addresses

When planning how many Internet Mail Services to install and where they should be placed in your organization, you should take SMTP addresses into consideration. The default SMTP domain name used for Exchange Server is based on your organization and site name. For example, if your organization's name is *mycompany* and your site's name is *NAmerica-E,* then your SMTP domain name is generated as *namerica-e.mycompany.com.* This domain name is added to the username to generate the SMTP email address for messages sent through the Internet Mail Service. You might want to install more than one Internet Mail Service to reflect correct site locations. Conversely, you might want to use the same SMTP email domain on all sites to avoid exposing your internal messaging topology.

Hardware Checklist

By now, you should have a concrete idea of the layout of your Exchange Server organization, including the number of sites and servers and the functions of each server. You should now consider what hardware and software are required to support your organization.

Exchange Server was developed to allow you to take advantage of the hardware you already have, both on the server and on the desktop. This allows you to get Exchange Server up and running using your existing hardware, saving additional expense.

However, to take full advantage of Exchange Server, you might find that some additional hardware installations and upgrades are necessary. Check your current hardware to make sure it matches requirements for server and client computers. Also, design server hardware to meet the expected load. Then, plan hardware and software upgrades if needed as part of the rollout schedule.

Planning ahead enables you to select hardware to allow for future growth through easy expandability and upgradability. For example, if a bottleneck occurs after installation, you can eliminate it with a minor upgrade rather than by installing a new server or changing the site layout. Or, as the number of users and connectors in a site grows, you can reconfigure the existing hardware on current servers instead of adding more servers.

Planning your hardware requirements involves the following tasks:

1. Make sure each server satisfies the necessary hardware requirements to run Exchange Server 5.5.

2. Determine what hardware upgrades are needed to optimize performance and fulfill the services each server will provide:

   Assess CPU needs.

   Assess memory needs.

   Assess I/O subsystem needs.

   Assess network adapter needs.

   Assess hardware needs for remote users.

3. Ensure that any computers that will be running Exchange Server client applications meet the minimum hardware requirements.

Table 3.8   Minimum and recommended hardware requirements for Intel-based systems.

	Processor	Disk Space	RAM
Minimum Requirements	Intel Pentium 90MHz or faster	At least 250MB after Windows NT Server has been installed	24MB
Recommended Hardware	Intel Pentium 166MHz or faster	1GB	48MB

Server Hardware Requirements

Table 3.8 outlines the minimum and recommended hardware requirements for Exchange Server running on Intel and Intel-compatible systems.

Table 3.9 outlines the minimum and recommended hardware requirements for Exchange Server running on Reduced Instruction Set Computer (RISC)-based systems.

● ● ● *Tip* ● ● ● ●

While planning server hardware needs, make sure that additional hardware is not required to support the Exchange Server services you plan to host on that server. For example, including a site connector or a connector to a foreign system on a server can require additional hardware installations (check the "Planning Site Connectors" and "Planning Connectors to Foreign Systems" sections earlier in this chapter for those requirements).

The hardware you can use with Exchange Server ranges from single-processor 486 computers to the most powerful configuration that Windows NT Server supports. Your hardware choices will significantly impact the performance of the Exchange Server organization.

Deciding how powerful your servers need to be depends on your company's needs and budget. You should also consider load, such as the number of users hosted by each server and those users' email usage patterns, and use more powerful servers if you expect significant load. For example, a company that has large, centrally located, or well-connected sites might use a few expensive, high-end, multiprocessor servers that have large amounts of

Table 3.9   Minimum and recommended hardware requirements for RISC-based systems.

	Processor	Disk Space	RAM
Minimum Requirements	Digital Alpha 4/27	At least 300MB after Windows NT Server has been installed	32MB
Recommended Hardware	Digital Alpha 5/500	1GB	64MB

Table 3.10   Possible server configurations.

Server Type	Processors	RAM	Disk Configurations	Number of Users
Low-end	1 Intel Pentium	48MB	2 2GB	100-300
Middle	1 Intel Pentium	64MB	5 2GB	250-600
High-end	3 Intel Pentiums	256MB	8 2GB	500-1000

RAM and dozens of disk drives, placing as many users on each server as possible; a company that has many small, geographically diverse locations might choose several inexpensive, lower-end servers instead. Most companies want to use the most cost-effective hardware, but also need to consider other issues, such as the costs of maintenance and administration and available floor space. Table 3.10 shows some possible server configurations.

Assessing Other Hardware Needs

In addition to making sure your Exchange Server computers meet the minimum hardware requirements to support Exchange Server, you might find that you need to add hardware upgrades and installations to individual servers. This additional hardware might be required to comfortably sustain the actions of the users who are housed on the server, or it might be needed to support the optional Exchange Server services and other services you plan to host on the server. You should consider each server's configuration individually and plan for upgrading any of the following: processors, memory, I/O subsystem, network adapters, or hardware to support remote users.

Assessing CPU Needs

Exchange Server needs adequate processing power to handle requests from clients and other servers in the site as well as optional services, such as third-party gateways, connections to other sites, RAS servers, and file servers for client installations. The type and number of CPUs dictate the performance potential of the Exchange Server computer. For example, computers based on the Pentium processor offer better performance than computers based on the 486 chip, and a 133MHz Pentium performs better than a 100MHz Pentium that has a similar configuration.

• • • *Tip* • • •

Using multiple CPUs can significantly increase the performance of the server. Not all servers need multiple processors and not all hardware can support them, though, so make your choices accordingly. Also, upgrading the CPU or adding additional CPUs does not increase performance when other hardware resources, like the I/O subsystem, are the sources of bottlenecks. Chapter 6, "Optimizing Exchange Server," will help you solve hardware problems, such as bottlenecks.

three

Assessing Memory Needs

By default, Exchange Server makes the best use of available memory, but your servers still need enough physical memory for processing user requests to the directory, processing user connections to mailboxes, and transferring information to and from mailboxes. Increasing the amount of RAM can greatly improve performance and avoid heavy use of the pagefile. Adding more RAM also enables more of the database to be cached in memory. Keep in mind, though, that other hardware resources, like the CPU or I/O subsystem, can become bottlenecks as you increase the amount of RAM.

Assessing I/O Subsystem Needs

The I/O subsystem includes the type and number of disk controllers, the types of drives installed, and the choices required for disk fault tolerance and Redundant Array of Inexpensive Disks (RAID). You should optimize the I/O subsystem before installing Exchange Server. The following is the recommended disk configuration for each Exchange Server computer:

➤ A physical disk containing the operating system and pagefile.

➤ A physical disk for the transaction log files (you can mirror this disk to increase fault tolerance).

➤ A striped set consisting of multiple physical disks for all other Exchange Server components so that databases can be accessed efficiently.

You will need adequate disk space for the server software and the information store, directory service, and transaction log files, all of which grow over time. (The *transaction log file* provides fault tolerance in case data needs to be restored to the information store or directory database.) To expand disk space, configure your disk for easy volume set expansion before installing Exchange Server. You can also increase performance by adding more disk drives, especially if disk I/O is random in nature, as with the information store. All drives have mechanical limitations on performance, so adding more drives distributes the workload more effectively.

An important performance consideration is whether to put the information store transaction log file on its own physical disk. Using a dedicated physical disk increases fault tolerance and system performance. Use the Performance Optimizer to configure the transaction log files so that they reside on their own disk drive. (The *Performance Optimizer* is a planning and system optimization tool that you should run after installing Exchange Server and every time you change the system configuration.) NTFS is recommended if the server will be backed up infrequently or if the log files could grow to more than 2GB.

Tip

Use the Performance Optimizer to evaluate the I/O subsystem and recommend locations for relevant Exchange Server files. If new disks are being added to a server, you can also use the Performance Optimizer to experiment with I/O subsystem setup.

Because modifications to the directory database are usually infrequent, putting the directory transaction log files on a separate drive is not necessary. However, you might choose to put the log files on servers used for large directory imports, such as servers that run the directory synchronization component or servers that are used primarily for large directory modifications.

You can put transaction log files and databases on the same striped set if your Exchange Server computers have only a few drives, have a small amount of memory, and cannot support many users. However, the increased sensitivity to insufficient memory that this causes decreases performance as the server load increases. When in doubt, choose to dedicate a disk to the log files, because disks are cheaper than memory.

Configure multiple physical disks into one virtual disk or striped set to host Exchange Server databases. Hosting the pagefile on the same striped set as the databases also improves I/O performance, which is important for servers low in memory. If your computer has multiple disk drives, consider additional disk administration options, such as disk striping with parity and disk mirroring, to increase fault tolerance.

Choose high-speed caching controllers to increase the speed of disk-intensive processes and provide optimal performance. Your servers should optimally have caching disk controllers with high-speed bus interfaces, such as PCI SCSI. Many of these controllers support hardware disk striping, offering greater performance and less CPU use than Windows NT Server software striping.

Assessing Network Adapter Needs

Although Exchange Server was developed to make the best use of available network resources, you can optimize performance by using high-speed network adapters and network drivers, which achieve high throughput rates with low CPU use. Server hardware that separates I/O on different channels also helps optimize network performance.

Because multiple clients access the server simultaneously, you should install one or more high-performance network adapters, based on a high-speed bus like PCI or Extended Industry Standard Architecture (EISA). Using multiple adapters in a multiprocessor server enables a single server to handle more clients, with each adapter servicing a separate network segment or protocol.

The quality of the network itself is another important performance consideration. Putting a server on a Fiber Distributed Data Interface (FDDI) ring with a capacity of 100MB/s provides better connectivity and performance than a server attached to a token ring network, for example. An overloaded Ethernet segment can reduce performance. You should also consider WAN connectivity and quality, particularly when drawing site boundaries or determining whether clients should access servers across the WAN.

Assessing Hardware Needs For Remote Users

Exchange Server allows all clients to access mailboxes, private folders, and public folders remotely. Clients connect to the network through a remote network connection, using a variety of software and hardware. Once the client is connected to the network, the user can send outgoing mail and retrieve waiting mail from his or her home Exchange Server.

To determine remote hardware requirements, examine the existing mobile user *traffic patterns* of your current email system, if it supports remote access. These patterns include the following: the number of remote clients, the frequency and duration of connections, the volume of data sent and received, the times when calls most occur, convenience for remote clients, and connection speed. Make sure that you have sufficient modems, phone lines, and ISDN or X.25 connections for the expected traffic volume, while incorporating flexibility for future growth. You might also have to take security requirements into consideration. Note that your existing mail system might provide an underestimate of your needs, due to the fact that all Exchange Server clients are capable of mobile use and the number of portable and home computers is increasing.

Speed of connections is a very important consideration. If a remote client connects at a lower BPS, it keeps the connection busy longer than if it connects at a higher BPS. In asynchronous connections, the types of modems used and the highest transfer rates at which the two modems can connect limit the connection speed. In X.25 connections, either the bandwidth of the leased line or the modem speed of the PAD, whichever is lower, limits the speed. Exchange Server's support for high-speed connections, such as X.25 and ISDN connections, can decrease the number of connections needed.

Tip

If your Exchange Server site is supporting multiple remote connections, consider using a hunt system in your company's phone system. A *hunt system* enables a call to a single phone number to be switched to an available modem, rather than requiring a separate phone number for each modem, making it quicker and easier for mobile users to connect.

Client Hardware Requirements

You should make sure that each computer that will be running Exchange Server client applications meets the minimum hardware requirements for supporting the client. Table 3.11 describes the minimum and recommended hardware requirements for the Outlook client.

Software Checklist

As well as hardware needs, you should consider the software required to run Exchange Server. Planning software needs involves the following tasks:

1. Make sure you have the required software to support Exchange Server.

2. Make sure you have the required software to support any remote users.

3. Make sure you have the required software to support any additional Exchange Server services on each server.

Table 3.11   Hardware requirements for computers running the Outlook client.

Operating System	Network Protocols	Disk Space	RAM
Windows 95	IPX/SPX, TCP/IP (built-in stack), or NetBEUI	12MB minimum for local installation; 22MB recommended	8MB minimum; 12MB recommended; 16MB recommended for Forms Designer
Windows 3.1; Windows for Workgroups 3.11	IPX/SPX, TCP/IP (compatible with Windows Sockets), NetBEUI, or VINES IP	12MB minimum for local installation; 22MB recommended	8MB minimum; 12MB recommended; 16MB recommended for Forms Designer
Intel-based Windows NT Server 3.51 or later; Intel-based Windows NT Workstation 3.51 or later	IPX/SPX (NWLink), TCP/IP (built-in stack), NetBEUI, or VINES IP	26MB minimum for local installation; 46MB recommended	16MB minimum; 20MB recommended; 24MB recommended for Forms Designer
RISC-based Windows NT Server 3.51 or later; RISC-based Windows NT Workstation 3.51 or later	IPX/SPX (NWLink), TCP/IP (built-in stack), NetBEUI, or VINES IP	15MB minimum for local installation; 22MB recommended	20MB minimum; 24MB recommended
MS-DOS 5.0 or later	IPX/SPX, TCP/IP (Microsoft LAN Manager only), or NetBEUI	2MB minimum for local installation; 3MB recommended	1MB (460K free conventional memory)
68030, 68040, or Power Macintosh, System 7 or later	AppleTalk Network	12MB minimum for local installation; 22MB recommended	8MB minimum; 12MB recommended

Server Software Requirements

The following software must be installed on each server that will run Exchange Server 5.5:

➤ Windows NT Server, version 4.0 or later.

➤ Service Pack 3 (SP3), which can be downloaded from http://www.microsoft.com/.

Remote Access Software Requirements

You can choose any of the following remote access software to enable mobile users to connect remotely to your Exchange Server computers:

➤ Microsoft Windows NT RAS Server.

➤ Shiva LanRover.

➤ Any other remote access server software that is RAS-compatible or is compatible with the network software currently used by your remote users.

Assessing Other Software Needs

Additional software might also be required on different Exchange Server computers to support the Exchange Server services you plan to provide, as follows:

➤ TCP/IP for Windows NT (required if you plan to use any Internet protocols).

➤ Microsoft IIS, version 3.0 or later (required to run Active Server Components and Outlook Web Access).

➤ Microsoft IIS, version 4.0 or later (required to install KM server).

➤ Microsoft Certificate Server (required to install KM server).

➤ Microsoft Cluster Server software (required to install Exchange Server on a pair of clustered servers).

Exchange Server And Microsoft Cluster Server

Installing Exchange Server on a pair of clustered servers using *Microsoft Cluster Server* software provides greater reliability in the event of hardware failure. Each pair of clustered servers includes an active node—the primary mail server—and a secondary node—the backup mail server. If the active node goes down, or if a critical service fails, the secondary node takes its place without interrupting mail service or dropping client connections. The clustered servers where you install Exchange Server must have identical processors and the same amount of RAM. (For more information about using Exchange Server and Cluster Server together, consult your Cluster Server documentation.)

•• *Tip* •••

Servers that run connectors to other sites or foreign systems might also need additional software; check the "Planning Site Connectors" and "Planning Connectors to Foreign Systems" sections for requirements.

Administration Checklist

Before installing and configuring your Exchange Server system, you will find it useful to have an administrative plan in place. Establishing administrative policies ahead of time provides a clear focus when making installation and configuration decisions and ensures that the entire organization is administered in the same way.

Making a plan for the administration of Exchange Server includes the following steps.

1. Define policies for the administration of the organization:

   Establish permissions for administration of the system.

   Delegate administrative duties.

   Establish policies for information storage.

   Schedule regular backups.

   Prepare a disaster plan.

2. Establish naming conventions:

   Decide on an organization name.

   Establish conventions for naming sites.

   Establish conventions for naming servers.

   Establish conventions for naming user mailboxes.

   Establish conventions for foreign email addresses.

Setting Administrative Policies

The administrative policies you set influence how the Exchange Server organization is implemented and changed. Besides the decisions outlined in the following sections, you might also need to establish policies unique to your company needs during this step.

Establishing Permissions And Delegating Administrative Duties

Before implementing Exchange Server, define roles and tasks for every person who will be administering a part of the organization. Decide who will be responsible for administering each site and server in your organization. For example, you can choose one person to administer an entire site, or you can break down large sites into separate areas for administration by different people. You can even give one or more people the capability to administer the entire organization. Also consider whether you want to give administrators permission to view, but not to change, areas of the organization they are not directly responsible for, such as the organization's hierarchy, elements, or configuration.

● ● **Tip** ● ● ●

If a group of people is responsible for administering the Exchange Server system, you might find it helpful to create an Admin public folder to keep administrators informed about policies and system issues.

You can reduce administrative duties by creating a Windows NT Server global group that encompasses all administrator user accounts and to which you can add and remove members as needed. All members of the administrative group have the permissions granted to the group, allowing you to change the permissions for the entire group rather than for each user account. In a site with multiple domains, create this global administrative group and all user accounts for administrators in the domain where administrative functions are centralized, such as the master domain for the single master or multiple master domain model.

Establishing Storage Policies

As the Exchange Server system is put into use, the size of the information stores on Exchange Server computers will grow as the following increase: mailboxes, distribution lists, public folders, gateways, remote users, mail messages, and outbound mail in queues for gateways or other sites. Making a policy to limit space enables you to better control hard disk needs and improve performance of the entire organization. You can include any of the following in your policy:

➤ Limit the size of user mailboxes by imposing storage limits.

➤ Limit the size of user mailboxes by deleting old messages.

➤ Limit the size of user mailboxes by preventing users from using the Sent Mail folder.

➤ Limit the maximum size of messages that can be sent to other sites and systems.

➤ Decrease the volume of public folders by limiting the maximum age for items stored in the folders.

➤ Decrease the volume of public folders by imposing storage limits.

Scheduling Backups And Preparing For Disasters

Creating backups of your Exchange Server files enables you to restore the server in case of emergency. A regular backup schedule should be part of your administrative plan. You should also devise a plan that will be implemented in case of emergencies, which can

Preventing Disasters

From the very beginning when you install and configure your Exchange Server computers, you should implement practices designed to prevent disasters. The following tips can help you avoid a disastrous loss of data:

- Install servers in adequate, safe, and secure environments.
- Avoid making Exchange Server a PDC.
- Store transaction log files for the directory and information stores on separate hard disks.
- Protect servers with uninterruptible power supplies (UPS).
- Document all server configurations and keep records of all changes.
- Equip servers with sufficient hard disk space to allow for recovery.

range from common disasters, like hardware failures and software corruption, to major disasters, like fires, hurricanes, and earthquakes. With an emergency plan already in place, you can lessen the severity of disruptions to the entire organization caused by the failure of one server.

Your backup and emergency data recovery plan should include the following elements:

➤ Develop a schedule of timely backups that includes verifying and documenting backups.

➤ Choose backup devices.

➤ Use dedicated recovery systems and recovery toolkits.

➤ Train administrators to implement the disaster recovery plan.

➤ Design and configure servers to avoid disasters as much as possible.

For more information on backing up and restoring servers, see Chapter 5.

Establishing Naming Conventions

Each object in the Exchange Server directory is uniquely identified by a name (a *directory object* is a record in the directory, such as a mailbox, public folder, connector, server, or site). Planning naming conventions involves deciding how names will be set for every directory object in the organization. You should also take into consideration how naming conventions will translate when connecting to foreign systems, such as the Internet. It is important to plan these conventions ahead of time, because you must provide the site and organization names when you install Exchange Server, and many names cannot be changed without reinstalling the software.

A good naming strategy enables you to identify objects and add new objects to the organization easily. Meaningful, logical names simplify the administration and use of the Exchange Server system. They also minimize rework due to unplanned name changes. You might choose to base your naming conventions on geography, the structure of your company, building numbers, or any other system that makes the most sense for the organizational layout of your company. You should also choose names that will not be affected by any future organizational changes.

Organization Name

The organization name encompasses the entire enterprise. It must be unique, and it cannot be changed. When choosing the organization name, be aware that it is used to generate foreign email addresses and the distinguished names of all directory objects, such as mailboxes, public folders, and distribution lists. The organization name can contain as many as 64 characters, but for practical purposes, you might want to limit names to no more than 10 characters, especially if you are connecting to legacy systems.

Site Names

Site names identify separate Exchange Server sites and should follow a consistent naming scheme. You might choose to name sites by their geographical locations, such as countries, regions, and cities; by their physical locations, such as buildings; or by their functions, such as company divisions or departments. Site names are also used to generate foreign email addresses and distinguished names. They must be unique and cannot be changed. Again, you might want to limit site names to no more than 10 characters, although they can contain as many as 64 characters.

Server Names

The Windows NT Server computer name is used for the Exchange Server name by default, so you should plan naming conventions for your Exchange Server computers before installing Windows NT Server, if possible. Server names must be unique and cannot be changed without removing the server from the site, renaming the server, and reinstalling the server software. They can contain as many as 15 characters.

Tip

If you plan to run logon scripts, do not include spaces in the server names of domain controllers.

Mailbox Names

It often makes sense to choose a convention for naming user mailboxes based on your established company standards for phone and address books. Also, consider consolidating mailbox naming conventions with the naming scheme used for Windows NT user accounts or for previous email systems. If you are concerned about the sort order of mailbox names in the *Address Book*, establish naming conventions accordingly. If you have several users with the same name, choose naming conventions that distinguish the users.

Tip

Mailbox names are also used to display resources, such as conference rooms, so be consistent when naming all resources. For example, you can establish a naming convention for all conference rooms as *Conference Room, Building (Size of Room)*.

Configuring mailbox names requires specifying names for different fields, as described in Table 3.12.

Foreign Email Addresses

Before users can communicate with foreign email systems, they must have an *email address* in a format that the foreign system can understand. These addresses are used to route messages and are the method by which Exchange Server users are known to other mail systems. Users in the foreign system must also be represented by email addresses in Exchange Server as custom recipients (*custom recipients* are users whose addresses are on a foreign mail system).

Based on the organization and site names, Exchange Server automatically generates MS Mail (PC), X.400, and Internet SMTP addresses for each recipient according to the naming conventions for those systems. Third-party gateways use the Alias Name field of the mailbox name to generate email addresses according to the different limits and restrictions of the gateway.

Table 3.12   Parts of the mailbox name.

Field	Guideline	Restrictions
First Name	User's first name	16 characters maximum; can be changed
Last Name	User's last name	40 characters maximum; can be changed
Alias Name	Short name that identifies the user; should be easily recognizable and have some relationship to the user's name	64 characters maximum; can be changed
Display Name	Mailbox name displayed in the Administrator window and Address Book; should be consistent so that all mailboxes are displayed in the same way	256 characters maximum; can be changed
Directory Name	Used by Exchange Server for internal purposes only to identify an object and to route messages	64 characters maximum; must be unique; cannot be changed

If your Exchange Server organization is connected to a foreign system, consider the character restrictions the foreign system imposes on its addressing scheme when establishing naming conventions. For example, spaces are not allowed in SMTP addresses, so if you plan to establish a connection to the Internet, you should not include spaces in mailbox *alias names,* site names, or organization names, all of which are used to generate SMTP addresses for Exchange Server users. X.400, MS Mail (PC), and foreign systems connected by third-party gateways, such as PROFS and SNADS, also impose character restrictions that you should take into account.

Rollout Checklist

You are now nearly ready to begin the installation of your Exchange Server organization. When planning and scheduling the rollout of the Exchange Server system, you should complete the following tasks:

1. Test the prototype design.

2. Develop a migration strategy, if needed.

3. Establish a schedule for the rollout.

Testing The Prototype

You have designed a prototype installation of the Exchange Server organization that incorporates all the services and connectors to other systems that you plan to support. Before installing the system, you should test implementation issues, such as server and client installation procedures, hardware and network compatibility, network bandwidth, and coexistence with or *migration* from other mail systems.

Optimize the prototype design until it meets all user requirements. Validate your design by checking your decisions for the organization against projected server loads, client response times, error rates, peak-to-average message traffic ratios, and sustainable forwarding rates by various Exchange Servers. Modify your plans as necessary to maximize performance, reliability, and services to users and to minimize costs. Thoroughly testing the prototype installation helps you find potential problems and adjust your plans accordingly before rollout.

Developing A Migration Strategy

If you have an existing email system, you must develop a strategy for migrating users and data from that system to Exchange Server. Most users will already have mailboxes, folders, address books, and calendars on the existing system, all of which they will want to use on the new system. By planning migration beforehand, you can prevent downtime, data loss, and disruption of the information flow. You can also reduce your administrative duties before, during, and after the migration.

Tip

Plan to migrate information when the server is least active, such as during evenings and weekends, and back up data before migration.

Your strategy should include an assessment of the following:

➤ Which users to migrate first.

➤ Whether migration should be done in phases or all at once.

➤ Coexistence issues that arise while both systems are in operation.

➤ How to establish and maintain connections.

➤ How to maintain directories, foreign system addresses, mail, scheduling information, distribution lists, and messaging applications during and after migration.

➤ How to handle offsite users.

The Exchange Server migration tools work with your existing system to copy and import mailboxes, messages, folders, and scheduling information. They include the following:

➤ *Source extractors* for copying directory, message, and scheduling data from other systems.

➤ Templates for writing custom source extractors.

➤ The *Migration Wizard* for importing and converting data created with source extractors and for stepping you through the migration process.

Exchange Server's migration tools support the conversion of email and user account information from the following systems:

➤ Microsoft Mail for PC Networks, version 3.x.

➤ Microsoft Mail for AppleTalk Networks, version 3.x.

➤ Lotus cc:Mail, database version DB6 and DB8.

➤ Verimation MEMO MVS, version 3.2.1 or later.

➤ IBM PROFS/OfficeVision (all versions).

➤ Digital All-in-1, version 2.3 or later.

➤ Novell GroupWise, versions 4.1 and 4.1a.

➤ Netscape CollabraShare, versions 1.x and 2.x.

Single-Phase Or Multiphase Migration?

Single-phase migration moves everyone at one time. It might work better for your company if there is little data to move from your existing system, your company has the resources to move everyone at once, and all hardware and software required to run the Exchange Server system are already in place.

Multiphase migration moves users in groups at different times. Larger companies might not be able to switch everyone over to the Exchange Server system at once. Multiphase migration might also be a good choice if all departments cannot upgrade at the same time, you need to free hardware for redeployment in later phases, or you cannot migrate everyone within an acceptable downtime period.

Scheduling The Rollout

Now, schedule the procedures for implementing the new Exchange Server system and migrating users from existing systems to the new system. You should have already adjusted your prototype plans as needed to maximize efficiency, avoid problems, and meet your organization's requirements. You should also have developed a migration strategy that will be included in the rollout schedule. Roll out your plan in phases until all users are on the Exchange Server system.

When you plan the rollout, you create a schedule for implementing the different phases of installing the Exchange Server system. Include the following as needed in your schedule:

➤ Hardware and software upgrades.

➤ Exchange Server computer setup.

➤ Server administrative training.

➤ Client training and support.

➤ Migration from other systems.

➤ Implementing new naming conventions and administrative policies.

• • • *Tip* • • •

It is a good idea to inform employees about the phases of the rollout schedule, so they know when they will be migrated from their current systems to Exchange Server.

Moving On

In this chapter, you created a plan for implementing your company's Exchange Server organization. As part of the plan, you determined how to lay out Exchange Server sites and servers, the roles different servers will play, the site connectors and connectors to foreign systems that are needed, and the hardware and software that needs to be upgraded or installed. You also determined administrative policies and naming conventions for the new system, tested the prototype, decided on a strategy for migrating users from the old system to the new system, and created a schedule for the rollout of the new system. Now, you are ready to begin installation. Chapter 4 will take you through the steps of installing and setting up the Exchange Server system according to your implementation plans.

Installing
Exchange Server

Once you have your plan for your Exchange Server organization in place, you are ready to begin installing the system. This chapter will take you through the steps required to install the Exchange Server software on a Windows NT Server computer and set up an Exchange Server computer and site. Installing Exchange Server involves the following tasks:

➤ Validate the user account.

➤ Create the service account.

➤ Run Exchange Server Setup to install the server software and server components.

➤ Configure settings for the core server components and the Exchange Server site.

➤ Set up optional server components, including connectors.

➤ Create user mailboxes.

➤ Initiate directory replication.

Keep the organization planning worksheet you completed in the previous chapter handy while you install Exchange Server. You will need to refer to it during the installation and configuration process to identify which users' mailboxes should be created on each server, determine which components need to be installed, and assign names based on your established naming conventions, among other factors. Referring to the worksheet ensures that you set up your Exchange Server organization in accordance with your plans, avoiding time-consuming alterations later.

Exchange Server Installation

To install the Exchange Server software on a *Windows NT Server* computer, you will need to run the Exchange Server Setup program. Before running Setup, you should designate a Windows NT user account to use for the installation of Exchange Server and create a second Windows NT user account that will be dedicated to running Exchange Server services. Then, after performing some additional tasks, you will be ready to install the Exchange Server software. Follow the steps outlined in this section to install the Exchange Server software. You can also refer to Decision Tree 4.1, "What Are The Steps To Install Exchange Server?"

The User Account

Before running Setup, you will need to decide which Windows NT user account you are going to use for the installation process. The Windows NT *user account* that is logged on during installation is automatically granted Exchange Administrator permissions, enabling that account to open the Administrator program, configure directory objects, and grant permissions to other user accounts. This must be a domain account in the local administrator's group. Use this account to log on to the Windows NT Server before creating the service account, running Setup, and configuring the Exchange Server components in the Administrator program.

The Service Account

You will also need to create a new Windows NT Server user account called the *service account* for running the Exchange Server services before running Setup. The service account is the user account that Exchange Server services use to log on and run. The same service account is used for all Exchange Server computers in a site, so you only need to create it before installing the first Exchange Server computer in the site.

Tip

Do not use an administrator account as a service account. The service account is used only to validate services.

Follow these steps to create the service account:

1. Log on to the Windows NT Server as domain administrator.

2. Select User Manager For Domains in the Administrative Tools group.

3. Select New User from the User menu.

4. Type the name and password of the service account in the Username and Password fields; for example, you might name the account **Exchange Service**.

5. Clear the User Must Change Password At Next Logon check box.

6. Select the User Cannot Change Password check box.

7. Select the Password Never Expires check box.

8. Clear the Account Disabled check box.

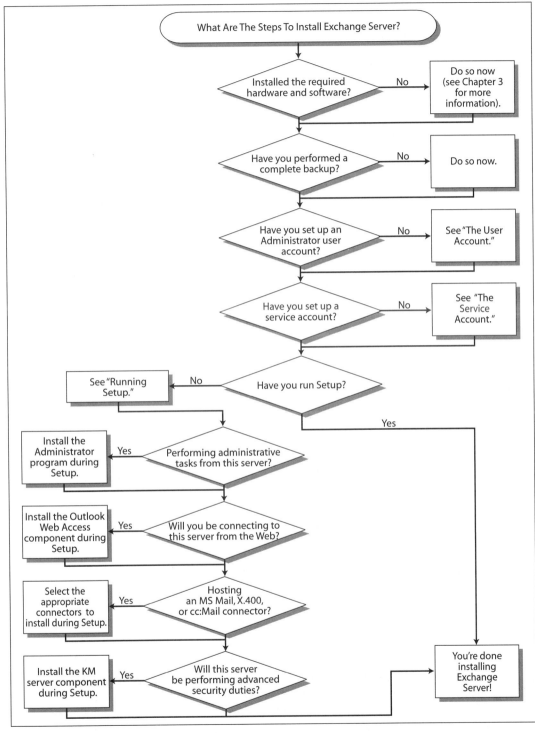

Decision Tree 4.1   What are the steps to install Exchange Server?

9. Click on Add.

10. Exit User Manager for Domains.

Before Running Setup

Before running Setup, perform the following tasks:

➤ Make sure that all required software and hardware are installed (see Chapter 3 for these requirements).

➤ Perform a complete backup on the computer where you're installing Exchange Server.

➤ Verify that the *Primary Domain Controller (PDC)* is running.

➤ Make sure that no messaging-aware applications are running.

➤ If you're installing Exchange Server on a pair of clustered servers, use the Cluster Administrator program to verify that an appropriate cluster group has been created (the group must contain a network name, an IP address, and a shared disk that is part of an external disk array).

Running Setup

Follow these steps to run Exchange Server Setup:

1. Log on to the Windows NT computer with the user account that will become the Exchange Server Administrator account.

2. Insert the Exchange Server compact disc into your CD-ROM drive and select Setup; the Welcome screen appears.

3. Read the license agreement and click on Accept; the Installation Options dialog box appears.

4. Select the Complete/Custom installation option, so you can choose which Exchange Server components to install as indicated in your installation plans.

5. If you do not want to install any of the components displayed in the next screen, clear the check boxes beside those components; otherwise, all of the components listed will be installed (see Figure 4.1).

• • • *Tip* • • •

Leave the Microsoft Exchange Server check box selected to install all the core components for a fully configured Exchange Server. Make sure that you install the Administrator program component on every server where you plan to perform administrative duties.

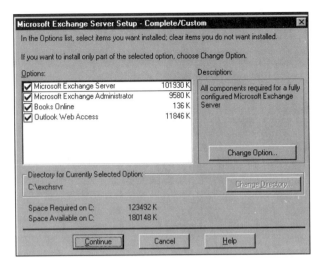

Figure 4.1   Selecting components to install.

6. Select Microsoft Exchange Server and click on Change Options to select which *connectors* and optional components you want to install.

7. Click on OK.

8. Click on Continue.

9. If any services must be temporarily stopped during the installation, Setup informs you now; click on OK to stop the services and continue.

10. The Licensing dialog box appears; select the I Agree That check box and click on Continue.

11. The Organization and Site dialog box appears (see Figure 4.2); click on the Create A New Site button.

12. Type the name of the organization in the Organization Name box.

13. Type the name of the site in the Site Name box.

Tip

If this is not the first Exchange Server computer you are installing in the site, click on the Join An Existing Site button in the Organization and Site dialog box, and type the name of an Exchange Server computer in the site you're joining in the Existing Server box.

14. Click on OK.

15. When asked if you're sure you would like to create a new site, click on Yes.

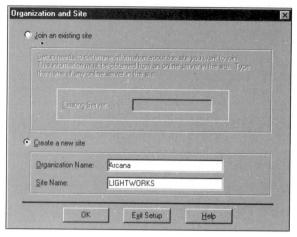

Figure 4.2   The Organization and Site dialog box.

16. In the Service Account dialog box, select the service account you created.

17. Type the service account password in the Account Password box.

18. Click on OK.

19. Setup then verifies the service account, copies the Exchange Server files, starts the Exchange Server services, builds the directory, and installs server components. When Setup is complete, click on Run Optimizer to run the Performance Optimizer.

● ● *Tip* ● ● ●

Running the *Performance Optimizer* is critical to the efficient operation of Exchange Server. If you skip this step during installation, make sure you run the Performance Optimizer manually before using the server. Refer to Chapter 6 for more information.

After installation and the Performance Optimizer have finished, verify that the Exchange Server components were installed and are functioning correctly. Do the following:

➤ Open the Services control panel, and verify that the Microsoft Exchange System Attendant, Directory, Information Store, and Message Transfer Agent (MTA) services have started.

➤ Open the Administrator program (select Microsoft Exchange Administrator from the Microsoft Exchange program group), and verify that your site and server objects are set up correctly and that the organization hierarchy looks like you intended.

Setting Up Core Components And The Site

Setup installs a set of core components, along with any additional components, such as connectors, that you selected. The core components provide the basic functionality of Exchange Server. Each component is installed with a default configuration, which you can customize. The core components are the MTA, directory, information store, and system attendant.

● ● ● *Tip* ● ● ●

You will use the Exchange Server *Administrator program* to configure settings for all Exchange Server components. See Chapter 5 to learn more about using the Administrator program.

You need to configure several settings pertaining to the site you created before you can begin using Exchange Server. These settings include site-wide configurations for the MTA, directory, and information store. Configuring additional settings for core components will be covered in later chapters.

The Message Transfer Agent

The *Message Transfer Agent (MTA)* enables message transfer on the Exchange Server system. It delivers messages to their destinations by moving them from one server to another. It also transfers messages between servers in different sites and to other mail systems.

You can change the local name of the MTA, which by default matches the Exchange Server name. You can also set an optional password to provide security for the MTA, which is required by some foreign systems when connecting to the MTA. Follow these steps:

1. Click on the Servers button in the Administrator window.

2. Select the server whose core components you're configuring.

3. Double-click on Message Transfer Agent.

4. Select the General tab (see Figure 4.3).

The System Attendant

The *system attendant* generates email addresses for new recipients using the *email address generator,* and it maintains *message tracking* logs. It also monitors the connection status among Exchange Server computers. You cannot change the default settings for the system attendant.

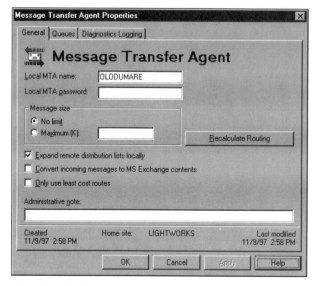

Figure 4.3   Setting the local MTA name and password.

    5. In the Local MTA Name box, type the new name.

    6. In the Local MTA Password box, type an optional password.

    7. Click on OK.

The Directory

The *directory* stores information about message *recipients* and other objects in the Exchange Server organization. There is a directory entry, which contains all the information you configure for an object using the Administrator program, for each *object* that appears in the Administrator window. See Chapter 5 to learn more about setting properties for directory objects using the Administrator program.

You can set various site-wide values for the directory, including settings for offline Address Books and tombstones. Remote users access *offline Address Books* on the offline Address Book server to get information about other users. (The *offline Address Book server* generates and stores the offline Address Book files.) A *tombstone* is a marker that indicates that you deleted an object from the server; it is replicated with the directory to update other servers with the deleted object.

Follow these steps to configure site-wide directory settings:

    1. Click on the Configuration button in the Administrator window.

    2. Double-click on DS Site Configuration.

    3. Select the General tab (see Figure 4.4).

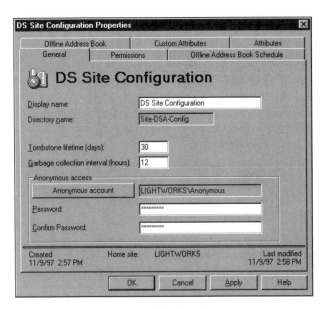

Figure 4.4 Configuring site-wide settings for the directory.

4. In the Tombstone Lifetime (Days) box, enter the number of days before a tombstone is removed.

5. In the Garbage Collection Interval (Hours) box, enter the interval between the removal of expired tombstones.

• • • *Tip* • • • •

Removing tombstones increases disk space and system efficiency.

6. Click on Anonymous Account to set up an internal account that enables the directory to access containers when anonymous users connect to Exchange Server.

7. Select either the Select An Existing Windows NT User Account option or the Create A New Windows NT User Account option and click on OK.

8. Select the existing account or specify the information for the new account and click on OK.

• • • *Tip* • • • •

The anonymous account should have minimal permissions and a password that does not expire.

9. Select the Offline Address Book tab (see Figure 4.5).

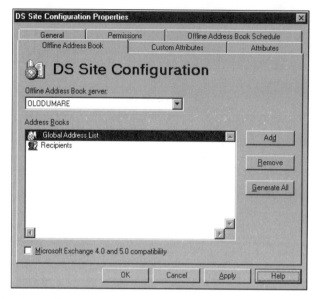

Figure 4.5   Configuring offline Address Book settings.

10. In the Offline Address Book Server box, select the server for generating the offline Address Book files and click on Add.

Tip

If there are many recipients in offline Address Books, you'll get the best performance by selecting an offline Address Book server that is not busy doing other tasks.

11. Select the recipients container to use for offline Address Book generation and click on OK.

Tip

Generally, you should select the Global Address List container for offline Address Book generation to ensure that remote users can send mail to any recipient in the organization.

12. Select the Microsoft Exchange 4.0 and 5.0 Compatibility check box if your users are running Exchange Client versions earlier than 5.0 or Outlook versions earlier than 8.03.

13. Select the Offline Address Book Schedule tab.

14. Click on the Always option to update offline Address Books continuously, or click on the Selected Times option to set a schedule in the grid.

15. Click on OK to save your changes.

The Information Store

The *information store* is the central repository for all mail messages and *public folders* stored on the Exchange Server computer. You can configure settings for all the information stores in your site, including assigning a public folders *container* where information about public folders is stored. Follow these steps:

1. Click on the Configuration button in the Administrator window.

2. Double-click on Information Store Site Configuration.

3. Select the General tab.

4. Click on Modify under Public Folder Container.

5. Select the public folder container and click on OK (see Figure 4.6).

6. Click on OK to apply your new settings.

Setting Up Connectors

During Setup, you can install three connectors: the MS Mail Connector, the X.400 Connector, and the Connector for Lotus cc:Mail. You can install the Site Connector, the Dynamic RAS Connector, and the Internet Mail Service in the Administrator program. After Exchange Server has been installed, you must set up the connection and configure settings for any connectors you installed.

Check your organization planning worksheet for the connectors that need to be installed and configured on each server. Be sure that you have installed the necessary hardware and software to support the connection, which should also be listed on your organization planning sheet (refer back to Chapter 3 for more information about connectors). See Decision Tree 4.2 for information on the steps needed to configure connectors.

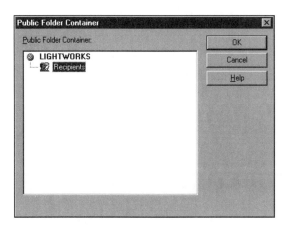

Figure 4.6   Selecting the public folder container.

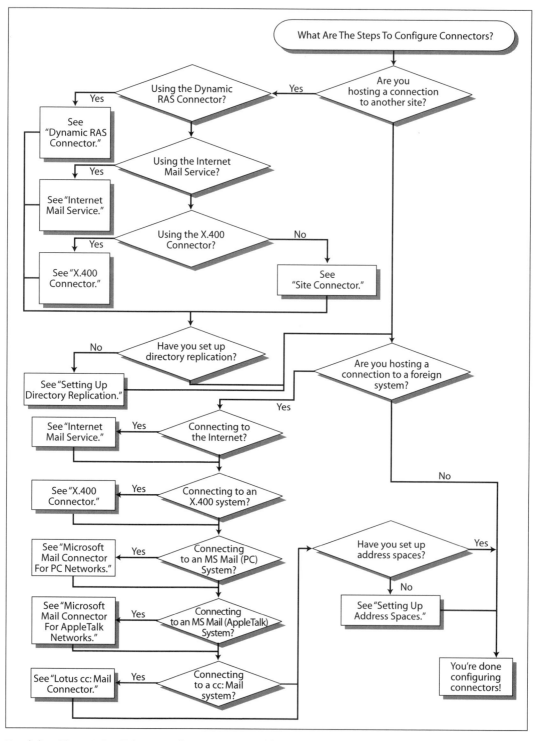

Decision Tree 4.2 What are the steps to configure connectors?

• • *Tip* • • •

If you are configuring a connector to a *foreign system,* you will need to consult that system's documentation to complete the connection processes.

Site Connector

The *Site Connector* joins two *Exchange Server sites* over a Local Area Network (LAN). To install the Site Connector, you need a logical map of your network, the name of at least one target server in the remote site that will provide message transfer through the connector, and Administrator permissions on both the local and remote sites.

> *Target server refers to the Exchange Server computer in each site that acts as the endpoint for the site connection. Local site refers to the Exchange Server site from which you're making the connection. Remote site refers to the Exchange Server site to which you're connecting.*

Follow these steps to install and configure the Site Connector:

1. Click on the Configuration button in the Administrator window.

2. Select Connections.

3. Select New Other from the File menu.

4. Select Site Connector.

5. Type the name of the target server in the remote site to which you want to connect and click on OK.

• • *Tip* • • •

If you'd like to edit the target server at a later time, double-click on Site Connector in the Administrator window and click on the Target Servers tab.

6. Type the name that will identify the Site Connector in the Administrator window in the Display Name box (see Figure 4.7).

7. Type the name that will identify the Site Connector in the directory in the Directory Name box.

8. Under Messaging Bridgehead In The Local Site, click on the Specific Server button to limit sending messages to the remote site to only the server you select.

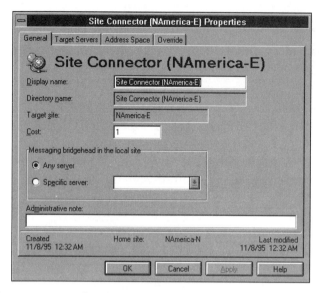

Figure 4.7 Setting properties for the Site Connector.

9. Select the Override tab if the service account for the local site doesn't have service account permissions for the remote site.

10. Type the name of the user who has access permissions for the remote site in the Windows NT Username box.

11. Type the password for the user account in the Password box.

12. Retype the password in the Confirm Password box.

13. Type the domain of the user account in the Windows NT Domain Name box.

14. Click on OK to save your changes.

After installing the Site Connector, you must create a corresponding Site Connector in the remote site that connects back to the server in the local site where the Site Connector is installed. Do so by logging on to a server in the remote site, opening the Administrator program on that server, and performing these same steps.

Dynamic RAS Connector

The *Dynamic RAS Connector* is used when there is no LAN connectivity between Exchange Server sites by using asynchronous, remote connections to connect the two sites. Before installing the Dynamic RAS Connector, you need the following:

➤ *Remote Access Service (RAS)* network software installed on the connecting Exchange Server computers.

➤ The service account for the remote site or a Windows NT user account with Send As and Mailbox Owner (User role) permissions for the Servers or Configuration containers in the remote site.

➤ The name and phone book entry of the server in the remote site to which you're connecting.

Installing The RAS MTA Transport Stack

Before you install the Dynamic RAS Connector, you must install and configure the RAS MTA transport stack on the server where the Dynamic RAS Connector will be located. Follow these steps:

1. Click on the Servers button in the Administrator window.

2. Select the server where you want to install the Dynamic RAS Connector.

3. Select New Other from the File menu.

4. Select MTA Transport Stack.

5. Select RAS MTA Transport Stack in the Type box.

6. Select the server on which to install the transport stack in the Server box.

7. Click on OK.

8. In the Display Name box, type the name of the RAS MTA transport stack (see Figure 4.8).

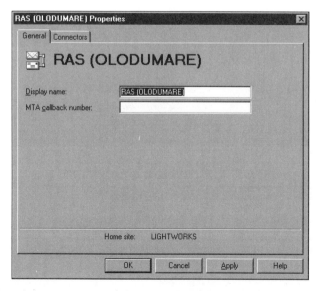

Figure 4.8   Setting the properties of the RAS MTA transport stack.

9. In the MTA Callback Number box, type the telephone number used to reach the server over a dial-up connection if you plan to use RAS callback security.

10. Click on OK to save your changes.

● ● *Tip* ● ● ●

Select the Connectors tab to view a list of all Dynamic RAS Connectors installed on the RAS MTA transport stack and to edit the properties of any of these connectors.

Installing The Dynamic RAS Connector

Now, you should install the Dynamic RAS Connector on the server where you installed the RAS MTA transport stack and configure properties for the connector. When you're finished, you need to install and configure the RAS MTA transport stack and Dynamic RAS Connector on the corresponding server in the remote site to enable the connection. Follow these steps:

1. Click on the Configuration button in the Administrator window.

2. Select Connections.

3. Select New Other from the File menu.

4. Select Dynamic RAS Connector (see Figure 4.9).

5. Type the name of the Dynamic RAS Connector that will be displayed in the Administrator window in the Display Name box.

Figure 4.9   Configuring general properties for the Dynamic RAS Connector.

6. Type the name that will permanently identify the Dynamic RAS Connector in the directory in the Directory Name box.

7. Type the name of the target server in the remote site in the Remote Server Name box.

8. Select the RAS MTA transport stack from the MTA Transport Stack menu.

9. In the Phone Book Entry menu, select the RAS phone book entry for the target server in the remote site (click on Refresh List to update the list of available phone book entries, or click on RAS Phone Book to add a new entry).

10. Select the Schedule tab.

11. Select one of the following options: Remote Initiated, to send messages only when the remote MTA connects to this MTA; Never, to disable the connector; Always, to send messages as they are queued; or Selected Times, to set a schedule for sending messages in the schedule grid.

12. Select the RAS Override tab (see Figure 4.10).

13. In the Windows NT Username box, type the name of the remote site's service account or the name of the user account used to log on to the remote site.

14. In the Password box, type the password associated with the account.

15. Type the password again in the Confirm Password box.

16. Type the domain of the account in the Windows NT Domain Name box.

Figure 4.10   Entering logon information for the remote site.

17. Under Optional Phone Numbers, type a callback number in the MTA Callback Number box if you want to override the callback number set for the RAS MTA transport stack.

18. Under Optional Phone Numbers, type a phone number in the Overriding Phone Number box if you want to override the number in the selected RAS phone book entry.

19. Select the MTA Override tab and modify the default values as needed to match the target server's MTA values.

Tip

Find the target server's MTA values by connecting to the target server in the remote site, double-clicking on MTA Site Configuration in the Administrator window, and selecting the Messaging Defaults tab.

20. Click on the Connected Sites tab.

21. Click on New (See Figure 4.11).

22. Type the name of the organization in the Organization box.

23. Type the name of the site you're connecting to in the Site box.

24. Select the Routing Address tab.

25. Fill out the fields with the X.400 address for the remote site and click on OK.

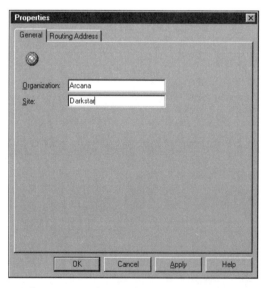

Figure 4.11   Specifying information about the connected site.

Tip

To find the X.400 address, connect to a server in the remote site, double-click on Site Addressing in the Administrator window, and select the Site Addressing tab. Copy the X.400 address exactly as shown.

26. Click on OK to save all your changes.

Internet Mail Service

The *Internet Mail Service* is used to send messages to and receive messages from the Internet. It can also connect two Exchange Server sites over a *Simple Mail Transport Protocol (SMTP)* backbone. To use the Internet Mail Service, you will need a direct or dial-up connection to the Internet. You should also gather the following information before installing the Internet Mail Service:

➤ The SMTP address for the site (double-click on Site Addressing in the Administrator window).

➤ The person to receive notifications if the Internet Mail Service fails.

➤ The host name and domain name of the computer on which the Internet Mail Service will be installed.

➤ Whether Domain Name System (DNS) will be used to provide domain name to IP address resolution.

➤ The IP address of the DNS server or SMTP server that will service the Internet Mail Service.

Before installing the Internet Mail Service, install and configure Windows NT Server *Transport Control Protocol/Internet Protocol (TCP/IP)* on the computer where the Internet Mail Service will reside; for improved security, this should be a computer using Windows NT Server File System (NTFS). If you are connecting two Exchange Server sites, install TCP/IP on each computer running the Internet Mail Service. Configure TCP/IP with a static IP address. In the TCP/IP DNS configuration, enter the server name as the host name, specify a domain name, and provide the IP address of the DNS server.

If you are using DNS, you also need to set up the DNS server using the Network applet in the Control Panel. On your DNS server, add an "A" and an "MX" record pointing to the Exchange Server computer that hosts the Internet Mail Service. If you are using a modem to access your Internet Service Provider (ISP), you must install RAS and create a phone book entry for the ISP on the Exchange Server computer.

Installing The Internet Mail Service

Follow these steps to install the Internet Mail Service:

1. Click on the Configuration button in the Administrator window.

2. Select Connections.

3. Select New Other from the File menu.

4. Select Internet Mail Service.

5. Click on Next.

6. Select the Exchange Server computer that you want to act as your Internet SMTP gateway (see Figure 4.12).

7. Select the Allow Internet Mail Through A Dial-Up Connection check box only if you are using a dial-up connection to connect to your ISP.

8. Click on Next.

9. If you are using a dial-up connection, select your RAS phone book entry and type the IP address of your ISP's mail host.

10. Click on Next.

11. Select the Route All Mail Through A Single Host option only if you are connecting to an ISP or have an existing SMTP server; enter the host name or IP address.

12. Click on Next.

13. Select the All Internet Mail Addresses option and click on Next.

14. When the default Internet address for your site is displayed, click on Next.

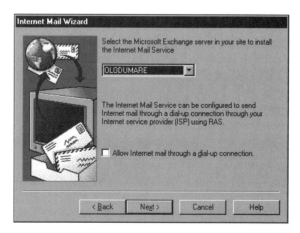

Figure 4.12 Selecting the server on which to install the Internet Mail Service.

15. Select the mailbox of the administrator to be notified if there are problems sending messages to the Internet and click on Next.

16. Select the service account for the Exchange Server site, type the password in the Password box, and click on Next.

17. Click on Finish; the Internet Mail Service is created and started.

Setting Up A Connection Between Sites

Follow these steps to connect two Exchange Server sites using the Internet Mail Service (you must install and configure a second Internet Mail Service separately on the target server in the remote site):

1. Click on the Configuration button in the Administrator window.

2. Select Connections.

3. Double-click on the Internet Mail Service that you want to configure as the connection to the remote site.

4. Click on the Connected Sites tab (see Figure 4.13).

5. Click on New.

6. Type the organization name in the Organization box.

7. Type the name of the site to connect to in the Site box.

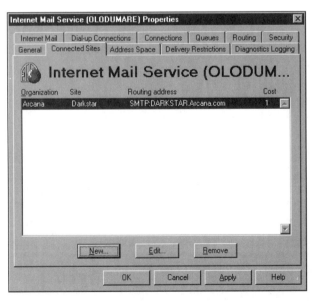

Figure 4.13   Setting up a connection between two sites using the Internet Mail Service.

8. Select the Routing Address tab.

9. Type **SMTP** in the Type box.

10. In the Address box, type the domain name or FQDN of the server hosting the Internet Mail Service in the remote site.

11. Click on OK twice to create the connection.

Configuring The Internet Mail Service

Follow these steps and review Decision Tree 4.3 before setting the properties of the Internet Mail Service:

1. Click on the Configuration button in the Administrator window.

2. Select Connections.

3. Double-click on the Internet Mail Service you're configuring.

4. Select the Internet Mail tab (see Figure 4.14).

5. Click on Notifications to set notification options for *non-delivery reports (NDRs)*.

6. Under Attachments (Outbound), select MIME or UUENCODE to specify encoding of outbound message attachments (the typical choice is MIME).

7. Under Character Sets, select the character sets to be used with MIME and non-MIME outbound messages.

Figure 4.14   Setting options for sending mail to the Internet.

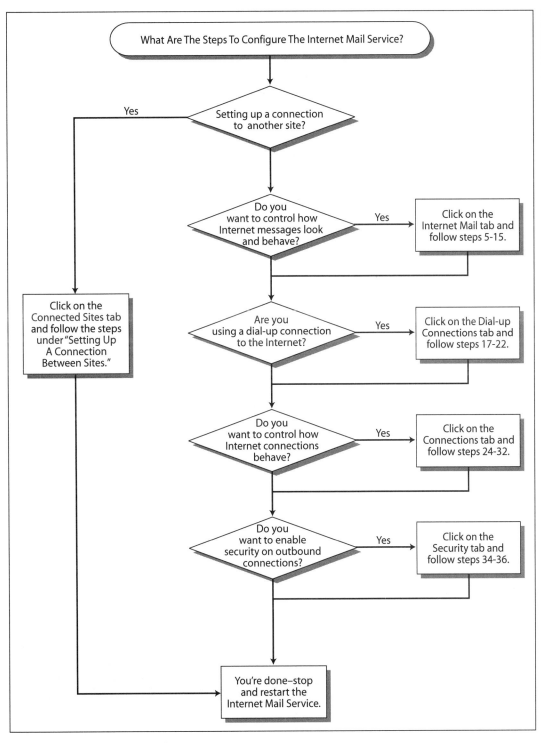

Decision Tree 4.3   What are the steps to configure the Internet Mail Service?

four

8. Select the Clients Support S/MIME Signatures check box if your users' clients support the S/MIME protocol.

9. Select the Convert Inbound Message To Fixed-Width Font check box to enable fixed-width characters to display.

••• *Tip* •••

Click on E-Mail Domain to set different encoding method, character set, and message size properties for individual domains.

10. Click on Advanced Options.

11. In the Send Microsoft Exchange Rich Text Formatting menu, select one of the following options: User, to send rich text only when it's enabled for the recipient; Always, to always send rich text; or Never, to never send rich text.

12. Clear the Disable Out Of Office Responses To The Internet check box to allow out-of-office messages.

13. Clear the Disable Automatic Replies To The Internet check box to allow automatic replies.

14. Select the Disable Sending Display Names To The Internet check box to turn off display names on messages sent through the Internet Mail Service.

15. Click on OK.

16. Select the Dial-up Connections tab only if you are using a dial-up connection to connect to the remote site or ISP (see Figure 4.15).

17. Under Available Connections, select the check box by the connection you want to activate.

18. In the Time-out After box, enter the amount of time to keep the RAS connection open.

19. Click on Mail Retrieval to specify a command that identifies you to the ISP, if your ISP requires it.

20. Click on Logon Information and specify the username, domain, and password information needed to log on to the ISP; click on OK.

21. Select one of the of the following options to set a schedule for the connection: Daily; Weekly; Every, to specify the time interval for connections; At, to specify the time to connect; or When Mail Queued, But At Most Every, to specify the number of minutes for the most frequent connection interval.

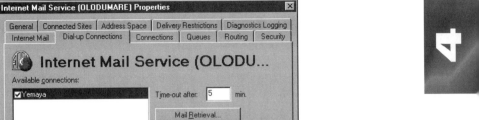

Figure 4.15   Setting dial-up connection properties.

22. If you choose the Every or When Mail Queued, But At Most Every option, enter the hours during which the schedule takes effect in the Start and End boxes, or select the All Day check box to make the schedule continuously active.

23. Click on the Connections tab (see Figure 4.16).

Figure 4.16   Setting properties for Internet connections.

24. Under Transfer Mode, select one of the following options: Inbound & Outbound; Inbound Only; Outbound Only; or None (Flush Queues), if you want to suspend further message activity.

Tip

Use Transfer Mode to balance the responsibility for sending and receiving Internet messages among multiple Internet Mail Services. If your organization has only one Internet Mail Service, you should set Transfer Mode to Inbound & Outbound.

25. Click on Advanced under Transfer Mode, fill out the options for the number of connections that can be made and accepted at one time, and click on OK.

26. Under Message Delivery, select the Use Domain Name System (DNS) option to route all outbound messages using DNS queries, or select the Forward All Messages To Host option and type the IP address of the host.

27. Select the Dial Using check box if you are using a dial-up connection, and choose the appropriate connection.

Tip

To define the way messages are delivered by individual domain, click on E-Mail Domain under Message Delivery.

28. Under Accept Connections, select one of the following options: From Any Host (Secure Or Non-secure), to accept messages from all hosts; Only From Hosts Using, and choose Authentication, Encryption, or Auth And Encrypt; or Hosts, and click on Add to create a list of IP addresses from which to accept or reject connections.

29. If you selected the Only From Hosts Using option, select the Clients Can Only Submit If Homed On This Server check box to restrict the sending of messages to users who are housed on the server.

30. If you selected the Only From Hosts Using option, select the Clients Can Only Submit If Authentication Account Matches Submission Address check box to restrict the sending of messages to users whose user account names match the name in the From field.

31. Under Service Message Queues, enter the number of hours to wait before retrying a failed connection in the Retry Intervals (Hrs) box.

32. Click on Time-outs to set time-out options for messages of different priorities.

33. Select the Security tab to enable security on outbound connections (see Figure 4.17).

Figure 4.17   Specifying security options for an email domain.

34. Click on Add.

35. Type the name of the domain for which you want to enable security in the E-mail Domain box.

36. Select one of the following security types: No Authentication Or Encryption; SASL/SSL Security, and select authentication and encryption options; or Windows NT Challenge/Response Authentication And Encryption, and select the Windows NT account to use for authentication.

Tip

For the greatest security, select SSL encryption or use a Windows NT account with a non-blank password.

37. Click on OK to close all dialog boxes.

Tip

After making any changes to the Internet Mail Service's properties, you must stop and restart the Internet Mail Service by selecting Microsoft Exchange Internet Mail Service in the Services control panel, clicking on Stop, and clicking on Start.

four

X.400 Connector

Use the *X.400 Connector* to connect two Exchange Server sites over an X.400 backbone or to connect the Exchange Server system with an X.400 messaging system. When connecting two sites, you must install the X.400 Connector on one *messaging bridgehead server* in each site. Before you install the X.400 Connector, you must complete the following tasks:

➤ Determine what type of MTA transport stack to use to connect to the remote site or foreign system: X.25, TCP/IP, or Transport Class 4/Connectionless Network Protocol (TP4/CLNP).

➤ Install the network transport protocols used by the MTA transport stack on the connecting server in each site or system.

➤ Obtain the address of the site or foreign system to which you're connecting.

Installing The MTA Transport Stack

The *MTA transport stack* contains configuration information about the network software and hardware responsible for routing messages over the X.400 connection. You can choose from the following MTA transport stacks: TP0/X.25, using an Eicon port adapter, TCP/IP, or TP4/CLNP. Pick the one that matches the network software and hardware you installed on the Exchange Server computer that hosts the X.400 Connector.

Follow these steps to install the MTA transport stack:

1. Click on the Servers button in the Administrator window.

2. Select the server where you're installing the X.400 Connector.

3. From the File menu, select New Other.

4. Select MTA Transport Stack.

5. Select the type of stack to use in the Type box.

6. Select the server on which to install the transport stack in the Server box.

7. Click on OK.

8. In the Name box, type the name of the transport stack.

9. If other applications or services are using the same transport stack, fill out the appropriate information under OSI Address Information.

10. Select the Hex button to display address information as hexadecimal values, or select the Text button to display address information as Text.

If you installed the TCP/IP or TP4 MTA transport stack, click on OK at this point. If you installed the X.25 MTA transport stack, continue with the following steps:

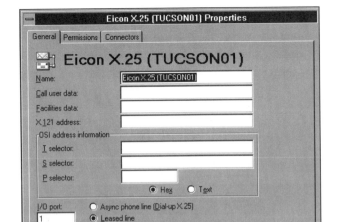

Figure 4.18   Configuring the X.25 MTA transport stack.

1. Type the call user data supplied by the X.25 provider in the Call User Data box (see Figure 4.18).

2. Enter any additional information about connection initiation in the Facilities Data box.

3. Type the local X.121 address as specified in the X.25 network service setup in the X.121 Address box.

4. Specify the I/O port where the Eicon adapter is installed in the I/O Port box.

5. Select whether the connection uses an Async Phone Line or a Leased Line.

6. Click on OK to install the transport stack.

● ● ● *Tip* ● ● ● ●

If you are connecting to a foreign system, you must configure the corresponding transport software to the MTA transport stack on the connecting X.400 server.

Installing The X.400 Connector

Follow these steps to add a new X.400 Connector to your Exchange Server computer:

1. Click on the Configuration button in the Administrator window.

2. Select Connections.

3. Select New Other from the File menu.

On Site

4. Select X.400 Connector.

5. In the Type box, select the type of MTA transport stack that you previously installed.

6. Click on OK.

7. Type the name that will identify the connector in the Administrator window in the Display Name box (see Figure 4.19).

8. Type the name that will identify the connector in the directory in the Directory Name box.

9. Type the name of the MTA on the server to which you're connecting in the Remote MTA Name box.

• • • *Tip* • • • •

If you're connecting to a remote site, find the name of the remote MTA by selecting the target server in the Administrator window, double-clicking on Message Transfer Agent, and selecting the General tab.

10. If a password for connecting to the remote MTA is required, type it in the Remote MTA Password box.

11. Select the MTA transport stack to use with the connector in the MTA Transport Stack menu.

Figure 4.19   Configuring general properties for the X.400 Connector.

12. Select one of the following options under Message Text Word-wrap: Never, to disable word-wrapping; or At Column, to specify the column where a carriage return is inserted in outgoing messages.

13. Clear the Remote Clients Support MAPI check box if email clients in the foreign system do not support rich-text formatting.

14. Select the Schedule tab.

15. Select one of the following options: Remote Initiated, to send queued messages when the remote MTA connects to the local system; Never, to disable the connector; Always, to connect whenever messages need to be transferred; or Selected Times, to assign specific times in the schedule grid.

16. Select the Stack tab.

17. Enter the appropriate information about the remote site or foreign system to which you're connecting; this information must match the transport configuration on the target server in the remote site or foreign system for the connection to work.

Tip

To obtain values for a remote site, select the target server in the Administrator window, select Properties under the File menu, and look at the General tab. To obtain values for a foreign system, check the system's transport configuration utility or ask the system administrator or service provider.

18. Select the Advanced tab (see Figure 4.20).

19. Under MTA Conformance, select a conformance mode that matches the conformance of the foreign system.

20. In the X.400 Bodypart Used For Message Text menu, select the bodypart type supported by the foreign system.

21. Under X.400 Link Options, select the Allow BP-15 (In Addition To BP-14) check box to send BP-15 attachments.

22. Under X.400 Link Options, select the Allow MS Exchange Contents check box to send message content formatted in the Exchange Server internal format whenever possible.

23. Under X.400 Link Options, select the Two Way Alternate check box to specify that the two connecting MTAs take turns sending and receiving messages.

24. Click on the Use The GDI From Site Addressing button; or click on the Use The GDI Specified Below button, and select the foreign system's GDI under Remote X.400 Global Domain Identifier.

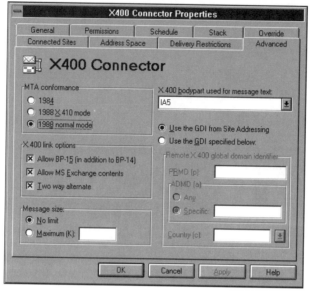

Figure 4.20   Setting advanced properties for the X.400 Connector.

Tip

Select the Override tab to change the default Exchange Server MTA attributes if necessary or to configure the connection to the foreign system manually.

25. Click on OK to save your changes.

Connecting To A Remote Site

Follow these steps to set up a connection between two Exchange Server sites using the X.400 Connector (you must also install the corresponding MTA transport stack and X.400 Connector on the target server in the remote site to which you want to establish the connection):

1. Click on the Configuration button in the Administrator window.

2. Select Connections.

3. Double-click on the X.400 Connector you just installed.

4. Select the Connected Sites tab.

5. Click on New.

6. Enter your organization's name in the Organization box.

7. Enter the name of the site to connect to in the Site box.

8. Click on the Routing Address tab.

9. Fill out the fields with the X.400 address for the remote site.

Tip

To find the X.400 address for the remote site, connect to a server in the remote site, double-click on Site Addressing in the Administrator window, and select the Site Addressing tab. Copy the X.400 address exactly as shown.

10. Click on OK twice to create the connection to the remote site.

Connecting To A Foreign System

It does not matter if you configure the Exchange Server X.400 Connector or the foreign X.400 system first when setting up a connection to a foreign X.400 system. However, you might find it easier to set up the connection on the foreign system after configuring the X.400 Connector on the Exchange Server computer, because you can gather most of the information you need for the foreign system's configuration from the X.400 Connector's property pages in the Administrator program. Use the configuration procedure or utility for the foreign system to configure the foreign MTA to receive messages from Exchange Server. Then, verify that the configuration of the X.400 Connector on Exchange Server and the foreign system's MTA match for the most reliable message exchange.

Microsoft Mail Connector For PC Networks

The MS Mail (PC) component of the *Microsoft Mail Connector* is used for information exchange between the Exchange Server system and an MS Mail for PC Networks system over a LAN, asynchronous, or X.25 connection. To configure the MS Mail (PC) Connector, you will need access to an MS Mail (PC) postoffice as an administrator and the network name and postoffice name of the postoffice. You will also need to set up a network connection between the Exchange Server computer and the MS Mail (PC) postoffice. See Decision Tree 4.4 for the steps needed to connect an MS Mail System.

Tip

To find the network name and postoffice name of the MS Mail (PC) postoffice, log on to the MS Mail Administrator program as the Administrator and choose Password from the Configuration menu.

Configuring The MS Mail Connector Interchange

The *Microsoft Mail Connector Interchange* is a Windows NT Server service that routes and transfers messages between Exchange Server and the MS Mail (PC) Connector postoffice. Follow these steps to configure the Interchange:

1. Click on the Configuration button in the Administrator window.

2. Select Connections.

3. Double-click on MS Mail Connector.

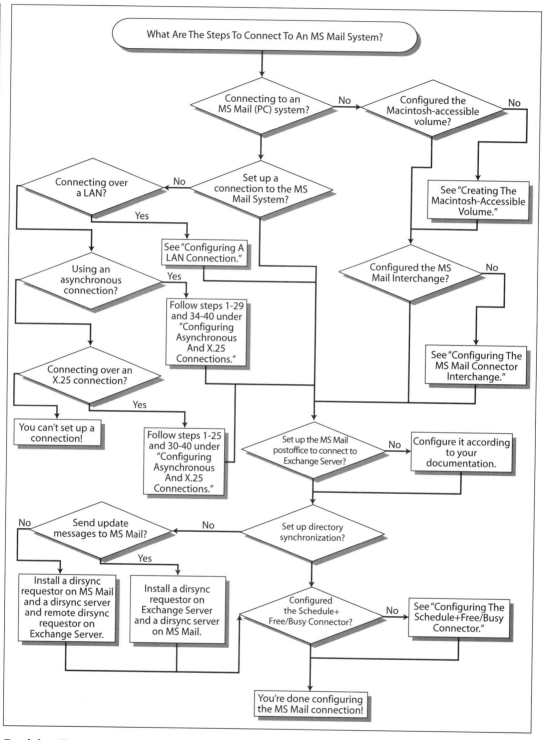

Decision Tree 4.4 What are the steps to connect to an MS Mail system?

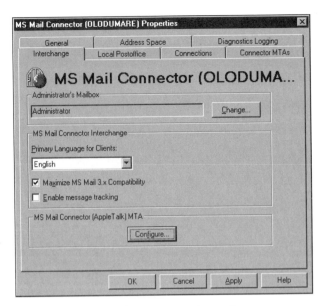

Figure 4.21 Configuring the MS Mail Connector Interchange.

4. Select the Interchange tab (see Figure 4.21).

5. Click on Change, select a recipient to receive delivery status messages for the connector, and click on OK.

Tip

You might want to create a new mailbox called "postmaster" to receive delivery messages.

6. In the Primary Language For Clients menu, select the language that most of your clients use.

7. Select the Maximize MS Mail 3.x Compatibility check box to enable MS Mail 3.x clients to view or save embedded objects sent from Exchange clients.

8. Click on OK.

Setting Up A Connection

Now, you need to configure the MS Mail (PC) Connector to connect to an MS Mail (PC) postoffice. These settings can differ, depending on whether you're connecting over a LAN, asynchronous, or X.25 connection.

Configuring A LAN Connection. Follow these steps to set up a connection to an MS Mail (PC) postoffice over a LAN connection:

1. Click on the Configuration button in the Administrator window.

2. Select Connections.

3. Double-click on the MS Mail Connector.

4. Select the Connections tab.

5. Click on Create (see Figure 4.22).

6. Under Connection Parameters, select LAN.

7. Click on Change.

8. Type the full path to the MS Mail (PC) postoffice using UNC format in the Path box: \\<server name>\<share name>\<postoffice location>, for example.

9. Type the logon identifier in the Connect As box and the account password in the Password box if you must use a specific account to make the network connection to the postoffice.

10. Click on OK.

11. In the Connection Attempts box, enter the number of attempts to send mail before returning an NDR.

Tip

Click on Upload Routing to display a list of any indirect postoffices connected to the MS Mail (PC) postoffice.

12. Click on OK to create the connection.

13. Select the Connector MTAs tab.

14. Click on New (see Figure 4.23).

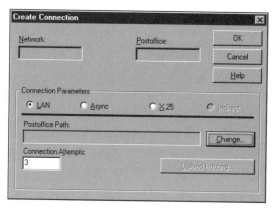

Figure 4.22   Creating a LAN connection.

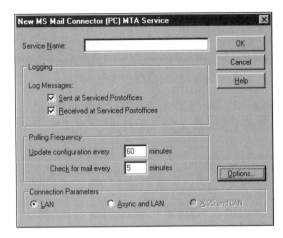

Figure 4.23   Creating the MS Mail (PC) Connector MTA.

15. Type the name for the new MS Mail (PC) Connector MTA in the Service Name box.

16. Under Logging, select the Sent At Serviced Postoffices check box and/or the Received At Serviced Postoffices check box to log messages delivered to and received from MS Mail (PC) postoffices.

17. In the Update Configuration Every box, enter how often the MS Mail (PC) Connector MTA checks the postoffices for updated user and network information.

18. In the Check For Mail Every box, enter how often the MS Mail (PC) Connector MTA checks the postoffices for mail.

19. Click on Options.

20. In the Close Postoffice If box, enter the minimum amount of disk space required on the destination postoffice for message transfer to go ahead.

21. In the Open Postoffice If box, enter the minimum amount of disk space required to restore the destination postoffice after it is closed.

22. Select the NetBIOS Notification check box to notify MS Mail (PC) users about new mail immediately using NetBIOS.

23. Select the Disable Mailer check box to prevent the MS Mail (PC) Connector MTA from distributing messages to users on LAN-connected postoffices.

24. Select the Disable Mail Dispatch check box to prevent the MS Mail (PC) Connector MTA from delivering messages to LAN-connected postoffices.

25. Select the Start Automatically At System Startup button to start the MS Mail (PC) Connector MTA with other system services, or select the Manual Start (From Control Panel) button to start the MS Mail (PC) Connector MTA manually.

26. Click on OK twice to create the MS Mail (PC) Connector MTA.

27. Click on List.

28. Under Available LAN Postoffices, select the postoffices you want to service, click on Add, and click on OK.

29. Type the name for logging on to the postoffice in the Account Name box.

30. Type the logon password in the Password box.

31. Select the Do Not Pick Up Mail At This Postoffice check box to send but not receive messages from this postoffice.

32. Click on OK twice to close all dialog boxes and save your changes.

Configuring An Asynchronous Or X.25 Connection

Follow these steps to set up a connection to an MS Mail (PC) postoffice over an asynchronous or X.25 connection:

1. Click on the Configuration button in the Administrator window.

2. Select Connections.

3. Double-click on MS Mail Connector.

4. Select the Connections tab.

5. Click on Create.

6. Under Connection Parameters, select Async or X.25 (see Figure 4.24).

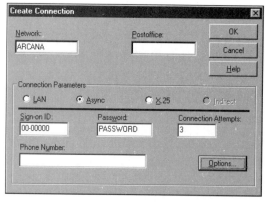

Figure 4.24   Creating an asynchronous connection.

7. In the Network box, type the network name for the postoffice to which you're connecting.

8. Type the postoffice name in the Postoffice box.

9. Type the serial number identifier for the postoffice in the Sign-on ID box.

10. Type the password used to log on to the postoffice in the Password box.

11. In the Connection Attempts box, enter the number of attempts to send mail before returning an NDR.

12. If you are configuring an asynchronous connection, type the entire dialing sequence used to reach the postoffice in the Phone Number box.

13. If you are configuring an X.25 connection, type the X.121 address of the postoffice in the X.121 Address box.

14. Click on Options.

15. In the Failed Connection Retry For Urgent Mail box, enter the interval range for urgent mail connection attempts.

16. In the Failed Connection Retry For Normal Mail box, enter the interval range for normal mail connection attempts.

17. In the Dial Every box, enter the interval range for dialing the modem.

18. Select the Allow Mail Reception After Sending check box to send and receive messages during the same connection.

19. Select the Return Registered Mail Confirmation check box to issue confirmation receipts automatically for registered mail messages.

20. Click on OK twice to create the connection.

21. Select the Connector MTAs tab.

22. Click on New.

23. Type a name for the MS Mail Connector (PC) MTA in the Service Name box.

24. Set the Logging and Polling Frequency options as described for the LAN connection above.

25. Select the Async And LAN button under Connection Parameters for an asynchronous connection, or select the X.25 And LAN button for an X.25 connection.

If you are using an asynchronous connection, continue with the following steps; if you are using an X.25 connection, skip to step 30.

26. Select the port configured for asynchronous communication in the Communication Port menu.

27. Select the modem script from the Modem Scripts menu.

28. In the Modem Timeout box, enter the amount of time the modem will try to establish a connection.

29. Select one of the following options: Two-way Mail Transfer, to set the MTA to transfer both incoming and outgoing mail; Transfer Incoming Mail Only; or Transfer Outgoing Mail Only.

If you are using an X.25 connection, continue with the following steps; if you are using an asynchronous connection, skip to step 34.

30. Type the X.121 address for the connector's MTA instance location in the X.121 Address box.

31. Type the X.25 adapter port number in the Port Number box.

32. Enter the listen user data information provided by your X.25 service provider in the X.25 Listen User Data box.

33. Enter the listen user facilities information provided by your X.25 service provider in the X.25 Listen User Facilities box.

34. Click on OK to create the MS Mail Connector (PC) MTA.

35. Click on List.

36. Under Available LAN Postoffices, select the postoffices you want to service, click on Add, and click on OK.

37. Type the name for logging on to the postoffice in the Account Name box.

38. Type the logon password in the Password box.

39. Select the Do Not Pick Up Mail At This Postoffice check box to send but not receive messages from this postoffice.

40. Click on OK twice to close all dialog boxes and save your changes.

Tip ● ● ● ●

After configuring the MS Mail (PC) Connector's components, you must start the MS Mail Connector Interchange and the MS Mail Connector (PC) MTA services from the Services control panel.

Connecting To The MS Mail Connector Postoffice

After setting up the MS Mail Connector, you need to configure each MS Mail (PC) postoffice that you identified to connect back to the Exchange Server computer. Use the MS Mail 3.x Administrator program to do this. You will need to know the postoffice and network names of the MS Mail (PC) Connector postoffice to make these configurations. You can find this information by double-clicking on MS Mail Connector in the Administrator window and selecting the Local Postoffice tab. The network name is displayed in the Network box, and the postoffice name is displayed in the Postoffice box. Although you can change these names, it is not recommended because they are used externally for routing services between Exchange Server and the MS Mail (PC) system.

Setting Up Directory Synchronization

If you use other messaging systems, you must maintain at least two sets of directories. *Directory synchronization* is the process of sharing address information with other messaging systems that use the MS Mail directory synchronization protocol to keep both directories up-to-date. To set up directory synchronization between Exchange Server and an MS Mail (PC) system, MS Mail (AppleTalk) system, or a system that supports the MS Mail (PC) 3.x directory synchronization protocol, you must install a directory synchronization component on both sides.

The Exchange Server directory synchronization component can function as one of two roles: dirsync requestor or dirsync server. The *dirsync requestor* periodically queries the Exchange Server directory for changes to recipient information and sends update messages to the MS Mail directory server postoffice. The *dirsync server* processes incoming update messages from MS Mail directory requestors and incorporates the updates into the directory as custom recipients. One dirsync server services all dirsync requestors on the site.

Install the directory synchronization component on the computer where you installed the MS Mail Connector. Before setting up directory synchronization, confirm that you have the MS Mail Dispatch program on a LAN to service the MS Mail directory requestors. Also, make sure that the Exchange Server computer and the MS Mail computers are running correctly and that message exchange between the systems is working properly.

Installing A Dirsync Requestor. Follow these steps to set up a dirsync requestor that will connect to an MS Mail directory server:

1. Click on the Configuration button in the Administrator window.

2. Select Connections.

3. Select New Other from the File menu.

4. Select Dirsync Requestor.

5. Select the directory server from the list of MS Mail postoffices.

6. Click on OK.

7. Type a name for the dirsync requestor in the Name box.

8. Select the Append To Imported Users' Display Name check box to put the requestor name after each custom recipient created by directory synchronization.

9. Accept the default dirsync address under Mail Addresses.

10. Under Address Types, select the check boxes by any other address types, other than MS Mail addresses, that the requestor will receive and request.

11. Select the primary language used in your MS Mail system from the Requestor Language menu.

12. Select the Exchange Server computer that will act as the dirsync requestor from the Server menu.

13. Select the Import Container tab (see Figure 4.25).

14. Click on Container, select the container in which to place imported recipients, and click on OK.

Tip

It's a good idea to create a new recipients container to hold MS Mail addresses. Create a new container by choosing New Other and Recipients Container from the File menu.

15. Set a trust level for the import container in the Trust Level menu.

16. Select the Export Containers tab.

17. Select a site from which to export recipients in the Site menu.

18. Select the recipients containers to export in the Recipient Containers window and click on Add.

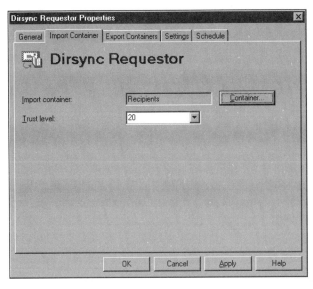

Figure 4.25   Selecting an import container for the dirsync requestor.

19. Select a trust level for the connection in the Trust Level menu.

20. Select the Export Custom Recipients check box to export custom recipients in the selected containers.

21. Select the Settings tab (see Figure 4.26).

22. Type a password, if required, in the Dirsync Password box (this must be the same as the password on the MS Mail directory server).

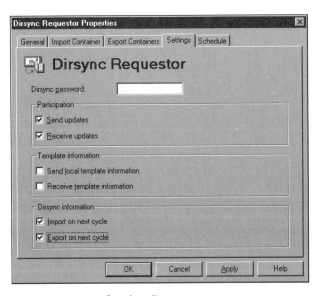

Figure 4.26   Configuring settings for the dirsync requestor.

23. Under Participation, select the Send Updates and Receive Updates check boxes to allow the dirsync requestor to send and request address updates to and from the directory server.

24. Under Template Information, select the Send Local Template Information and Receive Template Information check boxes to send and receive templates.

Tip

If you selected Send Local Template Information or Receive Template Information, you must configure template mappings by double-clicking on Directory Synchronization in the Administrator window and selecting the Incoming Templates and Outgoing Templates tabs.

25. Under Dirsync Information, select the Import On Next Cycle and Export On Next Cycle check boxes to import and export all available addresses on the next synchronization cycle.

26. Select the Schedule tab.

27. In the schedule grid, select the time for sending directory update messages to the directory server.

28. Click on OK to create the dirsync requestor.

After configuring the dirsync requestor, you must configure the MS Mail directory server to recognize the Exchange Server computer as a requestor. Use the MS Mail Administrator program to register the dirsync requestor with the directory server. Then, start the directory synchronization service on the Exchange Server computer by selecting Microsoft Exchange Directory Synchronization in the Services control panel and clicking on Start.

Installing A Dirsync Server. Follow these steps to create a dirsync server on an Exchange Server computer:

1. Click on the Configuration button in the Administrator window.

2. Select Connections.

3. Select New Other from the File menu.

4. Select Dirsync Server.

5. In the Name box, type the name of the dirsync server (see Figure 4.27).

6. Click on Dirsync Administrator, select the recipient who will receive directory synchronization messages, and click on OK.

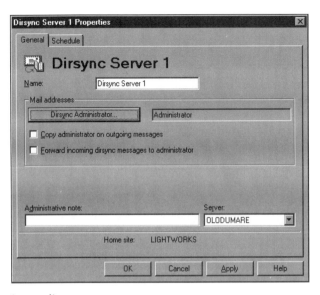

Figure 4.27   Creating a dirsync server.

7. Select the Copy Administrator On Outgoing Messages and the Forward Incoming Dirsync Messages To Administrator check boxes to receive each update message sent to and received from each requestor (typically used for troubleshooting).

8. Select the Exchange Server computer that will act as the dirsync server in the Server menu.

9. Select the Schedule tab.

10. In the schedule grid, select the time to send directory update messages to the directory requestors.

11. Click on OK to create the dirsync server.

12. Start directory synchronization by opening the Services control panel, selecting Microsoft Exchange Directory Synchronization, and clicking on Start.

Each remote MS Mail directory requestor to the dirsync server must be added to the Exchange Server directory as a *remote dirsync requestor*. You should also verify that each remote MS Mail directory requestor is set up as a requestor to the dirsync server (consult your MS Mail documentation for more help with this). Follow these steps to set up a remote dirsync requestor:

1. Click on the Configuration button in the Administrator window.

2. Select Connections.

3. Select the dirsync server you just created.

4. Select New Other from the File menu.

5. Select Remote Dirsync Requestor.

6. Select the requestor from the list of MS Mail postoffices.

7. Click on OK.

8. Type a name for the remote requestor postoffice in the Name box (Figure 4.28).

9. Select the Append To Imported Users' Display Name check box.

10. Accept the default dirsync address under Mail Addresses.

11. Type the password used by the remote requestor, if any, in the Password box.

12. Select MS in the Requestor Address Type menu.

13. Select the language used by the remote dirsync requestor in the Requestor Language menu.

14. Select the Export On Next Cycle check box.

15. Select the Import Container tab.

16. Click on Container, select the recipients container where imported address listings will be placed, and click on OK.

17. Select a trust level for the container in the Trust Level menu.

18. Select the Export Containers tab.

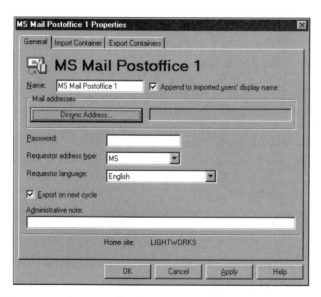

Figure 4.28   Setting general properties for a remote dirsync requestor.

19. Select the site that has the recipients container you want to export to the requestor in the Site menu.

20. Select the recipients container to export under Recipient Containers and click on Add.

21. Select a trust level for the connection from the Trust Level menu.

22. Select the Export Custom Recipients check box to export any custom recipients in the container.

23. Click on OK to create the remote dirsync requestor.

Configuring The Schedule+ Free/Busy Connector

The *Schedule+ Free/Busy Connector* is automatically installed when the MS Mail (PC) Connector is installed to enable Schedule+ free and busy information to be shared between the Exchange Server and MS Mail (PC) systems. Before using the Schedule+ Free/Busy Connector, you must complete the following steps on the MS Mail (PC) system with which you will be sharing scheduling information:

1. Create an AdminSch account on all MS Mail (PC) postoffices that will be sharing schedules with the Exchange Server system by running directory synchronization between Exchange Server and the MS Mail (PC) system to distribute AdminSch accounts across both systems.

2. Install the Schedule+ program files on an MS Mail (PC) postoffice server.

3. Install the Schedule+ Administrator program (Adminsch.exe) on a Windows-based workstation connected to the postoffice that contains the Schedule+ program files, and use it to configure and administer the Schedule+ system.

4. Configure the MS Mail Schdist.exe program.

You must then configure properties for the Schedule+ Free/Busy Connector by following these steps:

1. Select the site where the MS Mail (PC) Connector is installed in the Administrator window.

2. Double-click on Recipients.

3. Double-click on Microsoft Schedule+ Free/Busy Connector.

4. Select the Schedule+ Free/Busy Connector Options tab (see Figure 4.29).

5. Click on Change under Administrator Mailbox, select an administrator for the Schedule+ Free/Busy Connector, and click on OK; any mail messages that cannot be processed by the connector are sent as NDRs to the administrator's mailbox.

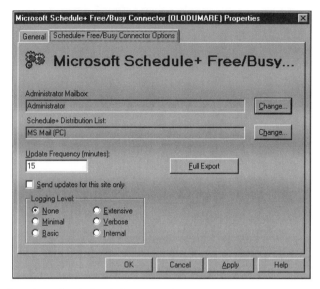

Figure 4.29   Configuring the Schedule+ Free/Busy Connector.

6. Click on Change under Schedule+ Distribution List, select the distribution list of MS Mail (PC) postoffices that will share free and busy information with the Exchange Server site, and click on OK; this list contains all AdminSch accounts.

7. In the Update Frequency (Minutes) box, enter how often free and busy information is sent to the distribution list; this number should be equal to the polling interval set for the Schdist program in the MS Mail system.

8. If your organization has more than one Schedule+ Free/Busy Connector, select the Send Updates For This Site Only check box.

9. Click on Full Export to export free and busy information to all postoffices in the distribution list, a step that is necessary whenever new postoffices are added to the list.

10. Select the General tab.

11. In the Display Name box, type a name that will identify the Schedule+ Free/Busy Connector in the Administrator window.

12. In the Alias Name box, type **AdminSch**.

13. Click on OK to save your changes.

14. Open the Services control panel, select the MS Schedule+ Free/Busy Connector Service, and click on Start.

Microsoft Mail Connector For AppleTalk Networks

The MS Mail Connector also provides a component that enables you to connect to an MS Mail (AppleTalk) server or a Quarterdeck Mail server from the Exchange Server system. Before setting up the MS Mail (AppleTalk) Connector, make sure you have the software necessary to support the connection installed on both the Exchange Server computer and the Macintosh computer to which you're connecting.

• • *Tip* • • • •

If you already configured the Exchange Server computer's instance of the MS Mail Connector as a connector to an MS Mail (PC) system, you cannot use it to connect to an MS Mail (AppleTalk) system. Instead, you must configure another MS Mail Connector on a separate Exchange Server computer.

Creating The Macintosh-Accessible Volume

The *Macintosh-accessible volume* is the directory that contains the MS Mail (AppleTalk) Connector postoffice on the Windows NT Server computer that is made available to Macintosh clients. This enables MS Mail (AppleTalk) postoffices to view and exchange files with the MS Mail (AppleTalk) Connector. Follow these steps to create the Macintosh-accessible volume:

1. Install Macintosh support on the Windows NT Server computer.

2. In Windows NT Explorer, select the exchsrvr\Connect\Msmcon\Maildata directory.

3. Select Create Volume from the MacFile menu.

4. Type a name for the volume in the Volume Name box.

5. Type a password for the volume in the Password box.

• • *Tip* • • • •

Don't enter a password if you want message transfer to start automatically when the connected Macintosh starts.

6. Retype the password in the Confirm Password box.

7. Under Volume Security, clear the This Volume Is Read-Only check box.

8. Under Volume Security, clear the Guests Can Use This Volume check box.

9. Under User Limit, select the Allow button and type a number in the Users box to limit simultaneous connections to the volume.

10. Click on Permissions.

11. Select the MS Mail (AppleTalk) administrator in the Owner menu.

12. Select all the check boxes beside the Owner menu.

13. Clear all the check boxes for the Everyone option.

14. Select the Replace Permissions On Subdirectories check box.

15. Clear the Cannot Move, Rename, Or Delete check box.

16. Click on OK twice to create the volume.

Configuring The MS Mail Connector Interchange

Configuring the MS Mail Connector Interchange specifies how to translate information between Exchange Server and the MS Mail (AppleTalk) Connector postoffice.
Follow these steps:

1. Click on the Configuration button in the Administrator window.

2. Select Connections.

3. Double-click on the Microsoft Mail Connector.

4. Select the Interchange tab.

5. Click on Change, select an administrator's mailbox for receiving delivery status
   messages, and click on OK.

6. Under MS Mail (AppleTalk) Connector MTA, click on Configure (see Figure 4.30).

7. Under Set Status, select the Enable MS Mail (AppleTalk) Connector MTA button.

8. Under Startup, select one of the following options for starting the MS Mail
   (AppleTalk) Connector MTA service: Start Automatically At System Startup or
   Manual Start (From Control Panel).

9. Click on OK twice to create the MS Mail Connector Interchange.

Figure 4.30   Configuring the MS Mail (AppleTalk) Connector MTA.

Setting Up The Connection

When connecting to the MS Mail (AppleTalk) Connector postoffice from the Macintosh computer, you will need to know the network and postoffice names of the MS Mail (AppleTalk) Connector postoffice. These names identify Exchange Server externally for routing services between MS Mail (AppleTalk) postoffices and the Exchange Server system. Find the network and postoffice names by selecting Connections in the Administrator window, double-clicking on MS Mail Connector, and selecting the Local Postoffice tab.

After connecting to the MS Mail (AppleTalk) Connector postoffice from the Macintosh computer, you will need to install and set up the Exchange Connection on the Macintosh computer. You will also need to set up times for connecting to the MS Mail (AppleTalk) Connector postoffice to transfer mail. Have the MS Mail (AppleTalk) administrator complete these tasks, or consult the Exchange Server documentation for more help with this.

Finally, start the MS Mail Connector Interchange and MS Mail (AppleTalk) Connector MTA services from the Services control panel to enable the connection. Then, set up directory synchronization between the Exchange Server and MS Mail (AppleTalk) systems, as described under "Setting Up Directory Synchronization" in the "Microsoft Mail For PC Networks Connector" section.

Connecting To Quarterdeck Mail Systems

When connecting Exchange Server to a Quarterdeck Mail server using the MS Mail (AppleTalk) Connector, you must add an addressing .DLL file to Exchange Server for the Quarterdeck Mail address type. Install this file before creating recipients to create the address type for all recipients automatically by following these steps:

1. In the Exchange\Address directory, create the following subdirectory: msa\<server type> where *server type* is your Exchange Server computer's platform.

2. Copy the file Macproxy.dll from the Connect\Msmcon\Bin subdirectory to the new subdirectory.

3. Run the address installation program (Addrinst.exe) located in the Support\Macproxy\platform\Msmcon directory with the following parameters: /sitedn=<site name> /name="Quarterdeck Mail proxy generator" / machine=<server type> /type=MSA /proxydll=<path to macproxy.dll> / server=<server name> /gwproxy=<gateway name on Mail server>.

four

Lotus cc:Mail Connector

Use the *Microsoft Exchange Connector for Lotus cc:Mail* to integrate Exchange Server into cc:Mail environments for exchanging messages and synchronizing directories. To set up this connector, you will need the name and password of the cc:Mail post office to which you want to connect. Before setting up the connector, make sure that the correct software is installed on the cc:Mail post office to support the connection and that the Import.exe and Export.exe programs are in the system path on the Exchange Server computer where the connector is installed. The service account for the connector must also have read-and-write permissions for the connected cc:Mail post office.

Follow these steps to configure the Lotus cc:Mail Connector:

1. Click on the Configuration button in the Administrator window.

2. Select Connections.

3. Double-click on Connector for cc:Mail.

4. Select the Post Office tab (see Figure 4.31).

5. Click on Change, select a recipient who will receive messages that cannot be converted by the connector, and click on OK.

6. Type the name of the cc:Mail post office to connect to in the Name box.

7. Type the password for connecting to the cc:Mail post office in the Password box.

Figure 4.31   Setting up a connection to a cc:Mail post office.

4

8. Type the network path to the cc:Mail post office database in UNC format in the Path box as \\<**server name\<share name>**, for example.

9. Under Import/Export Version, select the version of Import/Export installed on the cc:Mail post office.

10. Select a language used for text sent to and from the connector in the Post Office Language menu.

11. Select the Permit ADE To Propagate Entries Synched To cc:Mail To Downstream Post Offices if the cc:Mail post office has ADE selected.

12. Select the Preserve Forwarding History On Messages Sent From cc:Mail to Microsoft Exchange check box to retain the message forwarding history as an attached file.

13. Select the Export Containers tab.

14. Select the site to export recipients from in the Site menu.

15. Select a recipients container to export to the cc:Mail directory in the Recipient Containers window and click on Add.

16. Select a trust level for the connector in the Trust Level menu.

17. Select the Export Custom Recipients check box to include custom recipients in the export container.

18. Select the Import Container tab.

19. Click on Container, select the recipients container to store imported cc:Mail recipients, and click on OK.

Tip

It is a good idea to create a separate recipients container for storing imported cc:Mail addresses. Do so by selecting New Other and Recipients Container from the File menu.

20. Under Filtering, select one of the following options: Import All Directory Entries; Only Import Directory Entries Of These Formats, and specify the formats to import; or Do Not Import Directory Entries Of These Formats, and specify the formats not to import.

21. Click on Run Dir Synch Now to start synchronization of the Exchange Server and cc:Mail directories manually.

22. Select the Schedule tab.

four

23. Select one of the following options: Never, to disable directory synchronization; Always, to run directory synchronization at the default interval of 15 minutes; or Selected Times, to set the schedule in the schedule grid.

24. Click on OK to save your changes.

Setting Up Address Spaces

The *address space* is the path a connector uses to send messages outside the site. It identifies the recipient address types supported by the connector. Every connector must have at least one associated address space. When configuring address spaces, specify only as much of the address information as is needed to distinguish which messages should pass through the connector.

Address spaces for foreign systems are determined by the type of mail system to which you're connecting. For example, the X.400 Connector should have an associated X.400 address space, while the Internet Mail Service should have an associated SMTP address space. Address spaces to other Exchange Server sites should include every address type that you want to route to the remote site, which can encompass X.400 addresses, SMTP addresses, and other types of addresses.

Follow these steps to set up address spaces (you should set up address spaces for each connector installed on the server):

1. Click on the Configuration button in the Administrator window.

2. Select Connections.

3. Double-click on the connector for which you want to set up address spaces.

4. Select the Address Space tab (see Figure 4.32).

5. Click on New, choose an address type, and click on OK.

6. Fill out the template to create the appropriate address space (see Figure 4.33).

Tip

To insert a multicharacter wildcard in the address space, use an asterisk (*). To specify a single-character wildcard in the address space, use a percent sign (%).

7. Click on the Restrictions tab to control whose messages can flow through the connector by selecting one of the following options: Organization, This Site, or This Location.

8. Click on OK twice to create the new address space.

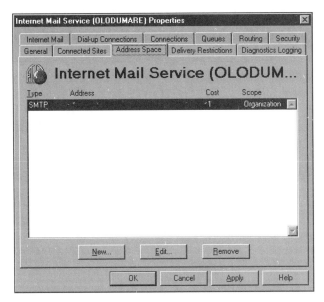

Figure 4.32 The Address Space tab for the Internet Mail Service.

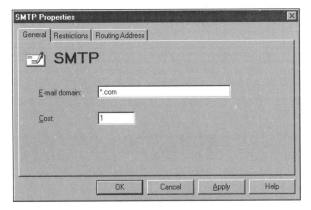

Figure 4.33 The template for the SMTP address type.

Setting Up Mailboxes

To enable users to start using the Exchange Server system, you must create *mailboxes* that are associated with the users' Windows NT user accounts on the users' *home server*. If you try to create a mailbox for which there is no associated user account, Exchange Server will ask you to create a new account.

Creating A New Mailbox

Follow these steps to create a new mailbox:

1. Click on the Recipients button in the Administrator window; this opens the recipients container, where mailboxes are stored.

Site Addressing

Exchange Server automatically generates addresses for the cc:Mail, MS Mail (PC), MS Mail (AppleTalk), SMTP, and X.400 address types for every recipient, based on your organization and site names. You might find it necessary to edit these site addresses, such as by removing characters that are not valid for the address type. You can also disable the automatic generation of address types that are not applicable to your organization. For example, you do not need to generate cc:Mail addresses if the cc:Mail Connector is not installed. Using only the address types you need reduces network traffic and disk space usage when creating new users. To edit or disable site addresses, double-click on Site Addressing in the Administrator window, select the Site Addressing tab, and select the address type you would like to edit or remove.

2. Select New Mailbox from the File menu (see Figure 4.34).

3. In the First Name box, type the first name of the mailbox's user.

4. In the Initials box, type the middle initial of the mailbox's user.

5. In the Last Name box, type the last name of the mailbox's user.

6. Click on the Primary Windows NT Account button.

7. Choose either Select An Existing Windows NT Account or Create A New Windows NT Account, and click on OK.

Figure 4.34   Creating a new mailbox.

8. If you chose to select an existing account, select the Windows NT user account that belongs to the person for whom you're creating the mailbox, click on Add, and click on OK.

9. If you chose to create a new account, select the NT domain for the account, type the account name, and click on OK; the account is generated with a blank password, which the user will have to change the first time he or she logs on.

10. Click on OK to create the mailbox.

Tip

To save time, you can create an associated Exchange Server mailbox whenever you create a new Windows NT user account. In User Manager for Domains, select Options from the Exchange menu and select the Always Create An Exchange Mailbox When Creating Windows NT Accounts check box. Select the Always Prompt For Microsoft Exchange Server check box to prompt for the user's home server name when the mailbox is created.

Auto Naming

When you enter a mailbox user's first name, initials, and last name, the *display name* and *alias name* for the mailbox are automatically generated. Use auto naming to set up the way in which they are generated according to your established naming conventions. Follow these steps:

1. Select Options from the Tools menu in the Administrator window.

2. Select the Auto Naming tab (see Figure 4.35).

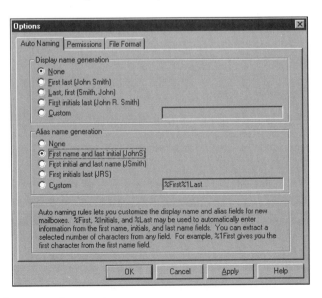

Figure 4.35 Setting up auto naming.

3. Under Display Name Generation, select None, to disable automatic display name generation; one of the options, to determine how display names are created based on the First Name, Last Name, and Initials fields; or Custom, to create a custom display name.

4. Under Alias Name Generation, select None, to disable automatic alias name generation; one of the options, to determine how alias names are created based on the First Name, Last Name, and Initials fields; or Custom, to create a custom alias name.

5. Click on OK to save your changes.

Configuring Mailbox Properties

After creating a new mailbox, you need to specify information about the owner of the mailbox. This information will be displayed in the *Address Book*. Many of these properties are optional. Follow these steps to configure the properties for a mailbox:

1. Click on the Recipients button in the Administrator window.

2. Double-click on the mailbox for which you want to set properties.

3. Select the General tab.

4. Fill in the fields with the appropriate information to identify the user associated with this mailbox.

5. Select the Organization tab.

6. If the mailbox owner has a manager, click on Modify under Manager, select the manager's name from the appropriate address list, and click on OK.

7. If the mailbox owner has any recipients who report directly to him or her, click on Modify under Direct Reports, select the recipients from the appropriate address list(s), click on Add, and click on OK.

8. Select the Phone/Notes tab.

9. Fill out the optional telephone number information in the appropriate fields.

10. Type any comments in the Notes window.

11. Select the Delivery Options tab.

12. Click on Modify under Give Send On Behalf Of Permission To, select the recipients who have *send-on-behalf-of permission* for the mailbox, click on Add, and click on OK.

13. Click on Modify under Alternate Recipient, select another recipient who can receive messages intended for the mailbox, and click on OK.

14. Select or clear the Deliver Messages To Both Recipient And Alternate Recipient check box.

15. Select the Advanced tab (see Figure 4.36).

16. In the Simple Display Name box, type a display name to be used by systems that cannot interpret all the characters in the mailbox's normal display name.

17. In the Trust Level menu, select a trust level for the mailbox.

Tip

The *trust level* determines whether the mailbox is sent to a connected MS Mail system during directory synchronization. If the mailbox's trust level exceeds the directory synchronization trust level, the mailbox is not sent.

18. If your organization uses Microsoft NetMeeting, type the name of the mailbox owner's ILS Server and ILS Account under On-line Listings Information.

19. In the Home Server menu, select the mailbox's home server.

20. Select the Downgrade High Priority X.400 Mail check box to keep the mailbox from sending mail messages marked high priority to an X.400 system.

21. Select the Hide From Address Book check box to prevent the mailbox from being displayed in the Address Book.

22. Click on OK to save your changes.

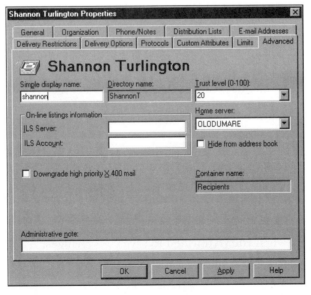

Figure 4.36   Setting advanced options for a mailbox.

Editing Email Addresses

Exchange Server uses email address information as the basis for message transfer. *Email addresses* identify recipients to the connectors to foreign messaging systems. Exchange Server automatically generates cc:Mail, MS Mail (PC), MS Mail (AppleTalk), X.400, and SMTP email addresses, but you might find it necessary to modify an individual user's or component's email addresses. To do so, double-click on the component or recipient in the Administrator window and select the Email Address tab. Click on New to create a new email address, select an email address in the window and click on Edit to modify it, or select an email address and click on Remove to delete it. Because many Exchange Server services make use of these default addresses, changing or removing them can cause message transfer and messaging-based services to fail.

Using Mailbox Templates

A *mailbox template* is a mailbox whose configuration is copied to new mailboxes as they are created. Use it to set default values for common properties shared by multiple mailboxes, such as company name, postal address, delivery restrictions, and trust level. All properties are copied except for the first name, last name, alias name, permissions, and email address fields. Mailbox templates can be used as the basis for creating new, individual mailboxes, when importing a batch of mailboxes, or when migrating mailboxes from an existing mail system.

Follow these steps to create a mailbox template:

1. Click on the Recipients button in the Administrator window.

2. Choose New Mailbox from the File menu.

3. Type a name for the template in the Display box.

4. Type an alias name for the template in the Alias box.

5. Click on OK to create the template.

6. Double-click on the mailbox template in the Administrator window.

7. Configure the properties for the mailbox template as for a mailbox object; only fill in the fields that you want copied to all new mailboxes based on the template.

8. Click on OK when you've finished to save your changes.

● ● ● *Tip* ● ● ● ●

You can create multiple mailbox templates that contain information related to different departments or geographic locations of the company and save them under names
that reflect the type of mailbox they should be used to create. For example, create a
template for the San Francisco office called SF Template, or create one for the marketing department called Mktg Template.

Follow these steps to use the mailbox template to create a new mailbox that has common
properties already filled in for you:

1. Click on the Recipients button in the Administrator window.

2. Select the mailbox template you created.

3. Select Duplicate from the File menu.

4. Fill out the First Name, Initials, and Last Name fields.

5. Click on the Primary Windows NT Account button and select the Windows NT
   user account for the new user.

6. Provide additional information and properties not filled in by the mailbox template.

7. Click on OK when you've finished.

Creating Custom Recipients

A *custom recipient* is a recipient outside the Exchange Server organization that appears in the
Address Book and can receive messages. Follow these steps to create a custom recipient:

1. Click on the Recipients button in the Administrator window.

2. Select New Custom Recipient from the File menu.

3. Select the custom recipient's address type and click on OK.

4. Type the custom recipient's email address, set any other properties for the email
   address, and click on OK (see Figure 4.37).

5. Fill out the First Name, Initials, and Last Name fields with the name of the
   custom recipient.

6. Click on OK to create the custom recipient.

7. In the Administrator window, double-click on the custom recipient you just created.

8. Fill out the user information and properties as for a mailbox; make sure to fill out
   the custom recipient options on the Advanced tab.

9. Click on OK when you've finished to save your changes.

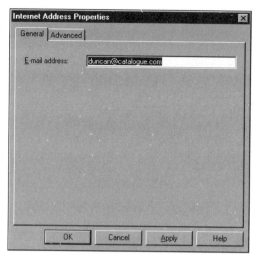

Figure 4.37   Entering a custom recipient's email address.

Importing Existing Mailboxes

Exchange Server provides import and extraction tools to migrate existing users on Novell NetWare, LAN Manager, and Windows NT networks to the Exchange Server system. These tools enable you to create mailboxes for large numbers of users who are not migrating from an existing mail system.

Importing LAN Manager And Windows NT Accounts

To create a batch of mailboxes for existing LAN Manager and Windows NT users, you should first extract the account information and then import it to Exchange Server using the *directory import* feature. To extract account information, you must have LAN Manager 2.x or Windows NT Server installed. You must also log on as a user or as an administrator and know the names of the PDC or *backup domain controller (BDC)* in the domain. Follow these steps to extract the account information and import it to Exchange Server:

1. Select Extract Windows NT Account List from the Tools menu in the Administrator window (see Figure 4.38).

2. Select the name of the domain that contains user accounts in the Windows NT Domain box.

3. Select the name of the PDC or BDC for this domain in the Windows NT Domain Controller box.

4. Click on Browse to specify a file to which the extracted account information will be written.

5. Click on OK to extract the account information.

6. Click on OK again once the extraction process is complete.

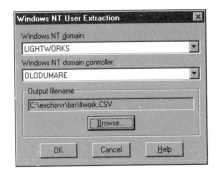

Figure 4.38 Extracting Windows NT account information.

 *Tip*

The extracted account information file contains an entry for each user in the domain. Before importing the file into Exchange Server, you can edit it to delete network accounts that do not need mailboxes, including guest and service accounts.

7. Select Directory Import from the Tools menu (see Figure 4.39).

8. Select the domain where new accounts will be created in the Windows NT Domain menu.

9. Select the server to house mailboxes in the MS Exchange Server menu.

10. To use a mailbox template, click on Recipient Template, select the template, and click on OK.

11. Click on Import File, select the file that contains the extracted account information, and click on Open.

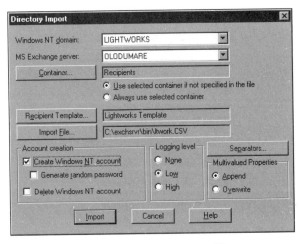

Figure 4.39 Importing extracted accounts as new mailboxes.

12. Select the Create Windows NT Account under Account Creation to create user accounts automatically when the mailboxes are imported.

13. Click on Import.

Importing NetWare Accounts

To create a batch of Exchange Server mailboxes from NetWare user account information, you should first extract the NetWare account information and then import it to Exchange Server. To extract the account information, you must have a Novell NetWare server, version 2.x, 3.x, or 4.x, running bindery emulation. If you are running NetWare 2.15, you also need a NetWare account and password with supervisor rights to the server. Follow these steps to extract the NetWare account information and import it into Exchange Server:

1. Select Extract NetWare Account List from the Tools menu in the Administrator window (see Figure 4.40).

2. Type the name of the NetWare server in the NetWare Server Name box.

3. Type the name of the user who has supervisor rights on the NetWare server in the NetWare User box.

4. Type the supervisor's password in the NetWare User Password box.

5. Click on Browse to specify a file to which the extracted account information will be written.

6. Click on OK to extract the account information.

7. Click on OK again when the extraction process is complete.

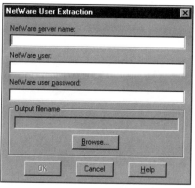

Figure 4.40 Extracting NetWare account information.

Tip

The extracted account information file contains an entry for each user in the bindery. Before importing the file into Exchange Server, you can edit it to delete network accounts that do not need mailboxes, including guest and service accounts.

8. Select Directory Import from the Tools menu.

9. Select the domain where new accounts will be created in the Windows NT Domain menu.

10. Select the server to house mailboxes in the MS Exchange Server menu.

11. To use a mailbox template, click on Recipient Template, select the template, and click on OK.

12. Click on Import File, select the file that contains the extracted account information, and click on Open.

13. Select the Create Windows NT Account under Account Creation to create user accounts automatically when the mailboxes are imported.

14. Click on Import.

Migrating User Information

Migration involves moving your existing mail system to Exchange Server, including copying mailboxes, distribution lists, public folders, messages, attachments, calendars, and addresses. The *Migration Wizard* imports migration files extracted from your existing system and creates mailboxes and addresses based on the files. It also acts as a *source extractor* for cc:Mail, MS Mail (PC), Novell GroupWise, and Collabra Share systems to copy the directory, message, and scheduling data to a migration file format. (If you are migrating from another system, use a separate source extractor, such as the ones provided on the companion CD-ROM.)

Tip

To use the Migration Wizard as a source extractor, choose to migrate from your existing system in the opening screen and follow the wizard's instructions to create the migration files.

Before running the Migration Wizard, review your migration plans and make sure that you are implementing your migration schedule correctly. You should move data when the server is least active. Unless you are using the Migration Wizard as a source extractor, stop the old service before migrating. You should also perform a complete system backup before running the Migration Wizard.

Follow these steps to run the Migration Wizard:

1. Select Microsoft Exchange Migration Wizard from the Microsoft Exchange program group.

2. Select Import From Migration Files and click on Next (see Figure 4.41).

3. Read the informational screen and click on Next.

4. Type or browse to the path to the packing list file in the Pathname For Migration Files box and click on Next.

5. Select the Migrate To A Microsoft Exchange Computer option and click on Next.

6. Type the name for the destination server in the Enter A Server Name box and click on Next.

7. If you are importing shared data to public folders, select the Shared Information Is Included In Migration Files option and click on Next.

8. Under Choose A Recipient Container, select the recipients container where custom recipients and mailboxes will be created (see Figure 4.42).

● ● *Tip* ● ● ● ●

If you are importing data for existing mailboxes, choose the container where the mailboxes have already been created.

9. To use a mailbox template, browse to the template's name in the Use This Account As A Template box.

10. Click on Next.

Figure 4.41   Importing migration files using the Migration Wizard.

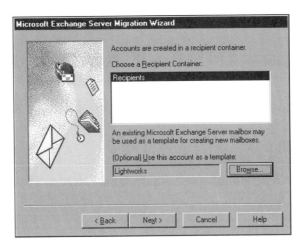

Figure 4.42   Selecting the recipients container.

11. Select an option in the For Users That Don't Have Windows NT Accounts box.

12. Select the domain where user accounts are located or are to be created.

13. Click on Next to begin the migration process.

14. Click on Finish when the Migration Wizard has finished importing the migration files.

Setting Up Directory Replication

Each Exchange Server computer has a local directory component. At any time, the local directories on two servers can be different because of changes made to the server's directory by the administrator. For example, if you create a new mailbox on one server, it will not show up on other servers until the servers are updated through directory replication.

Directory replication is the process of duplicating information in the directories on all Exchange Server computers within a site and between sites so that all directories reflect the same information. It ensures that directory data is current and updated throughout the organization. Sharing up-to-date, accurate information among servers is the cornerstone of administering the Exchange Server system. Directory replication between servers in the same site occurs automatically within five minutes after a change to the directory, so you do not need to set up directory replication within a site.

To establish directory replication between multiple sites, you must configure a *directory replication connector* between the two sites. One server is required at each end of a directory replication connector to request directory replication updates. These servers are called *directory replication bridgehead servers.*

If your organization has multiple sites, you need to plan directory replication topology to include all the sites in your organization, to grow as new sites are added, and to minimize the number of sites through which messages are replicated. You should also map directory replication topology to your messaging topology so that replication messages travel on the least costly connections.

Tip

If you have many sites, consider choosing a different directory replication bridgehead server for each site to balance the load of directory replication among servers.

Before setting up directory replication, make sure that all Exchange Server computers in the local and remote sites are installed and running correctly. Also, make sure that you can exchange messages between sites through some kind of site connector and that you have Administrator permissions for both sites. Finally, choose which servers will be the directory replication bridgehead servers.

Installing Directory Replication Connectors

If you are setting up directory replication between two sites on the same LAN, you can save time by installing the directory replication connector in the remote site at the same time that you install it in the local site. If you are setting up directory replication between two sites that do not have LAN connectivity, you must configure the directory replication connector in each site separately. Follow these steps to install the directory replication connector:

1. Select the site where you want to configure directory replication in the Administrator window.

2. Select New Other from the File menu.

3. Select Directory Replication Connector (see Figure 4.43).

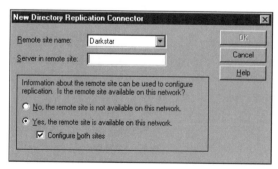

Figure 4.43   Installing the directory replication connector.

4. Select the site to which you want to replicate the directory in the Remote Site Name menu.

5. Type the name of the directory replication bridgehead server in the remote site in the Server In Remote Site box.

6. If the sites have LAN connectivity, select the Yes, The Remote Site Is Available On This Network check box; otherwise, select the No, The Remote Site Is Not Available On This Network check box.

7. If the sites have LAN connectivity, select the Configure Both Sites check box to configure a directory replication connector in the remote site automatically.

8. Click on OK.

Setting Directory Replication Connector Properties

Follow these steps to configure the properties of the directory replication connector:

1. Click on the Configuration button in the Administrator window.

2. Select Directory Replication.

3. Double-click on the Directory Replication Connector.

4. Select the General tab (see Figure 4.44).

5. Type the name that will identify the directory replication connector in the Administrator window in the Display Name box.

Figure 4.44   Setting general properties for the directory replication connector.

6. Type the name that will identify the directory replication connector in the directory in the Directory Name box.

7. In the Local Bridgehead Server menu, select the local server that will act as the directory replication bridgehead server.

Tip

If you change the local bridgehead server, you must specify the same server as the remote bridgehead server in the corresponding directory replication connector in the remote site.

8. In the Remote Bridgehead Server menu, select the server in the remote site that will act as the directory replication bridgehead server.

Tip

If you change the remote bridgehead server, you must configure a directory replication connector on that server connecting back to the local site.

9. Select the Sites tab to view the list of inbound and outbound sites; *inbound sites* send directory information to the local site, and *outbound sites* are remote sites to which the local site sends directory information.

10. To request updated directory information manually, select the site in the Inbound Sites box and click on Request Now.

11. Click on OK when you've finished.

Moving On

In this chapter, you learned how to install the Exchange Server software and set up the Exchange Server site, core components, optional components, mailboxes, and directory replication. These are all the basic tasks needed to start running your Exchange Server system. In the next chapter, you'll learn about the more in-depth tasks required to administer and maintain the system. Chapter 5 will cover working with Exchange Server services and directory objects, as well as such required administration tasks as setting up clients, setting up security, maintaining core components, monitoring the system, backing up servers, and managing log files. These maintenance tasks will help keep your Exchange Server system running smoothly.

PART III

Administering And Optimizing Microsoft Exchange Server

5

Administering Exchange Server

One of the primary goals in developing Exchange Server was to create a platform that would be easy to manage and administer, thus reducing operating costs. To this end, Exchange Server includes many features and tools that make the job of administering the messaging system faster and easier.

Exchange Server's key administrative feature is its ability to provide a single-seat view of the entire Exchange Server organization, even if that organization is dispersed over a wide geographic region. This means that you can administer the entire system from one computer and one program, including multiple, linked sites. Exchange Server is also tightly integrated with the Windows NT Server system that is its foundation by sharing a security context and integrating with Windows NT Server management tools.

Exchange Server's centralized management, combined with its system of monitors, alerts, and other built-in administrative tools, makes your job much easier by reducing the costs of managing a distributed system, avoiding redundant administrative efforts, and ensuring reliable performance. In this chapter, you will learn how to make effective use of these tools and features to administer the Exchange Server system. The following administrative tasks will be covered:

➤ Setting up Exchange client applications.

➤ Setting up Key Management (KM) server.

➤ Managing Exchange Server services.

➤ Using the Administrator program.

➤ Maintaining the Message Transfer Agent (MTA), information store, and directory on Exchange Server computers.

➤ Monitoring the performance of the Exchange Server system.

➤ Backing up and restoring servers.

➤ Managing transaction log files.

Setting Up Clients

After you install Exchange Server, one of the first things you should do is make client applications available to your users, so that users can begin interacting with the new messaging system. *Microsoft Outlook 97,* included with Exchange Server, is the strategic client for interacting with Exchange Server, providing full-featured functionality. However, if you are upgrading from an earlier version of Exchange Server, you can continue to use the basic *Exchange Client.*

In this section, you will learn how make the Outlook 97 client available to users through a client installation point or network share. You already should have identified the server or servers that will host the client installation point or network share during the planning process.

Client Installation Point

A *client installation point* is a shared directory on a file server to which users can connect to install clients to their local computers. Installing the client to a local computer increases performance, but uses more hard disk space on the client computer. Choose this type of installation if you do not want to use network resources for shared programs.

Outlook is available for both Windows and Macintosh operating systems. If your users will be installing clients to different desktop platforms, you need to set up a separate client installation point for each platform.

Windows

Users who have Windows 95, Windows NT, and Windows 3.x operating systems can install Outlook from the client installation point by connecting to the server and running Setup. Follow these steps to set up the client installation point:

1. Create a directory on the client installation point server to which users have read-only access, but to which you have full write, read, and delete permissions.

2. Disable virus detection software on the server to prevent triggering of virus detection during setup.

3. Insert the Outlook CD into the appropriate drive.

4. If there is more than one language on the CD, choose the directory for the appropriate language.

5. Double-click on Ucsetup.exe.

6. Provide information as prompted by the installation program.

7. Give access rights to the client installation point to all users.

Migrating To Outlook

The same Exchange Server system can host both Exchange Client and Outlook. Because Outlook is more robust than Exchange Client, it has several features that Exchange Client does not support. You should determine before setting up clients whether your users' needs will best be satisfied by Outlook, by a combination of Exchange Client and *Schedule+*, or by a mixture of all three clients.

Outlook was designed to be an easy upgrade from Exchange Client and Schedule+, so it can be easily integrated into your Exchange Server infrastructure. Outlook stores email messages and rich text with the same message properties and file format as Exchange Client. Outlook also supports all custom applications and electronic forms written for Exchange Client. This enables a smooth transition from Exchange Client to Outlook for your users.

By the same token, Outlook and Schedule+, versions 1.0 or 7.0, are completely compatible at the basic level of scheduling group meetings and browsing free and busy information. However, to use the delegate access feature, both users must be using the same client technology: Schedule+ 1.0, Schedule+ 7.0, or Outlook. To facilitate migration from Schedule+ to Outlook, users can maintain their Schedule+ 7.0 component while migrating the rest of their client to Outlook. After migration is complete, you can then switch users over to Outlook without revisiting the desktop.

Macintosh

Users who have the Macintosh operating system can install Outlook by connecting to the client installation point and choosing Setup. Follow these steps to set up a client installation point for Macintosh users:

1. Create a directory on the client installation point server to which users have read-only access, but to which you have full write, read, and delete permissions.

2. Disable virus detection software on the server to prevent triggering of virus detection during setup.

3. Create a folder on the server (the server must have enough room to hold the contents of the CD).

4. Insert the Outlook CD into the appropriate drive.

5. Double-click on the folder for the Macintosh client.

6. Copy the contents of the Macintosh folder to the new folder on the server.

7. Give access rights to the client installation point to all users.

five

Network Share

A *network share* is a directory on a file server where users can install and run the client from the server itself. Multiple users who have the same network operating system can connect to and use the client on a single network share. This option leaves most of the client files on the server, so multiple users can share them. Creating a network share reduces the amount of hard disk space required on client computers, but it also requires the client computer to have continuous access to the network share over the network while running the client. Also, when running the client on a network share, it will operate more slowly than when running it on the local hard drive.

Users can install Outlook by connecting to the network share and choosing the Run From Network Server installation. Follow these steps to set up a network share for the Outlook client:

1. Create a directory on the network share server to which users have read-only access, but to which you have full write, read, and delete permissions.

2. Disable virus detection software on the server to prevent triggering of virus detection during setup.

3. Insert the Outlook CD into the appropriate drive.

4. Choose Run from the Start menu.

5. Type: **Setup /a**.

6. Type the name of your organization (during client installation, Setup uses this name as the organization name for each user).

7. Type the product ID number printed on the CD or provided by your licensing agreement.

8. Type the name and path for the directory where you want to store the Outlook program files.

9. Type the name and path for the directory where you want to store the shared program files.

10. Under Network Location, type the server name and path for the shared programs folder (this is the path users will enter when they install Outlook).

11. Under Connect to Server Using, select one of the following options: Server Name to allow users to access the directory using a Universal Naming Convention (UNC) path; or Drive Letter if you want users to connect to the server using the drive letter you enter.

12. Give all users access to the network share.

Setting Up Key Management Server

Exchange Server's *advanced security* features enable users to keep data confidential during message transfer through *encryption* and to verify message originators through *digital signatures.* To use the advanced security features, you must install the *Key Management (KM) server* component on your organization's *Microsoft Certificate Server* computer. KM server stores and manages the security database, creates and maintains backups of public and private encryption keys, generates temporary keys, maintains the *Certification Revocation List (CRL),* and issues certificates for Certification Authorities in other organizations.

The Certificate Server acts as a *Certification Authority (CA)* and must be running at all times to certify public signing and encryption keys. This computer should be in the same domain where you centralize administration, should be physically secure and backed up regularly, and should use the Windows NT Server File System (NTFS) format. For maximum security, configure the CA as a dedicated server in a separate site.

• • • *Tip* • • •

After installing KM server, it is strongly recommended that you not move the KM server component to a new Exchange Server computer, as this will eliminate your ability to do key recovery.

Two passwords are required to install the KM server. Exchange Key Manager uses one password, and administrators use the other to perform advanced security tasks. During Setup, either copy the Exchange Key Manager password to a floppy disk when prompted or make a note of it, as you will need it when configuring advanced security.

Starting The KM Server

After installation, you must start the KM server to enable security features. (Unlike other Exchange Server services, the KM server does not start automatically.) After starting it, leave the KM server running at all times. Follow these steps:

1. Open the Services control panel.

2. Double-click on Microsoft Exchange Key Management Server.

3. Select This Account under Log On As.

4. Select the Exchange Server service account.

5. Click on OK.

6. Insert the disk containing the password that you made during Setup or type the password in the Startup Parameters box.

five

7. Select Microsoft Exchange Key Manager.

8. Click on Start.

Configuring CA Properties

After starting the KM server, you need to configure properties for the CA and for site-wide encryption. Follow these steps:

1. Select the site where the KM server is located in the Administrator window.

2. Select Configuration.

3. Double-click on CA.

4. In the Key Management Server Passwords box, type the advanced security administrator password, which is "password" until you change it, and click on OK.

Tip • • •

You must enter your advanced security administrator password before modifying any advanced security properties. Every time you open an advanced security-related property page, the Key Management Server Passwords dialog box will reappear. To perform some tasks, this box may prompt for the passwords of multiple advanced security administrators, depending on your company's multiple password policies.

5. Click on the General tab.

6. Type the name that identifies the CA in the Administrator window in the Display Name box.

7. Select the Administrators tab to assign other administrators as advanced security administrators.

8. Click on Add Administrators, select the recipient you want to make an advanced security administrator, and click on OK.

9. To change your advanced security password, click on Change My KM Server Password.

10. Type your advanced security administrator password in the Current Password box, type the new password in the New Password box, and retype the new password in the Verify Password box.

Tip • • •

All advanced security administrators receive a different advanced security password, which only they can change. Change your advanced security password immediately after starting the KM server and occasionally thereafter to preserve security.

11. Select the Remember Password For 5 Minutes check box to allow you to modify security properties for up to 5 minutes without retyping your password.

12. Click on OK.

13. Select the Passwords tab to set multiple password policies.

14. Set the number of administrator passwords that must be entered for each option and click on Apply to set your changes.

15. Select the Enrollment tab.

16. Select the Allow E-mail To Be Sent To The User With His Or Her Temporary Key And The Welcome Message check box to set a policy for allowing temporary keys to be sent to the user using email.

17. Click on Edit Welcome Message to edit the text of the welcome message sent with the temporary key.

18. Click on Bulk Enrollment to generate temporary keys in bulk for a large group of new users.

19. Under Container Name, click on Modify to select the recipients container with the users you want to enroll.

20. Click on Mail Temporary Keys To All Newly Enrolled Users to send temporary keys to users through email.

21. Click on Save Results In A File to save advanced security information to a file.

22. Click on OK when you're done.

23. Under Microsoft Exchange 4.0 And 5.0 Compatibility, select one of the following options: Issue Both V1 And V3 Certificates if any users are running Exchange Client 4.0, Exchange Client 5.0, or Outlook 8.0x; Issue X.509 V3 Certificates Only if all users are running an S/MIME-compatible client; or Issue X.509 V1 Certificates Only if the majority of users' clients are Exchange Client 4.0, Exchange Client 5.0, or Outlook 8.0x and you want to force S/MIME-compatible clients to use only the backward-compatible mode.

24. Click on Renew All Users to notify all users that they should initiate enrollment with the specified certificate type, to reset any changes made to the security message format, or to reset the issuing of V1 and V3 certificates, and click on Apply.

25. Select the Certificate Trust List tab.

26. Click on Import to import certificates from another CA and establish trust with another organization.

27. Click on Import A Certificate to import a certificate file you already received from an outside organization, or click on Import A CRL to import a CRL from a trusted organization.

28. In the File Name box, type the name of the certificate file or CRL to import, and click on OK.

29. To remove or untrust an imported certificate, select the certificate in the large window and click on Remove.

30. Click on Untrust Certificate to add the certificate to your CRL, or click on Remove Certificate to delete the certificate but not add it to your CRL.

31. Click on OK twice when you're done.

● ● *Tip* ● ● ●

To view the details of any certificate listed in the large window, including its validity, select the certificate and click on Properties.

Configuring Site Encryption Properties

Follow these steps to set site-wide encryption properties:

1. Select the site where the KM server is located in the Administrator window.

2. Select Configuration.

3. Double-click on Site Encryption Configuration.

4. In the Key Management Server Passwords box, type your advanced security administrator password and click on OK.

5. Select the General tab.

6. Type the name for the Site Encryption Configuration object in the Display Name box.

7. Select the Algorithms tab.

8. Under Preferred Microsoft Exchange 4.0 and 5.0 Encryption Algorithms or under Preferred S/MIME Encryption Algorithms, select an encryption method for the geographic location.

9. Click on OK to save your changes.

Enabling And Revoking Advanced Security

To enable advanced security for a user, you give the user a temporary key. The *temporary key* is used once by the user on the client to secure the connection between the KM server and the client. Follow these steps to enable advanced security for a user:

1. Click on the Recipients button in the Administrator window.

2. Double-click on a mailbox where you want to configure advanced security.

3. Select the Security tab; the status of the user's security is displayed in the top portion of the page.

4. Type your advanced security administrator password in the Key Management Server Passwords box and click on OK.

5. Click on Enable Advanced Security to create the temporary key.

6. Click on Send Enrollment Message to send an advanced security enrollment welcome message to the user through email, or click on Do Not Send E-Mail to give the temporary key to the user in another manner (these options may be dimmed according to the policies you previously set for the CA).

7. Enter your advanced security password again and click on OK.

Tip

You can reissue a user's key if the user loses his or her password, if the user removes local security information, or if security information gets corrupted by clicking on Recover Security Key.

Revoking a user's advanced security should be done only if the security of the user has been compromised. Revoke advanced security if it seems that someone is signing messages on behalf of the user or if someone has accessed the user's security file and password. Also, revoke the user's advanced security when the user leaves the company. After you revoke a user's advanced security, all other users are warned when they verify signed messages that contain that user's revoked certificate. You can enable advanced security for the user again by giving him or her another temporary key.

Tip

Limit *revocation,* because the performance of advanced security degrades as the size of the CRL increases.

Follow these steps to revoke a user's advanced security:

1. Click on the Recipients button in the Administrator window.

2. Double-click on the mailbox whose advanced security you want to revoke.

3. Select the Security tab.

4. In the Key Management Server Passwords box, type your advanced security administrator password and click on OK.

5. Click on Revoke Advanced Security.

6. Enter your advanced security administrator password again and click on OK.

Managing Exchange Server Services

All Exchange Server services are Windows NT services that run in the Windows NT Server environment. The Services control panel displays the services configured to run on the Windows NT Server computer and their current states (see Figure 5.1). The Startup column indicates which Exchange Server services start automatically when the Windows NT Server starts and which services must be started manually.

The Services control panel lets you control the Exchange Server services shown in Table 5.1 (some services might not be displayed in the control panel, depending on how your Exchange Server system is configured).

You might occasionally need to stop Exchange Server services when performing administrative or maintenance tasks or to restart a service manually after it has been stopped. Use the Services control panel to start, stop, pause, and continue Exchange Server services by following these steps:

1. Select Settings from the Start menu.

2. Select Control Panel.

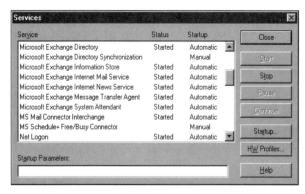

Figure 5.1 Exchange Server services displayed in the Services control panel.

3. Double-click on the Services icon in the Control Panel dialog box.

4. Scroll down the list of services to find the Exchange Server services.

5. Select the service you want to stop, start, pause, or continue, and click on the appropriate button.

6. Click on Close to close the Services dialog box.

The Administrator Program

The *Administrator program* is Exchange Server's graphical system administration application. Using the Administrator program, you can access and administer all Exchange Server components across the organization with a single set of commands and from one screen, including recipients, connectors, gateways, sites, and servers. The Administrator program displays objects in the Exchange Server organization in a hierarchical structure, making navigation intuitive and simplifying the management of objects at each level of the organization.

Table 5.1   Exchange Server services displayed in the Services control panel.

Service	Function
Microsoft Exchange Connector for Lotus cc:Mail	Connects the Exchange Server system and a Lotus cc:Mail system.
Microsoft Exchange Directory	Maintains the directory and replicates directory information.
Microsoft Exchange Directory Synchronization	Exchanges addressing information between Exchange Server and any system that is using the MS Mail directory synchronization protocol.
Microsoft Exchange Event Service	Runs public folder workflow applications.
Microsoft Exchange Information Store	Stores mailboxes and public folders.
Microsoft Exchange Internet Mail Service	Routes messages to the Internet.
Microsoft Internet News Service	Provides USENET newsfeeds.
Microsoft Exchange Key Management Server	Provides advanced security.
Microsoft Exchange Message Transfer Agent	Routes messages between servers in a site and between sites.
Microsoft Exchange System Attendant	Handles general administrative tasks.
MS Mail Connector Interchange	Translates Exchange Server information to MS Mail information and vice versa.
MS Mail (PC) Connector MTA	Transfers messages between the MS Mail (PC) Connector postoffice and MS Mail (PC) postoffices.
MS Schedule+ Free/Busy Connector	Distributes free and busy information to and from MS Mail and Schedule+ environments.

five

Yet, Exchange Server is flexible enough to enable separate sites and servers to be managed separately by different members of an administrative team, if you prefer. This is accomplished through the *permissions* model, which enables you to grant access and modification rights to other mailboxes. You can set up administrators of varying levels to share management of the system in accordance with your company's established administrative policies by granting them permission to modify different components, servers, and sites through the Administrator program.

You will be using the Administrator program to perform administrative tasks in this chapter and in every other chapter of this book, so you should become familiar with it now. Once you start working with the Administrator program, you will find it to be an intuitive, easy-to-use tool.

Running The Administrator Program

To run the Administrator program, you must have Administrator permissions for the site that contains the server where the Administrator program is installed. The only accounts that have Administrator permissions are the account that was logged on during Setup and the service account provided during Setup. After Setup, you can use the Administrator program to give other user accounts Administrator permissions.

Tip • • • •

The Administrator program can be installed on more than one server in a site, so that if one computer is unavailable, another can be used to perform administrative duties.

Follow these steps to start the Administrator program:

1. Select Programs from the Start menu.

2. Select Microsoft Exchange.

3. Select Microsoft Exchange Administrator.

4. In the Server box, type or select the name of the Exchange Server computer to which you want to connect.

After connecting, you can modify information about any object in the site that contains the server to which you are connected. All objects in other sites are read-only until you connect to a server in that site. A read-only object is dimmed in the Administrator window.

Tip • • • •

To connect to additional Exchange Server computers, showing each server in its own window, choose Connect To Server from the File menu and type or select the name of the server.

The Administrator Program Interface

The Administrator program window displays a graphical, hierarchical view of all objects in the Exchange Server organization (see Figure 5.2). Navigate through branches of the hierarchy to travel a complete layout of your organization.

The major areas of the Administrator program's interface are as follows:

➤ **Container area.** Located on the left side of the window, this display area shows all the containers in the organization.

➤ **Contents area.** Located on the right side of the window, this display area shows the contents of the selected container.

➤ **Split bar.** Drag the split bar between the Container and Contents areas to set the sizes of these areas.

➤ **Column sizing bars.** The column names above the Contents area are used to set the width of columns and sort the items in each column.

➤ **Title bar.** Located above the display areas, this bar displays the name of the server and site to which you are connected and the name of the selected container.

➤ **Server box.** This menu, located above the title bar, displays a list of the 20 most recently selected servers; quickly connect to a server by selecting its name from the menu or by typing the name of the server in the box.

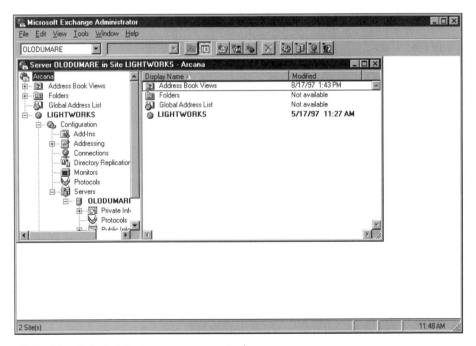

Figure 5.2   The Administrator program window.

five

➤ **View Filters box.** Choose filters from this box (to the right of the Server box) to view only custom recipients, distribution lists, mailboxes, public folders, or all of these combined in the display areas.

➤ **Toolbar.** The toolbar at the right of the View Filters box provides button shortcuts to common tasks.

➤ **Menus.** Located above the Server and View Filters boxes, the menus give access to all commands for the Administrator program.

Tip

As you read this chapter and later chapters, you will learn how to use many of the functions of the Administrator program, but basic operations will not be covered. To learn how to perform these operations, such as customizing the toolbar, consult the Administrator program help files.

Working With Directory Objects

Manage every aspect of your Exchange Server organization by using the Administrator program to change the directory structure or alter the properties of individual directory objects. *Directory objects* are the building blocks of the Exchange Server organization. The way they are linked together and their defined properties determine the organization's structure.

All objects in the Exchange Server directory are organized by containers in the *Container area*. A *container* is an object that contains other objects. Click on the plus (+) or minus (–) buttons next to a container to expand or hide the additional containers and objects in it. For example, clicking on the plus button next to the public folders container displays all public folder objects. Select a container to display the objects it contains in the *Contents area* (see Figure 5.3).

Each object is defined by a set of properties. Setting properties for an object enables you to change the object's performance and characteristics. You can easily define properties for different objects using the Administrator program. Simply select an object and choose Properties under the File menu (or double-click on the object) to display the property pages for that object (see Figure 5.4). *Property pages* group the object's properties logically as tabbed pages for easy reference.

Although the types of property pages for each object can vary considerably, every object has a General property page that allows you to change the object's display name, as well as other general properties. The General property page also has space for you to enter an administrative note about the object at the bottom of the page, and it displays the date and time when the object was created, the object's home site and home server, and the date and time the properties for the object were last modified.

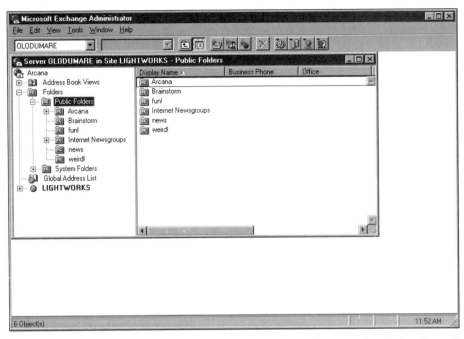

Figure 5.3   The contents of the public folders container shown in both the Container and Contents areas.

Figure 5.4   The set of property pages for a mailbox object, with the General property page displayed.

Table 5.2 outlines the containers and their objects available in the Container and Contents areas (depending on your organization's configuration, you might not see all of these objects in the directory object hierarchy).

five

Table 5.2   The hierarchy of directory objects displayed in the Administrator window.

Container	Objects	Description
Organization	All containers and objects	Exchange Server organization and the starting point of the directory, identified by the organization name.
Address Book Views	Address Book View subcontainers and objects	Groupings of recipients, identified by the names of Address Book views.
Folders	Public Folders System Folders	Hierarchy of public folders and system-related folders.
Global Address List	All recipient objects in the organization	Organization-wide Address Book.
Site	Configuration container Recipients container	Exchange Server site, identified by the site name.
Configuration	Add-Ins container Addressing container Connections container Directory Replication container Monitors container Protocols container Servers container DS Site Configuration Gateway Information Store Site Configuration MTA Site Configuration Site Addressing Certificate Authority Site Encryption Configuration	Site-wide configuration properties (containers and objects).
Add-Ins	Extension	Third-party add-ins.
Addressing	Details Templates Email Address Generators One-Off Address Templates	Site-wide addressing information.
Connections	Dynamic RAS Connector Connector for cc:Mail Internet Mail Service DirSync Server DirSync Requestor MS Mail Connector Site Connector X.400 Connector Newsfeed	Connections to foreign systems, to other sites, and to the Internet.
Directory Replication	Directory Replication Connector	Directory replication between sites.

Continued

Table 5.2   The hierarchy of directory objects displayed in the Administrator window (Continued).

Container	Objects	Description
Monitors	Link Monitor Server Monitor	Monitoring tools.
Protocols	HTTP (Web) Site Settings IMAP4 (Mail) Site Defaults LDAP (Directory) Site Defaults NNTP (News) Site Defaults POP3 (Mail) Site Defaults	Site-wide configuration information for Internet protocols.
Servers	Server container	All Exchange Server computers in the site, identified by server names.
Server	Protocols container Server Recipients container Directory Service Directory Synchronization Message Transfer Agent Private Information Store Public Information Store System Attendant MTA Transport Stack	Core components for a single server.
Protocols	IMAP4 (Mail) Settings LDAP (Directory) Settings NNTP (News) Settings POP3 (Mail) Settings	Server-wide Internet protocol configuration settings.
Server Recipients	All server-related recipient objects	All users on a single server.
Recipients	Custom Recipient Distribution List Mailbox Public Folder Mailbox Agent	Message recipients housed on the site; there can be multiple recipients containers for each site.

Setting Permissions

The permissions model lets you grant permissions to individual user accounts or global groups to access and modify objects in the directory hierarchy using the Administrator program. Each object has an access control list associated with it. An object's *access control list* is a list of Windows NT user accounts and groups that have been granted access to the object. You can edit the object's access control list in the object's Permissions property page.

Each time you give someone permission to access and modify a directory object, you must assign him or her a role. The *role* is the set of rights defining how much access and what kind of access each user or group has to the object. For example, the Admin role gives the user add child, modify user attributes, and delete permissions.

When planning the Exchange Server system, you should have decided how the system will be administered. In other words, will different people have the ability to administer different areas of the organization, such as sites and servers? If you decided on a model with multiple permissions, you need to set permissions through the Administrator program to give other administrators access to the areas of the organization they will be maintaining.

You do not have to set permissions individually for each object, because objects inherit the permissions defined for their containers. For example, you might choose to give administrators access to the site container or the configuration container based on your company's administrative model. Accounts and groups that have site permissions can perform administrative tasks on the site's recipients, such as adding custom recipients and creating new mailboxes. Accounts and groups that have configuration permissions can perform configuration-related administrative tasks, such as installing new connectors and servers and changing the property pages for the site.

Tip

Giving someone full administrative permissions means granting permissions on both the site and configuration containers.

Follow these steps to grant site and configuration container permissions (granting permissions to any directory object is performed in the same way):

1. In the Administrator window, select the site container or the configuration container under the site where you want to grant permissions.

2. Select Properties under the File menu.

3. Select the Permissions tab; a list of user accounts that have permission to access the container is displayed in the Windows NT Accounts With Permissions window (see Figure 5.5).

4. Click on Add to display the Add Users And Groups dialog box (see Figure 5.6).

5. Select the Windows NT domain from which you want to choose users and groups in the List Names From menu.

6. Select the user account or group to whom you want to grant permissions in the Names window.

7. Click on Add; the selected user or group appears in the Add Names box.

8. Repeat steps 5 through 7 to add additional users or groups.

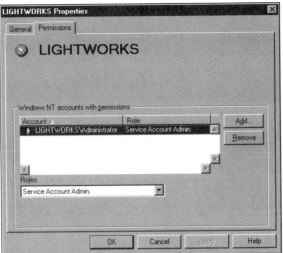

Figure 5.5   Configuring permissions for the site container.

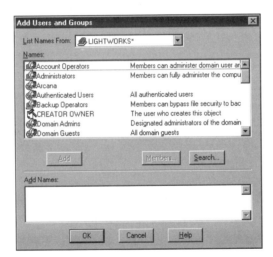

Figure 5.6   The Add Users And Groups dialog box.

9. Click on OK when you're finished; the additional users and groups you selected appear in the Windows NT Account With Permissions window.

10. Select a user or group you just added.

11. Select a role for the user or group from the Roles menu.

12. Repeat steps 10 through 11 for each user or group you added.

13. Click on OK when you're finished.

Tip

The Permissions property page is displayed for containers only by default. To configure permissions for individual objects, you must display their Permissions property pages by choosing Options from the Tools menu, selecting the Permissions tab, and selecting the Show Permissions Page For All Objects check box.

Maintaining Servers

The Administrator program makes it easy to manage the information flow and communications of your Exchange Server organization. Maintaining Exchange Server computers is essential to keeping the system performing at the highest and most reliable level. If you do not maintain servers, performance can degrade and the risk of server failures increases. You should develop a maintenance plan for all your Exchange Server computers.

Maintenance tasks ensure that message and information transfer is running smoothly. Maintaining Exchange Server consists of performing the following tasks on all your Exchange Server computers on a routine basis (depending on your organization design, you might find that you need to perform additional tasks):

➤ Verify that the MTA, connectors, and gateways are transferring messages correctly and in a reasonable amount of time.

➤ Verify that the information store is working correctly and providing adequate resources and performance.

➤ Verify that the directory is working correctly and that directory replication is sharing the correct information.

Maintaining The Message Transfer Agent

The *Message Transfer Agent (MTA)* is a core Exchange Server component that submits, routes, and delivers email messages to other MTAs, information stores, connectors, and third-party gateways. To maintain the MTA and make sure it is working properly, you might have to configure message size limits, rebuild the routing table, set local expansion of remote distribution lists, configure least-cost routing, and manipulate message queues. See Decision Tree 5.1 for more information on maintaining the MTA.

General Maintenance Of The MTA

You can change MTA settings to ensure that message transfer is performing adequately. If network performance has considerably slowed, you can set a size limit for all messages transferred by the MTA. Setting a message size limit prevents the MTA from processing any larger messages and returns those messages to their senders as non-deliverable. Knowing what size limit to set is generally a byproduct of experience; for example, you might find that messages larger than 1000K routinely clog the network, so you should set a maximum message size of 1000K.

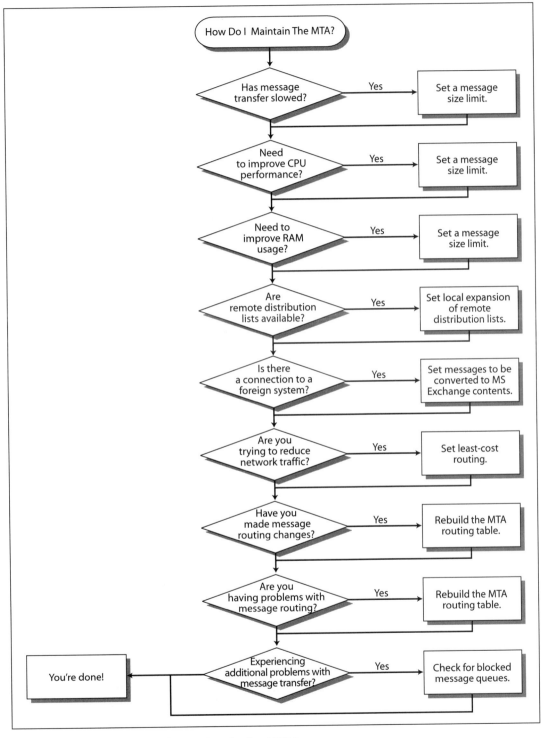

Decision Tree 5.1   How do I maintain the MTA?

The Maintenance Plan

When you put together a plan for maintaining your Exchange Server computers, consider including all the following tasks:

- Develop system-wide maintenance guidelines and procedures.
- Schedule and track maintenance to make sure that guidelines are being met.
- Document maintenance tasks as they are completed to create a record of past maintenance on the system.
- Develop topology maps that show all the major components in your system that must be regularly maintained.
- Configure the system so that duplicate components can continue to perform mission-critical operations during downtime caused by maintenance.
- Train other system administrators how to maintain their areas of the system, following the set guidelines and procedures.

Messages that pass through connectors and gateways for delivery outside the site are processed by the MTA for security, routing, and other purposes (with the exception of messages routed by the MS Mail Connector). The MTA *routing table* displays information about connectors and gateways. When you make *message routing* changes, such as changing the configuration of a connector, those changes are incorporated into the routing table. The routing table is rebuilt automatically after the change is made, as well as once a day. If the current routing information does not show recent changes to the routing information used by the MTA, or if you want your changes to take effect sooner, you must manually rebuild the routing table.

A *remote distribution list* is a list of recipients created for mass mailings on another site. Remote distribution lists can be made available to local users through replication of the directory. When local users send a message to a remote distribution list, Exchange Server prepares and delivers the message by expanding the remote distribution list. Setting local expansion of the distribution list determines the best routing for the message based on the recipients' locations, maximizing message transfer efficiency. Remember that processing large distribution lists can adversely affect server performance when using this setting.

You can also configure the MTA to send messages using only least-cost routes, without attempting any other routes. This setting prevents messages from being routed to connectors in other sites when a connector in the local site is unavailable. If a message cannot be routed through the least-cost route, a *non-delivery report (NDR)* is returned to the message sender.

Follow these steps to perform general maintenance tasks on the MTA:

1. Select Servers in the Administrator window.

2. Select the server whose MTA you want to maintain.

3. Double-click on Message Transfer Agent.

4. Select the General tab (see Figure 5.7).

5. To limit the size of messages that can be processed by the MTA, click on the Maximum (K) button under Message Size and enter the maximum size in kilobytes.

6. Select the Expand Remote Distribution Lists Locally check box to set the MTA to expand any remote distribution lists locally when messages are sent to those lists.

7. Select the Convert Incoming Messages To MS Exchange Contents check box to change the address and content for incoming messages to a *Message Application Programming Interface (MAPI)* and Exchange Server-compatible format.

8. Select the Only Use Least Cost Routes check box to configure least-cost routing for the MTA.

9. Click on Recalculate Routing to rebuild the routing table on the selected server and replicate the new information to other servers in the site, a process that can take several minutes.

10. Click on OK when you're finished.

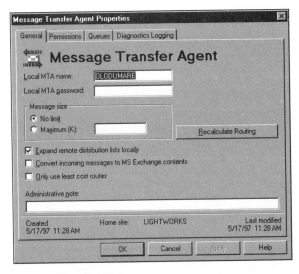

Figure 5.7   Setting options for the MTA.

Manipulating MTA Queues

When messages are waiting to be delivered by the MTA, Exchange Server places them into different *message queues* for each server in the site, as well as for any installed connectors and gateways. Normally, messages do not remain in the queue long. The buildup of message queues indicates service interruption somewhere in your organization, such as a problem with the physical connection between servers, a damaged message, a server or MTA configuration error, or an improperly configured connector.

There are two types of message queues: secured queues and unsecured queues. *Secured queues* are queues to the Internet Mail Service and MS Mail Connector. They do not appear in the queue list until the Internet Mail Service or MS Mail Connector sends messages to or retrieves messages from the MTA. *Unsecured queues* are queues to components on the MTA's server, other servers' MTAs in the same site, Site Connectors, Dynamic RAS Connectors, and X.400 Connectors. They appear in the queue list whenever the receiving service is running.

Use the MTA Queues property page to find out how many messages are in each queue, view detailed information about messages, change the priority of messages waiting to be delivered, or delete corrupted messages (see Figure 5.8).

You can view details about each message in the queues, including the originator of the message, the message ID, the time the message arrived in the MTA, the message's priority, and the message's size. Checking message details can be helpful when troubleshooting problems with message transfer. For example, if the same server is the originator of several problem messages, there might be a server configuration error. Compare the submit time to the time the message was sent to determine where delays are occurring.

Figure 5.8   The MTA Queues property page.

The Microsoft Mail (PC) Connector MTA

Messages are transferred between the Exchange Server system and an MS Mail (PC) system by the *Microsoft Mail Connector for PC Networks*. During message transfer, the message is picked up by the *Microsoft Mail Connector Interchange*, converted to MS Mail (PC) format, and placed in a temporary information store on the MS Mail (PC) Connector. The MS Mail (PC) Connector MTA retrieves the message and delivers it to the MS Mail (PC) postoffice. To view the MS Mail (PC) Connector MTA queue and delete or return messages that might be blocking this queue, select Connections, double-click on MS Mail Connector, select the Connections tab, and click on the Queue button.

Knowing the message ID lets you trace the message through the tracking log, event log, or other message queues.

Changing the priority of a message is an easy way to make sure an urgent message is delivered immediately or to take care of a message you suspect is blocking the queue (you can also choose to delete a message that is blocking the queue). A message that has High priority is moved to the top of the queue for faster delivery, while a message that has Low priority is moved to the end of the queue, so that other messages are delivered ahead of it. Messages that have the same priority are delivered in the order in which they are received. You can only change the priority of messages in unsecured queues, not in secured queues.

Follow these steps to view and manipulate MTA queues:

1. Select Servers in the Administrator window.

2. Select the server that contains the MTA you want to maintain.

3. Double-click on Message Transfer Agent.

4. Select the Queues tab.

5. Click on the Refresh button to update your view of the message queues.

6. Select a queue in the Queue Name menu (the number of items in the queue is listed beside the queue's name).

7. Click on a message in the large window to select it.

8. Click on the Details button to view detailed information about the selected message.

9. To change the order of the selected message in unsecured queues, click on Priority and select one of the following options: High, Normal (the default), or Low.

10. Click on Delete to return the selected message to the originator as non-deliver-able—if you suspect the message is blocking the queue, for example.

11. Click on OK when you've finished editing the queues.

Maintaining The Information Store

The *information store* is divided into two areas: the private information store and the public information store. A server's *private information store* contains all the mailboxes and their contents, such as messages and attachments, for Exchange Server users housed on the server. A server's *public information store* contains all public folders and public folder replicas on the server.

As well as storing public folders and email messages, the information store performs the following tasks:

➤ Provides rules and views.

➤ Maintains storage and age limits.

➤ Delivers email messages to users on the same server.

➤ Forwards email messages to the MTA to deliver to recipients on other servers and systems.

Monitor the information store's usage statistics to make sure it is being used most efficiently, and maintain the information store to keep old data from accumulating and cluttering up the server's storage space. Maintenance tasks include setting a maintenance schedule, setting mailbox and public folder age and storage limits, and periodically cleaning out mailboxes. You might also find that you occasionally must move mailboxes or public folders to free up server space. For more information on maintaining the information store, see Decision Tree 5.2, "How Do I Maintain The Information Store?".

Viewing Information Store Statistics

Using the Administrator application, you can easily monitor usage statistics for the public and private information stores. Checking the properties of the information store gives you an idea of how frequently and for what purposes the information store is being used. After noting usage patterns, you might want to reconfigure the locations of information stores on different servers to make the best use of available disk space and connection speeds. Statistics that you can monitor include the following:

➤ **Mailbox logons.** Displays information about users who have logged on to the private information store, including the user's name, mailbox, Windows NT user account, the date and time of the logon, the date and time of the last access, and the client version used to log on.

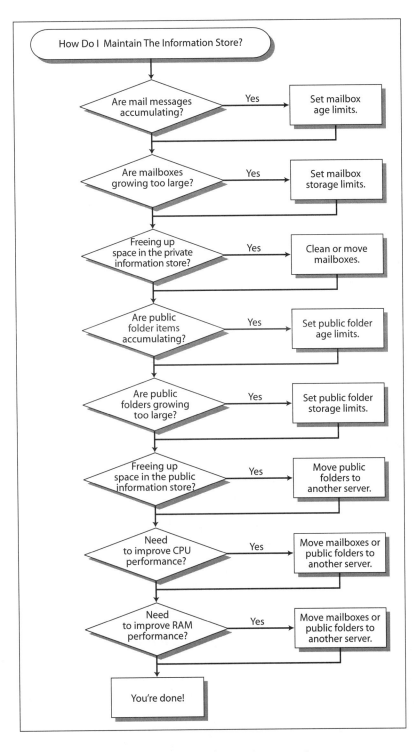

Decision Tree 5.2   How do I maintain the information store?

five

➤ **Mailbox resources.** Displays private information store statistics, so you can determine how mailboxes are being used and whether resources are sufficient; you can view the name and Windows NT user account of each mailbox in the private information store, mailbox sizes, the total number of items in mailboxes, and the last logon and logoff dates and times for each mailbox.

➤ **Folder replication status.** Displays information about public folder replication within the site, including the names of replicated folders, the last time replication messages were received, the number of replicas, and the replication status.

➤ **Public folder logons.** Displays information about users who have logged on to the public information store, including the user's name and Windows NT user account, the date and time of the logon, the date and time of the last access, and the client version used to log on.

➤ **Public folder resources.** Displays public information store statistics so you can determine which folders are being accessed and how they are being used; you can find the name of each folder in the public information store, folder sizes, the total number of items in each folder, the date and time each folder was created and when it was last accessed, and the number of owners and contacts for each folder.

➤ **Server replication status.** Displays the status of public folder replication between the server and other servers in the organization; you can view the server name, the replication status, the last time a replication message was received, the average transmission time of replication messages, and the last transmission time of replication messages.

To monitor the usage statistics of the information store, follow these steps:

1. Select Servers in the Administrator window.

2. Select the server that contains the information store whose statistics you want to monitor.

3. Double-click on either Public Information Store or Private Information Store.

4. In the Contents area, double-click on the property you want to monitor; the status information is displayed in the Contents area (see Figure 5.9).

5. To customize how the information is displayed, you can add, remove, move, or change the sizes of columns by choosing Columns from the View menu; columns display category names for status items (see Figure 5.10).

Setting The Maintenance Schedule

Exchange Server automatically performs maintenance of the information store on a scheduled basis. These automated tasks include cleaning up deleted items in mailboxes and public folders, deleting expired folder indexes and expired items from public folders,

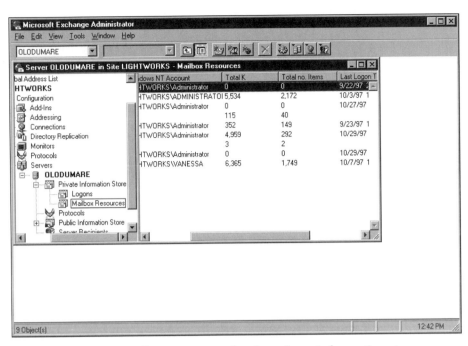

Figure 5.9   Monitoring mailbox resources for the private information store.

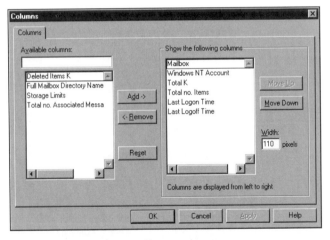

Figure 5.10   Modifying columns for mailbox resources.

synchronizing the information store with other servers, and removing expired public folder conflicts.

Regular maintenance prevents deterioration of the information store's performance when users are accessing it to view email messages and public folders. It is a good idea to run this maintenance schedule at least once each day, no matter what the size of your organization. Performance of the information store will significantly degenerate if you do not schedule information store maintenance or if you schedule maintenance only infrequently, particularly for large or heavily used information stores.

Use the server's IS Maintenance property page to schedule a time when information store maintenance will be performed (see Figure 5.11). The response times of the information store are significantly slowed while the server is performing maintenance tasks. You should therefore set the maintenance schedule for the time of day when the fewest users access information on the server.

Follow these steps to set the maintenance schedule:

1. Select Servers in the Administrator window.

2. Select the server that contains the information store for which you want to set up a maintenance schedule.

3. Select Properties from the File menu.

4. Click on the IS Maintenance tab.

5. Under Detail View, select a view for the schedule grid; you can choose to view the grid in one-hour or in 15-minute increments.

6. Select one of the maintenance options: Always to perform maintenance tasks at the default interval of 15 minutes (this option can adversely affect server performance and is not recommended), or Selected Times to select a block of time in the schedule grid when maintenance will occur.

7. Click on OK.

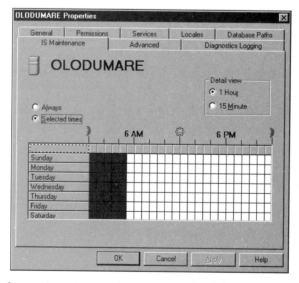

Figure 5.11   The information store maintenance schedule.

Maintaining Mailboxes

To conserve server storage space, you can set age and storage limits for users' mailboxes in the private information store. For example, you can set the maximum number of days that deleted mail messages are retained for possible recovery before they are permanently erased; the *age limit* keeps deleted messages from accumulating in the private information store.

You can configure the maximum amount of disk space that each mailbox can occupy before a warning message is sent to the mailbox's owner; you can also set the maximum amount of space the mailbox can occupy before you prohibit the mailbox from sending or receiving mail. Setting mailbox *storage limits* keeps mailboxes from growing too large, which can be important if a lot of users are housed on the same server or if storage space is limited.

Follow these steps to configure mailbox settings:

1. Select Servers in the Administrator window.

2. Select the server whose private information store you want to configure.

3. Select Private Information Store.

4. Select Properties from the File menu.

5. Click on the General tab (see Figure 5.12).

Figure 5.12 Setting mailbox limits for the private information store.

6. In the Deleted Item Retention Time (Days) box, enter the number of days that deleted items are retained before they are removed permanently.

7. Select the Don't Permanently Delete Items Until The Store Has Been Backed Up check box to ensure that items are not deleted until the information store has been backed up (even if the age limit for deleted items has been exceeded).

Tip

If you don't perform regular backups, selecting this option can adversely affect the performance of the server as items accumulate in the information store.

8. Select the Issue Warning (K) check box and enter the maximum mailbox storage limit before a warning message is sent.

9. Select the Prohibit Send (K) check box and enter the maximum mailbox storage limit before a mailbox is prohibited from sending mail.

10. Select the Prohibit Send And Receive (K) check box and enter the maximum mailbox storage limit before a mailbox is prohibited from sending and receiving mail.

11. Click on OK.

Tip

You can set message size and mailbox storage limits on individual mailboxes in the same way as you set them for the entire private information store. Individual mailbox settings override the private information store settings. Double-click on the mailbox in the recipients container in the Administrator window and select the Limits tab to make these settings.

Cleaning Mailboxes

The maintenance task of cleaning a mailbox deletes messages from the user's mailbox that are stored on the server and recovers space in the private information store. You can clean single or multiple mailboxes for users, whether the mailboxes are open or closed. However, you cannot clean mailboxes for distribution lists, custom recipients, or public folders.

Follow these steps to clean a mailbox:

1. Select Recipients in the Administrator window.

2. Select the mailbox you want to clean.

3. Select Clean Mailbox from the Tools menu (see Figure 5.13).

Figure 5.13   Setting options for cleaning a mailbox.

4. To set an age limit for email messages, type a number in the All Messages Older Than (Days) box; all messages older than the specified number of days are deleted.

5. To set a storage limit for email messages, type a number in the All Messages Greater Than (K) box; all messages larger than the specified number of kilobytes are deleted.

6. To delete all messages marked with a specific sensitivity level, select an option in the Sensitivity area: Normal, Personal, Private, or Confidential.

7. To delete messages based on whether they have been read, select an option in the Read Items area: Read Items, Unread Items, or Read And Unread Items.

8. Select the Only Delete Mail Messages check box to delete email messages only; if this check box is cleared, email messages and messages that contain contact, calendar, and task information are deleted.

9. Select the Delete Deferred Action Messages check box to delete messages in the deferred actions folder (deferred action messages contain commands that are queued for the email client to perform the next time it logs on, such as rules).

10. In the Action area, select an option to indicate what action is taken on deleted messages: Delete Items Immediately permanently deletes all messages that meet the criteria you set; Move Items To Deleted Items Folder sends all messages that meet the criteria you set to the user's Deleted Items folder, so the user can retrieve the messages for viewing or for moving to another folder.

11. Click on OK when you've finished to clean the mailbox.

Moving Mailboxes

Occasionally, you will need to move mailboxes from one server to another to accommodate load balancing between servers, free up space in an overloaded server's private information store, or take a server offline. As users move around physically, you might also need to move their mailboxes to a new home server.

Follow these steps to move a mailbox between two servers in the same site:

1. Select Recipients in the Administrator window.

2. Select the mailbox or group of mailboxes you want to move.

3. Select Move Mailbox from the Tools menu (see Figure 5.14).

4. Select the server where you want to move the mailbox in the Move Mailbox To box (this server must be in the same site).

5. Click on OK.

Maintaining Public Folders

Setting public folder age and storage limits helps conserve server storage space and control the size of the public information store as the number of public folders grows. As with mailboxes, you can set the age limit for retaining deleted items in the public information store for possible recovery before they are deleted permanently. The storage limit represents the most space the public folder and its contents can occupy in the public information store. Once the limit is exceeded, a warning message is sent to the owner of the overlarge folder.

Tip

The storage limits you set for the public information store will be the default for all public folders on the server, unless you override the setting in the individual public folder's property pages.

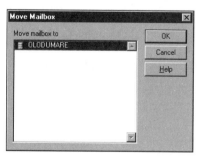

Figure 5.14   Moving a mailbox.

Follow these steps to set storage limits for the public information store:

1. Select Servers in the Administrator window.

2. Select the server whose public information store you want to configure.

3. Select Public Information Store.

4. Select Properties from the File menu.

5. Click on the General tab (see Figure 5.15).

6. In the Deleted Item Retention Time (Days) box, enter the maximum number of days that deleted items in the public information store are retained before they are deleted permanently.

7. Select the Don't Permanently Delete Items Until The Store Has Been Backed Up check box to keep items from being permanently deleted until the information store has been backed up (even if the age limit for deleted items has been exceeded).

Tip

If you don't perform regular backups, selecting this option can adversely affect the performance of the server as items accumulate in the information store.

8. Select the Issue Warning (K) check box and enter the maximum public folder size.

9. Click on OK.

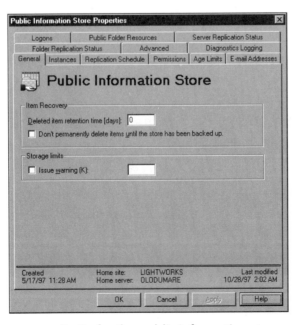

Figure 5.15 Setting storage limits for the public information store.

Moving Public Folders

You might sometimes find it necessary to move a public folder to a new server to free up space in the public information store. If most of the users of a public folder are located on another server, moving the folder to that server can also reduce traffic across the network. Moving the public folder is an alternative to public folder replication, which can cause too much network traffic through the replication process for an infrequently used folder.

Public folder replication is used to move the folder from one server to another. The public folder is replicated to the new server according to the schedule set in the Replication Schedule property page. The folder remains on its original server until the replication process is complete, when it is removed permanently from the old server. To learn how to configure public folder replication, see Chapter 6.

To move a public folder, follow these steps:

1. Select Folders in the Administrator window.

2. Select Public Folders to display the hierarchy of public folders.

3. Double-click on the public folder you want to move.

4. Select the Replicas tab.

5. Select the server where you want to move the public folder in the Servers box.

6. Click on Add.

7. Select the server from which you are moving the public folder in the Replicate Folders To box.

8. Click on Remove.

9. Click on OK.

Setting The Schedule For Storage Warnings

After setting maximum storage limits for mailboxes and public folders, you need to configure the times when notification messages about storage limit violations are sent to the owners of the mailboxes and public folders. This enables you to configure how often and at what times to send out storage warnings. For example, you might choose to send out storage warnings once a week or once a day. Follow these steps:

1. Click on the Configuration button in the Administrator window.

2. Double-click on Information Store Site Configuration.

3. Select the Storage Warnings tab (see Figure 5.16).

Figure 5.16   Setting a schedule for sending storage warnings.

4. Under Detail View, select a view for the schedule grid; you can view the grid in either one-hour or 15-minute increments.

5. Select one of the following options: Never (to disable sending out storage warnings), Always (to send storage warnings continuously at the default interval of 15 minutes), or Selected Times (to set a schedule for sending storage warnings in the schedule grid).

6. Click on OK.

Maintaining Directory Replication

The Exchange Server *directory* stores information about the organization's users and resources, including mailboxes, distribution lists, and public folders. This information is automatically replicated to all the servers in the site through *directory replication*, so that the directory remains consistent across the organization.

One large facet of maintaining the directory is periodically verifying that the directory information replicated is correct and consistent. As part of your maintenance schedule, you should make a consistency check of all directories in your organization to check for errors and to make sure information about new servers and sites is replicated properly.

You can then update the directory or verify that all information in the site is synchronized. You might need to resynchronize the directory with other servers if a new server is added to the site, if a server goes offline temporarily, or if you find an error. If a new site was recently added, the connection to another site was temporarily down, or a replication error between sites occurred, you can also initiate an immediate directory replication request to the outside site.

On Site

Follow these steps to maintain directory replication:

1. Select Servers in the Administrator window.

2. Select the server whose directory you want to maintain.

3. Double-click on Directory Service.

4. Click on the General tab (see Figure 5.17).

5. Click on Check Now to check the consistency of all the directories in your organization (see Figure 5.18).

6. Click on Update Now to request updates from other servers within the site and thus resynchronize the directories of all servers in the site.

7. Click on OK when you're finished.

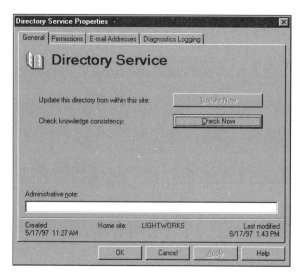

Figure 5.17   Maintaining directory replication.

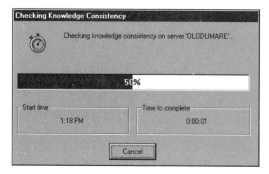

Figure 5.18   Checking the knowledge consistency of the directory.

Monitoring The Organization

Monitoring the Exchange Server organization involves checking for problems with servers, connections, gateways, and services, and then fixing those problems. Proper monitoring of the system often enables you to find and fix problems before they impact your users.

You can monitor the performance of the Exchange Server system and troubleshoot problems using a series of built-in tools, including the Server Monitor and the Link Monitor. These tools alert you to any problems, so you can take action immediately to avert system failures. Because Exchange Server is built on top of the Windows NT Server system, it is integrated with Windows NT Server management tools, including the Windows NT Performance Monitor. This enables you to use the same tools for monitoring the performance of Exchange Server that you use for monitoring Windows NT Server. Monitoring cannot be used to check all Exchange Server features, such as directory and public folder replication.

Server Monitor

In a distributed environment like the Exchange Server system, you must be aware of every server in the organization. If a server goes down or starts performing poorly, the productivity of all users who rely on that server can decrease. The *Server Monitor* enables you to get system feedback and view server statistics quickly from any location in the organization.

The Server Monitor tests all core and optional server components, including installed connectors, the directory service, the MTA, the information store, and other key services, to ensure that they are running properly. You do not have to search for the information you need; instead, one interface shows the status of all servers.

By monitoring servers closely using the Server Monitor, you can often eliminate problems before they occur. The Server Monitor can automatically take predetermined actions if a problem does arise, such as restarting a stopped service. The Server Monitor's display helps you research the cause of the problem.

This monitor is installed by default, so you do not have to purchase and install an add-on product to do this necessary job. You should configure and start all necessary Server Monitors as soon as possible after installing the Exchange Server system. If you are the only system administrator, you can set up one Server Monitor to monitor all servers. If a different administrator is responsible for maintaining different servers, you can create multiple Server Monitors for each server or group of servers and run them all from one Administrator program, so that problems are reported to the appropriate administrator.

Configuring The Server Monitor

Before using the Server Monitor, you must configure it and set up its alert system and the predetermined actions you want it to take to fix server problems. Setting up the Server Monitor involves adding it to the directory hierarchy in the Administrator window, creating log files, and setting polling intervals, notifications, and the servers and services to monitor.

The Server Monitor log file stores information about monitored servers, so you can keep an archive of the status of your servers. Although creating log files is not required, they are helpful for troubleshooting problems with Exchange Server services.

Polling intervals indicate how often the Server Monitor checks Exchange Server services. You can set the polling intervals for both a normal site and a critical site to any duration. In a *normal site,* services are running and the clock is not off by more than the specified interval. A *critical site* does not meet the criteria defined for a normal site and thus is in a warning state or an alert state. Therefore, the polling interval for a normal site should be longer than that for a critical site.

Follow these steps to set up the Server Monitor:

1. Select the site where you want to configure the Server Monitor in the Administrator window.

2. Select Configuration.

3. Select Monitors.

4. Select New Other from the File menu.

5. Select Server Monitor.

6. Click on the General tab (see Figure 5.19).

7. In the Directory Name box, type the name that the system will use to identify the Server Monitor.

8. In the Display Name box, type the name used to identify the Server Monitor in the Administrator window.

9. Click on Browse to create the log file.

10. Type or select the pathname and file name for the log file and click on Save; the log file will be easier to find on the network if you specify the path using the UNC, such as: \\Servername\C$\S1m1hour.log.

11. In the Normal box, enter a number that represents the polling interval for a normal site, and select Seconds, Minutes, or Hours for the duration; the default is 15 minutes.

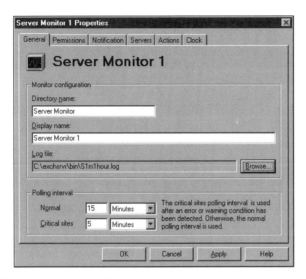

Figure 5.19   Configuring a Server Monitor.

12. In the Critical Sites box, enter a number that represents the polling interval for a critical site, and select Seconds, Minutes, or Hours for the duration; the default is five minutes.

13. Click on OK.

Setting Notifications. You need to specify how to notify administrators or system personnel when the Server Monitor detects that the server is in a warning or alert state. A warning state indicates a possible problem and occurs when the clock is off by a small amount. An alert state indicates a serious problem and occurs when a service is not running, when a server does not respond, or when the clock is off by a large amount.

There are three choices for delivering notifications: notification applications, mail messages, or network alerts. Notification applications alert users who are not logged on to the network, such as an administrator who monitors the network remotely using a pager program. Mail messages send an email notification to the mailbox of the administrator, which is useful for historical tracking of notifications. *Network alerts* send the alert message to a specific computer or person logged on to the network (the alert message cannot be delivered if the computer is turned off or if no one is logged into the computer). Network alerts appear in real time and require immediate attention.

Configuring an *escalation path* creates a prioritized list of primary and secondary support personnel to notify when the Server Monitor enters a warning or alert state. For example, you might choose to notify the primary support person immediately when the monitor enters a warning state and wait to notify secondary personnel until the monitor enters an alert state. Set up an escalation path by configuring the Notifications property page separately for each person to notify.

Follow these steps to set up notifications:

1. Click on the Configuration button in the Administrator window.

2. Select Monitors.

3. Double-click on the Server Monitor you are configuring.

4. Click on the Notification tab (see Figure 5.20).

5. Click on New.

6. In the New Notification box, select Launch Process to set up a notification application, Mail Message to send a notification email message, or Windows NT Alert to send a network alert.

7. Click on OK.

8. If you chose Launch Process, select a file name to appear in the Launch Process box by clicking on File, type special command-line parameters in the Command Line Parameters box if needed, and select the Append Notification Text To Parameter List check box to attach the standard notification text to the parameters list (see Figure 5.21).

9. If you chose Mail Message, click on Recipient and select the person to send the message to; this name appears in the Mailbox To Notify box (see Figure 5.22).

10. If you chose Windows NT Alert, type the name of the computer to receive the alert message in the Computer To Alert box (see Figure 5.23).

Figure 5.20   Setting notifications for the Server Monitor.

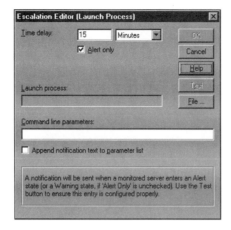

Figure 5.21   Setting options for the Launch Process notification.

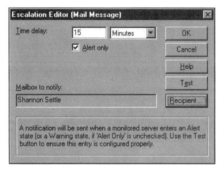

Figure 5.22   Setting options for the Mail Message notification.

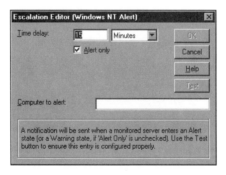

Figure 5.23   Setting options for the Windows NT Alert notification.

11. In the Time Delay box, enter the amount of time after the monitor enters an alert or warning state that you want the notification process to start and select Minutes or Hours; the default is 15 minutes.

12. Select the Alert Only check box to send the notification only if the monitor enters an alert state; otherwise, the notification occurs at both the warning and alert states.

13. Click on Test to verify that the process works correctly.

14. Click on OK.

15. Repeat steps 5 through 14 to set up an escalation path of multiple people to notify.

16. Click on OK when you've finished to close the Notifications property page.

● ● ● *Tip* ● ● ● ●

You can modify the notification settings at any time by selecting a notification, clicking on Edit, and making the appropriate changes in the Escalation Editor dialog box. When you no longer want to use a particular notification, select it and click on Remove.

Setting The Servers And Services To Monitor. Now, you should specify which servers the Server Monitor you have set up should monitor. All servers monitored by a single Server Monitor must have LAN connectivity.

The Server Monitor monitors only the directory, information store, and MTA services by default. However, you can use the Server Monitor to monitor any additional Windows NT Server service running on the Exchange Server computer. When you configure additional services to monitor, that information is stored in the directory and replicated to all servers in the organization, where all Server Monitors can access it. (Monitors that are already running do not pick up changes, so you must restart them after the changed data is replicated.)

Follow these steps to indicate which servers and services should be monitored by the Server Monitor:

1. Click on the Configuration button in the Administrator window.

2. Select Monitors.

3. Double-click on the Server Monitor you're configuring.

4. Select the Servers tab (see Figure 5.24).

5. Select the server you want to monitor in the Servers window.

6. Click on Add to add the selected server to the list of monitored servers.

7. To monitor additional services, click on the Services button (see Figure 5.25).

8. Select the services you want to monitor in the Installed Services window and click on Add to add them to the Monitored Services window.

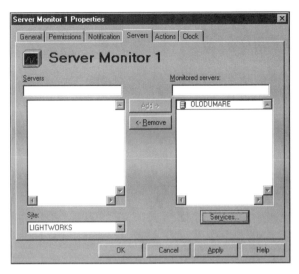

Figure 5.24   Setting up servers to monitor.

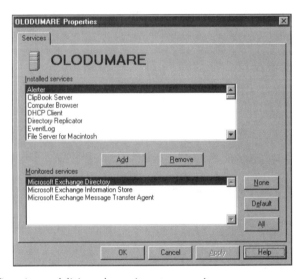

Figure 5.25   Configuring additional services to monitor.

 *Tip*

Click on None to turn off monitoring of all services, or click on Default to return to the default monitored services.

9. Click on OK when you've finished.

10. Repeat steps 5 through 8 for each additional server you want to monitor with the same Server Monitor.

11. Click on OK to close the Servers property page.

Tip

If you no longer need to monitor a specific server, remove it from the Monitored Servers list by selecting it and clicking on Remove.

Setting Escalation Actions. You can set up automatic processes to take action when a service stops. These escalation actions occur after a failed attempt to start a stopped service and continue until the service is successfully started. For example, you might configure the first step as taking no action, the second step as restarting the service, and the third step as restarting the computer.

The same set of actions is used for all monitored servers, so you should configure separate Server Monitors if you want to take different actions on different servers. Escalation actions are independent of notifications, so you can specify that notifications occur before, during, or after action is taken.

Follow these steps to set up escalation actions:

1. Click on the Configuration button in the Administrator window.

2. Select Monitors.

3. Double-click on the Server Monitor you're configuring.

4. Select the Actions tab (see Figure 5.26).

5. Under Action When A Service Is Stopped, select one of the following options in each attempt box: Take No Action if the Server Monitor should only notify you of a stopped service, Restart The Service if the Server Monitor should try to restart

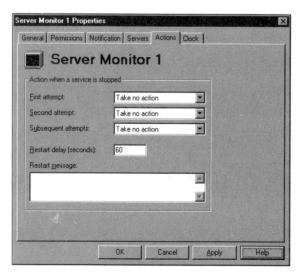

Figure 5.26   Configuring escalation actions.

the stopped service, or Restart The Computer if the Server Monitor should try to restart the computer with the stopped service.

6. If you chose Restart The Computer as one of the escalation actions, enter the delay until the computer restarts in the Restart Delay (Seconds) box to give users time to save their work before the computer shuts down.

Tip

Do not set the Restart Delay (Seconds) option to be less than the time it takes to restart the computer; otherwise, the action will repeatedly fail. Also, remember that restarting the computer can interfere with non-Exchange Server services.

7. If you chose Restart The Computer as one of the escalation actions, type a message in the Restart Message box that appears in the Restart Warning box on the server to be restarted.

8. Click on OK.

Setting Clock Notifications. You can initiate an alert if one of the monitored servers' internal clocks is off by more than a specified number of seconds. If you are monitoring servers in other time zones, you can also synchronize the clocks of monitored servers with the clock of the monitoring computer, or the computer that is hosting the Server Monitor. (Synchronization ensures that monitors function correctly with servers in other time zones and that time-based events like message tracking and event logs are recorded correctly.)

Follow these steps to set the clock notifications:

1. Click on the Configuration button in the Administrator window.

2. Select Monitors.

3. Double-click on the Server Monitor you're configuring.

4. Click on the Clock tab (see Figure 5.27).

5. In the Warning If Off By More Than box, type the minimum number of seconds clocks can differ by before a warning notification is sent.

6. In the Alert If Off By More Than box, type the minimum number of seconds clocks can differ by before an alert notification is sent.

7. Select the Synchronize check box to synchronize the clocks of monitored servers with the Server Monitor's server clock.

8. Click on OK.

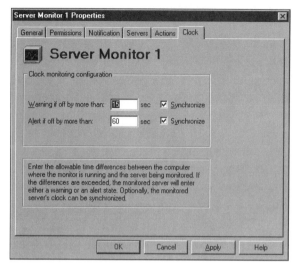

Figure 5.27   Setting clock notifications.

Starting The Server Monitor

Once you have configured the Server Monitor, you must start it to begin monitoring the specified servers. Follow these steps to start the Server Monitor:

1. Click on the Configuration button in the Administrator window.

2. Select Monitors.

3. Select the Server Monitor you want to start.

4. Select Start Monitor from the Tools menu.

5. Type the name or browse to the server to which you want to connect.

6. Click on OK.

You can also set the Server Monitor to restart automatically whenever you start the Administrator program, so you do not have to start each monitor manually. Follow these steps:

1. Select Settings from the Start menu.

2. Select Taskbar.

3. Select the Start Menu Items tab.

4. Click on Add.

5. Click on Browse.

6. Locate the Exchange Server Admin.exe program, and double-click on the program icon; this program is generally located in the \Exchsrvr\bin subdirectory.

Server Monitor Permissions

Use the Permissions property page for the Server Monitor to indicate which Windows NT user accounts have permission to modify the Server Monitor. These accounts should correspond to the additional administrators you decided on for that Server Monitor, if there are any.

7. In the Command Line box, add the /m option with the site name, monitor name, and server name in the following format: [path]\admin.exe /m[site name]\ [monitor name]\[server name]. To start multiple monitors, add additional entries in this format: [path]\admin.exe /m[site name]\[monitor name]\[server name] /m[monitor name]\[server name] /m[monitor name]\[server name].

8. Click on Next.

9. Double-click on the StartUp folder.

10. Type the name that you want to see on the StartUp menu.

11. Click on Finish.

12. In the Taskbar Properties window, click on OK.

The Server Monitor Display

After the Server Monitor is started, it begins checking that Exchange Server services are running and alerts you to problems. The Server Monitor display appears, showing the configuration of all servers monitored by a single Server Monitor (see Figure 5.28). The display gives an immediate picture of the health of all your Exchange Server computers. It is updated in real time with each polling interval.

The display shows all monitored servers, with each line representing a separate server. An upward green arrow indicates that all services on the server are running normally. A downward red arrow indicates that one or more services on the server have stopped, and the Server Monitor considers the server to be down. The display also tells you the last time each server was polled and the last time the condition of any service on the server changed, along with comments about the server status.

Monitoring Server Status. If you are alerted to a problem, check the Server Monitor display first to determine which server or servers are down. Then, check the status for each individual server where there is a problem to view the current status of each service. You can also use the status information to determine how well an individual server is performing. Server status is displayed in real time and is updated at each polling interval.

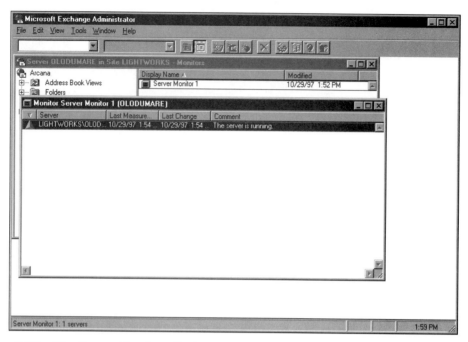

Figure 5.28   The Server Monitor display.

Follow these steps to monitor the status of an individual server using the Server Monitor:

1. In the Server Monitor display, double-click on the monitored server you want to check.

2. Click on the Actions tab (see Figure 5.29).

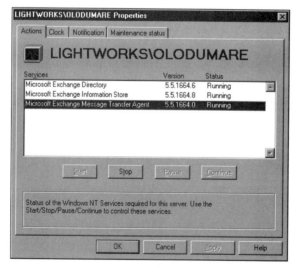

Figure 5.29   Checking the status of a monitored server.

3. The Services window lists the monitored components and connectors of the server, the version of each service, and the current status of each service; select a service by clicking on it.

4. Click on Start to start a stopped service.

5. Click on Stop to stop a running service.

6. Click on Pause to stop a running service temporarily.

7. Click on Continue to restart a paused service.

8. Click on OK when you've finished.

Monitoring The Clock. You can use the Server Monitor to view measurement results and time zone information for a monitored server, including the time when the last check occurred, the difference between the monitored server's clock and the clock on the Server Monitor's server, and daylight savings time information for the monitored server.

Follow these steps to view statistics for the server clock:

1. Double-click on the monitored server you want to check in the Server Monitor display.

2. Click on the Clock tab (see Figure 5.30).

3. Click on OK when you've finished.

Monitoring Notifications History. When a component on a monitored server does not respond to the Server Monitor's poll, the Server Monitor begins processing the notification instructions you previously set. For any monitored server, you can see who has been

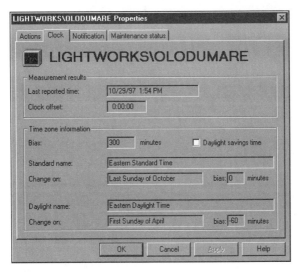

Figure 5.30 Monitoring the server clock.

notified, the time they were notified, and how they were notified, which lets you know if notification instructions are being carried out correctly and anticipate notifications if a problem continues. Also, whenever you test notifications, the test message displays on this page.

Follow these steps to track the history of notifications:

1. Double-click on the monitored server in the Server Monitor display whose notifications you want to check.

2. Select the Notification tab (see Figure 5.31).

3. Click on OK when you've finished.

Checking Maintenance Status. To determine if a monitored server is down for scheduled maintenance, rather than for any problem, use the server's Maintenance Status property page. This page indicates whether notifications or repairs are suspended during maintenance of the server and displays information about the last server modification.

Follow these steps to check the maintenance status of a monitored server:

1. Double-click on the monitored server you want to check in the Server Monitor display.

2. Select the Maintenance Status tab (see Figure 5.32).

3. Click on OK when you've finished.

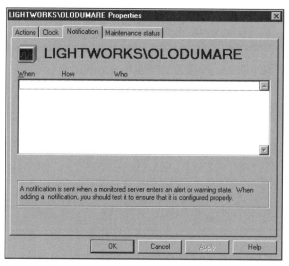

Figure 5.31   Monitoring a server's notification history.

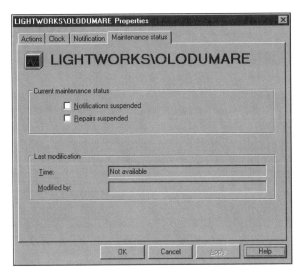

Figure 5.32   Monitoring a server's maintenance status.

The Server Monitor Log

The Server Monitor retains a log file of recent server monitoring events, so you can review recent events when researching a problem. To find the name of the log file, check the Server Monitor's General property page by double-clicking on the name of the Server Monitor in the Administrator window and selecting the General tab. The log file can be opened by any word processor, spreadsheet, or database (see Figure 5.33). Scroll to the bottom of the page to find the most recent events.

Stopping The Server Monitor

When taking down a server for maintenance or to perform a backup, you can stop the Server Monitor for that server. Stopping the monitor also suspends any notifications or escalation actions to avoid unnecessary alerts and system repairs. To temporarily suspend the Server Monitor, type one of the commands in an automated process for scheduled maintenance or from the command line as shown in Table 5.3.

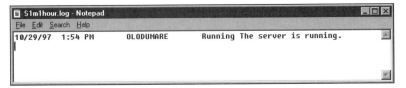

Figure 5.33   The Server Monitor log file.

five

Table 5.3   Commands for temporarily suspending the Server Monitor for maintenance.

Command	Function
admin /t	Temporarily suspends the Server Monitor.
admin /t –r	Suspends repairs but continues sending notifications.
admin /t –n	Suspends notifications but continues making any repairs.
admin /t –nr	Suspends both notifications and repairs.
admin /t –t	Resets the Server Monitor to normal mode.

Link Monitor

Exchange Server supports connections to multiple sites, to foreign systems, and to the Internet, transforming your dispersed organization into a uniform system spanning multiple locations. You must be able to monitor the status of these connections, so you can prevent potential problems and respond to problems quickly when they do occur. The *Link Monitor* lets you monitor the state of intersite connections, as well as connections to sites that do not have Microsoft messaging systems, from one management console.

The Link Monitor sends test messages, called *ping messages,* between servers and connections and alerts you if the messages take longer than expected to make the round trip. When ping messages travel between Exchange Server computers, the system attendant on each server recognizes them and replies to them. When traveling to foreign systems, ping messages are sent to nonexistent recipients so that they are returned as nondeliverable. In this way, ping messages always return to the sending server unless they are manually deleted along the way, ensuring that the round-trip time can be measured and monitored.

Use this monitor to ensure that connections are available and that messages are making the round trip between connections in an acceptable amount of time. If a connection goes down, the Link Monitor alerts you so you can fix it quickly and avoid a major problem. The information displayed by the Link Monitor can also help you diagnose the cause of a problem.

Like the Server Monitor, the Link Monitor is included with Exchange Server and is installed by default. It should be configured and started soon after installing your Exchange Server system, so you can begin monitoring connections as part of your routine maintenance chores.

Tip

It is not necessary to run the Link Monitor if your Exchange Server organization does not encompass multiple sites, connectors to foreign systems, or a connection to the Internet.

Configuring The Link Monitor

You can configure the Link Monitor according to your organization's specific needs. Setting up the monitor involves creating log files, programming polling intervals, configuring bounce times, setting up notifications, and indicating which servers and foreign systems to monitor.

Polling intervals indicate how often ping messages are sent to check connections. In normal sites, ping messages return within the specified bounce time. Critical sites do not meet the criteria defined for a normal site and so are in a warning or alert state, so the default polling interval for a critical site should be shorter than that for a normal site. Polling intervals for both normal and critical sites can be set to any duration.

Follow these steps to set up a new Link Monitor:

1. Select the site where you want to configure the Link Monitor in the Administrator window.

2. Select Configuration.

3. Select Monitors.

4. Select New Other from the File menu.

5. Select Link Monitor.

6. Click on the General tab (see Figure 5.34).

7. In the Directory Name box, type a name that identifies the Link Monitor to the system.

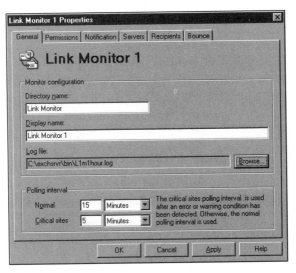

Figure 5.34   Setting up a Link Monitor.

five

8. In the Display Name box, type the name of the Link Monitor that is displayed in the Administrator window.

9. Click on Browse.

10. Type or select the directory and file name for the log file and click on Save; to make the log file easy to find on the network, specify the path using the UNC.

11. In the Normal box, enter a number indicating the polling interval for ping messages on normal sites, and select Seconds, Minutes, or Hours; the default is 15 minutes.

12. In the Critical Sites box, enter a number indicating the polling interval for ping messages on critical sites, and select Seconds, Minutes, or Hours; the default is five minutes.

13. Click on OK.

Setting Bounce Durations. The bounce duration is the longest acceptable time for a ping message to make the round trip between the Link Monitor's server and a server in a remote site or in a foreign system. This value is usually determined by tests you previously performed. You set both warning and alert bounce durations for each Link Monitor. The alert bounce duration indicates a more serious problem than a warning bounce duration. Since the Link Monitor uses one set of bounce durations for all monitored connections, you should create multiple Link Monitors if you want to assign different bounce durations to different connections.

 Tip

Be careful when configuring bounce durations—if they are set too low, fully operational connections can go into warning or alert states.

Follow these steps to set bounce durations:

1. Click on the Configuration button in the Administrator window.

2. Select Monitors.

3. Double-click on the Link Monitor you're configuring.

4. Click on the Bounce tab (see Figure 5.35).

5. In the Enter Warning State After box, enter a number that indicates the warning bounce duration, and select Seconds, Minutes, or Hours; the default is 30 minutes.

6. In the Enter Alert State After box, enter a number that indicates the alert bounce duration, and select Seconds, Minutes, or Hours; the default is 60 minutes.

7. Click on OK.

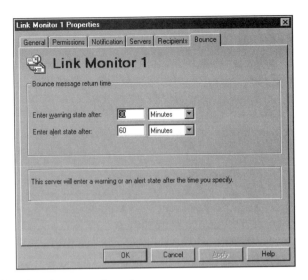

Figure 5.35   Configuring bounce durations.

Setting Notifications. Notifications indicate how the Link Monitor notifies administrators and support personnel of a connection's warning or alert state. Notifications are also sent when connections are restored. As with the Server Monitor, notifications can be delivered as notification applications, mail messages, or network alerts. You can also set an escalation path, or a prioritized list of people to notify, by configuring the Notification property page separately for each person to notify.

To set notifications for the Link Monitor, follow these steps:

1. Click on the Configuration button in the Administrator window.

2. Select Monitors.

3. Double-click on the Link Monitor you're configuring.

4. Click on the Notification tab.

See "Setting Notifications" under the "Server Monitor" section previously in this chapter to review the process for configuring notifications.

Setting Site Connections To Monitor. You must indicate which Exchange Server computers should receive ping messages from the Link Monitor. All servers specified must be in your organization, but they can be in different sites. Specifying a server in a different site than the one where the Link Monitor is configured tests the connection between the sites.

Follow these steps to set monitored servers:

1. Click on the Configuration button in the Administrator window.

2. Select Monitors.

3. Double-click on the Link Monitor you're configuring.

4. Select the Servers tab.

5. Select the server you want to monitor in the Servers box.

6. Click on Add to add the selected server to the list of monitored servers.

7. Repeat steps 5 through 6 for each additional server to monitor.

8. Click on OK when you're finished.

Setting Foreign System Connections To Monitor. You can also configure the Link Monitor to check connections to foreign systems or the Internet. The Link Monitor sends a ping message to a nonexistent recipient on the foreign system and determines whether the connection is working based on whether an NDR is returned. (If you specify an existing recipient, you will not receive an NDR, so you will not know if the connection is working.)

When the Link Monitor receives a reply to the ping message from a foreign system, it does not read the contents of the message, but instead looks for the subject of the original message. You must specify how you expect the subject of the original message to be returned. For example, if you know that the foreign system has an automatic reply program and that the program puts the original subject text in the reply subject field, choose the Message Subject Returned From option; this option saves time because the message body does not need to be opened. If you do not know how the system will return the subject, choose the Message Subject Or Body Returned From option.

Follow these steps to set up monitoring of a connection to a foreign system:

1. Create a custom recipient for an invalid recipient on the foreign system you want to monitor.

2. Use the custom recipient's Advanced property page to hide the custom recipient from the Address Book; this prevents users from accidentally sending messages to that address.

3. Click on the Configuration button in the Administrator window.

4. Select Monitors.

5. Double-click on the Link Monitor you're configuring.

6. Click on the Recipients tab (see Figure 5.36).

7. Click on Modify under either the Message Subject Returned From or Message Subject Or Body Returned From option.

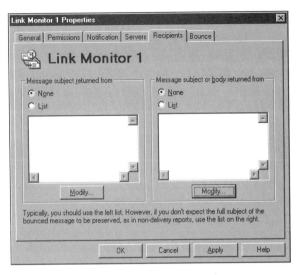

Figure 5.36   Setting up monitoring of connections to foreign systems.

8. Type or select the name of the invalid custom recipient you created, click on Add, and click on OK.

9. Click on OK.

Starting The Link Monitor

You must start the Link Monitor to begin monitoring connections in your Exchange Server organization. Follow these steps:

1. Click on the Configuration button in the Administrator window.

2. Select Monitors.

3. Select the Link Monitor you want to start.

4. Choose Start Monitor from the Tools menu.

5. Type the name or browse to the server to which you want to connect.

6. Click on OK.

You can also set the Link Monitor to start automatically whenever you start the Administrator program, so you do not have to start each monitor manually. Follow these steps:

1. Select Settings from the Start menu.

2. Select Taskbar.

3. Select the Start Menu Items tab.

4. Click on Add.

Link Monitor Permissions

As with the Server Monitor, you can set permissions for specific Windows NT user accounts to modify the Link Monitor. This allows administrators of different sites or servers to control the Link Monitors for their areas of the system.

5. Click on Browse.

6. Locate the Exchange Server Admin.exe program and double-click on the program icon; this program is generally located in the \Exchsrvr\bin subdirectory.

7. In the Command Line box, add the /m option with the site name, monitor name, and server name in the following format: **[path]\admin.exe /m[site name]\ [monitor name]\[server name]**. To start multiple monitors, add additional entries in this format: **[path]\admin.exe /m[site name]\[monitor name]\[server name] /m[monitor name]\[server name] /m[monitor name]\[server name]**.

8. Click on Next.

9. Double-click on the StartUp folder.

10. Type the name that you want to see on the StartUp menu.

11. Click on Finish.

12. In the Taskbar Properties window, click on OK.

The Link Monitor Display

After you start the Link Monitor, the Link Monitor display opens, showing the status of all monitored connections in one window, so you can quickly determine which connections are working properly and where there are connection problems (see Figure 5.37). Check the Link Monitor display first when you become aware of a connection problem to find out how many connections are affected by the problem.

Each line in the display represents one monitored connection. Sort these entries using the column-heading buttons or change the widths of the columns to make the display easier to read. For example, clicking on the column-heading button over the symbols sorts the display by status, grouping problem connections together. The display also tells you the name of the server or connection being monitored, the time the last ping message was sent, the time the status of a connection last changed, and the round-trip time of the last returned ping message. Comments based on the configured bounce durations describe the status of connections.

Monitoring Link Status. When you find a problem connection in the Link Monitor display, you can examine details about the connection to determine its status. The Link

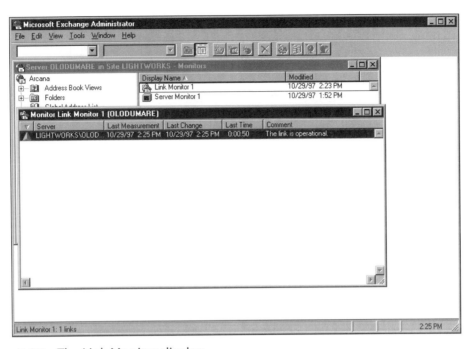

Figure 5.37   The Link Monitor display.

Monitor must have been running for at least the time of the specified bounce durations before link status can be checked. The link status provides information about the last ping message sent, along with details about the time the message spent between key points in the path. Ping messages that have been sent but have not yet returned appear in the Pending Request box.

Follow these steps to monitor the status of an individual link:

1. Double-click on the monitored connection you want to check in the Link Monitor display.

2. Click on the General tab (see Figure 5.38).

3. Click on OK when you've finished.

Monitoring The Notification Status. If the delayed return of a ping message exceeds the bounce durations you set, the Link Monitor begins notifying people of the problem. You can view the status of notifications sent in response to alerts, including current outstanding notifications. Follow these steps to view the status of link notifications:

1. Double-click on the connection you want to check in the Link Monitor display.

2. Select the Notification tab.

3. Click on OK when you've finished.

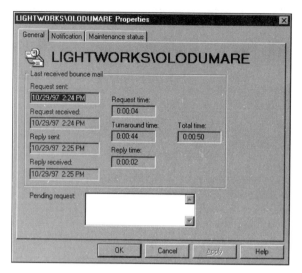

Figure 5.38 Viewing details about an individual connection.

This page is not updated in real time, so close and reopen the page to see the current notification status.

Monitoring The Maintenance Status. The maintenance status shows the current condition of maintenance notifications and repairs, such as the time of the last modification, the name of the person who made the modification, and whether notifications and repairs are suspended during maintenance of the destination server. Follow these steps to view the maintenance status of links:

1. Double-click on the connection you want to monitor in the Link Monitor display.

2. Select the Maintenance Status tab.

3. Click on OK when you've finished.

The Link Monitor Log

The Link Monitor keeps a log of recent connection problems, including the dates and times when connections started, slowed, or stopped, as well as all the information shown by the Link Monitor display. The file name for the log is displayed in the Link Monitor's General property page, which you can open by double-clicking on the Link Monitor in the Administrator window and clicking on the General tab. You can view this log with any text editor or word processor, even if the Link Monitor is not operating (see Figure 5.39). Scroll to the bottom of the page to find the most recent entries. Checking the Link Monitor log can be helpful when gathering data on a connection problem.

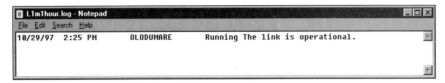

Figure 5.39   The Link Monitor log.

Stopping The Link Monitor

When taking down a server for maintenance or to perform a backup, you can temporarily stop the Link Monitor for that server. Stopping the monitor also suspends any notifications configured for that server to avoid unnecessary alerts. To suspend the Link Monitor, type one of the commands (in Table 5.4) in an automated process for scheduled maintenance or from the command line.

Troubleshooting Failed Connections

Troubleshooting failed connections is often a process of elimination, involving looking for patterns in connections that are not running as opposed to those that are. If you find that you have connection problems, keep the following points in mind to help solve the problems:

➤ If multiple connections are down, check for a common feature of the problem connections that might be causing the failures, such as a server, router, bridge, gateway, or leased line.

➤ If only one connection is down or if there is a long delay between one hop and the next on the ping message's route, a bottleneck or failing connection is indicated; try to find components in the ping message's path that might be down.

➤ If a ping message does not return, check the message queues and information stores of the sending and receiving servers, or use the message tracking log to trace the ping message and find where along its route the problem lies.

➤ Most problems that cause a Link Monitor alert also cause a large backlog of messages; check the message queue sizes along the ping message's route, looking for one or more servers that have large queues.

Table 5.4   Commands for temporarily suspending the Link Monitor for maintenance.

Command	Function
admin /t	Temporarily suspends the Link Monitor.
admin /t –r	Suspends repairs but continues sending notifications.
admin /t –n	Suspends notifications but continues making repairs.
admin /t –nr	Suspends both notifications and repairs.
admin /t –t	Resets the Link Monitor to normal mode.

five

➤ Use the Server Monitor to see if any servers along the ping message's route are down.

➤ Use the Performance Monitor to see if connectors and gateways along the ping message's route are processing mail.

Performance Monitor

The *Performance Monitor* is a graphical Windows NT Server tool that tracks statistics on more than 300 system characteristics, including processors, memory, disks, and the network. It can be configured to provide information about any Exchange Server service, such as the directory, the MTA, and the information store. This information can be accessed from any Windows NT Server on the network.

When you monitor the system using the Performance Monitor, you look at the different components of the system, such as an individual process, section of shared memory, or physical device. Each of these components can have several counters associated with it in the Performance Monitor. The Performance Monitor provides alerts to discrepancies in system performance, displays data in charts and reports, and logs a history of monitored data. When a problem occurs, use this information to determine the scope and onset of the problem, find patterns in errors, and locate failing objects in large networks.

You can use the Performance Monitor to identify trends in system performance. This lets you diagnose problems as they develop and identify the changing needs of your organization. Based on trends, you can add system resources or reconfigure the system as needed. For example, as new users are added to your system and message traffic increases, monitoring trends enables you to anticipate load imbalances and message bottlenecks. Then you can adjust routing costs and add more servers, information stores, and connectors to avoid problems.

Running The Performance Monitor

Follow these steps to start the Performance Monitor:

1. Choose Programs from the Start menu.

2. Select Administrative Tools.

3. Select Performance Monitor (see Figure 5.40).

Ideally, your monitors should run 24 hours a day, just as your system runs 24 hours a day. You can configure the Performance Monitor to start automatically by adding it to the StartUp folder, but the command-line argument is limited to one alert file that has previously been created and saved (see the "Configuring Alerts" section following this one).

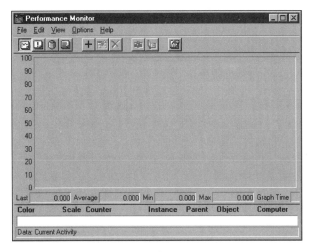

Figure 5.40   The Performance Monitor window.

Follow these steps to start the Performance Monitor automatically:

1. Select Settings from the Start menu.

2. Select Taskbar.

3. Select the Start Menu Items tab.

4. Click on Add.

5. Click on Browse.

6. Locate the Windows NT Server Performance Monitor program (Perfmon.exe), and double-click on the program icon; this program is generally located in the Winnt\System32 subdirectory.

7. In the Command Line box, add the pathname and file name for the Performance Monitor alert file using this format: **perfmon.exe [pathname]\[filename]**.

8. Click on Next.

9. Double-click on the StartUp folder.

10. Type the name that you want to see on the StartUp menu.

11. Click on Finish.

12. In the Taskbar Properties window, click on OK.

Configuring Alerts

The Performance Monitor's alert view monitors the performance of several selected counters at one time, tracks events, and notifies you of any problems, such as if a counter exceeds or falls below a certain value. Alerts also occur if a computer that has a monitored object shuts down or reconnects. Configure alerts by creating an *alert log*.

Follow these steps to open alert view and create an alert log:

1. With the Performance Monitor open, select Alert from the View menu.

2. Choose New Alert Settings from the File menu.

3. Choose Add To Alert from the Edit menu (see Figure 5.41).

4. Select the computer to monitor by clicking on the button beside the Computer box.

5. From the Object menu, select an object to monitor; the Counter and Instance windows change to display items available for that object.

6. Select one or more counters to monitor from the Counter window.

7. To find out what a selected counter measures, click on Explain; an explanation displays in the Counter Definition box at the bottom of the window.

8. Select one or more instances for the object, if appropriate, from the Instance window.

9. Select a color to be assigned to counters from the Color menu.

10. In the Alert If box, select either the Over or Under option and specify the appropriate value.

11. In the Run Program On Alert box, select either the First Time or Every Time option, and type the complete path of the program or macro you want to run if an alert occurs.

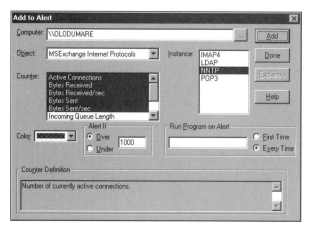

Figure 5.41   Creating an alert log.

On Site

12. Click on Add to add your selections to the alert log.

13. Repeat steps 4 through 12 for any additional objects or computers you want to monitor.

14. When you've finished, click on Done to return to the Performance Monitor window.

Save the alert log by choosing Save Alert Settings As from the File menu. Then, you can open the alert log at any time by choosing Open from the File menu and typing the file name of the settings file you saved.

After you create the alert log, the alert view window displays. This window shows current activity in the Alert Log box, the information you selected for logging in the Alert Legend box, and how often you want to monitor the system in the Alert Interval box (see Figure 5.42). If you are not in alert view, alert symbols appear in the status bar, indicating the number of alerts that occurred since you were last in alert view.

Tip

You can change alert log settings at any time by double-clicking on a counter in the Alert Legend box and editing the Add To Alert dialog box that appears.

Performance Monitor Counters

After starting the Performance Monitor, you can monitor the values of various counters to determine how the Exchange Server organization is performing or to track error conditions. Tables 5.5 through 5.11 describe the Performance Monitor counters specific

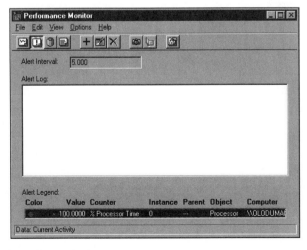

Figure 5.42   The alert view window.

to Exchange Server functions (there are many more counters available besides these—consult your Windows NT Server documentation for more information).

Table 5.5   General counters relevant to Exchange Server.

Object	Counter	Measurement	Monitoring Use
LogicalDisk	% Disk Time	Percentage of time a hard drive is writing or reading.	A sustained value over 90% indicates that the hard drive is a performance bottleneck.
Memory	Pages/Sec	Paging of memory from or to the pagefile.	A high average value indicates that the computer is low on memory.
Processor	% Processor Time	Percentage of time the processor is running non-idle threads.	An average value below 20% indicates the server is unused or services are down; an average value above 90% indicates the server is overburdened.
Process	Elapsed Time	Number of seconds a process has been running.	Provides a quick way to see if a server or service has recently been restarted.
Redirector	Bytes Total/Sec	Number of bytes per second sent and received by the network redirector.	Compare the maximum throughput of your network card to the maximum value of this counter to see if network traffic is a bottleneck.
Redirector	Network Errors/Sec	Number of unexpected errors received by the redirector.	If you suspect network problems, check if the counter is above zero, and check the event log for details on the network error.

Table 5.6   MTA-specific counters in the Performance Monitor.

Object	Counter	Measurement	Monitoring Use
MSExchange MTA	Messages/Sec	Average number of messages sent and received by the MTA each second.	Measures traffic sent to other servers.
MSExchange MTA	Work Queue Length	Number of messages in message queues awaiting delivery or processing.	Divide this value by Messages/Sec to estimate the message delay in the queue; a high number indicates a problem in performance or in transmitting to other servers.
MSExchange MTA Connections	Queue Size	Number of objects in message queues to and from each connection.	Check this counter to find blocked or backlogged message queues.

Table 5.7   Directory-specific counters in the Performance Monitor.

Object	Counter	Measurement	Monitoring Use
MSExchange DS	Pending Replication Synchronization	Synchronization requests sent by the directory that are still unanswered.	Check this counter after resynchronizing the directory; it should start high and decrease as synchronization messages arrive.
MSExchange DS	Remaining Replication Updates	Synchronization updates waiting to be applied to the directory.	When this counter and Pending Replication Synchronization counter both reach zero, directory synchronization is complete.

Table 5.8   Information store-specific counters on the Performance Monitor.

Object	Counter	Measurement	Monitoring Use
MSExchange ISPriv, MSExchange ISPub	Average Time for Delivery	Average time the last 10 messages waited in the information store queue to the MTA.	A high value indicates an MTA performance problem.
MSExchange ISPriv, MSExchange ISPub	Average Time for Local Delivery	Average time the last 10 local delivery messages waited for transport to a mailbox in the same information store.	A high value indicates a private information store performance problem.
MSExchange ISPriv, MSExchange ISPub	Logon Count	Clients logged on to the information store.	Assess public folder and mailbox usage.
MSExchange ISPriv, MSExchange ISPub	Logon Active Count	Clients logged on to the information store who initiated server activity in the last 10 minutes.	Assess public folder and mailbox activity.
MSExchange ISPriv, MSExchange ISPub	Messages Delivered/Min	Average number of messages delivered to the information store per minute by clients on the server and by the MTA.	Assess message volume.
MSExchange ISPriv, MSExchange ISPub	Message Recipients Delivered/Min	Average number of messages sent per minute divided by the number of recipients to whom they were sent.	Gives a clear picture of the actual number of deliveries.
MSExchange ISPriv, MSExchange ISPub	Messages Sent/Min	Average number of messages sent per minute from the information store to the MTA for transfer to other servers and gateways.	Assess message traffic off the home server.

five

Table 5.9 MS Mail Connector-specific counters on the Performance Monitor.

Object	Counter	Measurement	Monitoring Use
MsExchange MSMI	Messages Received	Number of messages received by Exchange Server from the MS Mail Connector.	If this number is not changing, there could be a problem with the connector or there is no mail to transfer.
MSExchange PCMTA	File Contentions/Hour	Number of file contentions per hour.	If too many file contentions occur, it indicates a file is locked open or too much traffic is going through a particular postoffice.
MSExchange PCMTA	LAN/WAN Messages Moved/Hour	MS Mail (PC) Connector MTA performance.	Investigate any strong deviance from the expected value

Table 5.10 Internet Mail Service-specific counters in the Performance Monitor.

Object	Counter	Measurement
MSExchangeIMC	Queued MTS-IN	Messages awaiting final delivery in Exchange Server.
MSExchangeIMC	Bytes Queued MTS-IN	Size of messages that have been converted from Internet mail and are awaiting final delivery in Exchange Server.
MSExchangeIMC	Messages Entering MTS-IN	Messages entering the MTS-IN folder after conversion from Internet mail format.
MSExchangeIMC	Queued MTS-OUT	Messages waiting to be converted to Internet mail format.
MSExchangeIMC	Bytes Queued MTS-OUT	Size of messages waiting to be converted to Internet mail format.
MSExchangeIMC	Messages Entering MTS-OUT	Messages entering the MTS-OUT folder for conversion to Internet mail format.
MSExchangeIMC	Messages Leaving MTS-OUT	Messages entering the outbound queue.
MSExchangeIMC	Connections Inbound	SMTP connections to the Internet Mail Service established by other SMTP hosts.
MSExchangeIMC	Connections Outbound	SMTP connections established to other SMTP hosts by the Internet Mail Service.
MSExchangeIMC	Connections Total Outbound	Number of successful SMTP connections established by the Internet Mail Service since it was started.
MSExchangeIMC	Connections Total Inbound	Number of SMTP connections accepted by the Internet Mail Service since it was started.

Continued

Table 5.10   Internet Mail Service-specific counters in the Performance Monitor (Continued).

Object	Counter	Measurement
MSExchangeIMC	Connections Total Rejected	Number of SMTP connections rejected by the Internet Mail Service since it was started.
MSExchangeIMC	Connections Total Failed	Number of failed SMTP connections attempted by the Internet Mail Service since it was started.
MSExchangeIMC	Queued Outbound	Messages from Exchange Server queued for delivery to the Internet.
MSExchangeIMC	Queued Inbound	Messages received from the Internet for Exchange Server.
MSExchangeIMC	NDRs Total Inbound	Number of NDRs generated for inbound mail.
MSExchangeIMC	NDRs Total Outbound	Number of NDRs generated for outbound mail.
MSExchangeIMC	Total Inbound Kilobytes	Total number of kilobytes transferred to Exchange Server.
MSExchangeIMC	Total Outbound Kilobytes	Total number of kilobytes transferred from Exchange Server.
MSExchangeIMC	Inbound Messages Total	Total number of Internet messages delivered to Exchange Server.
MSExchangeIMC	Outbound Messages Total	Total number of outbound messages delivered to their destinations.

Table 5.11   Lotus cc:Mail Connector-specific counters on the Performance Monitor.

Object	Counter	Measurement
MSExchange CCMC	NDRs to Microsoft Exchange	Number of NDRs submitted to Exchange Server by the connector since it was started.
MSExchange CCMC	NDRs to Lotus cc:Mail	Number of NDRs submitted to cc:Mail by the connector since it was started.
MSExchange CCMC	Messages Sent to Microsoft Exchange/Hour	Average number of messages sent per hour from cc:Mail to Exchange Server.
MSExchange CCMC	Messages Sent to Lotus cc:Mail/Hour	Average number of messages sent per hour from Exchange Server to cc:Mail.
MSExchange CCMC	Microsoft Exchange MTS-IN	Number of messages in the MTS-IN queue awaiting delivery to Exchange Server.
MSExchange CCMC	Microsoft Exchange MTS-OUT	Number of messages in the MTS-OUT queue awaiting delivery to the cc:Mail Connector information store.

Continued

five

Table 5.11   Lotus cc:Mail Connector-specific counters on the Performance Monitor (Continued).

Object	Counter	Measurement
MSExchange CCMC	Messages Sent to Microsoft Exchange	Number of messages sent to Exchange Server from cc:Mail since the connector was started.
MSExchange CCMC	Messages Sent to Lotus cc:Mail	Number of messages sent to cc:Mail from Exchange Server since the connector was started.
MSExchange CCMC	DirSync to Microsoft Exchange	Number of updated directory entries in the Global Address List since the last directory synchronization cycle.
MSExchange CCMC	DirSync to Lotus cc:Mail	Number of updated directory entries in the cc:Mail address list since the last directory synchronization cycle.

Backing Up And Restoring Servers

The ability to restore data in the event of hardware failure or software corruption is an integral part of maintaining your Exchange Server system, so Exchange Server was developed with the goal of making backing up and restoring data faster and easier. For example, Exchange Server allows for hot backup and backups while the server is still online, and it has improved backup performance. Exchange Server can back up 15GB of data per hour, compared to the 2 to 3GB/hour rate of most systems, letting you take advantage of the most advanced parallel tape drives.

Types Of Backup Routines

The Backup program supports full, differential, and incremental backups. A *full backup* (or normal backup) backs up the entire directory or information store. An *incremental backup* backs up directory or information store data that was changed since the last full or incremental backup. A *differential backup* backs up data in the information store or directory that has changed since the last full backup. Full and incremental backups also back up transaction log files, deleting those that have all transactions committed to the database; differential backups back up transaction log files, but do not delete them.

Choosing a backup routine is based on the time required to perform the backup, performance impact, the amount of data to back up, tape drive capacity, personnel resources, and the value, priority, and security of data to be saved. Most organizations use a combination of all methods, rotating full backups with differential or incremental backups.

Choosing A Backup Device

The Backup program works with any tape drive compatible with Windows NT Server. Your tape drive choice should be large and fast enough to support the amount of data you need to back up. The tape drive must be directly connected to the computer running the Backup program (although the server you are backing up can be anywhere on the network). You can provide tape drives on multiple servers to prevent backing up data across the network. When choosing which server to connect the tape drive to, take into consideration how the additional load will impact the services provided by the server.

When planning your Exchange Server organization, you should have developed a backup and disaster recovery plan to ensure the optimal performance of your system. Your backup schedule should include periodic backups of the entire file system offline, including the Windows NT Registry, to preserve server configuration changes. It should also include incremental or differential backups of the directory and information store online, using the *Backup program*, according to the backup rotation indicated by your backup plan.

The Backup Program

Exchange Server includes an enhanced version of the Windows NT Server Backup application, which combines all the standard file and directory backup functions with the capability for backing up and restoring Exchange Server directories and information stores. These backups are made while the server is online, so no downtime is necessary. The directory and information store are backed up as objects, so you do not need to know which files make up the services, only the servers and components you want to back up. (You can also perform offline backups, but this entails stopping the service you are backing up and then backing up individual databases.)

When you start the Backup program from an Exchange Server computer, you get a view of all the Exchange Server computers in your organization. Even if you are not running the Backup program from an Exchange Server computer, you only have to enter the name of a server to see this hierarchy. This allows you to back up and restore any Exchange Server computer in your organization from one location and one interface.

Backing Up Databases

Follow these steps to perform an online backup of the information store and directory:

1. Select Programs from the Start menu.

2. Select Administrative Tools.

3. Select Backup (see Figure 5.43).

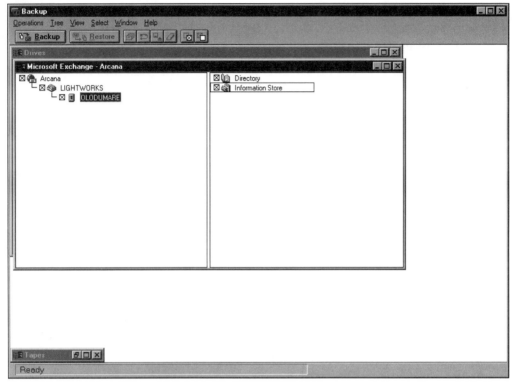

Figure 5.43   The Backup program interface.

4. If the Exchange Server organization is not displayed, choose Microsoft Exchange from the Operations menu, type the name of any Exchange Server computer, select Connect to Organization, and click on OK.

5. Select the sites you want to back up in the Backup window.

6. Select the servers in each site that you want to back up.

7. Select the components of each server that you want to back up.

8. Click on Backup to start the backup.

Tip

To automate backups, use the At.exe utility provided with Windows NT to schedule the times of automatic backups. Alternatively, you can use the Winat.exe utility, which has a graphical user interface. The Winat.exe utility is contained in the Windows NT Resource Kit. In either case you must also turn on the Schedule service using the Services utility in the Control Panel.

Archiving Backups

Documenting the backup strategy, including backup types and rotation, provides guidelines on how backups can be used to restore data. You should label all backup tapes and keep them in a secure location, preferably offsite so that important data is preserved in case of a disaster, like a fire.

The Backup program's Copy option lets you create a full backup without disturbing ongoing incremental or differential backups. Creating these *copy backups* on a regular basis and adding them to your archives provides additional protection. Consider performing copy backups once a month or after significantly changing the configuration of servers.

During backup, the Backup Status dialog box is displayed. It shows the bytes of the directory and information store components, the elapsed time of the backup, and major operations, including whether the backups completed successfully. You can stop the backup operation by clicking on Abort.

Restoring Backups

Use backups of your Exchange Server computers to restore servers or data if data is lost, hardware fails, software is corrupted, or there is a similar emergency. The last full backup is required to restore from a full backup. The last full backup and each incremental backup since then are required to restore from an incremental backup. The last full backup and the differential backup are required to restore from a differential backup. Exchange Server services are stopped while information is being restored, and users cannot use the services until the server is fully restored.

Follow these steps to restore an information store and directory to the same server from the one where they were backed up:

1. Select Programs from the Start menu.

2. Select Administrative Tools.

3. Select Backup.

4. Select the sets you want to restore from the Tapes window.

5. Select the Destination Server, or the server to which the backup will be restored.

6. Select the Private and Public check boxes.

7. Select the Erase All Existing Data check box to erase all data currently on the hard disk that pertains to the database being restored.

8. Select the Start Service After Restore check box to restart the directory and information store services after the restore has finished.

9. Select the Verify After Restore check box to verify the contents of the files restored to disk from files on tape and log any exceptions.

10. Click on Restore.

After the restore process is complete, the restore status screen displays a summary of what occurred and the amount of time it took to restore the information. You can choose either Summary Only or Full Detail from the Restore Information dialog box to see the results of the restore process. The Summary Only option logs the major operations of the restore process, such as loading a tape, starting the restore, and failing to create a file. The Full Detail option logs all information about the restore process, including the names of all files and directories that are restored. Choose the Don't Log option to skip logging the restore operations.

You might choose to restore the information store and directory to a different Exchange Server computer from the one where you backed them up. Do so as a last-resort method if you want to recover individual items, like messages or folders, without restoring over a server in use. Also do so to validate that backups are being performed correctly (see the section, "Verifying Backups," later in this chapter). Restoring to a different server requires an additional computer that has enough hard drive space to store the entire backup and that meets the hardware requirements to run an Exchange Server computer. The alternative server cannot replicate its directory with the organization.

Follow these steps to restore the information store and directory to a different server from the one where they were backed up:

1. Set up Exchange Server on the alternate server with the same organization and site name as the tape being restored, but do not add this server to an existing site.

2. Start the Backup program.

3. Select the sets you want to restore from the Tapes window.

4. Type the alternate server name for the Destination Server.

5. Select the Private and Public check boxes.

6. Select the Erase All Existing Data check box.

7. Select the Start Service After Restore check box.

8. Click on Restore.

9. After the restore process is finished, use the Administrator window to open the Advanced property page for the server.

Backing Up And Restoring Advanced Security Data

If you installed the KM server component of Exchange Server, then you should incorporate backing up of advanced security data into your backup schedule. Current security data is important for recovering lost keys or corrupted security files. Advanced security data is stored in the Kmsdata subdirectory of the Exchange Server directory. Before backing up, stop the Microsoft Key Management Server service. Then, use the Backup program to back up all files and subdirectories of the Kmsdata subdirectory. Note that you cannot automate backing up of advanced security data because you must manually stop and start the Microsoft Key Management Server service.

10. Locate DS/IS Consistency Adjustment and choose All Inconsistencies.

11. Click on Adjust.

12. To recover deleted messages, select a mailbox account to view mail on the alternate server with the restored information store, and give yourself Mailbox Owner permissions for that account.

13. Log on to the client and move the data from the mailbox to a personal folder file, which you can give to the user.

Validating Backups

The ability to recover servers and restore data when needed depends on the quality of your backups, so validating backup tapes and verifying backup procedures should be an integral part of your backup schedule. To verify backups, always use the Verify feature of the Backup program. Review the daily backup logs to check if backups are being completed as scheduled. Periodically, you should also restore the backups to ensure that information is being backed up correctly and that no information is lost.

To validate a backup, you must restore a server from tape backup to a nonproduction server and verify that you can log on to mailboxes and public folders on the restored server. Follow these steps:

1. Restore the information store and directory to an alternative server from tape backup, as described in the previous section.

2. Use the Administrator program to select a mailbox account to view mail, and give yourself Mailbox Owner permission on that account.

3. Create a client profile and log on to the mailbox.

4. Check to see that mail is in the mailbox; send yourself a message to verify delivery.

5. Use the Administrator program to view the Mailbox Resources property page on the private information store to verify the total kilobytes per user.

Managing Log Files

Two database files are associated with each Exchange Server—the information store database and the directory database. Exchange Server uses write-ahead *transaction log files* to improve server data write performance and to provide fault tolerance. Directory data and information store data are written synchronously at high speed and simultaneously to a sequential transaction log file and to a memory cache. The data in the cache is later written to the transaction log files as necessary. When a log file has 5MB of transactions, a new log file is generated. Transaction log files are named with hexadecimal serial numbers.

Tip

To find the locations of the directory and information store databases and transaction log files for a server, select the server in the Administrator window, select Properties from the File menu, and click on the Database Paths tab.

Dedicated Recovery Systems And Disaster Recovery Kits

Dedicated recovery systems and disaster recovery kits make it easier to recover from disasters and minimize recovery time for your organization. A *dedicated recovery system* is one or more Exchange Server computers that are used only when a disaster occurs. These computers should have sufficient capacity for the server file system, directory, and information store, and a storage device that is compatible with the device used for backing up the system. They are connected to the network, but are not configured as members of a site until they are needed. Using a dedicated recovery system avoids the tasks of locating the necessary server hardware and software, installing the server, and configuring the server for recovery after a server fails. Instead, you can restore the failed server's information store, directory, and configuration to the recovery server and use the recovery server to replace the failed server.

A *disaster recovery toolkit* contains all the needed materials to survive a disaster. It can include any of the following: operating system configuration sheets; EISA/Micro Channel Architecture (MCA) configuration disks; RAID configuration sheets; hardware configuration sheets; Exchange Server computer configuration sheet; Windows NT emergency repair disk; and Performance Optimizer settings sheet.

5

If a power outage or abnormal system shutdown occurs before data in the cache is written to the database, Exchange Server reconstructs the database at restart by reading from the transaction log files. If a database is corrupted, the transaction log files on the hard disk can be used to reconstruct the database from a backup (if an uninterrupted sequence of transaction log files exists from the time of the backup).

Transaction log files normally accumulate sequentially until a full or incremental backup is performed. These types of backups delete log files that have all transactions committed to the database, whereas differential backups back up the transaction log files, but leave them on the hard disk.

Diagnostics Logging

Each Exchange Server component logs *events,* or any significant occurrences in a system or application. Each event generated by Exchange Server is assigned a number from 0 (most significant) to 5 (least significant) and is logged to an event log file. This enables you to track significant events, such as a server that has a full disk or an interrupted power supply.

Because events differ considerably in significance, *diagnostics logging* is used to regulate the level of detail of information written to the event log. *Logging levels* determine which Exchange Server events are written to the event log. They represent a progression of detail from recording only highly significant events, such as an application failure, through moderately important events, such as the receipt of messages across a gateway, to events relevant only to debugging.

Circular Logging

Circular logging recycles transaction log files by overwriting them after the data they contain has been written to the database. Circular logging reduces the required disk storage space and prevents the buildup of transaction log files, but reduces the ability to recover data. Information can be restored only to the last full backup, not to the last transaction. Also, you cannot perform incremental or differential backups when using circular logging.

The circular logging feature of Exchange Server is turned on by default. If you would like to turn off circular logging to increase backup options and your ability to recover data, use the server's Advanced property page in the Administrator program. It is recommended in most cases that you turn off circular logging, but you might want to leave it on if your server has limited hard disk space or if the server contains only noncritical data, such as a news server.

Logging levels are set by category, or group of related functions, for each service and component. The Exchange Server service categories were established for their use in troubleshooting. When a service or component generates an event that has a significance number less than or equal to the logging level, the event is recorded in the event log. If the significance number is greater than the logging level, the event is ignored. As you adjust the logging levels for categories of a service, you can see the results in the event log.

You primarily use diagnostics logging to troubleshoot a problem. Normally, you should log only error events and critical error events that have a significance number of 0 by setting the diagnostics logging level to None for every category of every service on every server. Otherwise, the volume of logging information would be overwhelming and would probably degrade server performance. When problems occur, you can increase logging levels on the aspects of a service that might be related to the problem. This method allows the capturing of more detailed information that can help in diagnosing the problem. However, setting a level too high can produce an event log that is confusing and irrelevant to the investigation of the problem.

Configuring Diagnostics Logging Levels

Set the level of detail of logged events by configuring the Diagnostics Logging property page on different Exchange Server components. The logging level set for a server component applies only to that component and does not affect the levels set for other components on the same server or for like components on different servers. Diagnostics logging is available for the following services and components: the directory, directory synchronization, the information store, the Internet Mail Service, the KM Server, the MTA, the Lotus cc:Mail Connector, the MS Mail Connector, the Schedule+ Free/Busy Connector, Internet Message Access Protocol 4 (IMAP4), Network News Transport Protocol (NNTP), and Post Office Protocol 3 (POP3).

Follow these steps to open a component's Diagnostics Logging property page:

1. Select a server in the Administrator window if you're configuring diagnostics logging for a server component, or select Connections if you're configuring diagnostics logging for a connector.

2. Select the component or connector for which you want to configure diagnostics logging.

3. Select Properties from the File menu.

4. Click on the Diagnostics Logging tab.

Each component and connector has a similar Diagnostics Logging property page (with the exception of the Schedule+ Free/Busy Connector). The property page displays the application name of the service in the Services window and a list of diagnostic categories and the current logging level for each category in the Category window (see Figure 5.44).

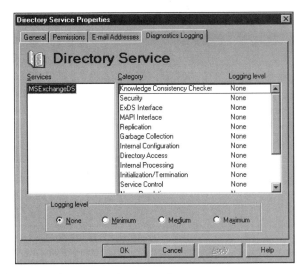

Figure 5.44   The directory's Diagnostics Logging property page.

Follow these steps to change the diagnostics logging level for a category:

1. With the Diagnostics Logging page open for the component or connector for which you're setting logging levels, select a category from the Category window.

2. Select one of the options described in Table 5.12 from the Logging Level box to set the logging level for the selected category.

3. Click on OK when you're finished.

You can also change the logging levels of several components on a single server from the server's Diagnostics Logging property page (see Figure 5.45). This has the same result as if you set levels individually by using the Diagnostics Logging property page for each

Table 5.12	Diagnostics logging levels.		
Option	**Significance Numbers**	**Events Logged**	**Troubleshooting Use**
None (default)	0	Critical events and error events	Change only if a problem occurs.
Minimum	0-1	High-level events, such as major tasks performed by the server	Used for beginning an investigation when the problem location is unknown.
Medium	0-3	Medium-level events, such as steps taken to run a task	Used when the problem has been narrowed to a particular service or group of categories.
Maximum	0-5	All events	Used when the problem has been traced to a particular category or small set of categories.

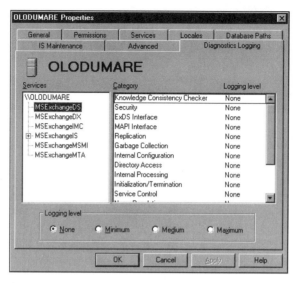

Figure 5.45   The Diagnostics Logging property page for a server.

component. Open the server's Diagnostics Logging property page by selecting the server in the Administrator window, choosing Properties from the File menu, and selecting the Diagnostics Logging tab. The logging levels of server components are displayed in a hierarchy in the server's Diagnostics Logging property page.

The following sections describe diagnostics logging operations specific to individual services or components.

MTA Diagnostics Logging

The MTA's Diagnostics Logging property page allows you to create Interoperability and Application Protocol Data Unit (APDU) text logs. Diagnostics logging levels of Medium or Maximum in the Interface and Interoperability categories trigger *Interoperability logs,* which consist of the binary contents of X.400 protocol messages transported by the MTA. These logs can be instrumental when tracking down MTA configuration problems, but are valuable only if you are familiar with ASCII translations of X.400 protocol. They can grow quickly, affecting server performance. Interoperability logs are stored in the Mtadata directory; the current log is named Ap0.log and old logs are named Ap*x*.log, with *x* increasing with the age of the log.

Setting the diagnostic logging levels of the X.400 Service and APDU categories triggers the creation of *APDU logs,* which are binary representations of communication among MTAs in different sites and between the MTA and clients within a site. Setting these categories to Minimum writes APDU logs when any of the following events occur: bad APDU transferred from another MTA, bad APDU submitted to this MTA, APDU delivery failed temporarily, and APDU delivery failed permanently. Setting these categories to Maximum writes APDU logs when any of the previous events occur, as well as when the APDU sent and APDU received events occur. APDU logs can also be helpful in solving problems with the MTA; but, like Interoperability logs, they are useful only to those who are familiar with ASCII translations of the X.400 protocol. They can also grow very quickly, affecting server performance. APDU logs are stored in the Mtadata directory, with the current log named Bf0.log and old logs named Bf*x*.log, with the *x* increasing with the age of the log.

Follow these steps to create Interoperability and APDU logs:

1. Select the server that contains the MTA for which you want to set logging levels in the Administrator window; the MTA on each server has its own diagnostics logging page, so make sure you select the correct one.

2. Double-click on Message Transfer Agent.

3. Select the Diagnostics Logging tab (see Figure 5.46).

4. To create Interoperability logs, set the Interoperability and Interface categories to either a Medium or Maximum logging level.

5. To create APDU logs, set the APDU and X.400 Service categories to either a Medium or Maximum logging level.

6. Click on OK when you've finished.

Information Store Diagnostics Logging

Events generated by the information store include establishing and maintaining connections, sending and receiving messages, applying rules set by users, and replicating public folders, among others. Unlike other components, information store events are

Figure 5.46   The MTA's Diagnostics Logging property page.

categorized first by the subcomponent that generated the event, and then they are divided into category groups, which are further divided into categories of events. The application name of the subcomponent that generated the event is listed as the source of the event in the event log.

You can use the Diagnostics Logging property page of either the public information store or the private information store to set logging levels for any subcomponent of the information store on that server. These levels are set by category, just like for other services, but the categories are used only to group events and are not written to the event log. Event log entries include the subcomponents and category groups instead.

When the information store generates critical events, they are always written to the event log, regardless of the set logging levels for any category. The categories for critical events for the information store do not appear on the Diagnostics Logging property page, but they do appear as the following categories in the Event Viewer: Performance, Recovery, DS/IS Consistency, and None.

Follow these steps to set logging levels for the public or private information store:

1. Select the server that contains the information store where you want to set logging levels in the Administrator window.

2. Select Private Information Store or Public Information Store.

3. Select Properties from the File menu.

4. Click on the Diagnostics Logging tab (see Figure 5.47).

5. Double-click on a subcomponent.

6. Select a category group.

7. Select a category.

8. Select a logging level.

9. Click on OK when you've finished.

Categories for the information store diagnostics logging are very specific. Therefore, getting the information you need to have to solve a problem with the information store could be as easy as increasing the level on just one category. For example, you want to use diagnostics logging to track down a problem with public folder replication. This could involve increasing the logging level of the Replication State Update category to Minimum to log events when replication configurations are added or deleted, increasing the logging level of the Incoming Messages and Outgoing Messages categories to Maximum to log all replication messages sent to or received by public folders, or both. Combining the information from the event log with the message tracking log, Link

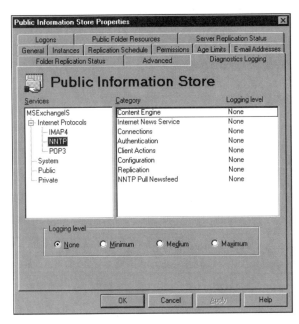

Figure 5.47   The public information store's Diagnostics Logging property page.

Monitor logs, and MTA logs can help you narrow your search and diagnose problems with the information store, as well.

Internet Mail Service Diagnostics Logging

Each Internet Mail Service configured on an Exchange Server computer establishes multiple connections, and each of those connections can generate events. A trace of those events can be useful in diagnosing problems with the Internet Mail Service. Using the Internet Mail Service's Diagnostics Logging property page, you can log Simple Mail Transport Protocol (SMTP) information and create message archives, as well as change logging levels.

SMTP events are generated by Internet Mail Service connections. Increasing the logging level for the SMTP Protocol Log category triggers *SMTP protocol logs* by writing these events to text files. Each transmission message is preceded by a code, which indicates normal transmission, temporary problems, or permanent problems that require repair (for more information, see RFC 821). Each concurrent connection logs its events to a separate file, found in the path Exchsrvr\Imcdata\Log. Note that the very large log files this generates can adversely affect server performance.

Solving some problems with Internet mail might require examining the entire text of an SMTP message. Setting the logging level for the Message Archival category to Medium or Maximum triggers *message archives,* which move each message sent or received by the Internet Mail Service to the Archive directory. Inbound messages are stored in

Imcdata\In\Archive, and outbound messages are stored in Imcdata\Out\Archive. Message archives can also log a large amount of information, adversely affecting server performance.

Follow these steps to create SMTP protocol logs and message archives:

1. Choose Connections in the Administrator window.

2. Double-click on the Internet Mail Service for which you want to set logging levels.

3. Select the Diagnostics Logging tab.

4. To create SMTP protocol logs, set the SMTP Protocol Log category to one of the following levels: Minimum to write connection information; Medium to write SMTP commands and headers; or Maximum to write complete, unformatted protocol packets.

5. To create message archives, set the Message Archival category to the Medium or Maximum logging level.

6. Click on OK when you've finished.

7. After changing the logging level, stop and restart the Internet Mail Service to make the change take effect.

Microsoft Mail Connector Diagnostics Logging

Diagnostics logging levels for the MS Mail Connector are set by subcomponent, not category. Events are generated by three subcomponents of each MS Mail Connector: Microsoft Mail Interchange, Microsoft Mail (PC) Message Transfer Agent, and Microsoft Mail (AppleTalk) Message Transfer Agent. When events generated by these subcomponents are logged, the application name of the subcomponent appears as the source of the event. The event also includes the category of the subcomponent that generated the event, but these categories do not appear in the Diagnostics Logging property page.

When investigating an MS Mail problem in Exchange Server or tracing mail through the gateway, you should increase the logging levels of more than one subcomponent, as well as of the Exchange Server MTA. The logging levels for each subcomponent are set separately.

Follow these steps to change the diagnostics logging levels for the subcomponents of the MS Mail Connector:

1. Select Connections in the Administrator window.

2. Double-click on the Microsoft Mail Connector for which you want to configure diagnostics logging levels.

3. Click on the Diagnostics Logging tab (see Figure 5.48).

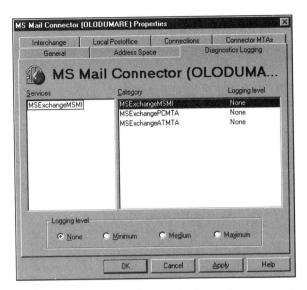

Figure 5.48   The MS Mail Connector's Diagnostics Logging property page.

4. Select one or more subcomponents.

5. Select the logging level for each subcomponent.

6. Click on OK when you've finished.

Schedule+ Free/Busy Connector Diagnostics Logging

The Schedule+ Free/Busy Connector is an extension of the MS Mail Connector and is represented as a recipient mailbox agent. This connector has six logging levels, and no categories are associated with it. Selecting a level causes events at that level and all higher levels to be written to the event log.

Follow these steps to set logging levels for the Schedule+ Free/Busy Connector:

1. Select Recipients in the Administrator window.

2. Double-click on Microsoft Schedule+ Free/Busy Connector.

3. Select the Schedule+ Free/Busy Connector Options tab (see Figure 5.49).

4. In the Logging Level box, select one of the following options: None, the default, to log only critical and error events; Minimal, the same level as None; Basic, to log the number of messages received and the number of information messages created; Extensive, to log the number of changes made and the number of users receiving messages from the connector; Verbose, the same level as Extensive; or Internal, to log all events.

5. Click on OK.

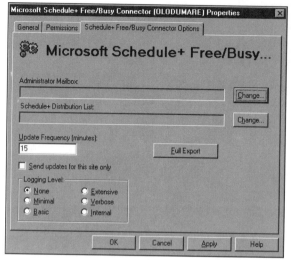

Figure 5.49   Setting logging levels for the Schedule+ Free/Busy Connector.

The Event Viewer

The Windows NT *Event Viewer* is a graphical tool for viewing logs of application, security, and system events and is used to report information on system status. These event logs are the first places to look for evidence of server problems. Use the Event Viewer to display, search, and maintain the event logs and to set alerts to notify you of problems. The service name and categories in the Diagnostics Logging property pages generally correspond to the source name in the Source box of the event log, and the categories of events correspond to the categories displayed in the Category box of the event log.

Events are classified by type in the left column of the Event Viewer. There are five types of events:

➤ An *error event* means a significant problem, such as data or function loss; it might be logged if a service was not loaded during the startup of Windows NT Server.

➤ A *warning event* is an event that is not necessarily significant, but can indicate problems in the future; a warning event might be logged when disk space is low.

➤ An *information event* is an infrequent significant event that describes successful operations of major services; an information event might be logged when an information store program loads successfully.

➤ A *success audit event* indicates an audited security access attempt that was successful; when a user logs on to the system successfully, it might be logged as a success audit event.

➤ A *failure audit event* indicates an audited security access attempt that failed; if a user tried to access a network drive unsuccessfully, it might be logged as a failure audit event.

Starting The Event Viewer

Follow these steps to start running the Event Viewer:

1. Select Programs from the Start menu.

2. Select Administrative Tools.

3. Select Event Viewer.

4. Select Application from the Log menu (see Figure 5.50).

Searching Event Logs

Once you have started the Event Viewer, you can view or search the application event log to find events generated by a specific server component, service, or connector. You can also search for events that were generated when a specific user was logged on or by a specific computer. Each line in the event log represents one event. Simply double-click on an event to display explanatory text. Follow these steps:

1. From the Event Viewer's View menu, select Find (see Figure 5.51).

2. Select one or more severity types to search for in the Types box.

3. If desired, type or select the name of the component or service that generated the event in the Source box (the Source usually matches the name in the Services column in the Diagnostics Logging property page for the component).

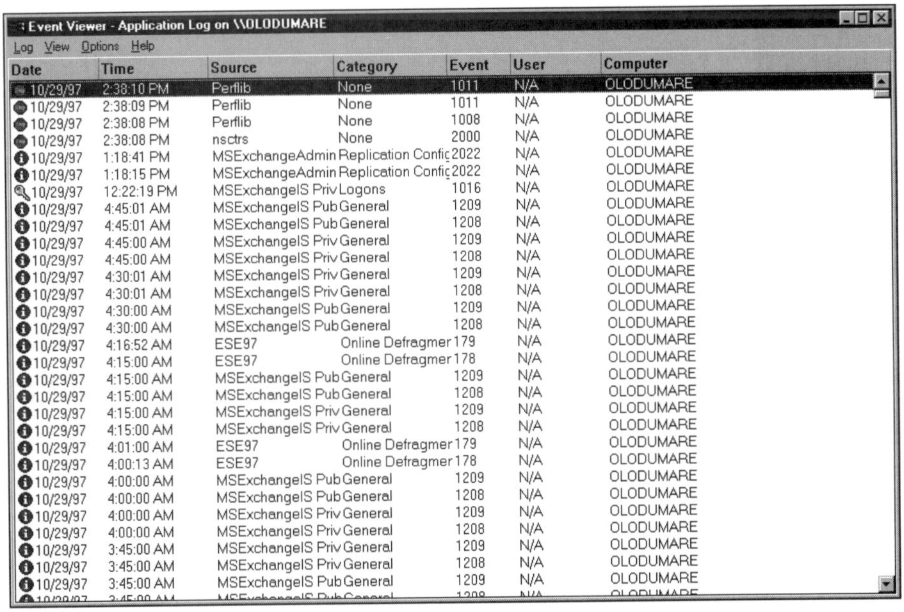

Figure 5.50   The event log as displayed in the Event Viewer.

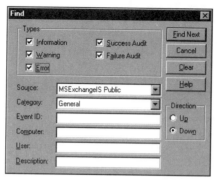

Figure 5.51   Searching the event log for a particular event category.

4. If desired, type or select the category that generated the event in the Category box (the Category generally matches the Category column in the Diagnostics Logging page for the component).

5. If desired, type the event ID number in the Event ID box.

6. If desired, type the name of the computer that generated the event in the Computer box.

7. If desired, type the name of the user who was logged on when the event occurred in the User box.

8. If desired, type a word or phrase from the event text in the Description box.

9. Select a search direction.

10. Click on Find Next to search.

Filtering Event Logs

Filtering limits the events displayed in the Event Viewer to those that meet your criteria. Unlike searching, filtering shows only those events that meet all the search criteria. Follow these steps to filter the event log:

1. From the Event Viewer's View menu, select Filter Events (see Figure 5.52).

2. Under View From, either select First Event or select Events On and enter the time from which to start viewing events.

3. In the View Through box, either select Last Event or select Events On and enter the time through which to view events.

4. Select search criteria as described in the previous section, including the Types, Source, Category, User, Computer, and Event ID, if desired.

5. Click on OK to filter events.

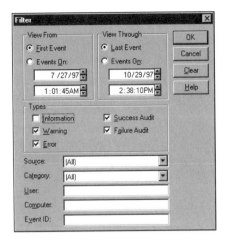

Figure 5.52   Filtering events in the event log.

Moving On

In this chapter, you learned how to administer and maintain your new Exchange Server organization, including setting up clients; setting up advanced security; maintaining the directory, MTA, and information store; monitoring the performance of the Exchange Server organization; backing up and restoring servers; and managing transaction log files and diagnostics logging. Many of these activities can be used to track down and diagnose problems with the Exchange Server system. The next chapter addresses methods for optimizing the system, including hardware, software, and topology optimization, to solve those problems, to address changing user needs, and to adapt as your organization grows.

Optimizing Exchange Server

Your Exchange Server system is not static; it is constantly growing and changing due to a large number of factors. One of the biggest factors that affects the Exchange Server system is its user community. Not only will you continue to add new users as your company grows, but you will also be moving users from server to server as their physical locations, job descriptions, and workgroups change. The needs of individual users and user groups are also changing constantly, affecting how each user connects to the Exchange Server system and implements Exchange Server services from day to day.

Because your users' needs are constantly changing, you need to make sure that the Exchange Server system is evolving to meet them. Configuration of Exchange Server's hardware resources, software resources, and topology does not stop after you finish planning and installing the new system. Instead, it is an ongoing process that you must continually reevaluate and adjust. Optimizing the Exchange Server system to meet the growing and changing needs of your users is therefore a fundamental part of administering Exchange Server.

When optimizing your Exchange Server system, you should concentrate on two main areas: server optimization and topology optimization. Optimizing your Exchange Server computers involves constantly monitoring and reevaluating the performance, hardware resources, and software resources of your servers to make sure they are keeping up with users' needs and are not causing problems that adversely affect user actions. Topology optimization includes monitoring and evaluating *network traffic* between servers and sites to ensure that message routing is performing at peak efficiency and is best serving your users' messaging needs.

Server Optimization

To provide your users with the fastest, most reliable service that Exchange Server is capable of, you should optimize your servers to take advantage of the hardware and software resources you already have. As your Exchange Server organization grows—along with increases in users, network traffic, and storage requirements—you might find it necessary to reconfigure servers or to add new hardware and software resources to continue providing the best service.

six

Ensuring that your Exchange Server computers perform reliably and at peak levels is the most important part of server optimization. Built-in tools like the Windows NT Performance Monitor and the Exchange Server Performance Optimizer make it easy to evaluate and optimize the performance of your Exchange Server computers. If your Exchange Server computers are not performing up to standards, you can also balance hardware resources through a variety of methods to increase their performance.

Monitoring Performance Trends

In Chapter 5, you learned how to use the *Performance Monitor* to monitor different components and services of the Exchange Server system and to be alerted to potential problems. You can also use the Performance Monitor to identify performance trends, which help you pin down overall server problems and keep up with the changing needs of your organization.

When you installed Exchange Server, a number of pre-configured Performance Monitor charts were installed along with it. These charts were designed to provide ongoing reports on crucial Exchange Server performance trends, including server health, system history, *message queues,* statistics, network traffic, server load, the *Internet Mail Service,* and user actions (see Figure 6.1). Simply select the report you're interested in monitoring from Microsoft Exchange in the Programs menu to open it and begin monitoring these trends in the Performance Monitor.

Table 6.1 describes each of these Performance Monitor trend analysis reports.

You can analyze these constantly updated reports of system data to identify performance trends and problem areas. For example, trend analysis can help you anticipate load imbalances and message bottlenecks. Based on these trends, you can reconfigure the server

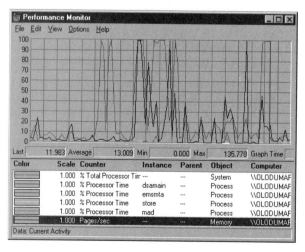

Figure 6.1   Analyzing the health of Exchange Server using a pre-configured Performance Monitor report.

Table 6.1   Pre-configured Performance Monitor reports available for analyzing the performance of Exchange Server.

Report Name	Monitored Trends
Microsoft Exchange Server Health	Total time all processors are busy, percentage of processor time used by different processes, and paging.
Microsoft Exchange Server History	Total number of users connected to the information store, number of outstanding messages to be processed by the MTA, and paging.
Microsoft Exchange Server IMS Queues	Message queues created by sending messages to and receiving messages from the Internet.
Microsoft Exchange Server IMS Statistics	Total number of messages sent to and received from the Internet by this Exchange Server computer.
Microsoft Exchange Server IMS Traffic	Hourly average of messages sent to or received from the Internet, and the current number of connections established to and received from SMTP hosts by the Internet Mail Service.
Microsoft Exchange Server Load	Load caused by messages being received and submitted, open associations to other MTAs, RPC packets being processed, browsing and reading of the Address Book, and directory replication.
Microsoft Exchange Server Queues	Total number of messages waiting in the MTA, private information store, and public information store queues.
Microsoft Exchange Server Users	Total number of users currently connected to the information store.

or add hardware or software resources as needed to keep up with the expanding and changing needs of your users. Different problems will require different solutions. It might be necessary to add more servers, information stores, or connectors based on what you find when analyzing performance trends. (See the section, "Balancing Hardware Resources," later in this chapter for solutions to common performance problems.)

The Performance Optimizer

When optimizing your Exchange Server system, you will find the Performance Optimizer to be an invaluable help. The *Performance Optimizer* is a planning and system optimization tool included with Exchange Server that helps you get the best performance from your Exchange Server computers. It analyzes the Exchange Server computer's hardware and memory resources and makes recommendations about file locations, memory uses, and other system parameters that affect performance, based on your system's unique configuration. In this way, the Performance Optimizer is an easy-to-use tool for optimizing disk access and server performance.

six

What The Performance Optimizer Does

Whenever you run the Performance Optimizer, it analyzes the Exchange Server computer's disk and memory configurations. Using this analysis, it determines the best location for the information store, directory, Message Transfer Agent (MTA), and *transaction log files*. It also recommends the amount of memory that should be dedicated to the information store and directory, based on the server's total available memory. If you accept the Performance Optimizer's recommendations, it reconfigures file locations and memory allocations for you.

The Performance Optimizer analyzes the server's hard disk configuration to determine which drives provide the best performance for different Exchange Server service data files. During the analysis process, it determines which logical drives (not physical disks) provide the fastest sequential access time and random access time. Then, the Performance Optimizer assigns the transaction log files to the drive that has the fastest sequential access time. It also places the files for the selected server type on the fastest random access drive; for example, if you are running the Performance Optimizer on a public folder server, it automatically locates the public information store on the fastest random access drive.

The Performance Optimizer also detects the amount of physical memory available in the server. It calculates the size of the directory and information store caches, based on information you provide about how the server is used. Although larger caches might provide better performance in some cases, performance depends mainly on the amount of available physical memory, so the default values for the caches are sufficient for most installations.

Note that Exchange Server uses all available RAM by default, and the size of the database cache is set automatically whenever you run the Performance Optimizer. However, setting the database cache too large can make even servers that have a lot of RAM thrash severely, while setting it too small can cause excessive input/output (I/O) operations to the database because not enough information is cached in RAM for the amount of load on the server. If you run other applications on your servers, you can use the Performance Optimizer to restrict the amount of memory used by Exchange Server.

Running The Performance Optimizer

You should run the Performance Optimizer whenever you do any of the following:

➤ Install the Exchange Server software.

➤ Change the configuration of server hardware.

➤ Change the role of a server, such as when you add or remove a connector.

➤ Move files to other physical disks.

➤ Experiment with different parameter settings.

To run the Performance Optimizer, follow these steps:

1. Select Programs from the Start menu.

2. Select Microsoft Exchange.

3. Select Microsoft Exchange Optimizer; the Performance Optimizer welcome screen appears.

4. The Performance Optimizer must stop all Exchange Server services to perform its tasks; these services will be restarted automatically at the end of the optimization process. To stop the services, click on Next, or click on Cancel to abort the process (see Figure 6.2).

5. The next screen that displays requests information about how the Exchange Server computer is used; the Performance Optimizer uses this information to optimize the expected services and load for your unique server configuration (see Figure 6.3).

Tip

You should rerun the Performance Optimizer whenever you change how you use a server, such as when you install new components or services on the server, to optimize the new server configuration.

6. Under Users On This Server, select the button by the maximum number of users you expect to be housed on the server.

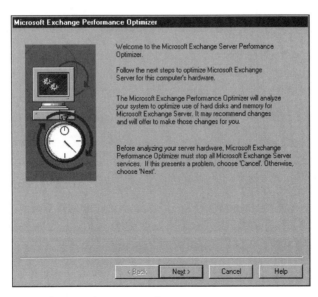

Figure 6.2   Stopping Exchange Server services.

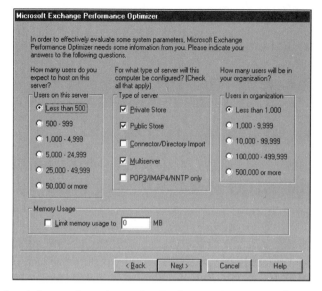

Figure 6.3   Entering information about the Exchange Server configuration.

7. Under Type of Server, select all of the following options that apply: Private Store, if the server stores user mailboxes; Public Store, if the server stores public folders; Connector/Directory Import, if the server includes a connector or imports or exports directory information; Multiserver, if the server connects to other servers and/or connectors; and POP3/IMAP4/NNTP Only, if the server hosts only Internet protocol clients (not MAPI clients).

8. Under Users In Organization, select the button by the total number of users expected to be hosted on all the Exchange Server computers in your organization.

9. Under Memory Usage, select the check box if you want to limit the amount of memory Exchange Server can access to free memory for non-Exchange Server applications that run on the same server.

10. If you selected the Memory Usage check box, enter a number that represents the total amount of memory allocated to Exchange Server in the Limit Memory Usage To box; this number should be 24 or greater.

11. Click on Next when you've finished.

12. The Performance Optimizer then analyzes the hard disk drives to determine the best locations for Exchange Server files; click on Cancel to abort this process, or click on Next when it is finished (see Figure 6.4).

13. The Performance Optimizer suggests new locations for Exchange Server files based on your hardware configuration, the hard disk analysis, and your indications of how the server will be used; the current location and suggested location of each

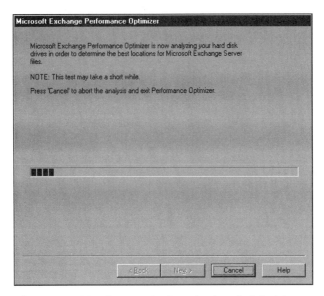

Figure 6.4   The Performance Monitor analyzing the hard disk drives.

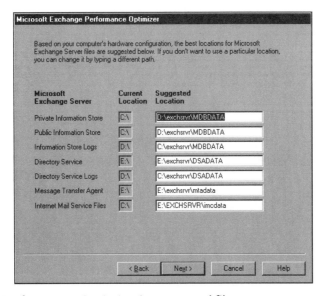

Figure 6.5   The Performance Optimizer's suggested file moves.

file are listed (see Figure 6.5). Type a new path in the Suggested Location window if you want to change the location of any file, or click on Next to accept the suggested file moves.1

14. The Performance Optimizer asks you to verify the file moves; clear the Move Files Automatically check box to leave files where they are and reject the suggested locations (see Figure 6.6).

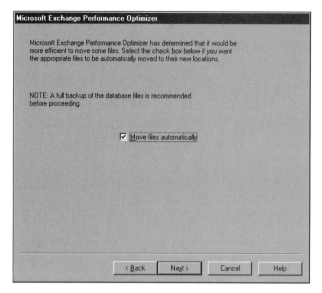

Figure 6.6   Verifying the suggested moves.

Tip

A full backup of the database files is recommended before changing file locations.

15. Click on Next to move Exchange Server files.

16. The Performance Optimizer has now optimized the configuration of your Exchange Server computer; the next screen informs you of the location of the Performance Optimizer's log file, lists the stopped Exchange Server services, and prompts you to restart these services. Select the Do Not Restart These Services check box to restart the stopped services manually at a later time, or click on Finish to restart the stopped services and save the new Exchange Server parameter settings (see Figure 6.7).

Tip

The Performance Optimizer log file records information that can be used to track changes made to your server and report problems. Log entries are appended to this file each time you run the Performance Optimizer. Make a note of the log file's location, so you can consult it if needed.

Balancing Hardware Resources

When you planned your Exchange Server organization, you determined the number of users to place on each server, based on user needs, physical locations, and groups that habitually worked together. However, none of these factors is static. Instead, how your

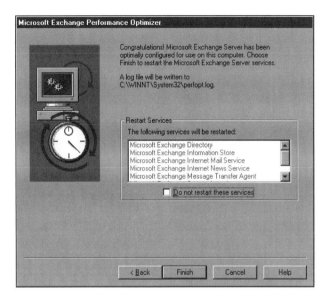

Figure 6.7   Restarting stopped Exchange Server services.

users work with Exchange Server and the number of users on the system are constantly changing. The load users place on your servers continually affects server performance in different ways.

As your company grows, more users connect to the server and the server performs more background actions. Server actions begin to overlap and compete for hardware resources. *Bottlenecks* occur when the server must wait for hardware resources, such as processors, RAM, disks, the I/O subsystem, and network hardware, to become available to complete tasks. Bottlenecks put the server under load so that all actions take longer to complete, resulting in a slower server response time to user requests. Once a server is under load and is exhibiting poor performance, it is time to make changes in the server's hardware resources.

• • *Tip* • • • •

Remember that actions that cause load are not evenly distributed over time. You might notice a burst of activity in the early morning, when users catch up on the night's mail. Conversely, you might discover lulls in activity during lunch times or on weekends. It is important that the server perform as reliably during peak times as it does at every other time.

Balancing your servers' hardware resources is an essential part of optimizing server performance. Because all of a server's hardware resources work together to accomplish user actions and background actions, it can be difficult to find where a bottleneck is located. Often, when one resource appears to be operating inefficiently, another resource is actually at fault. The Performance Monitor is a useful tool for detecting the sources of bottlenecks. See Decision Tree 6.1 for more information on how to reduce bottlenecks.

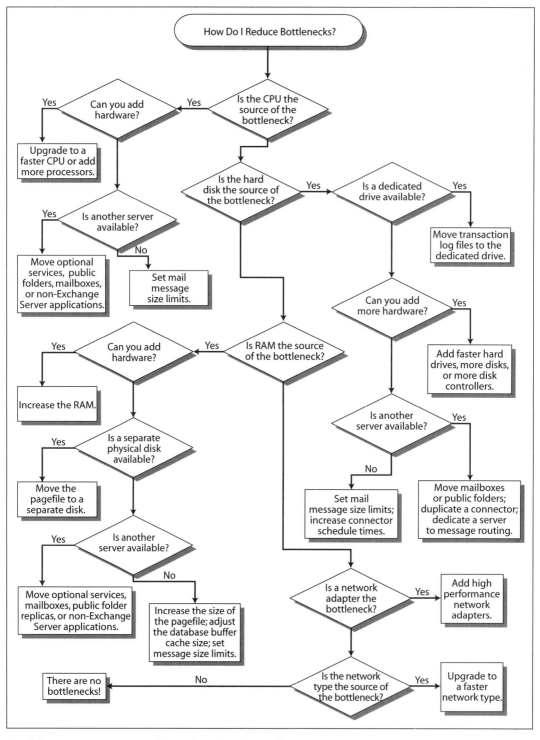

Decision Tree 6.1 How do I reduce bottlenecks?

When you balance the hardware resources on your servers, you minimize bottlenecks in each resource to ensure that they are working together reliably. You should consider the following resources when optimizing the performance of your servers: processors, disks, RAM, and network hardware.

Optimizing Processor Usage

If the server's CPU is the source of a bottleneck, you should consider upgrading to a faster processor or increasing the number of processors to raise the server's performance potential. Exchange Server's improved scalability enables the system to run on very large, multiprocessor servers. You might also consider upgrading to a CPU that has more Level 2 caching, which is faster than RAM.

You can, however, improve CPU performance without making hardware adjustments by trying one of the following solutions (refer to Chapters 4 and 5 to review how to perform many of these tasks):

➤ Optimize the way the system responds to foreground and background applications: Open the System control panel, select Tasking, and select the Foreground And Background Applications Equally Responsive check box.

➤ Move optional Exchange Server components to another Exchange Server computer that is underutilized or to a new computer.

➤ Set restrictions on the size of mail messages that users can send.

➤ Move some user mailboxes to an underutilized or new Exchange Server computer.

➤ Move public folder replicas to another Exchange Server computer.

➤ Dedicate your Exchange Server computers to Exchange Server services only by moving non-Exchange Server applications to another computer.

How Other Applications Affect Performance

Often, the performance of an Exchange Server computer is adversely affected by non-Exchange Server applications that are running on the same server. Ideally, your Exchange Server computers should be dedicated to Exchange Server services. However, if you must simultaneously provide other services on the same server, choose services that don't require the server to respond to client requests and so aren't resource-intensive. Move those resource-intensive applications—SMS Server, SQL Server, and SNA Server, to name a few—to another computer that is not running Exchange Server.

Optimizing Disk Usage

One of the most important considerations when optimizing disk usage is the location of transaction log files. Exchange Server writes changes to transaction log files sequentially. Sequential disk access is much faster than random disk access, because the disk head does not need to physically move from one disk location to another to access contiguous pieces of data. Putting the transaction log files on a dedicated physical disk drive is the best way to take advantage of this sequential disk access feature. Because there are no other sources of disk I/O on the drive, good performance for writing to disk is ensured. Using a separate disk controller from the one for the disk that contains the information store and directory databases also enhances performance.

You can also add additional hard drives, increase the speed of the hard drive, add more disks to the stripe set, or use multiple disk controllers to free up a bottleneck in the server's disks. When adding disk controllers, consider using disk controllers that cache read and write operations, providing optimal performance for Exchange Server. Many of these kinds of controllers also support hardware *disk striping*, which offers greater performance and less CPU use than Windows NT Server software striping.

If you do not have the means to upgrade disks or disk controllers, you might try one of the following strategies to adjust the available disk space (see Chapters 4 and 5 to review how to perform many of these tasks):

➤ Set restrictions on the size of mail messages that users can send.

➤ Move some user mailboxes to an underutilized or new Exchange Server computer.

➤ Regroup the mailboxes of users who habitually work together or send mail to each other on the same server to maximize the use of the *local delivery* and *single-instance message storage* features.

➤ Move the public information store or the private information store to another hard drive.

➤ Dedicate an Exchange Server computer to public folders only.

➤ Move some public folders to an underutilized or new Exchange Server computer and do not replicate them.

➤ Add another connector on a second Exchange Server computer to balance the load of connections to outside sites and systems.

➤ Increase the frequency of scheduled connection times to other sites and systems to reduce the size of outbound message queues.

➤ Dedicate one Exchange Server computer to message routing to reduce MTA traffic.

Optimizing RAM Usage

Windows NT Server uses virtual memory to move data between physical memory and a temporary paging file on the disk if Exchange Server needs more memory than is available. Most often, the more frequently accessed data is stored in physical memory, and data is moved to the pagefile when it is no longer needed. Windows NT Server then pages the data back into physical memory if it is needed again.

If the most frequently accessed data cannot fit in the available physical memory, excessive paging—or *thrashing*—occurs. Thrashing, a common cause of unacceptable performance, results when the system expends too much effort passing pages between physical memory and the pagefile. One indication of thrashing is that the CPU is underused, but the I/O subsystem is working excessively. You can try to prevent thrashing by adding more memory—not more disk space—to the server.

Tip

Check the Pages/Sec counter in the Performance Monitor to determine the amount of paging.

On Exchange Server, data is moved between the database cache in physical memory when needed and the databases on the server's disk when it is no longer needed, in a process similar to paging. Again, adding more RAM can improve performance, because more of the database can be cached in memory. You can also adjust the size of the database cache using the Performance Optimizer.

The following are some methods you can try to eliminate a memory bottleneck without adding more RAM (return to Chapters 4 and 5 to review how to do many of these tasks):

➤ Move the pagefile to a separate physical disk.

➤ Increase the size of the pagefile: Open the System control panel, click on Virtual Memory, and set a new pagefile size under Paging File Size For Selected Drive; calculate the appropriate pagefile size by adding 125MB to the amount of available RAM.

➤ Optimize Exchange Server for network applications: Open the Network control panel, select Server from the list of installed network software, click on Configure, and select the Maximize Throughput For Network Applications check box.

➤ Adjust the size of database buffer caches by typing **perfwiz** –v at the command prompt; you should reduce the buffer cache by 10 to 30 percent.

➤ Dedicate your Exchange Server computers to Exchange Server services only by moving non-Exchange Server applications to another computer.

➤ Move optional Exchange Server components to another Exchange Server computer that is underutilized or to a new computer.

➤ Set restrictions on the size of mail messages that users can send.

➤ Move some user mailboxes to an underutilized or new Exchange Server computer.

➤ Move public folder replicas to another server.

Optimizing Network Hardware Usage

Optimal network performance depends on the kinds of network adapters used and the type of network medium, such as twisted pair cable, fiber optic cable, and coaxial cable. Network adapter characteristics that most affect performance include the bus type, bus width, and throughput rates.

You should consider installing one or more high performance network adapters and multithreaded drivers in the server if the network adapter is causing a bottleneck. You can also segment the network by using multiple network adapters in a single server. If the network type is causing a performance bottleneck, try upgrading to a higher speed network type, such as fiber optic or 100MB/second Fast Ethernet. Finally, try reducing the number of protocols used to improve network performance.

Topology Optimization

Exchange Server features a customizable topology that can grow as your organization grows and can be adjusted to the changing needs of your company. Because there are no limits to how many Exchange Server computers can reside in a single site, you can tailor your site configuration to match the network environment. You can also easily add additional servers to the site as needed. For example, you can add new servers to balance the hardware resources on your existing servers. They can act as public folder servers, house new user groups or reduce the user load on existing servers, or be used as new connector points.

Adding a new server to an Exchange Server site is no longer a time-intensive process. Every computer that runs Exchange Server has the built-in capability to join a site and start communicating with other servers in the site automatically, with very little need for configuration by the administrator. The existing servers automatically detect the new server and add it to the directory and public folder replication schedule.

Optimizing the topology of your Exchange Server organization involves monitoring the network traffic between clients and servers, between servers, and between sites, and making sure that *network bandwidth* is adequate to handle the traffic. Most network traffic consists of one of two kinds of messages: mail messages sent between recipients on different servers, between recipients in different sites, and to and from *foreign systems;* and replication messages caused by updating of the directory and replicated public folders. Therefore, you should take care to optimize both of these kinds of traffic.

Reducing Pass-Through Traffic

Pass-through traffic is traffic that originates in one site and flows through a second, destined for a third site or foreign system, and it can really increase the load on the servers it passes through. Traffic flows between Exchange Server sites through the servers that are configured with any one of the available site connectors. Traffic can also flow out of a site to a foreign system through the servers that are configured with a *connector* to the foreign system. Consider using any of the following methods to reduce pass-through traffic:

- Dedicate an Exchange Server computer that has no users as a *messaging bridgehead server.*

- Have traffic flow into a site to one Exchange Server computer and out of the site from another Exchange Server computer, with neither computer hosting any users.

- Distribute the load on all servers by having traffic flow in and out of the site on all servers.

Optimizing Message Routing

Because transferring messages between servers in the same site is point-to-point, message routing within a site requires no special configuration. However, when sending messages between sites or to foreign systems by using connectors, you need to optimize message routing to reduce network traffic and provide the most efficient message delivery. *Message routing* is the process of determining all the connectors that can deliver a message and then identifying the most efficient connector to use to transfer the message.

Tip

To prevent users from sending large attachments across the network, limit the sizes of messages that can be sent.

When delivering messages to outside sites and foreign systems, connectors create paths represented by address spaces. An *address space* is a set of address components that the connector uses to identify the messages it is responsible for processing. Each connector has at least one address space and one or more connected sites associated with it, which you defined when you configured the connector.

These configurations are used to create the *Gateway Routing Table (GWART)*, a table of all possible message routes in the Exchange Server organization. The MTA compares each message recipient's *email address* type with the data in the GWART to determine which connectors have similar address spaces and so can deliver the message. The GWART is automatically replicated throughout the organization, so each server is aware of all possible message routes. The GWART is also automatically updated every time a message routing change is caused by a connector being added to or removed from the site or by a change in a connector's address space or connected sites' settings.

If the MTA determines that more than one connector can deliver a message, it implements a connector selection process to determine the most efficient connector to use. Often, the connector selection process applies only to connectors between sites; connectors to foreign systems are chosen based on their address spaces. Each time a connector meets the connector selection criteria, it is passed to the next step of the selection process. You can optimize message routing to the most efficient connectors by configuring the settings used in the connector selection process. You can also assign costs to connectors to route messages along the most efficient paths.

Configuring And Viewing The GWART

Follow these steps to set up the server responsible for creating and replicating the GWART:

1. Click on the Configuration button in the Administrator window.

2. Double-click on Site Addressing.

3. Select the General tab.

4. Select the server responsible for recalculating and replicating the GWART in the Routing Calculation Server menu (see Figure 6.8).

5. Click on OK.

Figure 6.8   Setting the routing calculation server.

Sharing An Address Space

It is possible for an Exchange Server site to share the same address space with an X.400 system. In this case, if Exchange Server receives a message from the X.400 system and cannot find the recipient, the message can be routed to the system that is sharing the address space, preventing unnecessary *non-delivery reports (NDRs)*. To set this up, click on the Configuration button in the Administrator window, double-click on Site Addressing, select the General tab, and select the Share Address Space With Other X.400 Systems check box.

Delivery Restrictions

Delivery restrictions can be set on the Dynamic RAS Connector, the Internet Mail Service, the X.400 Connector, the Lotus cc:Mail Connector, and individual mailboxes to prevent certain users from sending messages through those connectors or to those mailboxes. Use delivery restrictions to restrict connector use to a small group of users or to reduce network traffic by preventing users who habitually send large messages from sending mail to certain connectors or mailboxes in other sites.

Follow these steps to set up delivery restrictions:

1. Select the connector or mailbox object in the Administrator program window.
2. Select Properties under the File menu.
3. Select the Delivery Restrictions tab.
4. To accept messages from every user, select the All button under Accept Messages From.
5. To reject messages from every user, select the All button under Reject Messages From.
6. Select the List button under Accept Messages For or Reject Messages From to specify which individual users can or can't send messages through the connector.
7. Click on the Modify button and select names from the list to add to the Accept Messages From or Reject Messages From window (specifying even one name in the Accept Messages From list automatically rejects messages from all other recipients, and specifying even one name in the Reject Messages From list automatically accepts messages from all other recipients).
8. Click on Add.
9. Click on OK.

You can view the GWART at any time, seeing the possible routes a message might take and troubleshooting delivery problems. The GWART displays the address spaces for each connector, along with the cost of sending a message to that connector and the connectors used for each message route.

After making any routing changes, the GWART must be recalculated so that messages continue to be sent correctly. The system automatically recalculates the GWART when it detects a change that affects routing, but you can manually force recalculation at any time. You can also set up a schedule for recalculation.

Follow these steps to view and manually recalculate the GWART:

1. Click on the Configuration button in the Administrator window.

2. Double-click on Site Addressing.

3. Select the Routing tab; the large window displays the GWART (see Figure 6.9).

4. Select a connector in the GWART and click on Details to display more detailed routing information about the connector, including associated addresses and address spaces, the cost of sending a message along that route, and the path of remote connectors used to route a message along that route (see Figure 6.10).

5. Click on the Recalculate Routing button to recalculate the routing table manually.

6. To save a snapshot of the routing table, click on the Save As button.

7. Click on OK when you've finished.

Figure 6.9   Viewing the message routing table.

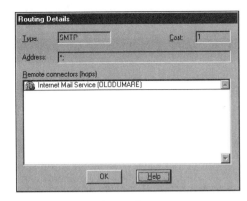

Figure 6.10 Viewing details about a selected connector.

Follow these steps to set up a schedule for recalculation of the GWART:

1. Click on the Configuration button in the Administrator window.

2. Double-click on Site Addressing.

3. Select the Routing Calculation Schedule tab (see Figure 6.11).

4. Select one of the following options: Never (to set up the GWART so it is always recalculated manually); Always (to set up automatic recalculation of the GWART); or Selected Times (and set a schedule in the schedule grid for when routing calculations are updated).

5. Click on OK.

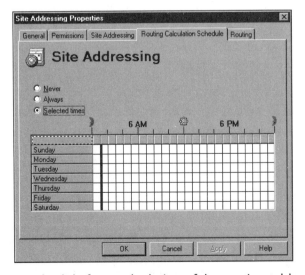

Figure 6.11 Setting a schedule for recalculation of the routing table.

Setting Message Routing Defaults

You can change the settings used in the connector selection process to optimize message transfer to the most efficient routes (see Decision Tree 6.2 for more information on how to optimize message routing). The most important of these settings is the *max open retries setting*. The max open retries setting specifies the number of times a connector can attempt to transfer a message. Connectors that have an open retry count of less than the max open retry value are chosen in the selection process (the *open retry count* is the number of times the MTA has tried to transfer a message through the connector and failed). Otherwise, connectors that have the lowest open retry counts are chosen.

You can also set the Reliable Transfer Service (RTS) values, which determine how often information is verified as it is transferred, how long to wait after an error to restart message transfer, and how often you want other systems to verify that they received your transfers. For example, you can set a checkpoint in your messages; if an error occurs, retransferring starts from the most recent checkpoint. Setting a checkpoint reduces transmission speed, so you should use low checkpoint values only on less reliable connections.

Finally, you can set *associations*, or paths that are opened to other systems. Associations are contained within a connection and are used to transfer messages to a foreign system. And you can assign transfer time-out values, or the amount of time to wait before sending an NDR when message transfer fails. The transfer timeout can be adjusted according to the priority of the message.

Follow these steps to set the max open retries setting and other site-wide message routing settings:

1. Click on the Configuration button in the Administrator window.

2. Double-click on MTA Site Configuration.

3. Select the Messaging Defaults tab.

4. Under RTS Values, enter a number in the Checkpoint Size (K) box that represents the amount of data to be transferred before inserting a checkpoint; 30 is the default, and 0 sets no checkpoint.

5. Under RTS Values, enter a number in the Recovery Timeout (Sec) box that represents the amount of time after an error occurs that the MTA waits for a reconnection before deleting checkpointed information and restarting the transfer; 60 is the default.

6. Under RTS Values, enter a number in the Window Size box that represents the number of checkpoints that can go unacknowledged before data transfer is suspended (if the checkpoint size is more than 0); the default is 5, and transfer rate increases as window size increases.

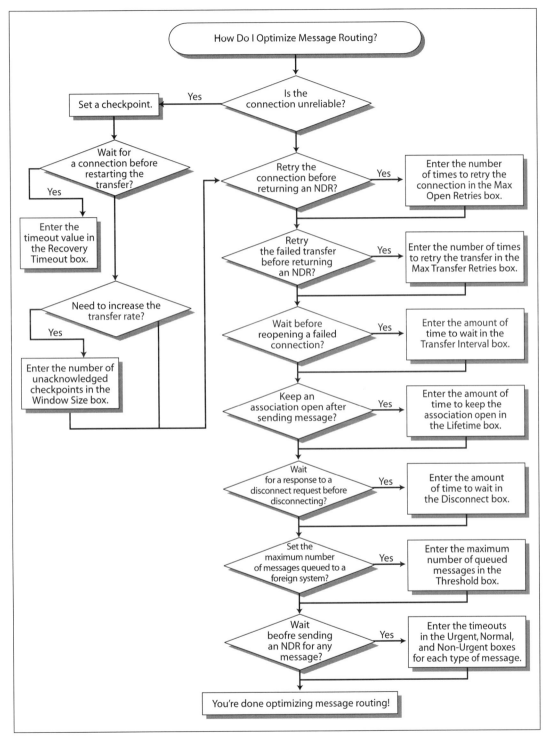

Decision Tree 6.2   How do I optimize message routing?

six

7. Under Connection Retry Values, enter a number in the Max Open Retries box that represents the maximum number of times a connection is tried; the default is 144.

8. Under Connection Retry Values, enter a number in the Max Transfer Retries box that represents the maximum number of times the system tries to transfer a message across an open connection; the default is 2.

9. Under Connection Retry Values, enter a number in the Open Interval (Sec) box that represents the amount of time to wait before trying to reopen a connection after an error; the default is 600.

10. Under Connection Retry Values, enter a number in the Transfer Interval (Sec) box that represents the amount of time to wait before trying to resend a message across an open connection after a previous attempt failed; the default is 120.

11. Under Association Parameters, enter a number in the Lifetime (Sec) box that represents the amount of time to keep an association to a remote system open after the message is sent; the default is 300.

12. Under Association Parameters, enter a number in the Disconnect (Sec) box that represents the amount of time to wait for a response to a disconnect request before closing the connection; the default is 120.

13. Under Association Parameters, enter a number in the Threshold (Msgs) box that represents the maximum number of queued messages to a foreign system (another association is opened when this number is exceeded); the default is 50.

14. Under Transfer Timeouts (Sec/K), enter a number in the Urgent box that represents the amount of time to wait before sending an NDR for an urgent message; the default is 1000.

15. Under Transfer Timeouts (Sec/K), enter a number in the Normal box that represents the transfer timeout for messages that have normal priority; the default is 2000.

16. Under Transfer Timeouts (Sec/K), enter a number in the Non-Urgent box that represents the transfer timeout for messages that have non-urgent priority; the default is 3000.

17. Click on OK when you've finished.

Tip

To return all messaging values to their original settings, click on Reset Default Values.

Choosing Local Connectors

A connector on the same server as a message's originator can send the message directly to the remote site. Otherwise, the message must be passed by the MTA to a connector on a remote server before being passed to the remote site. Therefore, using local connectors wherever possible reduces the processing power and bandwidth required to transfer the message.

Assigning Costs

Load balancing is implemented when more than one route is chosen to deliver a message. Load balancing randomly selects one of the routes to transfer the message, so that the load placed on all routes is roughly equal. You can influence which routes are used more frequently by adjusting the cost value of each route.

The *cost* is a number of 1 to 100 that represents the desirability of one route as compared to other routes, with 1 being the most desirable (least expensive) and 100 being the least desirable (most expensive). Routes that have the lowest costs are tried first. Most often, you assign costs to identify the primary and backup paths for message transfer based on the dollar cost of each network connection. For example, you can assign a leased-line connection a cost of 1, a frame-relay connection a cost of 5, and a satellite connection a cost of 50.

Connected site costs optimize message routing between Exchange Server sites. They are most often based on the expense of sending messages between two sites. For example, a site connected by a Site Connector on the same physical local area network (LAN) using *Remote Procedure Calls (RPCs)* would probably have a lower connected site cost than a site connected by an X.400 Connector using X.25. For more information on assigning connector costs, see Decision Tree 6.3.

Follow these steps to set a connector's connected site costs:

1. Select the Configuration button in the Administrator window.

2. Double-click on the connector for which you want to configure connected site costs.

3. Click on the Connected Sites tab; the large window displays all the connected sites for that connector (see Figure 6.12).

4. Select a connected site whose cost you want to change (the default cost for all connected sites is 1).

5. Click on the Edit button.

6. Enter the new cost (a number between 1 and 100) in the Cost box.

7. Click on OK twice to close both dialog boxes.

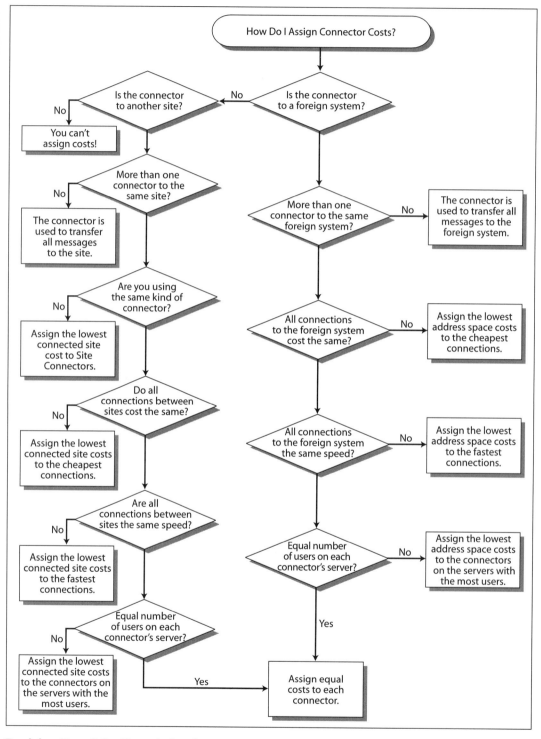

Decision Tree 6.3   How do I assign connector costs?

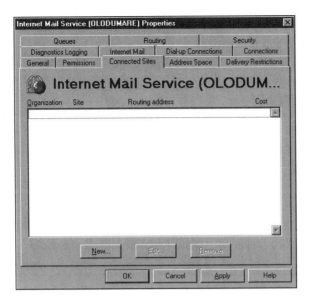

Figure 6.12 Setting connected site costs for the Internet Mail Service.

Address space costs optimize message routing between sites or to foreign systems. If more than one address space is available, then the address space that has the lowest cost is used.

Follow these steps to set a connector's address space cost:

1. Click on Configuration in the Administrator window.

2. Double-click on the connector for which you want to assign an address space cost.

3. Select the Address Space tab; the large window displays all the address spaces for that connector, along with each address space's type, scope, and cost (see Figure 6.13).

4. Select the address space for which you want to assign a cost (the default cost for all address spaces is 1).

5. Click on the Edit button.

6. Type the cost (a number between 1 and 100) in the Cost box (Figure 6.14).

7. Click on OK twice to close both dialog boxes.

Tip

You can set the maximum message size for each connector to restrict large messages from passing through certain connectors. Do so by double-clicking on the connector in the Administrator window, selecting the General tab, and entering the maximum message size in kilobytes in the Maximum (K) box.

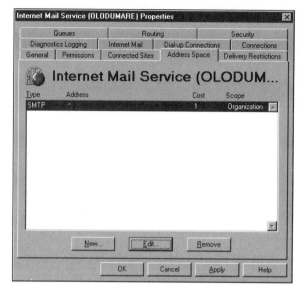

Figure 6.13 Configuring the address space cost for the Internet Mail Service.

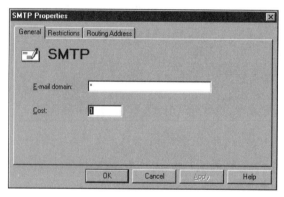

Figure 6.14 Setting the cost of an address space.

Optimizing Replication

Replication messages account for a large amount of traffic between servers and between sites. *Replication* is the process of copying new and updated information in the directory and the public information store from one server to another. All information in the directory and in replicated public folders is sent the first time that replication occurs. After that, only modifications and new entries are sent. You can optimize replication by setting up a schedule for directory and public folder replication and by choosing whether to use public folder replication or public folder affinity.

Setting The Directory Replication Schedule

You already configured *directory replication* when setting up the Exchange Server system. To optimize replication and make use of limited bandwidth, you can set a schedule for

Optimizing The Internet Mail Service

The Internet Mail Service is often a problem connector because the amount of mail sent to and received from the Internet is often higher than with other foreign systems. If you are regularly experiencing backlogs in the Internet Mail Service's message queues or interruption in mail transfer to and from the Internet, consider adding additional Internet Mail Service connectors to the site (only one Internet Mail Service connector can be installed on each Exchange Server computer). When adding additional Internet Mail Services, you may need to perform the following tasks to optimize message transfer to and from the Internet:

- Assign costs to the address spaces of each Internet Mail Service to determine which connectors are used primarily.

- Configure one Internet Mail Service to process only incoming messages and another to process only outgoing messages to balance processing of Internet mail.

- Configure each Internet Mail Service to process mail for specific domains if the amount of mail to those domains can be divided.

- Set the maximum number of inbound and outbound connections of each Internet Mail Service to limit Internet connections for each connector.

directory replication between sites. This lets you control the flow of replication messages between sites to occur during off-hours and lull times, so directory replication does not impact the transfer of mail messages. If two sites are connected by a slow connection, you can schedule replication so that the slow connection is used only occasionally, improving performance.

Tip

Be careful when setting up a directory replication schedule. If replication is set too frequently, the *directory replication bridgehead servers* won't be able to process replication messages before new updates arrive, resulting in redundant requests and increased message traffic. However, if replication is scheduled too infrequently, the directory might not reflect the latest, crucial information.

Follow these steps to set the directory replication schedule:

1. Click on the Configuration button in the Administrator window.

2. Select Directory Replication.

3. Double-click on the connector you want to use for directory replication.

4. Select the Replication Schedule tab.

5. Under Detail View, select a view for the schedule grid; you can choose to view the grid in one-hour or 15-minute increments.

6. Select one of the following options: Never (to disable directory replication); Always (to run replication at the default time of every 15 minutes); or Selected Times (and set the schedule for replication in the schedule grid).

7. Click on OK.

Configuring Public Folder Replication

You can use the Exchange Server replication engine to distribute any *public folder* throughout the sites and servers of the organization in a process called *public folder replication*. Although the list of available public folders (called the *public folder hierarchy)* is automatically replicated to every *public folder server,* the content, permissions, and design elements of a particular folder are distributed only to the servers where you have set up public folder replicas. The client must connect to a server that contains the original public folder or one of its replicas before it can display the information contained in the public folder. Exchange Server manages the distribution of the folder and ensures that any changes to the folder on one server are automatically reflected in the replicas of the folder on other servers.

Administering public folder replication includes deciding which replicas each public folder server will have, setting schedules for public folder replication, and setting up public folder affinity between sites in your organization. Use Decision Tree 6.4 to help you decide when you should replicate a public folder.

Replicating The Schedule + Free/Busy Information Folder

Although it is not required, replicating the *Schedule + Free/Busy Information public folder* within a site can help with load balancing. For example, if the site contains hundreds of users who heavily use the *group scheduling* feature, that can generate a lot of traffic on the server that houses the free/busy folder, because it is responsible for processing all updates to and requests for scheduling information. If the server that stores the free/busy folder shows a decrease in performance, you can create a replica of the folder on another server in the site. When there are two or more replicas of the folder in the site, requests and updates are directed to different replicas randomly, reducing the traffic on all the servers that house the folder.

However, to share group scheduling information among multiple sites, you must replicate all free/busy folders in all sites to the servers in each site that host the free/busy folder for that site. Alternatively, you can set up public folder affinity to enable users in other sites to connect to free/busy folders not in their sites.

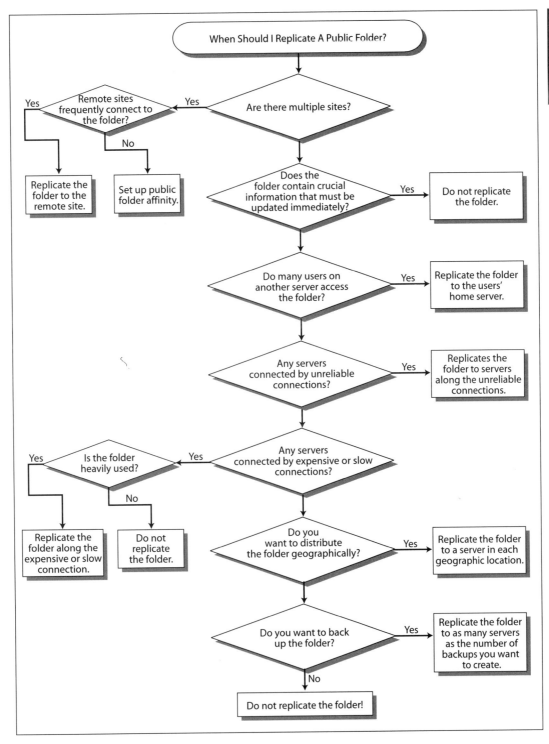

Decision Tree 6.4   When should I replicate a public folder?

Creating Public Folder Replicas. If the users of your site frequently access public folders in another site, it's a good idea to replicate the public folders to the local site. This minimizes traffic across the site connection, because users will not have to connect directly to the outside site to access the folder's contents. Replicas are also useful for distributing public folders geographically or as a means of backing up folder data. However, if a folder contains critical information that must be updated immediately as soon as new data is received, that folder should not be replicated.

When there is more than one replica of a public folder, user connections to the folder are automatically distributed across all replicas in a site. The first attempted connection is to the public folder replica on the user's *home server*, if one exists. If a connection cannot be made because a server is down or a network connection fails, then a connection to a replica on a different server in the same site is attempted. Each replica in the site is thus tried in turn. If no replicas in the site can be accessed and you have set up public folder affinity, replicas in different sites are then tried.

Tip

It's always a good idea to test a folder replica on a small scale before replicating it to a large number of servers.

Follow these steps to set up a public folder replica:

1. Click on the Servers button in the Administrator window.

2. Double-click on the server where you want to create the replica.

3. Select Public Information Store.

4. Select Properties from the File menu.

5. Select the Instances tab (see Figure 6.15).

6. In the Site menu, select the site that contains the public folder you want to replicate.

7. Select a public folder to replicate in the Public Folders window; this window lists all the public folders available within the selected site that are not replicated to the server.

8. Click on Add to create an instance of the public folder in the information store and add the folder to the list displayed in the Folders On This Information Store window.

9. Repeat steps 7 through 8 for each public folder replica you want to create on this server.

10. Click on OK.

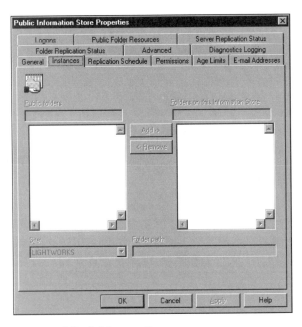

Figure 6.15   Setting up a public folder replica.

Tip

You might later choose to remove a public folder replica from the server. For example, you might decide that you no longer want users in your site to have access to the information in the public folder, or another replica of the public folder might be available on another server in the site. Select the folder to remove in the Folders On This Information Store window and click on the Remove button.

Setting A Replication Schedule. Public folder replication is the process of updating public folder replicas on other servers. The server where the original public folder is stored connects to servers that contain replicas of the folder and updates the information in those replicas according to a set schedule. The public folder server's information store sends changes to all other information stores that contain a replica of the folder via email messages. This means that replicas will not be identical at all times. As users add, edit, or delete items in the folder, the replicas will contain different information until the next replication schedule.

When setting a replication schedule, you should schedule replication messages to be sent during off-hours and lull times to minimize message traffic. You can also limit the size of replication messages so that large messages do not cause delays. If a folder contains time-critical information, you will want to set up a more frequent replication schedule to keep all replicas current. However, if a folder contains information that doesn't change very often, such as company policies, you can safely schedule less frequent replication.

Follow these steps to set up the replication schedule:

1. Double-click on Public Folders in the Administrator window.

2. Select the public folder for which you want to configure a replication schedule.

3. Select Properties from the File menu.

4. Select the Replication Schedule tab (see Figure 6.16).

5. Select either a one-hour or a 15-minute view of the schedule grid under Detail View.

6. Select one of the following options: Use Information Store Schedule (to use the schedule set in the Public Information Store Replication Schedule property page); Never (to disable public folder replication); Always (to run replication all the time at the default interval of every 15 minutes); or Selected Times (to assign specific replication times in the schedule grid).

7. Click on OK.

You can also set a replication schedule for all public folders on a public folder server. However, if you've set up a replication schedule for a particular public folder, it will override the server's schedule. Follow these steps:

1. Click on the Servers button in the Administrator window.

2. Double-click on the server for which you want to set a replication schedule.

3. Select Public Information Store.

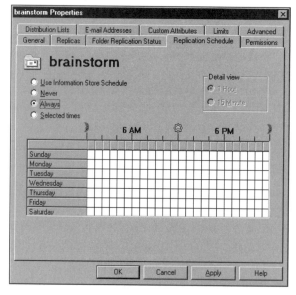

Figure 6.16   Setting the replication schedule for a single public folder.

4. Select Properties from the File menu.

5. Select the Replication Schedule tab.

6. Set the replication schedule in the same way you did for the individual folder.

7. Click on OK.

You can limit the size of replication messages by specifying a message size limit. Setting a size limit is useful if you are replicating folders across a connector or *gateway* that has a restriction on the size of messages that can flow through. It also ensures that large replication messages will not cause delays in a gateway or MTA message queue when traveling over slow links. Be aware, though, that an item in a public folder cannot be broken up into multiple replication messages, so messages larger than the set limit will not be replicated.

You can also define the replication interval if you set the replication schedule to the Always option. This changes the default value of 15 minutes to an interval of your choosing.

Follow these steps to set the size limit and replication interval:

1. Click on the Servers button in the Administrator window.

2. Double-click on the server for which you want to configure replication options.

3. Select Public Information Store.

4. Select Properties from the File menu.

5. Select the Advanced tab (see Figure 6.17).

6. In the Replicate Always Interval (Minutes) box, enter a number that represents the interval at which replication occurs; the default is 15.

7. In the Replication Message Size Limit (K) box, enter a number that represents the maximum size of replication messages in kilobytes.

8. Click on OK.

Tip

To see if replicas are up to date and view the status of public folder replication, select the public information store in the Administrator window and click on Folder Replication Status. This displays information about the replication schedule, including the last time replication occurred and the average transmission time of replication messages for each public folder server.

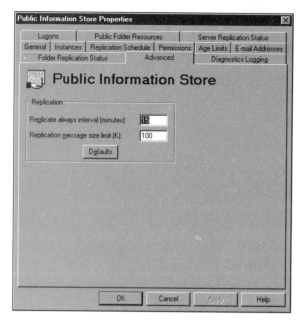

Figure 6.17   Setting properties for public folder replication.

Setting Up Public Folder Affinity. Public folder affinity enables users in one site to connect to public folders on servers in other sites without replicating the folders to the local site. Users must have network connectivity to the remote site before they can access a public folder on that site. Public folder affinity helps reduce the network traffic caused by sending replication messages across site connections and reduces the required storage space on the local site. However, if users are frequently connecting to a public folder on an outside site, creating a replica of the folder on the local site will reduce network traffic better than setting up public folder affinity.

When setting up public folder affinity, you associate a cost with each site. The cost determines the order in which the client attempts to connect to outside sites to access a public folder. For example, if the public folder has replicas in multiple outside sites, the first connection will be made to the site that has the lowest cost. Typically, sites that have higher bandwidth connections should have lower costs.

Follow these steps to set up public folder affinity:

1. Click on the Configuration button in the Administrator window.

2. Double-click on Information Store Site Configuration.

3. Select the Public Folder Affinity tab (see Figure 6.18).

4. Select the site to which you want to connect from the Sites window.

5. Click on Add to add the site to the Public Folder Affinity window.

Figure 6.18   Setting up public folder affinity.

6. Enter the cost for the site (a number from 1 to 100) in the Connected Site Cost box.

7. Click on the Set Value button to set the site cost.

8. Click on OK.

Creating Server Locations

Grouping servers within a site into *locations* can help optimize public folder replication. Servers in the same location are generally grouped together on the same *network segment*. When a user attempts to access a public folder replica, Exchange Server first searches for replicas within the user's home server's location. It only searches servers outside the location if the folder can't be found inside the location. Server locations can be used to load balance your servers or to prevent users from accessing public folders across a slow connection.

Follow these steps to set up a server location:

1. Click on the Servers button in the Administrator window.

2. Select the server you want to assign to a location.

3. Select Properties from the File menu.

4. Select the General tab.

5. Type or select the name of the location in the Server Location menu (see Figure 6.19).

6. Click on OK.

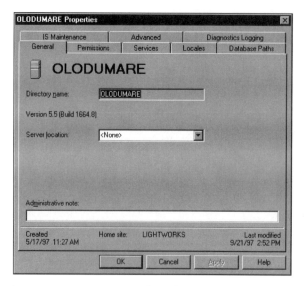

Figure 6.19   Assigning a server to a server location.

Moving On

Now that you've installed your Exchange Server system and learned how to administer and optimize it, you're ready to discover what you can do with your new system. The next few chapters will cover specific ways your business can make the most of Exchange Server, from creating virtual teams to publishing information to becoming a part of the Internet. Chapter 7 focuses on Exchange Server's capability for letting virtual workgroups work together across the organization. You'll learn how to use client applications like Outlook and Team Manager 97 for group scheduling, group tasks, sharing folders, and other ways your users can work together more efficiently on Exchange Server.

PART IV

Communication And Collaboration With Microsoft Exchange Server

Using Microsoft Client Applications

Exchange Server works with client applications to give users access to the information stored on the server and to enable users to send email across the server to other users in the organization. As the system administrator of a small- to medium-sized business, you are likely to use an Exchange Server client application to perform day-to-day computing tasks. Even if you do not use the client applications, it will benefit you to understand how they work with Exchange Server and the extent of the tasks that they can perform, so that you can more easily help the system's users when they come to you with problems. This chapter is designed to give you an understanding of how client applications work with the server and the range of communication and collaboration activities they can perform together.

This chapter provides examples of the many ways you and your users can employ Microsoft Outlook 97 as a client application to Exchange Server. *Outlook,* which ships with Exchange Server, is a full-featured information management tool that enables users to perform basic, day-to-day computing activities. Outlook makes users more productive by allowing them to organize and manage their desktop information in one place and work with it from one graphical interface. Outlook was also developed to make collaborating with others across the server easier, with its functionality for such communication and group activities as electronic mail, *group scheduling,* sharing information, and managing group tasks. Finally, Outlook integrates with other desktop programs—for example, Office applications and Microsoft Team Manager 97—to further streamline common group tasks, such as sharing files and working with a virtual team.

The scope of this chapter does not include the basic operations of Outlook and Team Manager; for more help with these, consult the help files or one of the commercially available books on these programs.

Outlook Basics

When Microsoft developed Outlook, its goal was to design an integrated desktop environment that helps users stay organized and in control of daily activities. Microsoft created Outlook to make it easy to organize personal, public, and online information all in one place, view that information in a variety of ways, and easily find information anywhere on the desktop or on Exchange Server.

How Outlook Organizes Information

Outlook is customized for each user through the *personal user profile,* a group of settings that defines how the user is set up to work with Outlook. The personal user profile enables users to send and receive email messages over the Internet or to access mailboxes on Exchange Server, for example.

A group of settings called an *information service* specifies how to send, store, and receive Outlook items and email messages and where to store Outlook information. There can be multiple information services in one user profile. For example, a personal user profile might include the Exchange Server information service for sending and receiving email messages and a Personal Address Book information service for storing personal distribution lists.

Outlook is organized around *Outlook items.* Different types of items include email messages, appointments, contacts, journal entries, tasks, and notes. To help keep items organized, they are sorted by type and separated into different folders. For example, email messages are stored together in the Inbox folder, and tasks are stored in the Tasks folder. Folders that contain Outlook items are grouped together so that you can quickly find, categorize, and archive your Outlook items.

The Outlook interface is composed of three distinct areas (see Figure 7.1):

➤ **Outlook Bar.** Located at the far left, the *Outlook Bar* contains several shortcuts, enabling favorite or frequently used folders to be opened quickly.

➤ **Folder List.** Located to the right of the Outlook Bar, the *Folder List* displays the hierarchy of folders and subfolders that can be accessed from Outlook. The Folder List is also used to navigate, open, and manipulate personal folders on the desktop, folders that contain Outlook items, and public folders stored on Exchange Server.

➤ **Information Viewer.** The *Information Viewer* is the large window at the far right that displays items or files in the open folder.

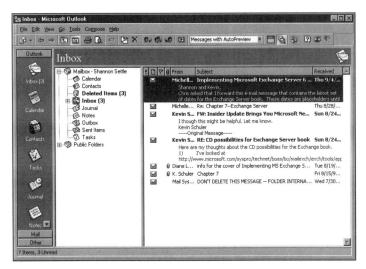

Figure 7.1   The Outlook interface.

Working With Outlook Information

Outlook provides several productivity tools, called *modules*. Each module is actually a folder containing a specific type of Outlook item. The module includes predefined forms for creating new items and updating existing ones, predefined views for organizing items, and miscellaneous tools for manipulating items.

Tip

This section briefly reviews Outlook's modules. Learning the basic operations of each module is largely intuitive and will not be covered in this chapter; if you need assistance, consult Outlook's detailed help files.

Outlook's modules include the following:

➤ **Universal Inbox:** Outlook's full-fledged electronic mail program for sending email to other Exchange Server users and to users on outside email systems, and for organizing and processing email messages.

➤ **Calendar:** Scheduling module for managing appointments, assigning time to work on tasks, and planning group meetings.

➤ **Contacts:** Outlook's address book for organizing and maintaining a detailed listing of personal and business contacts.

➤ **Tasks:** Outlook's to-do list for creating, organizing, and tracking the progress of personal and business tasks and for making task assignments to others.

seven

➤ **Journal**: A log of completed activities related to particular contacts or files that are automatically recorded by Outlook.

➤ **Notes:** Sticky notes for jotting down short reminders or copying text to be used later.

Outlook can be used for many productivity and group tasks beyond those supported by the Outlook modules. Users can create, open, work on, and otherwise manage files and folders on the desktop or on Exchange Server from the Folder List. Outlook integrates with the family of Office programs for creating and editing Office files from within Outlook and for sharing those files with others. Users can also share Outlook files and folders to communicate more effectively or to delegate tasks. Finally, Outlook is fully customizable, so that information is organized in the way that makes the most sense to each individual user.

Customizing Information In Outlook

Outlook provides many easy-to-use features for organizing Outlook items, including the following:

➤ Change views and create new views.

➤ Sort items.

➤ Group items.

➤ Filter items.

➤ Create rules to process email messages.

When you learn how to create public folders in Chapter 8, you will apply all these techniques to organizing information inside public folder applications.

Customizing Views

Outlook's *views* provide preset ways to display items contained in the same folder. Using views helps control the amount of detail shown for items and emphasizes certain details. Standard views are available for each module in the Current View menu on the toolbar. For example, an Address Cards view in the Contacts module displays names and addresses in blocks that look like paper business cards, making it convenient to find a mailing address (see Figure 7.2).

Each Outlook view is composed of a view type, fields that can be filled in with information about the items, a sort order, formatting, and other settings. The *view type* is the basic structure of a view that determines how information is arranged and formatted. The five view types include table, timeline, day/week/month, card, and icon. Customize

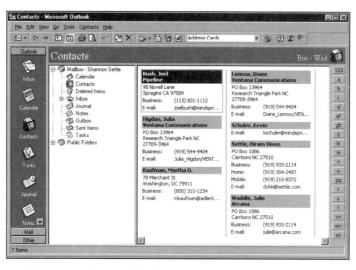

Figure 7.2   The Address Cards view for the Contacts module.

any view by selecting Format View from the View menu. Different options enable fonts, font sizes, actions allowed on different areas, dimensions, labels, and more to be changed, depending on the view type being customized. After making changes to a predefined view, save it as a new view by typing the new view name directly into the Current View menu on the toolbar and pressing Enter. To set for which folders the new view is available, click on an option under Can Be Used On.

Tip

Reset a customized view back to the standard view by choosing Define Views from the View menu; in the Views For Folder box, select the view to change back to its original settings and click on Reset.

Sorting Items

Sorting items arranges them in ascending or descending order based on some criteria. For example, email messages can be sorted by the date and time they were received, either chronologically or from the latest date and time to the earliest. Items can also be sorted on multiple fields, such as sorting email messages by the sender of the message and then by the subject of the message. Doing so sorts all items by the first field and then sorts again by the second field within the confines of the first sort.

To sort items, follow these steps:

1. In the Current View menu on the Outlook toolbar, select a table, card, or icon view type (time-based views, such as day/week/month and timeline, cannot be sorted).

2. Select Sort from the View menu (see Figure 7.3).

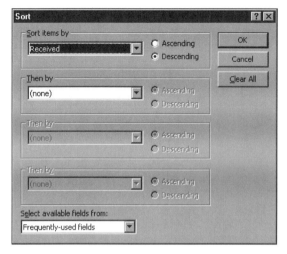

Figure 7.3   Sorting email messages by date.

3. In the Sort Items By menu, select a field to sort by; if the field isn't shown in the Sort Items By menu, choose a different field set in the Select Available Fields From menu.

4. Click on either Ascending or Descending for the sort order.

5. To sort by an additional field, select the second field in the Then By menu and choose Ascending or Descending; you can sort by up to four different fields.

6. Click on OK.

● ● ● *Tip* ● ● ● ●

To quickly sort items in a table, click on the column heading in the Information Viewer by which you want to sort. Click on the column heading again to change the order of the sort. To remove sorting, choose Sort from the View menu and click on Clear All.

Grouping Items

A group is a set of items with something in common, such as tasks that have the same due dates. Grouping items in tables and on timelines puts related items under the same heading, as with an outline. For example, group email messages by the From field to organize the messages by the person who sent them. Once items are grouped, the headings for related groups of items are shown, such as the names of the senders of email messages (see Figure 7.4). Expand or collapse headings to see the items in the group.

When items are grouped by a field that can contain more than one entry, such as the Categories field, the items might appear more than once in the table or timeline. For example, grouping by category causes an item assigned to two categories to be listed

Figure 7.4   Email messages grouped by sender in a table view.

under both category headings. Though the item is displayed in the table or timeline more than once, it still only exists as one item. Any changes made to one instance of the item are stored with all instances of the item, no matter where they might be grouped.

Tip

You can view all items (except email messages) grouped by category by choosing the By Category view from the Current View menu.

To group items, follow these steps:

1. In the Current View menu, choose a table or timeline view type (other view types cannot be grouped).

2. From the View menu, select Group By.

3. In the Group Items By menu, select a field to group items by; if the field you want isn't shown, select a different field set in the Select Available Fields From menu.

4. Click on either Ascending or Descending to set the sort order of the group headings.

5. To show the field you're grouping items by, click on the Show Field In View check box.

6. To further group items by subgroups, select a field in the Then By menu and choose Ascending or Descending; you can group by up to four fields.

7. Click on OK.

seven

Tip

● ● ● ● ● ●

To group items directly in the table, click on the Group By Box toolbar button and drag the column heading you want to group items by into the Group By Box at the top of the table. Continue dragging column headings to further group by more than one field. Use the double-arrow marker to position the column headings before or after other headings in the Group By Box.

Filtering Items

Filtering items shows only the items that meet predefined criteria. For example, email messages can be filtered to show only the messages where a manager's name appears in the From field. Filtering items does not remove all the other items in the folder; just remove the filter to see them again. When a filter is applied to a folder, Outlook's status bar displays "Filter Applied" in the lower-left corner.

To filter items or files, follow these steps:

1. Select the folder in the Folder List to which you want to apply a filter.

2. Select Filter from the View menu (see Figure 7.5).

3. Select the filter options you want to apply; filter options vary depending on the type of item.

4. To filter using additional criteria, such as a category, file size, or priority level, click on the More Choices tab and select the options you want.

5. To filter using custom fields, click on the Advanced tab and type in the new fields.

6. When you're finished selecting all fields, click on OK.

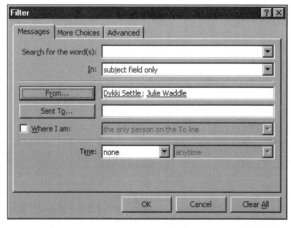

Figure 7.5   Filtering email messages by sender's name.

Tip

To remove a filter, select Filter from the View menu. In the lower-right corner, click on Clear All.

Customizing The Inbox With Rules

When using Outlook with Exchange Server, the *Inbox Assistant* can be used to create *rules* to help process and organize email messages in the Inbox. For example, a rule might automatically move all messages from a manager into a separate folder or might automatically forward all messages from a specific coworker to the rest of a team.

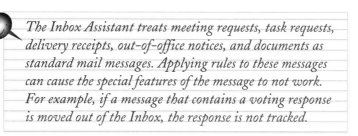

The Inbox Assistant treats meeting requests, task requests, delivery receipts, out-of-office notices, and documents as standard mail messages. Applying rules to these messages can cause the special features of the message to not work. For example, if a message that contains a voting response is moved out of the Inbox, the response is not tracked.

Follow these steps to create a new rule:

1. Select Inbox Assistant from the Tools menu (see Figure 7.6).

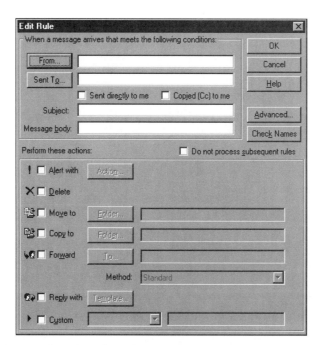

Figure 7.6   Creating a rule using the Inbox Assistant.

2. Under When A Message Arrives That Meets The Following Conditions, select the conditions the message must match for the rule to be invoked. For example, to process all messages sent by a specific person, type the sender's name in the From box.

3. To set more advanced conditions, click on the Advanced button (see Figure 7.7). For example, to process only messages received during a specific period of time, click on Advanced and set the dates in the Received box. Then click on OK.

4. Under Perform These Actions, set the action that will automatically be taken when the conditions for a rule are met. For example, to move a message to a folder, click on the Move To check box and type the name of the folder in the box.

5. Click on OK to add the new rule to the rules list of the Inbox Assistant.

6. Click on OK to close the Inbox Assistant.

After creating multiple rules, move the rules in the Inbox Assistant's window to change the order in which they are applied to messages. Do so by opening the Inbox Assistant from the Tools menu, selecting the rule to move, and clicking on Move Up or Move Down. Modify a rule by clicking on the Edit Rule button.

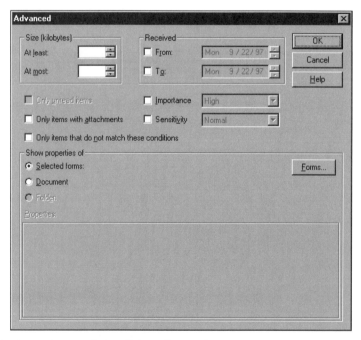

Figure 7.7 Setting advanced conditions for a rule.

Out-Of-Office Messages

If you are going to be out of the office for an extended period of time, such as for a vacation, you might find it convenient to set up a rule that automatically notifies everyone who sends you an email message that you are out of the office. To do so, use the *Out of Office Assistant,* available under the Tools menu. Click on the I Am Currently Out Of The Office button and type a short message that will be sent while you are away; for example, you might want to notify others of the date when you will be available again. Your out-of-office message will be sent automatically until you turn off the rule by reopening the Out of Office Assistant and clicking on the I Am Currently In The Office button.

Working With Outlook And Exchange Server

When Outlook is used as a stand-alone application, it is simply a useful desktop information management tool. However, when Outlook is used as a client program to access Exchange Server, its functionality greatly increases. Integrating Outlook as a client application to Exchange Server transforms Outlook from a productivity tool into a full-fledged communication and collaboration application that allows users to work with others connected to the server and with information stored on the server in a variety of ways.

Integrating Outlook with Exchange Server enables users to perform all the following important tasks:

➤ Send email to other users of Exchange Server.

➤ Track sent email messages.

➤ Plan meetings using meeting requests and shared schedules.

➤ Make and respond to task assignments and track the progress and status of those assignments.

➤ Send secure email with encryption and digital signatures.

➤ Share information in personal folders with other users.

➤ Allow others to view and manage your Outlook modules using the Delegate Access feature.

➤ Access the Exchange Server directory through the Address Book.

➤ Access information stored on Exchange Server through public folders.

➤ Create and publish public folders, electronic forms, and collaboration applications.

seven

Tip ● ● ●

To learn more about accessing the Exchange Server directory and public folders, and about publishing public folders, electronic forms, and collaboration applications, see Chapter 8.

In this section, we'll follow along as a member of a workgroup uses Outlook and Exchange Server to accomplish a wide variety of individual and group tasks to complete her part of a group project.

Jane works in the sales department of a medium-sized software company. Whenever the company develops a new product, a workgroup composed of members from different departments is formed to guide the product from initial development to the stores. Jane has been assigned to a workgroup for a new graphics program. As part of the workgroup, she works with members of the production, design, advertising, and promotion departments. A project coordinator makes sure that the entire team is working together efficiently and meeting deadlines.

Jane's duties include gathering marketing information about the product, creating fact sheets, and making sure the fact sheets are distributed to the regional sales directors across the country who will sell the product to the retail stores. Using Outlook, Jane can manage her tasks on the long-term project, coordinate with other members of the workgroup and people outside the workgroup, and share needed information with members of her team.

Creating A Personal Distribution List

Jane creates a personal distribution list, called Paintergroup, of all members of the workgroup so she can easily send messages to all members of the team. A *personal distribution list* is a collection of email addresses that is added to the Personal Address Book as one address. Since all members of the workgroup work for the company and are included in the Exchange Server directory, she can simply select their names from the Address Book for her personal distribution list.

Before creating a personal distribution list, Jane must set up a Personal Address Book in her personal user profile. Follow these steps to add a Personal Address Book to the personal user profile and create the personal distribution list:

1. Select Services from the Tools menu.

2. Click on Add.

3. In the Available Information Services box, click on Personal Address Book.

4. Click on OK.

The Address Book

> The *Address Book* includes the Global Address List, the Outlook Address Book, and the Personal Address Book. The *Global Address List* is based on the Exchange Server directory and contains all the email addresses for users, groups, and company-wide distribution lists in the organization. The *Outlook Address Book* is automatically created from all the contacts in the Contacts folder that have an entry in the email address field or fax number field; it can include people inside and outside the organization. The *Personal Address Book* is a customizable address list used to store personal distribution lists.

5. On the Personal Address Book tab, enter a name for the Personal Address Book in the Name box (see Figure 7.8).

6. In the Path box, enter the path for the Personal Address Book.

7. Click on OK twice.

8. Exit and restart Outlook.

9. Click on the Address Book button in the toolbar.

10. Click on the New Entry toolbar button.

11. Click on Personal Distribution List in the Select The Entry Type box.

12. Click on OK.

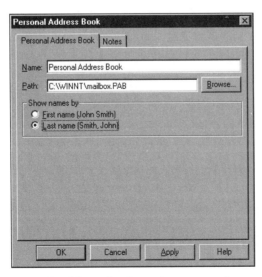

Figure 7.8 Adding a Personal Address Book to the personal user profile.

13. Type a name for the list in the Name box, such as **Paintergroup**.

14. Click on Add/Remove Members.

15. In the Show Names From The menu, select the Address Book that contains the names you want to add to the list; in this case, select the Global Address List (see Figure 7.9).

16. In the Type Name Or Select From List box, type or select each name you want to add to the personal distribution list and click on the Members button. Jane chooses all members of the workgroup to add to the list.

17. Click on OK.

18. Click on the Notes tab to enter any reminder notes about the new personal distribution list.

19. Click on OK; the personal distribution list is displayed in the Personal Address Book.

Tip

When sending an email message to a personal distribution list, particularly a large one, it's always a good idea to address the list in the Bcc box of the email message and address it to yourself in the To box. Otherwise, the message will be preceded by a list of everyone on the personal distribution list, which will annoy recipients of the message and might choke some email systems. If the Bcc box is not displayed when you are composing a message, select Bcc Field from the View menu to show it.

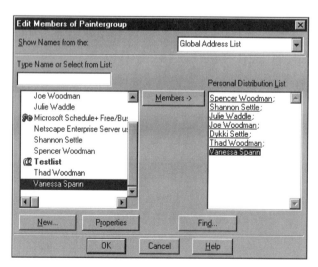

Figure 7.9   Adding names to the personal distribution list from the Global Address List.

Tracking Messages

Using the Inbox's *message tracking* features, you can keep abreast of what happens to your messages after they are sent on Exchange Server. The tracking features notify you when messages you sent are delivered or when they are read. When you're composing a message, select the Tell Me When This Message Has Been Delivered check box or the Tell Me When This Message Has Been Read check box from the Options tab. To review the tracking results, open the original message from the Sent Items folder and click on the Tracking tab.

Setting Up Security

Outlook works with Exchange Server to provide security features that protect any sensitive information sent through email from unauthorized readers. For example, as Jane is trading messages with the workgroup, she can use *advanced security* features to protect sensitive product data from being accessed. She can sign a message with a *digital signature* to ensure that the message is not altered during transit. Or she can encode the message with *encryption* to ensure that the message and its attachments are not readable by anyone other than the message's recipients. The recipients of the message must also have set up security to decode the message.

Tip

Users cannot employ Outlook's security features until the KM server has been set up and each user has been issued a temporary key, as described in Chapter 5.

Set up email security by following these steps:

1. From the Tools menu, select Options.

2. Click on the Security tab.

3. Click on Set Up Advanced Security.

4. In the Token box, type your temporary key.

5. Type your password in the Password box; passwords must be at least six characters long and are case sensitive.

6. Type your password again in the Confirm Password box.

To send a digitally signed or sealed message, click on the Digitally Sign Message toolbar button or click on the Seal Message With Encryption toolbar button after composing the message. After clicking on Send, type your security password into the Password box.

Tip

Add a digital signature to all messages you send by selecting Options on the Tools menu, clicking on the Security tab, and selecting the Add Digital Signature To Message check box. Select the Encrypt Message Contents And Attachments check box to seal all messages you send.

Working With Group Tasks

Now Jane is ready to compile a task list for the project. Using the Tasks module and Exchange Server, Jane can accept or reject task assignments, create tasks, make task assignments to others, and track the progress of assigned tasks.

Working With Task Requests

Jane receives a task assignment request from her project coordinator to create fact sheets for the product and distribute them to the sales directors. In the task request message, Jane can choose to accept, decline, or reassign the task. She accepts the request by following these steps:

1. Open the task request email message from the Inbox (see Figure 7.10).

2. Click on the Accept button to accept the task assignment, or click on the Decline button to decline the task assignment. Jane clicks on Accept.

3. To return a comment with the request response, click on Edit The Response and type the comments in the text box.

4. Click on the Send button to send the response to the task request.

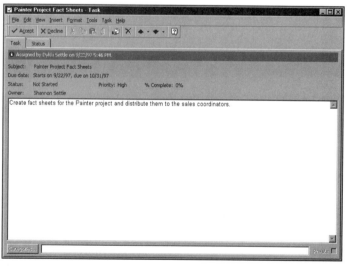

Figure 7.10 The task request message.

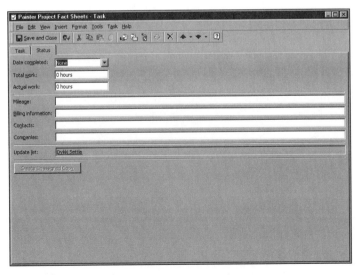

Tip

Drag a task request from the Inbox to the Tasks folder to automatically accept the request. Outlook transfers ownership of the task to you, adds the task to your task list, and sends an acceptance reply to the person who assigned the task.

Once Jane accepts the task assignment, Outlook automatically adds it to her task list. Now she can edit the task and record her progress on the task as she works. Anyone who owned the task before her, including the first person to assign the task and anyone who might have reassigned the task, can track the progress of her work. Every time she makes a change to the task, the change is automatically made to the copies of the task in their task lists. When she marks the task as completed, a status report is then sent out to anyone who requested one. Jane can view a list of all those keeping an updated copy of the assigned task by opening the task and clicking on the Status tab; the names are displayed in the Update List window (see Figure 7.11).

Tip

After accepting a task request or creating a new task and adding it to your task list, schedule time to work on the task by opening the Calendar module and dragging the task from the *TaskPad* to a block of time on the calendar.

Completing A Task Assignment

When Jane is finished with her assigned task, she marks the task complete and sends off a status report to the project coordinator. To send a status report, open the completed task and choose Send Status Report from the Tasks menu (see Figure 7.12). Outlook

Figure 7.11 Viewing the Update List of the task request.

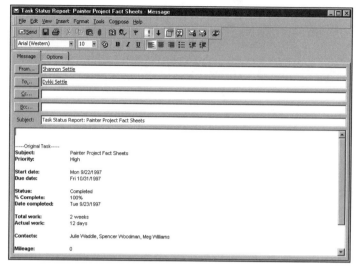

Figure 7.12 Creating a status report for a completed task assignment.

automatically creates the status report from the task and sends it in an email message to everyone on the update list. Fill out the status report with details about work on the task, such as the hours spent working on the task. Just click on Send to mail the report.

Making Task Assignments

Jane breaks the task assignment down into three separate tasks, assigning herself the task of gathering the marketing information. She delegates the rest of the work to others by making task assignments. First, she assigns a task to one of her employees to create the text for the fact sheets by following these steps:

1. Open the Tasks module.

2. Click on the New Task Request button in the toolbar (see Figure 7.13).

3. In the To box, type the name of the person you want to assign the task to, or click on the To button to select the name from the Address Book; Outlook automatically sends the task request through email to that person. Jane enters the name of the employee.

4. Type a task name in the Subject box, such as **Write text for Painter fact sheets**.

5. Select the task's due date.

6. Click on the Keep An Updated Copy Of This Task On My Task List check box to check progress on the task as the assignee works on it.

7. Click on the Send Me A Status Report When This Task Is Complete check box to receive a status report when the assignee finishes the task.

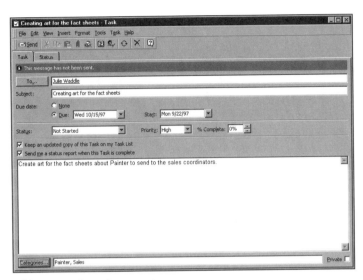

Figure 7.13 Making a task assignment.

8. In the text box, type any additional instructions or information about the task.

9. Select any other options, such as a priority, you want to give the task. Jane assigns the task a High priority and selects the Painter and Sales categories.

10. Click on the Send button; Outlook sends the task request through email.

Tip

Cancel a task request before you send it by clicking on the Cancel Assignment toolbar button.

The employee accepts the task assignment. He becomes the new owner of the task, and the task is automatically added to his task list so he can record progress on the task. Since Jane chose to keep an updated copy of the task in her task list, she can track her employee's work on the task. However, she can no longer change information related to the task; only the new owner can do that.

Jane also assigns a task to a coworker in the art department to create art for the fact sheets. The first person Jane assigns the task to is too busy and declines the task. Jane reassigns it to another member of the art department, who accepts the task, by following these steps:

1. Open the declined task request message in the Inbox (see Figure 7.14).

2. Click on Assign Task.

3. Enter a new name in the To box.

4. Click on the Send button.

On Site

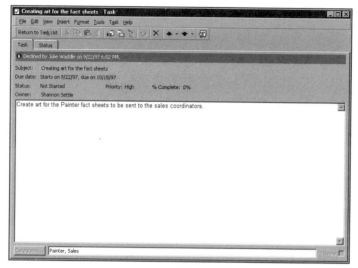

Figure 7.14   A declined task request message.

Reclaim ownership of a declined task request by opening the task request message and selecting Return To Task List from the Tasks menu.

Tracking Task Assignments

Jane tracks the progress of the tasks she assigned to her employee and to the member of the art department to make sure they are being completed as scheduled. To check the status of assigned tasks, Jane opens the Tasks module and chooses the Assignment view from the Current View menu (see Figure 7.15).

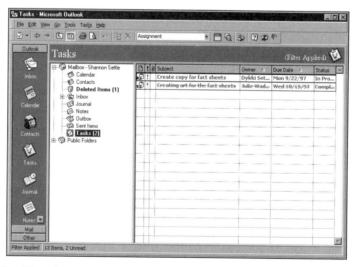

Figure 7.15   Tracking the progress on assigned tasks.

The art for the fact sheets is finished, and Jane automatically receives a status report via email. Jane updates her assigned task with the information that the art for the fact sheets is finished so the project coordinator can track the progress.

The other task is not making the progress that Jane expected. Jane sends an email to her employee to discuss the problem and receives a reply that the assignee would like to set up an appointment to discuss it.

Working With Group Scheduling

Jane sets up an appointment with her employee to discuss the problem. She creates the appointment directly from the employee's mail message by dragging the message onto the Calendar icon. Outlook's AutoCreate feature automatically fills in the subject of the appointment and includes the text of the message in the appointment's text box, so that Jane can review the reason for the appointment. Jane fills in the rest of the appointment information in the Appointment dialog box. The appointment is displayed in her calendar, along with other scheduled appointments, meetings, and events.

Planning A Group Meeting

After setting up the appointment, Jane decides to use Outlook's *Meeting Planner* tool to make the appointment a group meeting. She wants to include one of the software developers in the group meeting, so that he can answer the employee's questions directly. Follow these steps to plan a group meeting:

1. Open the scheduled appointment in the Calendar.

2. Click on the Meeting Planner tab (see Figure 7.16).

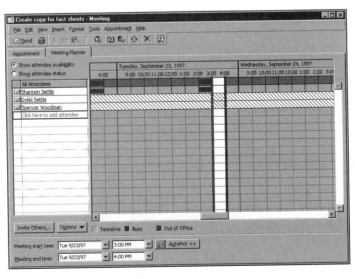

Figure 7.16   Planning a group meeting.

AutoCreate

With Outlook's *AutoCreate* feature, you can create one type of item from another by dragging an item to a folder that contains a different type of item, as Jane created an appointment from an email message. Also, use AutoCreate to create a task request for a contact, create an appointment with a contact, or record a meeting in the Journal, for example.

3. Click on Invite Others.

4. In the Type Name Or Select From List box, select the name of each person you want to invite to the meeting; Jane selects the software developer's name and her employee's name and clicks on Required for each name.

5. Select any resources, such as conference rooms and computer equipment, to reserve for the meeting and click on Resources for each resource.

6. Click on OK.

7. To automatically pick the next free time when everyone invited can attend the meeting, click on the AutoPick button.

8. After choosing a time, click on Make Meeting.

9. In the email message that opens, type a description of the meeting in the Subject box (see Figure 7.17).

10. If you did not schedule a room for the meeting, type the location in the Location box.

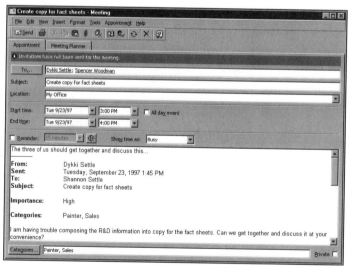

Figure 7.17   Filling out a meeting request message.

AutoPick

The *AutoPick* feature automatically chooses the next time when all invitees to a group meeting are available to attend the meeting. Outlook does this by accessing the *Schedule+ Free Busy Information public folder* on the Exchange Server system and checking the scheduling information for all invitees until a common free time is found. Outlook then suggests this time as the time for the meeting. Using Outlook's AutoPick feature in conjunction with Exchange Server's Schedule+ Free Busy Information folder saves time by automating the process of scheduling group meetings.

11. Select any additional options, such as notes, recurrences, and assigned categories.

12. Click on the Send button to send out the meeting requests.

The meeting time is then automatically blocked out in Jane's calendar. Responses to her meeting request appear as email messages in the Inbox. She tracks responses to see how many people will be attending the meeting by following these steps:

1. Open the Calendar.

2. Open the meeting.

3. Click on the Meeting Planner tab.

4. Click on Show Attendee Status (see Figure 7.18).

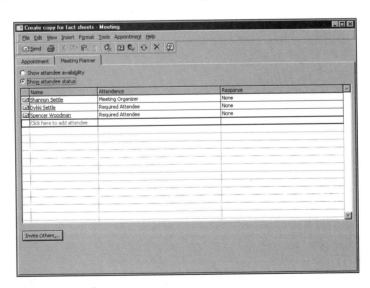

Figure 7.18   Tracking meeting responses.

Tip ● ● ●

To cancel a meeting that you've organized, open the meeting and select Cancel Meeting from the Appointment menu. The meeting time will then be removed from your Calendar and meeting cancellation notifications will be sent to all attendees.

Responding To A Meeting Request

Jane receives a meeting request from another member of the workgroup (see Figure 7.19). There has been a problem with the development of the software, which might cause delays in getting it to market. The entire group is invited to the meeting to discuss the delays. Jane accepts the meeting by clicking on Accept in the meeting request message, so it is added to her Calendar. At the meeting, the group discusses whether to push back the deadline. Jane adds notes about the meeting to the meeting request's journal entry.

Tip ● ● ●

If you drag a meeting request from your Inbox to your Calendar, the request is automatically accepted. Outlook blocks out the meeting in your Calendar and sends an acceptance message to the person who organized the meeting.

Working With Shared Private Folders

The software developer member of the team has given every member of the workgroup access to one of his private folders where he keeps the most updated information about the software product. Using Outlook on Exchange Server enables information in folders on the desktop to be shared with other users of the server. Jane checks this *shared private folder* frequently for updated system requirements and software capabilities.

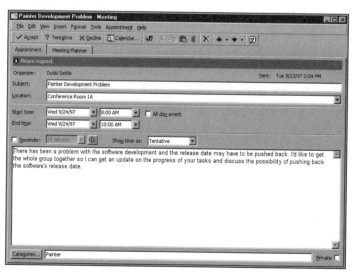

Figure 7.19   A meeting request message.

Sharing A Private Folder

To share a private folder with someone else, follow these steps:

1. On the Outlook Bar, click on the Other group.

2. Click on My Computer.

3. Locate the personal desktop folder you want to share in your Folder List and right-click on it.

4. Select Sharing from the shortcut menu.

5. Click on the Shared As button (see Figure 7.20).

6. Set the sharing options, such as the Share Name and any comments.

7. Click on the Permissions button (see Figure 7.21).

8. Click on Add.

9. In the Names box, select the group that contains the name of the person to whom you want to grant sharing permission.

10. Click on the Members button to show members of the group.

11. Select the name of the person to whom you want to grant sharing permission.

12. Click on Add; the name is added to the Add Names box.

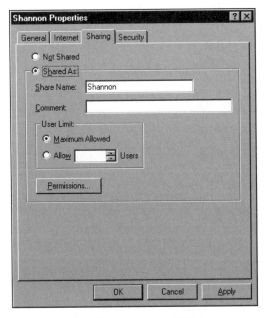

Figure 7.20   Setting sharing options for a personal folder.

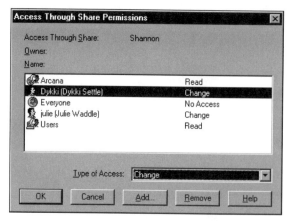

Figure 7.21   Setting permissions for a shared private folder.

13. In the Type Of Access menu, select the permission level you want to set for that person. For example, if you only want the person to be able to read items in the folder, select Read.

14. Repeat steps 9 through 13 for every person with whom you want to share the folder.

15. Click on OK until you have closed all the dialog boxes.

To remove someone's access to one of your folders, right-click on the folder and se-lect Properties. Click on the Sharing tab, click on the Permissions button, select the name of the person you want to remove in the Name box, and click on Remove.

Accessing A Shared Private Folder

Because the software developer member of the team has shared his private folder with the rest of the team, Jane can open it and view files inside it from within Outlook. Follow these steps to open a shared private folder:

1. Select Open Special Folder from the File menu.

2. Select Exchange Server Folder.

3. In the Exchange Server Folder dialog box, type the name of the owner of the folder or click on the Name button and select the owner's name from the Type Name Or Select From List box.

4. Select the type of folder to access from the Folder menu.

5. Click on OK. The folder opens in a separate window (see Figure 7.22).

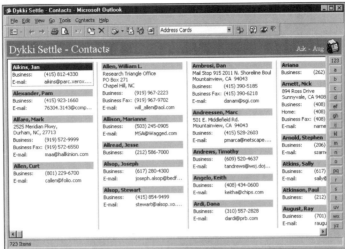

Figure 7.22   A shared private folder.

Working With Delegate Access

Another way to share information with others across the Exchange Server system is to use Outlook's *Delegate Access* feature. Jane uses Delegate Access to give permission to her assistant to access and manage her Outlook items on her behalf. Using Delegate Access, Jane's assistant can open her Outlook folders, create and manage items, and respond to requests and email for Jane.

Assigning Delegate Access

Jane sets up Delegate Access for her assistant by following these steps:

1. Choose Options from the Tools menu.

2. Click on the Delegates tab (see Figure 7.23).

3. Click on Add.

4. Type or click on the name of the person to grant delegate access to in the Type Name Or Select From List box. Jane chooses her assistant's name.

5. Click on Add.

6. Click on OK.

7. In the Delegates box, click on the name of the delegate you just added.

8. Click on Permissions.

9. Select the permission level for each Outlook folder to which you want the delegate to have access (see Table 7.1 for an explanation of permissions).

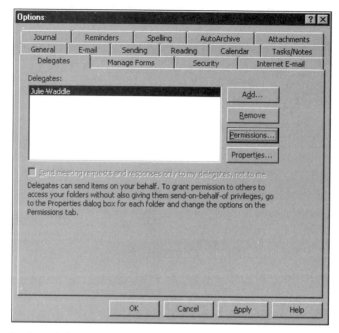

Figure 7.23 Assigning delegate access.

10. To send a message to notify the delegate of his or her delegate access status and level of permissions, select the Automatically Send A Message To Delegate Summarizing These Permissions check box.

11. Click on OK twice.

To add multiple delegates simultaneously, select multiple names in the Add Users dialog box. The permissions you select will apply to all delegates.

As with shared private folders, you determine the level of access your delegate has. Table 7.1 describes the different levels of delegate access:

Table 7.1   Levels of delegate access permissions.

Access Level	Allowed Activities
Author	Create items; read, modify, and delete own items.
Editor	Read, create, modify, and delete any item.
Reviewer	Read items only.
Custom	Perform activities you define.
None	No permission; can't open the folder.

Jane might give her assistant Author permission so that the delegate can create task requests and meeting requests directly in her Tasks and Calendar folders and then send those items on her behalf. Or Jane might give her assistant Reviewer access so that the delegate can read her email messages and reply on her behalf (but can't create new items).

Giving a person any level of delegate access means that the person also has *send-on-behalf-of permission*. The delegate can send an email message on your behalf. Messages sent this way contain both your name in the Sent on Behalf Of field and the delegate's name in the From field.

Tip

To remove sharing permissions for a delegate, select Options from the Tools menu and click on the Delegates tab. In the Delegates box, select the delegate you want to remove and click on Remove.

When the assistant receives notification that she has been granted delegate access permission by Jane, she can then open Jane's Outlook folders by choosing Open Special Folder on the File menu and clicking on Exchange Server Folder. In the Name box, type the name of the person who granted delegate access permission or click on Name to select from a list. In the Folder box, click on the other person's Outlook folder to open.

Tip

If you manage several folders for someone else, you might want to create a new group and Shortcuts on the Outlook Bar to store those folders together and allow quick access. To create a new group, right-click on the background of the Outlook Bar and select Add New Group; then, type in a name for your new group. Open the group and add Shortcuts to it by right-clicking on the background of the Outlook Bar and selecting Add To Outlook Bar; then, choose the folders to which you want to create Shortcuts.

Using Delegate Access To Manage Email

To send email on behalf of Jane, Jane's assistant opens Jane's Inbox and starts a new message by following these steps:

1. Select the From field on the View menu before composing the message.

2. In the From box, enter the name of the person on whose behalf you are sending the message.

3. Fill out the message as normal.

4. Click on the Send toolbar button.

Giving the assistant delegate access to Jane's Inbox ensures that she can perform many functions other than simply replying to messages on Jane's behalf. For example, with Author or Editor permission, the delegate can read Jane's messages and delete unwanted mail. The delegate can also send messages that appear to be composed and sent directly by Jane. Replies to the messages are sent to the delegate, not to Jane; sent mail is saved in the delegate's Sent Items folder; and message-tracking notifications are sent to the delegate. In this way, a delegate can manage Jane's email for her, leaving Jane free to concentrate on other activities.

Using Delegate Access To Manage Calendars And Tasks

Jane also wants her assistant to manage her schedule and to do list for her, so she must give the delegate Editor permission in the Calendar and Tasks folders and Reviewer permission in the Inbox. The delegate can then open her Calendar and Tasks folder and review her task list and appointments. The delegate can also create and modify tasks and appointments; any items the delegate creates are stored in Jane's task list or schedule, not the delegate's. Finally, the delegate can send and respond to task requests and meeting requests by opening Jane's Inbox. (The delegate cannot change the order of Jane's task list unless Jane has given the delegate Owner permission to the Tasks folder.)

Tip

If you select the Send Meeting Requests And Responses Only To My Delegates, Not To Me check box on the Delegates tab, then the delegate does not need Reviewer permission; instead, your meeting and task requests are sent directly to the delegate's Inbox. If you prefer that your delegate be sent copies of your meeting and task requests, select the Delegate Receives Copies Of Meeting-Related Messages Sent To Me check box; the delegate will still need Reviewer access to your Inbox.

Working With Office Files In Outlook

Jane's employee has finished his assignment and sent her a status report, so Jane combines the art and text of the fact sheets in an Office program and shares them with the group through email. The group makes comments and Jane revises the fact sheets accordingly.

Follow these steps to create a new Office file in Outlook and send it via email:

1. Open the folder in the Folder List where you want the new file to be located.

2. Click on the New Office Document toolbar button.

3. Double-click on the type of Office file you want to create.

4. After creating and saving the file, open a new email message and address it to the workgroup personal distribution list.

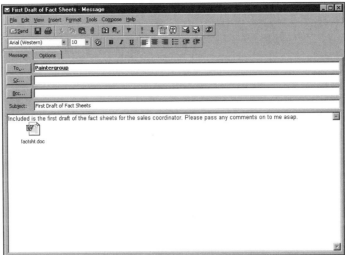

Figure 7.24 Sending a Word document as an attachment to an email message.

5. To send the file as an attachment to the email message, choose File from the Insert menu and select the file you just created (see Figure 7.24).

Using Outlook's Journal module, Jane can automatically record her work on the fact sheets and find the file based on when she last worked on it, rather than searching for a filename or path. After setting a type of file to be recorded automatically, the Journal creates an entry whenever she works on a file of that type and records the amount of time spent working on the file, which she can review later (see Figure 7.25). The journal entry is also a shortcut to the file, so that she can open the file directly from the text box

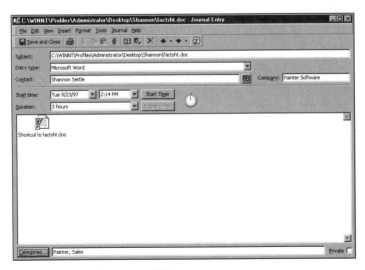

Figure 7.25 A journal entry for a Word file.

of the journal entry. She can also use the journal entry to record notes about the document or to assign categories to the document.

Follow these steps to record work on Office files in the Journal automatically:

1. Select Options from the Tools menu.

2. Click on the Journal tab.

3. In the Also Record Files From box, select the check boxes next to the Office programs whose files you want to record automatically.

4. Click on OK.

Jane then sends the finished version of the fact sheets to the regional sales directors by inserting it into an email message.

AutoArchive

Just as papers pile up on your desk, Outlook items pile up in your Inbox and other folders. Outlook provides a convenience feature called *AutoArchive* that automatically files or deletes old items according to the criteria you specify, keeping folders from getting cluttered with older items. For example, Jane might consider archiving all old items relating to her completed projects. The AutoArchive process runs automatically whenever you start Outlook, so you don't even have to think about cleaning out your old items.

AutoArchive is a two-step process: First turn on AutoArchive, and then set the AutoArchive properties for each Outlook folder. The items that are archived and when they are archived are determined at the folder level. The AutoArchive properties set for each folder are checked by date, and old items are moved to the designated personal folder, removing them from the original folders while maintaining copies of the items in case they are needed later. Items in the Deleted Items folder are removed entirely. AutoArchive preserves the existing folder structure in the archive folder, retaining the folder organization set up in Outlook.

To set up AutoArchive, follow these steps:

1. Choose Options from the Tools menu.

2. Click on the AutoArchive tab (see Figure 7.26).

3. Set AutoArchive to turn on when you start Outlook by selecting the AutoArchive Every check box.

4. Enter a number in the Days At Startup box to specify how often the AutoArchive process will run.

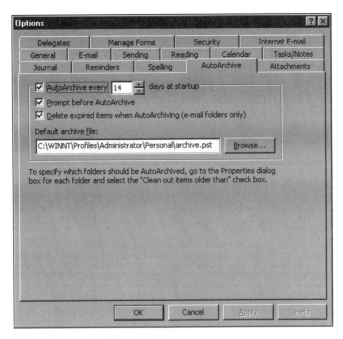

Figure 7.26 Setting up AutoArchive.

5. If you would like to be notified before items are archived, select the Prompt Before AutoArchive check box.

6. In the Default Archive File box, type a filename for the archived items to be transferred to or click on Browse to select from a list of files.

7. Click on OK.

Then, you must set AutoArchive properties for each Outlook folder individually to activate AutoArchive. Follow these steps:

1. In the Folder List, right-click on the folder you want to AutoArchive. For example, if you want to AutoArchive old email messages, right-click on the Inbox folder.

2. Select Properties from the shortcut menu.

3. Click on the AutoArchive tab (see Figure 7.27).

4. To enable AutoArchive of the folder, select the Clean Out Items Older Than check box.

5. Enter a number in the Months box to specify how old items should be before being automatically transferred to your archive file (you can also specify the age in weeks or days by clicking on the arrow to the right of the Months box).

On Site

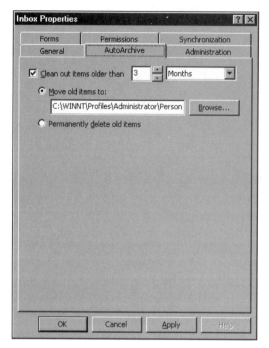

Figure 7.27 Setting AutoArchive properties for a folder.

6. In the Move Old Items To box, type a filename for the archived items to be transferred to or click on Browse to select from a list; you can also choose to delete old items rather than archiving them by clicking on the Permanently Delete Old Items button.

7. Click on OK.

Tip

Several Outlook modules are installed with AutoArchive turned on, although the settings can be altered to fit each user's needs. These include the Calendar, Tasks, Journal, Sent Items, and Deleted Items folders.

Retrieve archived items either by adding the archive file to a personal user profile or by importing the archive file. To add the archive file to the personal user profile, you must add an additional information service to the profile, which attaches the archive file to your mailbox and retains a separate file that contains all the archived items. If you import the archive file instead, the archived items are moved back into your mailbox.

Follow these steps to add the archive file to the personal user profile:

1. Select Services from the Tools menu.

2. Click on the Services tab.

3. Click on Add.

4. In the Available Information Services box, click on the information service you want to add—the archive file, in this case.

5. Click on OK.

6. If required, select the file name, location, and other options of the archive file.

7. Click on OK twice.

8. Exit and restart Outlook.

To import archived items into your mailbox, follow these steps:

1. Choose Import And Export from the File menu.

2. Click on Import From A Personal Folder File.

3. Follow the instructions on the Import And Export Wizard.

Outlook And Team Manager

Team Manager is a workgroup tool that makes it easy for a team to assign, coordinate, track, and consolidate all team tasks. It brings all the existing information about the work of a group to one central location, so that every member of the group can access the information. Each team member's workload, tasks, and progress are combined into one team file that shows the most updated information on team activities.

Using Team Manager, team members can coordinate their individual activities with overall team activities. Team members can add new tasks, change deadlines, enter actual work, and change reporting periods. Team Manager also tracks tasks and reports details using task and status management tools. Team Manager is an easy way to build a more collaborative and productive team.

Team Manager integrates easily with many different email systems, including Exchange Server, and with desktop clients, including Outlook, to extend group tasks management capabilities. By integrating the two clients, members of the team can use Outlook to view and keep track of their task assignments and use Team Manager to communicate with each other about the progress of group tasks.

This section describes how Team Manager can be integrated with Outlook and Exchange Server to further extend your system's collaboration capabilities. It is intended to illustrate how various client applications can work together on Exchange Server to create workgroup and collaboration solutions for businesses. This section assumes that you are already familiar with the basic operations of Team Manager. If not, consult your documentation or the program's help files.

Integrating Team Manager With Outlook

Team Manager integrates with Outlook by synchronizing the task lists in the two clients. Any task entered into Team Manager is also added to the Outlook task list. Both task lists are automatically updated whenever Team Manager is opened or closed and whenever a Team Member Settings message or team task update message is accepted in Outlook email. Team members can also create and work with all their Team Manager tasks directly in Outlook. Menu items are automatically added to Outlook so that team members can send Team Manager messages and view the status of tasks directly from their Outlook task lists.

Team Manager extends the capabilities of Outlook's Tasks module for assigning, managing, and tracking team tasks with additional features. For example, Team Manager adds the following functionality:

➤ Team Manager permits any team member to change a task; Outlook permits only the task owner to change a task.

➤ Team Manager permits assignment of more than one task at a time, unlike Outlook.

➤ Team Manager supports sending and receiving of status reports on more than one task at a time, unlike Outlook.

➤ Team Manager provides a team file of group tasks that reports the progress for everyone on the team; Outlook requires viewing of personal and team tasks together in one list.

To use Team Manager with Outlook, your users must install Team Manager on their client computers. Users also must accept a Team Member Settings message from their team managers in order to use Outlook to keep track of Team Manager tasks.

Working With Team Manager And Outlook Tasks

There are many ways that Team Manager and Outlook work together to help manage group tasks. This section outlines some of the most common activities performed by using Outlook and Team Manager together.

Integrating Team Manager Tasks With The Outlook Task List

Create an Outlook view that displays Team Manager tasks in Outlook together with the Outlook task list (see Figure 7.28). This view allows users to view, update, and report on Team Manager tasks from within Outlook's Tasks module. Follow these steps:

1. Open the Tasks module.

2. Select Detailed List from the Current View menu.

3. From the View menu, select Field Chooser.

4. Drag the Team Task field to the column heading row; use the double-arrow marker to position the column heading in the column heading row.

5. Close the Field Chooser.

6. Click in the Current View menu.

7. Type **Team Manager Tasks** and press Enter to create and save the new view.

Tip

When working on Team Manager tasks from within Outlook, open the Tasks module and select the Team Manager Tasks view from the Current View menu.

Follow these steps to integrate Team Manager tasks with the Outlook task list:

1. Open the Tasks module and switch to Team Manager Tasks view.

2. Select Team Manager For Team Members from the Tasks menu; Team Manager will open.

3. In Team Manager, click on the Options button on the Tasks tab.

4. In the Add Team Manager Tasks Created In Outlook Or Schedule+ box, select the name of the team file that you want to integrate into your Outlook task list.

Tip

If you work on tasks for more than one team or use more than one team file, you can only specify one team file at a time to integrate with your task list.

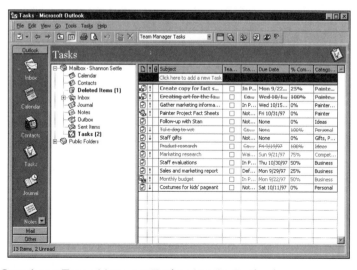

Figure 7.28   Creating a Team Manager Tasks view in Outlook.

Tasks can then be created in Outlook and turned into Team Manager tasks so that whenever a task update is sent to the team manager, any additions, changes, or deletions to the Team Manager tasks in Outlook are automatically reported. To do so, make sure that the Team Manager Tasks view is open in Outlook's Tasks module. In the task list, find the task that you want to make a Team Manager task and select the check box for that task in the Team Task column (see Figure 7.29). Repeat this step for each Outlook task to be identified as a Team Manager task.

To see more details about team tasks, start Team Manager from directly inside Outlook and view tasks from the team file; however, this does not allow you to make permanent changes to the team file. To do so, switch to the Team Manager Task view and select Team Manager For Team Members from the Tasks menu. Team Manager will then open. To view the team file and track the status for everyone on the team, select View Team Status from the Tasks menu.

If users work on more than one Team Manager team, they can also view tasks from another team file within Outlook. In the Send To box on the Task tab in Team Manager, click on the initials of the manager's team file to open. If a manager has more than one team file linked to a team member task list, a number follows his or her initials to help choose the correct file.

Tracking Progress And Status Of Team Manager Tasks In Outlook

Outlook can be used to track the progress of Team Manager tasks and to update the Team Manager team file. Whenever changes or new tasks need to be shared with the team, the team member making the changes sends a task update message to the manager via email. Team Manager then checks the status of all team members' tasks in its

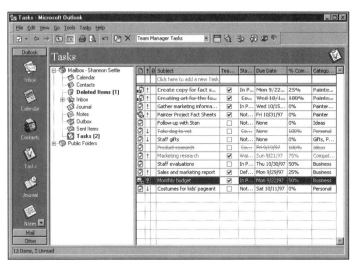

Figure 7.29 Identifying Outlook tasks as Team Manager tasks.

current database against the last task list the team member sent to the manager and sends an exceptions list to the manager. The manager can either accept the updated information as is or accept only parts of the update.

To send a task update message to the team manager, make sure the Team Manager Task view is open in Outlook's Tasks module. From the Tasks menu, select Send Updates. Make sure Task Updates is selected and click on Next. Then, change the subject, type a message into the text box, and change information in any editable column of the task list at the bottom of the message window. Click on the Send toolbar button to send a new status report to the manager. The manager uses the update message to update the team file with progress on individuals' tasks.

Send a team task status report to the manager via Outlook email to give the manager a narrative account of work on team tasks. Team Manager then merges the status report with the status reports of other team members into a single team Status Report. From the Tasks menu, select Send Updates. Click on Status Report and Next. Then, write the status report for Team Manager tasks using the section headings provided. The status report message reflects the reporting format that the team manager set up and sent to the team, along with the section headings the manager wants to be reported on. Be sure not to alter the section headings, or the report will not integrate properly with the rest of the team status reports. Click on the Send toolbar button to send the status report.

Whenever the team manager creates new team tasks or changes existing tasks, the changes are sent to all team members via email in a team task update message. When a team task update arrives from the manager in Outlook's Inbox, it is used to update Team Manager tasks with any changes that have been made to the team file. Open the team task update messages in the order that they were received, and review the task list at the bottom of the message to find whether each team task is new, changed, or deleted. Click on Accept to incorporate the updated task information into the task list in Outlook and Team Manager. To change the task information and send an explanation back to the manager before incorporating the updated information, click on Reply; make changes to the tasks in the table provided and click on the Send button.

Negotiate team tasks with a manager via Outlook email, as well. For example, negotiate changing information, such as the due date or work estimate of a task. In the Inbox, open the team task update messages in the order they were received and click on Reply. To decline a task assignment, change "Yes" to "No" in the OK? column and edit any task information. In the text box, type the message to the manager. Click on the Send button to send the message to the manager's Inbox. The tasks, along with the changed information, are incorporated into both Outlook and Team Manager.

seven

Moving On

In this chapter, you learned how to use the client applications Outlook and Team Manager to complete a variety of communication and collaboration activities on Exchange Server. The following chapter will show how Exchange Server can be used to publish information stored on the server for access by members of the organization and others outside the network. Exchange Server provides many options for publishing information so that the information is worked hardest—keep reading to learn about them all.

Publishing Information With Exchange Server

In this information age, it's no surprise that information is becoming business's most valuable commodity. Succeeding in an information-rich environment requires that all members of a team have access to a common set of data so that they can react more quickly, communicate more effectively, provide better services, and become more responsive to customers' needs. Whether the virtual team is made up of members of a workgroup, an entire organization, or an organization and its customers, it is critical that the virtual team can access needed information quickly and easily and understand it intuitively. And, in a business environment where information can change from minute to minute, it is necessary that information be as up-to-date as possible.

Recognizing the need to make information sharing easier, faster, and more flexible, Microsoft developed Exchange Server with many different capabilities for publishing information, both for users of the network and for customers out in the wider world. In this chapter, you will learn how to set up, administer, and make the most of these information publishing methods, including the following:

➤ Knowledge bases, instant groupware, and other applications that use public folders.

➤ Applications and public folders that use electronic forms.

➤ Corporate white pages, using the Exchange Server directory.

➤ Mass mailings, using Exchange Server distribution lists.

Never before have you had so many choices for sharing information with your employees, members of your workgroup, and customers and business partners outside your organization. Exchange Server not only makes these information-sharing benefits possible, but also, with its centralized administration and client/server architecture, makes maintaining and accessing different types of information easier than ever before.

Storing Public Information On Exchange Server

Exchange Server stores information on a single server or on multiple servers networked throughout your organization. That information can then be accessed, viewed, and manipulated by a variety of client programs that connect to the servers. You can configure the sites in your organization to exchange information stored on the various servers. This is called *information flow*. Earlier in this book, you learned how to control information flow throughout the various sites to make best use of available connection speed and data volume.

The Exchange Server *public information store* is a key component of the server for sharing and managing publicly accessible information contained on the servers in your site. The public information store is Exchange Server's centrally replicating store of public information that can be accessed globally by all users of the server, making it possible for users to access information in *public folders*. It holds the entire hierarchy of public folders and public folder replicas configured for the server.

The Public Folder Hierarchy

The public folders system on Exchange Server has two parts: the public folder hierarchy and the public folder content. The *public folder hierarchy* is the structure of all the server's public folders as they appear to the user in the client program. The *public folder content* is the information contained inside a public folder. Before allowing users to create public folders on the server, you should design and implement an easily understood public folder hierarchy. As users create new public folders, those folders will be added to the hierarchy but will still conform to the design you set up, keeping the ever-growing tree of public folders organized and easy to access.

The set of public folders available to Exchange Server users is displayed as a hierarchy, which can be viewed from Outlook, the Exchange Client, or the Administrator program. Public folders are stored in *folder sets,* containers used to organize and manage folders on Exchange Server. Although the same public folder hierarchy is available on all servers in the site, the information contained in the folders is distributed on different servers throughout the organization. This distribution is invisible to the user, who does not need to know the name or location of the server where public folder information is stored in order to access that information.

You should carefully plan the public folder hierarchy. As part of the planning process, determine how you want public folders to be organized. For example, you might want to organize *top-level folders* in the hierarchy by topic, language, or department. Subfolders contained within each top-level folder will cover a narrower range of information but still be related to the top-level folder in some way. This creates a consistent structure that your users will be able to navigate easily.

For example, suppose you decide to organize top-level folders in the hierarchy by department. When users open the list of public folders in the client program, they will see one public folder for each department, labeled with that department's name. For example, they will find a Sales & Marketing folder, an Accounting folder, a Customer Service folder, and so on, as well as a top-level folder that contains general information of interest to the entire company. Any additional public folders relating to a department will be created only within that department's top-level public folder. These departmental subfolders might include public folders used by workgroups for specific projects, folders that contain information of general interest to the entire department, and more. And these subfolders might contain even more subfolders on more specialized but related topics. Therefore, users accessing the public folder hierarchy can easily navigate through the top-level folders and subfolders to the information they need.

After planning the public folder hierarchy, you should decide which users can create public folders in the top level of the hierarchy and which servers in your site will be used to store public folders. You'll use the Administrator program to configure these settings.

Creating Top-Level Public Folders

To control the growth and organization of the public folder hierarchy, you'll probably want to restrict the number of people who can create folders in the top level or highest tier of the hierarchy. You can specify that all members of your organization have the right to create top-level folders, or you can limit those who can create top-level folders to individuals or to a distribution list. For example, if you decide to organize the top-level folders by company department, you will probably want to give only the head of each department permission to create the top-level folder for his or her department.

All other public folders will then be organized as subfolders of these top-level folders. The person who created the top-level folder (or its owner) controls which users can create these subordinate folders inside the top-level folder. By limiting the number of people who can create top-level folders, you can better ensure that the number of top-level folders is kept to a minimum and that the public folder hierarchy doesn't mushroom out of control. You can also coordinate with those users to whom you gave permission to create top-level folders to keep to the design of the hierarchy as you've previously mapped out.

Follow these steps to specify which users can create top-level public folders:

1. Click on the Configuration button in the Administrator window.

2. Double-click on Information Store Site Configuration.

3. Select the Top Level Folder Creation tab (see Figure 8.1).

4. Under Allowed To Create Top Level Folders, click on Modify.

Figure 8.1   Assigning top-level folder creation privileges.

5. Select the individual name or distribution list to which you want to give top-level folder creation privileges.

6. Click on the Add button to add your selection to the Allowed To Create Top Level Folders box.

7. Repeat steps 5 through 6 to add additional names to the Allowed To Create Top Level Folders box.

8. When you're finished, click on OK twice.

Tip

If you specify a distribution list in the Allowed To Create Top Level Folders box, you can restrict individual members of the list by entering their names in the Not Allowed To Create Top Level Folders box. If both boxes are empty, every user in the Global Address List can create top-level folders.

Public Folder Servers

Every server in your site can maintain public folders in the public information store. However, depending on how you've planned and set up your site, you might want to dedicate one server for maintaining all public folders, called a *public folder server*. This is the server that users connect to with the client to view the public folder hierarchy, and it has the responsibility for storing and managing all public folders. It is also where top-level folders are created and the first place that the server attempts to locate the contents of a folder that a client is trying to view. Dedicating one server to storing public folders provides several advantages:

➤ Planning and administration of servers is simplified.

➤ Memory, CPU, and disk requirements on the mailbox servers are reduced.

➤ Mail delivery performance is improved.

➤ Backing up of public folders is made easier.

When choosing a public folder server, you should take into account the server's storage capacity, processing power, and future expandability. Keep in mind that the public folder hierarchy will continue to grow, and the number of users connecting to the server to access public folders will grow along with it. You might consider increasing the RAM and CPU power of the public folder server, especially if you plan to store large folders or if folders will be searched or sorted.

To dedicate a server to maintaining only public folders, follow these steps:

1. In the Administrator window, click on the Servers button.

2. Select the server that you want to configure as the public folder server.

3. Double-click on Private Information Store.

4. Choose Properties from the File menu.

5. Select the General tab.

6. In the Public Folder Server menu, select the new public folder server (see Figure 8.2).

7. Click on OK.

Publishing Information With Public Folders

Using Exchange Server's public folders, you can maintain *knowledge bases* of publicly accessible information stored on the server. Knowledge bases improve the flow of communication in the company by providing a central location for submitting, viewing, and otherwise sharing a library of documents with a workgroup; a department; the entire organization; or business partners, vendors, and customers outside the organization. Documents inside the library can be reviewed and updated by users of the knowledge base and can include marketing requirements, product specifications, prototypes, testing plans, project schedules, newsletters, sales reports, or any other kind of document that needs to be shared across a group of users. The folder itself can store any type of file or Outlook item, including email messages, Office documents, spreadsheets, OLE objects, URLs to useful Web sites, voice mail, and graphics.

Figure 8.2   Configuring a dedicated public folder server.

Knowledge bases should be configured to hold information about a specific subject. For example, a project manager can create a public folder to store background information about the project that the entire team can access. A development workgroup might create a public folder as a specifications knowledge base for storing, organizing, and reviewing product specifications. A technical support department can create a public folder to store commonly asked questions and answers about a product. An employee information knowledge base could contain such reference material as employee handbooks, company policies, and human resources information.

Public folders not only provide an easy way to publish and share information among a group of people on Exchange Server through a knowledge base, but also enable you to create group applications for manipulating that information. Any public folder is actually an application that lets users store, manage, and exchange information on the server. Knowledge base folders are one type of public folder application that enables a group to store, organize, share, review, and update reference information, such as documents or graphics. Other commonly used public folder applications include online discussion applications and tracking applications. An online discussion public folder, often called an *electronic bulletin board,* is an easy way to facilitate group discussion about a particular issue or topic. Electronic bulletin boards serve as a central location where users can submit, share, and respond to ideas. For example, an electronic bulletin board for a technical users group enables members of the group to submit technical problems, review problems, and respond with solutions to the problems. A workgroup electronic bulletin board can be used for brainstorming sessions, where members of the group can submit new ideas about a product, respond to and expand upon the submitted ideas, and review the progression of conversation relating to a particular idea.

Tracking public folders enable a group to record and track information that is constantly updated. For example, a customer service request tracking application enables users to record and manage the workload for a customer service department of a company. In this kind of public folder, the application records the length of time that each request is open, provides a history of requests for spotting trends, and stores historic information to save time when responding to recurrent requests. Another type of tracking application is a meeting tracking folder, where users can propose and share meeting agendas, track discussions leading up to a meeting, record meeting minutes, and track action items resulting from the meeting. A client-tracking folder enables users to submit and store company contact profiles and record the history of the company's interaction with a particular client.

Creating A Public Folder

Users can create public folders with the Outlook client. To create a public folder, you must have permission to create subfolders in an existing public folder. For more information on the steps to creating a public folder, see Decision Tree 8.1.

Generally, a small number of people have permission to create public folders in the top level of the public folder hierarchy, such as the department heads. The owners of the top-level folders then grant permissions to others to use the folders and to create subfolders inside the top-level folders on narrower topics. For example, the department heads might grant permission to project coordinators within their departments to create subfolders relating to projects, workgroups, products, and other topics. The owners of the subfolders can then give permission to others to access the subfolders and to create additional subfolders inside them. And so on.

Before trying to create a subfolder, you should check your level of permission for the folder where the subfolder will be located to find out if you can access it and what actions you can perform inside the folder. Follow these steps to check your permission level:

1. From the Other group on the Outlook Bar, click on the Public Folders shortcut.

2. Right-click on the public folder where you want to create the subfolder in the Folder List.

3. Select Properties from the shortcut menu.

4. Click on the Summary tab; your permission level appears under Your Permissions (see Figure 8.3).

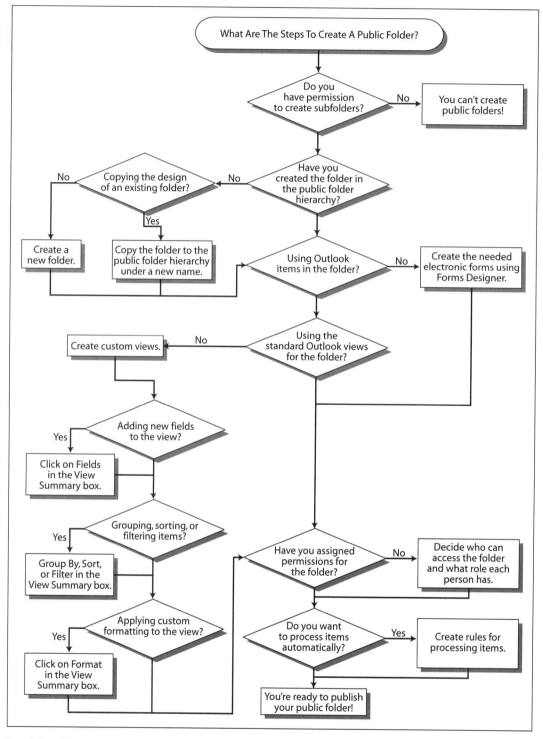

Decision Tree 8.1 What are the steps to create a public folder?

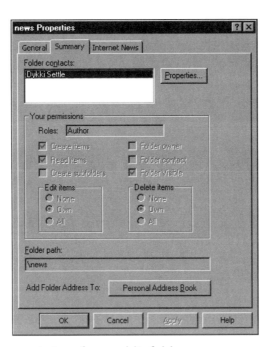

Figure 8.3   Checking permissions for a public folder.

Tip

If the Permissions tab appears instead of the Summary tab, you have owner access to the folder. If neither tab appears, you don't have permission to access the folder.

Parts Of A Public Folder

Each public folder is made up of the following parts:

➤ **Views for finding and organizing information.** Public folder *views* determine how items posted in the folder are displayed and how these items are grouped, sorted, and filtered. Multiple predefined and custom views can be associated with each folder. Users can choose from the different views in an open folder to change the way information in the folder is displayed and organized.

➤ **Forms for posting information.** *Forms* provide users with predefined templates for creating new items in a folder and responding to existing items. They ensure that information in the folder is consistently structured and organized and is easy to find. Each folder has an associated forms library into which the forms used for interacting with information in the folder are installed.

➤ **Permissions for determining who can view and use the folder.** Public folder *permissions* determine who can access the public folder and what actions each user can perform on the information contained in the folder. Some folders, such as a workgroup's folder, limit access to only a few people. Others, such as a company-wide folder, grant access to many users but limit the number of people who can add or change items in the folder. The users who can access a folder are determined by an *access control list*. Each user on the access control list is then assigned permissions to specify which actions he or she can perform.

➤ **Rules for routing posted information.** *Rules* are used to process incoming items to the folder. A rule is made up of a set of conditions and the actions that occur if the conditions are met by an incoming item to the folder. For example, you might create rules that reply to, forward, delete, or return specific items when they are posted to a folder.

Planning Your Public Folder

Before creating a new folder, you should plan its design so that it will best meet the needs of the folder's intended users. When the need for a new public folder arises, you should identify the folder's potential users, their needs, and the solutions the folder will provide.

As part of the planning process, decide which types of Outlook items the folder should contain to best meet the needs of the folder's users. For example, a reference library folder probably contains email messages that users can post to share information on a particular topic, while a group tasks tracking folder should contain task items that can be tracked by the folder's users on a timeline. The design plan should also include preliminary drawings of any custom forms and views that will be used in the folder.

For example, as a member of the Research and Development department, you decide to create a department-wide public folder where users can brainstorm about product ideas and other users can respond to those ideas. This simple type of public folder will require two forms—one for posting new ideas and one for responding to those ideas in the form of email messages. All members of the department should have access to the folder and be able to read and post new items. Let's go through the steps of creating this type of public folder.

Creating A New Folder

To create the new public folder, follow these steps:

1. From the File menu, choose New Folder.

2. In the Name box, type a name for the public folder: **Brainstorm** (see Figure 8.4).

3. In the Folder Contains menu, click on the type of Outlook item the folder will contain: Mail Items.

4. In the Make This Folder A Subfolder Of box, click on the public folder in which you want the new folder to appear. For example, if the public folder hierarchy is

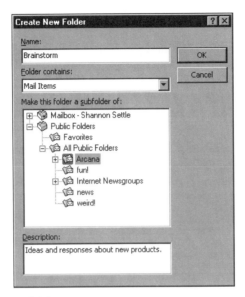

Figure 8.4   Creating a new folder.

organized by department-related folders, you will want to make this folder a subfolder of the R&D public folder.

5. In the Description box, type a description of the folder: **Ideas and responses about new products**.

6. Click on OK.

Copying An Existing Folder

If you want to create a new folder based on the design of an existing personal or public folder, you can copy the design of the existing folder and modify it. Copying the design ensures that the permissions, rules, forms, and views of the folder are maintained in the new folder. All the items in the folder will also be copied to the new public folder.

This method also applies if you want to make significant changes to an existing folder. You can copy the existing folder to a new folder, make the changes, and then copy the folder back. The existing folder remains available to other users while you are making changes to its copy.

 *Tip* • • • •

Remember that you must have owner permissions for the existing personal or public folder to copy its design or to modify it.

To copy an existing folder to a new public folder for later modification, follow these steps:

1. Select the public folder to which you want to copy the design of another folder in the Folder List.

2. Select Folder from the File menu.

3. Select Copy Folder Design (see Figure 8.5).

4. In the Copy Design From This Folder box, select the folder whose design you want to copy.

5. Under Copy Design Of, select one or more of the following check boxes to copy the corresponding design elements: Permissions, Rules, Description, or Forms & Views.

6. Click on OK.

Tip

If you only want to make minor changes to an existing public folder, you can modify it directly, without copying the folder design to a new folder.

Assigning Forms

After creating a new folder, you must specify the forms others will use to post information in the folder. Generally, you will specify one form for posting a new item and a second for responding to a previously posted item. For the simplest folders, you can use the default forms associated with the type of Outlook item the folder contains. For example, a public folder that contains contact items automatically uses the default form for composing a new contact to post items to the folder if no other form is specified. In

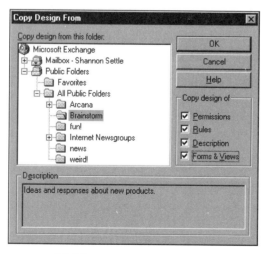

Figure 8.5   Copying a personal folder to a new public folder.

the case of our Brainstorm public folder, we're going to use the default email post and response forms. Later in this chapter, you'll learn more about modifying and creating new electronic forms that you might choose to copy to other public folders you create.

Creating Views

You should now create the views for the public folder, which are used to organize and find information in the folder. You can create any number of views based on different combinations of fields, groupings, sorts, and filters. Each view is given a name that the folder's users can choose from the Views menu to change the organization of the information in the folder.

Tip

Note that the Exchange Client will be unable to display custom table views created in Outlook. When creating the folder, you can specify that custom table views are made available to Exchange Client users with only the features that the Exchange Client supports. To do so, right-click on the folder and choose Properties on the shortcut menu. Select the General tab and select the Automatically Generate Microsoft Exchange Views check box.

Because our Brainstorm folder contains Outlook email message items, all the standard Inbox views will automatically be applied to the folder, including a By Conversation Topic view that allows users to organize postings in the folder by the conversation thread. However, we'd like to add an extra view that groups messages by sender and then sorts them by subject.

Follow these steps to create a new view for the folder:

1. Select the folder in the Folder List.
2. Select Define Views from the View menu.
3. Click on New (see Figure 8.6).
4. In the Name Of New View box, type a name for your view: **Sender by Subject.**
5. Choose a view type from the Type Of View box: Table.
6. Under Can Be Used On, select the This Folder, Visible To Everyone button.
7. Click on OK.

Tip

When naming your views, use a consistent naming convention throughout the folder. For example, if you create a view that categorizes items by Company Name and then sorts by date, name the view "Company Name by Date."

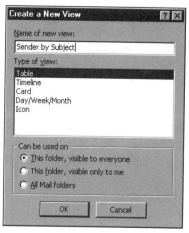

Figure 8.6   Creating a new view.

When you choose to create a new view, the View Summary dialog box opens. This dialog box lets you define fields or columns, groupings, sorts, filters, and formatting for your new view (see Figure 8.7).

With the Fields or Columns option, you can define the columns of information to display in the view. You can add or delete columns, rearrange their order, and change their widths. The properties provided in the Columns or Fields dialog box are a combination of default Exchange Sever properties and properties based on the forms you chose for the folder.

Follow these steps to add columns or fields to the view:

1. Click on Fields to open the Show Fields dialog box (see Figure 8.8).

2. Select the field you want under Available Fields; we'd like to add a field to our view that shows when the post was created, so select the Created option.

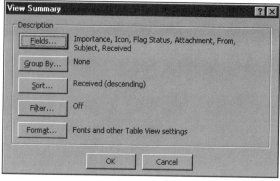

Figure 8.7   The View Summary dialog box.

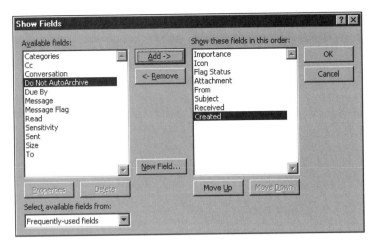

Figure 8.8 Choosing fields for your view.

If the field you want isn't listed, select a new option in the Select Available Fields From menu or click on the New Field button to create a new field.

3. Click on Add to add the column or field to the view.

4. To change the order of the displayed fields, click on a field name in the Show These Fields In This Order box and click on either Move Up or Move Down.

5. Click on OK.

Tip

To remove a column or field from the view, select it under Show These Fields In This Order and click on the Remove button.

From the Group By dialog box, you can group how items are displayed in the view. Grouping items is similar to creating an outline. You group items by standard form field properties, such as From, Sent To, and Attachment, and by fields that are determined by the columns or fields you previously selected. You can group by up to four fields and then sort the items in the groups.

Follow these steps to group items:

1. Click on the Group By button to open the Group By dialog box (see Figure 8.9).

2. Under Group Items By, select a field for grouping items; we've already determined that we're going to group items by sender, so click on From.

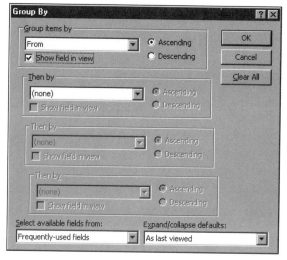

Figure 8.9   The Group By dialog box.

3. Click on either the Ascending or Descending button to choose an order for displaying the group; in this case, click on Ascending to show senders in alphabetical order.

4. To continue grouping items, choose another field from the next available Then By box; you can group by up to four fields.

5. Click on OK.

Sorting items in a view provides a way for the user to track an item and the history of responses to that item. You can sort by standard form fields and by the fields in the forms you added to the folder. If the items are already grouped, the sort applies to the last group in the hierarchy.

Follow these steps to sort items in the view:

1. Click on the Sort button to open the Sort dialog box (see Figure 8.10).

2. In the Sort Items By menu, select a field to sort items by; we decided to sort items by subject, so select Subject.

3. Click on Ascending or Descending for the sort order; in this case, choose Ascending to show sorted items in alphabetical order.

4. To continue sorting items, choose another field from the next available Then By box and select Ascending or Descending; you can sort by up to four fields.

5. Click on OK.

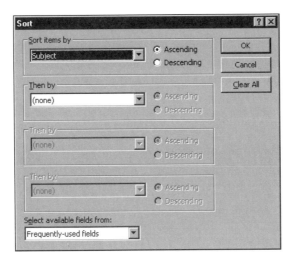

Figure 8.10   The Sort dialog box.

Filters let users quickly find information in the view. When a filter is applied, only the items that meet the filter's conditions are displayed; all other items are hidden.

In the case of our view for the Brainstorm folder, we're going to leave the filter option off. However, if you'd like to create a filter for the view, follow these steps:

1. Click on the Filter button to open the Filter dialog box (see Figure 8.11).

2. Specify the filter conditions from the options provided; for example, you can filter by the name of the sender or by a word in the subject or body text.

3. To find additional filter conditions, click on the More Choices tab.

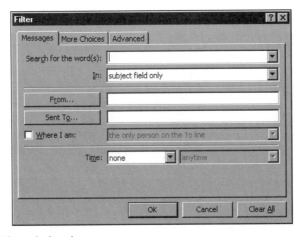

Figure 8.11   The Filter dialog box.

4. To define advanced filter conditions, click on the Advanced tab.

5. Click on OK when you've finished setting conditions for the filter.

You can also designate custom fonts and other settings for the type of view you have chosen. Follow these steps:

1. Click on the Format button to open the Format View dialog box (see Figure 8.12).

2. Choose from the options provided, which vary depending on the view type that you've chosen; for example, let's turn on the AutoPreview feature of new messages posted to the folder by clicking on the button beside Preview Unread Items.

3. Click on OK.

4. Click on OK again to close the View Summary dialog box.

5. Click on Close to close the Define Views dialog box.

After creating many views for the folder, you'll probably want to define the default view or the view that automatically opens whenever anyone opens the folder. Follow these steps to specify that the new view we just created is the default view for the folder:

1. Select the new public folder.

2. Select Folder Properties from the File menu.

3. Click on the Administration tab.

4. In the Initial View On Folder menu, select the name of the default view: Sender by Subject (see Figure 8.13).

5. Click on OK.

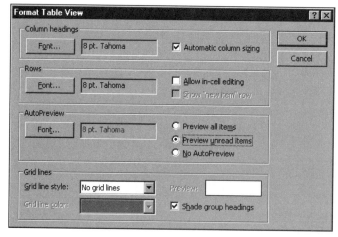

Figure 8.12 The Format Table View dialog box.

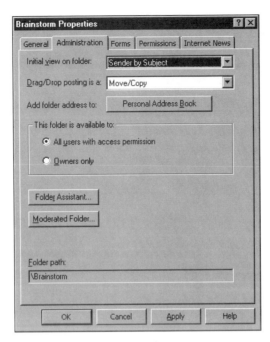

Figure 8.13   Defining the default view for the folder.

Tip

When setting the default view for a folder, choose Normal to show the default Outlook view for the type of items the folder contains.

Testing The Forms And Views

You should now test that your new forms and views work correctly, so you can make any necessary changes before going on with the design process. In this step, you're going to test the form for posting a new message and replying to a posted message. You're also going to test that the custom view you created displays posted messages correctly. Follow these steps:

1. Open the Brainstorm folder in the Folder List.

2. Select New Post in This Folder from the Compose menu; the default message form should open (see Figure 8.14).

3. Type **test** in the Subject box.

4. Type a short test message into the body of the message.

5. Click on the Post button to post the item in the folder; the test message appears in the list of items in the folder.

6. Double-click on the item you just posted to open it and make sure information is displayed correctly.

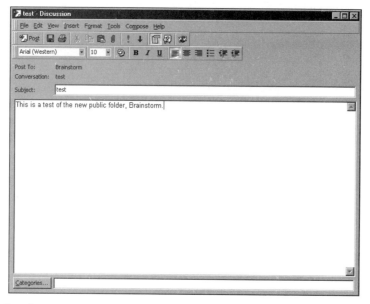

Figure 8.14   Posting a test message to the folder.

7. Click on the plus (+) button by the Sender group to expand the messages in that group and show your test message.

8. Select the test message.

9. Select Post A Reply In This Folder from the Compose menu.

10. Type **test reply** for the subject in the default form that opens.

11. Type a short reply message into the body of the message.

12. Click on the Post button.

13. Open the response and make sure that the information is also displayed correctly.

● ● *Tip* ● ● ●

You should test any additional forms you copied to the folder in this same way.

Finally, view the test items you posted to the folder using the various views you created. To switch to a different view, select the view from the Current View menu. The new Sender by Subject view should have opened automatically when you opened the folder. It should show a grouping by sender name, with the two test messages listed in the group by subject (see Figure 8.15). Any messages you haven't read should be previewed in the view as well. Test all the folder views you created to make sure that the items are in the folder display and are sorted, grouped, and filtered in the way that you planned. When you have finished testing the forms and views, delete the test items you posted in the folder.

Figure 8.15   Testing the Sender by Subject view.

Assigning Permissions

As the owner of the folder, you determine who can access the folder and what activities users can perform inside the folder. You must first add user, distribution list, and other public folder names to the folder's access control list to allow those users access to the folder. You can then specify permissions for each user on the access control list. Permissions indicate the activities each user can perform within the folder.

One item in the access control list is Default. Any permissions defined for Default are automatically granted to all users who have access to the folder and for whom you didn't individually set permissions. While testing the folder, it's a good idea to set the Default permission to None and grant access to a limited number of users who can test the folder. When you're sure the folder is working correctly, you can change the Default permissions.

In the case of our Brainstorm folder, we're going to allow all members of the Research and Development department to access the folder. Most users will only be able to read and create items in the folder and modify their own items. However, the department head would like a higher level of permission so he can manage all items posted to the folder. We'd also like to define a custom *role*, or group of permissions, for an assistant, making the assistant the contact person for the folder.

Folder Contacts

Folder contacts are the people users contact to report problems with the folder or to request changes to the folder. They also receive automatic conflict notifications for the folder, such as replication conflict messages.

Follow these steps to add users to the access control list and set permissions:

1. Select the folder in the Folder List.

2. Select Folder Properties from the File menu.

3. Select the Permissions tab.

4. Click on the Add button.

5. In the Type Name Or Select From List box, select the user, distribution list, or public folder you want to add to the access control list; in this case, select a member of the R&D department (see Figure 8.16).

Tip

If the user you want to add is not listed in the Type Name Or Select From List box, change the displayed Address Book by selecting a new one in the Show Names From The menu.

6. Click on the Add button.

7. Repeat steps 5 through 6 for every user, distribution list, and public folder you want to add to the access control list; in this case, continue adding all the members of the R&D department to the access control list.

8. Click on OK.

9. In the Name/Role box, select the name of the user to whom you granted access; first, choose the name of the department head (see Figure 8.17).

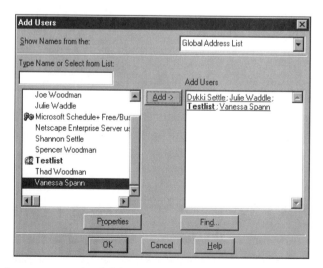

Figure 8.16 Adding users to the folder's access control list.

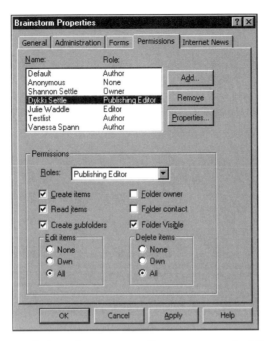

Figure 8.17 Setting permissions for users on the access control list.

10. Under Permissions, select the permission you want to give that user from the Roles menu; for the department head, choose Publishing Editor to allow the head to create, modify, read, and delete all items in the folder and to create subfolders in the folder.

11. In the Name/Role box, select the name of another user to whom you granted access; choose the name of the assistant.

12. Under Permissions, select the Editor role from the Roles menu to give the assistant the ability to create, read, modify, and delete items in the folder.

13. Underneath the Roles menu, select the Folder Contact check box to assign the assistant as the contact for the folder; this essentially creates a custom role.

Tip

You can continue to assign individual predefined or custom roles to anyone in the access control list by clicking on a name in the Name/Role box and then assigning roles under Permissions.

14. All other members of the access control list will have the same level of permissions, so to save time, we can assign a role to the Default setting; this automatically gives all users to whom we didn't individually assign permissions the same role. Click on Default in the Name/Role box.

eight

Making Folders Available Outside The Organization

Many times, you want to make your public folder knowledge bases available to users outside the organization. You can set up an Anonymous permission so that users who don't have an Exchange Server mailbox can access the folder. While setting permissions, choose Anonymous from the Name/Role box and then select the permissions for anonymous users from the Roles menu.

15. Choose Author in the Roles menu under Permissions; this gives all other users the ability to read and create items in the folder and to edit and delete any items they might have posted to the folder.

16. Click on OK when you're finished.

• • **Tip** • • •

Adding a distribution list to the folder's access control list provides a convenient way to assign a role to a group of users. For example, you might want to assign a custom role to a workgroup in the R&D department. You must first create a distribution list that contains the names of everyone in the workgroup (see the section "Creating Distribution Lists," later in this chapter). Then add the distribution list name to the access control list and assign the custom role to the entire distribution list.

Many predefined roles are provided that assign permissions to perform different kinds of activities. Table 8.1 describes the predefined roles and their associated activities that are available from the Permissions dialog box.

Table 8.1   Predefined roles that can be assigned to public folder users.

Role	Activities Allowed
Owner	Create, read, modify, and delete all items in the folder; create subfolders; change permission levels for the folder.
Publishing Editor	Create, read, modify, and delete all items in the folder; create subfolders.
Editor	Create, read, modify, and delete all items in the folder.
Publishing Author	Create and read all items; modify and delete items you created; create subfolders.
Author	Create and read all items; modify and delete items you created.
Reviewer	Read all items in the folder.
Contributor	Create items only; the contents of the folder are not shown.
None	Cannot access the folder.

Table 8.2   Activities that can be allowed in a public folder.

Activity	Definition
Create Items	Post items to the folder.
Read Items	Open any item posted to the folder.
Create Subfolder	Create subfolders located in the folder.
Edit Items	Specify None to indicate that the user cannot make changes to any item, specify Own to indicate that the user can modify items s/he created, or specify All to indicate that the user can modify any item.
Delete Items	Specify None to indicate that the user cannot delete any item, specify Own to indicate that the user can delete items s/he created, or specify All to indicate that the user can delete any item.

You can also designate that the user can perform different individual activities to create a custom role. Table 8.2 describes the activities that can be combined to create a custom role.

Setting Administration Properties

Administration properties are miscellaneous options that affect the general functionality of the folder. To display the administration options, select the folder, choose Folder Properties from the File menu, and select the Administration tab. From the Administration tab, you can enable drag-and-drop posting, add the folder to your Personal Address Book, and set other miscellaneous options (see Figure 8.18).

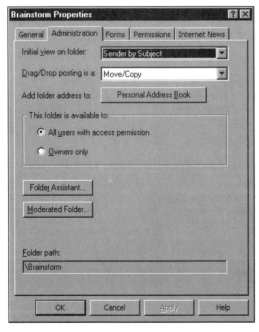

Figure 8.18   Setting the Administration properties for a public folder.

Tip ● ● ● ● ● ●

You can instantly create a moderated discussion group by right-clicking on an electronic bulletin board folder, choosing Properties from the shortcut menu, clicking on the Administration tab, and selecting Moderated Folder.

If you are creating a new folder or extensively modifying an existing folder's design, select the Owners Only button under the This Folder Is Available To option on the Administration tab. Doing so gives only those who have owner permissions access to the folder. After the folder is tested, you can select the All Users With Access Permission option to make the folder available for public use. Using the This Folder Is Available To option does not prevent access to subfolders contained within the folder you're modifying, so users can continue to work with the subfolders while the parent folder is being tested.

Creating Rules

Rules automatically process items as they arrive in the folder. For example, you might configure a rule to automatically delete posted items based on specified criteria or to automatically return certain kinds of items to the poster of the items. A rule consists of two parts: a set of conditions applied to an incoming item, and an action that is taken if the conditions are met.

Conditions can range from simple to advanced. A simple condition, such as "From: John Doe," specifies that when items are posted to the folder by John Doe, an action is taken. An example of a more advanced set of conditions is: "Only Messages That Do Not Match This Criteria; From: John Doe; Harry Jones; Jane Johnson." This rule states that if items submitted to the folder are not from John Doe, Harry Jones, or Jane Johnson, an action is taken.

In the case of the Brainstorm folder, we're going to create a rule that automatically returns any message from a specific user that is larger than an allowed size limit. You use Outlook's *Folder Assistant* tool to create rules for public folders. Follow these steps to create the rule:

1. Select the folder in the Folder List.

2. Select Folder Properties from the File menu.

3. Click on the Administration tab.

4. Click on Folder Assistant (see Figure 8.19).

5. To create a new rule, click on Add Rule, or to modify an existing rule, select a rule in the list and click on Edit Rule; in this case, we're going to create a new rule.

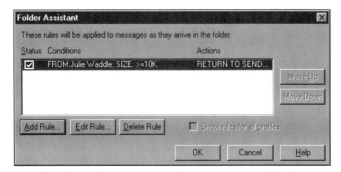

Figure 8.19   Using the Folder Assistant to create rules for a folder.

6. Enter the conditions the posted item must meet under When A Message Arrives That Meets The Following Conditions. For example, to specify that the rule applies to every message sent by a specific user, click on the From button and choose the user from the Type Name Or Select From List box; then click on the From button and click on OK (see Figure 8.20).

7. To configure advanced conditions, click on the Advanced button. In this case, we're going to specify a size limit of 10K for the message; click on the Advanced button, type 10 in the At Least box under Size (Kilobytes), leave the At Most box blank, and click on OK (see Figure 8.21).

8. Select the actions that will occur when the conditions are met under Perform These Actions. In this case, we're going to return the message, so select the check box beside Return To Sender.

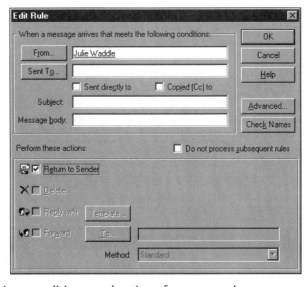

Figure 8.20   Setting conditions and actions for a new rule.

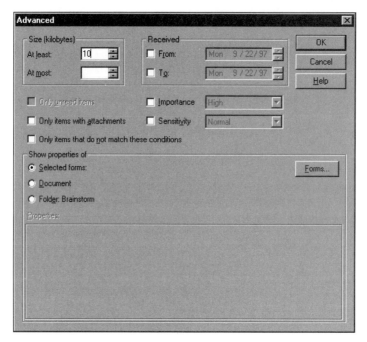

Figure 8.21   Setting advanced conditions for a new rule.

9. Click on OK when you're finished; the new rule will be displayed in the list in the Folder Assistant dialog box.

10. You can continue to add new rules or edit existing ones; when you're finished, click on OK to close the Folder Assistant dialog box.

11. Click on OK to close the Properties dialog box.

Tip

Multiple rules will be processed in the order in which they appear in the list in the Folder Assistant dialog box. To change the order in which rules are processed, select a rule in the list and click on the Move Up or Move Down button to change where the rule falls in the list. You can also remove a rule by selecting it and clicking on the Delete Rule button.

Testing And Releasing The Folder

Before making a new folder available for public use, you should test and debug it yourself and pilot test it with a limited number of users. During the testing process, you and the other testers should compose, submit, and open items in the folder and check forms, views, permissions, and rules to make sure they are working as planned. You can then make the folder available for general use on Exchange Server by copying the folder to a set of public folders, if you haven't done so already.

Searching Public Folders

You can search for a particular item in the set of all folders to find posted items that match criteria in which you're interested. To do so, select Find Items from the Tools menu. Select the type of item you're looking for in the Look For box. Select Public Folders in the In box to search all public folders, or choose a subset of public folders to search by clicking on the Browse button. Then type the criteria for your search and click on Find Now to start searching.

Once you've finished creating the public folder, you should notify everyone to whom you granted permission to access the folder that the folder is now available. To send a shortcut to the new folder using email, follow these steps:

1. Open the new public folder.

2. Open a new mail message.

3. Fill out the To and Cc fields with the names of everyone to whom you granted access to the folder.

4. Drag the icon for the public folder from the right side of the Folder Banner to the Mail Message button on the Windows taskbar and then to the text box of the email message (see Figure 8.22).

5. Click on Send.

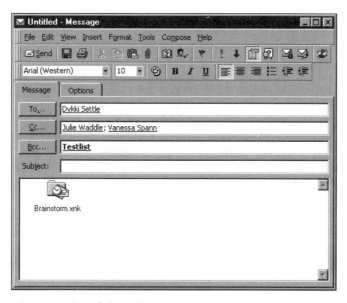

Figure 8.22 Sending a public folder shortcut in an email message.

Instant Groupware

When you create a public folder that contains Outlook items, the built-in Outlook module that handles that type of item becomes available from the folder. Any user of the folder who has the appropriate permissions can then use the Outlook module from inside the public folder to create, view, edit, and delete the Outlook items in the folder. That information is shared among all users of the folder. Therefore, simply moving Outlook items into a public folder creates a full-fledged group application—*instant groupware*. Programming code and creating custom forms become unnecessary, because the groupware application takes advantage of the existing forms and behavior of the Outlook module. The module can also be customized without programming to meet specific needs.

Common applications for instant groupware public folders include sharing email messages in an electronic bulletin board, scheduling group events, managing group tasks, and sharing and maintaining a customer contact list among a workgroup. All these groupware applications have the advantage of enabling users to easily share, edit, and review information that is constantly updated—using the functions of Outlook with which they are already familiar.

For example, simply creating a public folder that contains email messages produces an electronic bulletin board application where users can submit, share, and respond to ideas in one central location. Electronic bulletin boards help members of the group stay up to date on issues that affect the group. They can participate in the discussion at any time and from any location. A technical users group made up of either customers or internal users can post solutions, ideas, and problems related to a product to an electronic bulletin board; technicians can then review and respond to submissions. A customer support bulletin board might record customer questions, the preferred response, and how the call was resolved, with information organized in any number of useful ways, such as by product or by customer.

By Conversation Topic View

When viewing electronic bulletin boards, you can access a By Conversation Topic view that organizes messages by conversation thread. The By Conversation Topic view is the default view for electronic bulletin boards unless otherwise specified. This view enables users to show the history of responses to a particular post and follow the discussion related to that post. Conversation threading also provides an overview of the different topics under discussion. Conversation threads are grouped by subject and are sorted by the date of the last change, so that the most recently edited conversation threads appear at the top of the list. To view the messages in the folder by conversation thread, choose the By Conversation Topic view after opening the folder.

A team tasks folder using Outlook's Tasks module might be used to help everyone on the team keep track of the group's work on a project by displaying who is responsible for different group tasks and the status of those tasks. Members of the group can add the tasks they are required to complete as their part of the project to the workgroup's task list or create task requests for other members of the workgroup. Users can then update the progress of posted tasks as work is completed, giving the entire team an overall view of the progress of the project.

Tip

When you add tasks to a public tasks folder, you shouldn't create a task request from a private folder to assign a task to the public folder; the due date for the task will not be visible.

Items in Outlook's Calendar module can be shared to create a group schedule of appointments, meetings, and events that can be accessed and updated by any member of the group. For example, a company calendar might provide an organization-wide schedule of vacations, holidays, and important company events. A Calendar public folder might also be used to share group schedules, post the significant events in a marketing campaign, or make a class schedule publicly available.

Publishing the items in a Contacts folder to a public folder enables a group to create, review, and update contacts in a shared master contact list. For example, a workgroup could access and update a list of contacts related to the group's project, a sales department might share a list of leads, or the entire organization could share a list of vendors in a Contacts public folder.

Copying Public Folder Items

You might occasionally find it useful to copy an Outlook item, such as an appointment, contact, or task, from a public folder to one of your private Outlook folders. This enables you to add personal notes about the item and to view the item in the same list as your other appointments, contacts, or tasks. You must have permission to read items in the folder to do this. Right-click on the item in the public folder that you want to copy, and drag the item to your private folder. You can even drag the item to one of your private folders that doesn't contain items of the same type. For example, you can drag an appointment from a public Contacts folder to your private Inbox to attach the appointment to an email message. Then you can send the contact to someone who doesn't have permission to access the public folder.

Posting Office Documents To Folders

Public folders provide a convenient way to share Office documents with coworkers, who can then read and edit the documents. For example, you might choose to post sales projections or quarterly sales reports as Excel workbooks to a Sales and Marketing knowledge base, so that everyone in the department can review and edit the latest information. To post an Office document to a public folder, you must have the Office program installed on your computer, and you must have permission to create items in the folder. To post an Excel workbook, for instance, open the workbook in Excel. Choose Send To from the File menu and click on Exchange Folder; then double-click on the public folder where you want to post the workbook. You can also create the Excel workbook directly from the public folder. Simply open the folder and choose New Office Document from the File menu. When prompted, choose Post The Document In This Folder. Then, create the document as normal and click on the Post button when you're finished.

For example, the marketing department creates a public folder to track potential customers using contact items. Each potential customer is added to the folder as a contact. By creating a custom view with two new fields—Not Interested and Materials Sent—members of the marketing department can track potential customers' interest in the product from the public folder. If the potential customer is not interested in the product, the marketing staff member only needs to check the Not Interested field to notify the rest of the department not to contact the prospect. If the potential customer is interested, the marketing staff member can enter information in the Materials Sent field to show other members of the department at a glance when marketing materials were sent and to let them know when they should follow up with the prospect. Simply by adding new fields to a view, the contacts groupware application is customized to effectively communicate information your business or department needs to know.

Sample Applications

Sample applications are an easy way to create useful, full-fledged, public folder applications. They provide real-world solutions to common business problems and serve as examples for the kinds of more complex public folder applications that you can build. They can be used as-is to fulfill a wide variety of information-sharing and communication needs. They can also easily be customized by modifying the applications' views, forms, and rules, and thus are a good starting point for building new public folder applications. Several sample applications are included with your Exchange Server software, and additional applications are available from Microsoft and third-party vendors. See Appendix B for pointers to Web sites where you can download sample applications.

The sample applications included with Exchange Server provide solutions to many common business problems. For example, the Help Desk sample application provides an online help desk that enables employees or customers to request assistance from customer service staff; then, the customer service manager can assign tasks to customer service staff members based on these requests and track the progress of the tasks (see Figure 8.23). The Contact Tracking application enables users to create and view company contact profiles and respond with action items, correspondence reports, and miscellaneous activity reports related to contacts. The Classified Ads application provides a place where users can submit classified ads, read the posted ads, and respond with a purchase order for buying advertised items. These are just a few examples of the hundreds of sample applications available for use on your Exchange Server system.

You can immediately start using any sample application by installing it to the public folder set from the Exchange Server CD-ROM or from the Web and setting permissions for users who can access the folder. You can also copy the folder design to a new folder and then modify the sample application's design to suit the needs of your organization or workgroup.

Follow these steps to install and open a sample application in Outlook:

1. Copy the sample application's executable file from the Exchange Server CD-ROM or download it from the Web to the directory of your choice.

2. Double-click on the executable file to start the Setup program.

3. Follow the installation instructions; be sure to make a note of the directory where the sample application is installed.

Figure 8.23 The Help Desk sample application.

4. In Outlook, select Open Special Folder from the File menu.

5. Select Personal Folder.

6. In the Connect to Personal Folders dialog box, select the sample application's .PST file from the directory where the application was installed.

Tip
••• •••

If you want to install all the sample applications included with Exchange Server, select the Sampapps.pst file.

7. Click on OK; the public folder is opened in Outlook (see Figure 8.24).

After installing and opening the sample application, take some time to learn how it works before modifying it or installing it to the public folder hierarchy. View the application's forms by opening any existing item, or try to create a new item in the folder by choosing New Post In This Folder from the Compose menu. After becoming familiar with the sample application, you can customize its forms, views, rules, and permissions if you want using the methods described in the "Creating A Public Folder" section earlier in this chapter. When you're done modifying the application, you can copy the application to the public folders set to make it available across the Exchange Server organization.

Follow these steps to copy the folder to the public folder hierarchy:

1. From the Folder List, click on the sample application folder.

2. Select Folder Copy from the File menu.

Figure 8.24 The Contact Tracking sample application.

Creating Shortcuts To Favorite Public Folders

You might want to create Shortcuts on the Outlook Bar to public folders you use often. That way, you can open the folder directly from the Outlook Bar instead of navigating through the Folder List. Open the group where you want to place the Shortcut and select Add To Outlook Bar from the File menu. Click on Outlook in the Look In box and choose the public folder you want to create a Shortcut to from the Folder Name box. You can also add a public folder shortcut to your Favorites folder for easy access by dragging the public folder from the Folder List to the Favorites icon on the Outlook Bar.

3. In the Copy The Selected Folder To The Folder box, select an existing public folder where you want to add the new folder as a subfolder (see Figure 8.25).

4. Click on OK.

Publishing Electronic Forms

Electronic forms are customized applications that automate business tasks and replace their paper equivalents. Any type of request or reporting process in your organization can be automated and distributed electronically using electronic forms. For example, you could create forms for making and processing purchase orders, requesting travel information, requesting vacation or sick leave, distributing surveys, collecting feedback on a product or service, making charitable donations online, gauging public opinion about a topic, making expense reports, sending telephone messages, or submitting status reports. For help in determining the steps needed to create an electronic form, see Decision Tree 8.2.

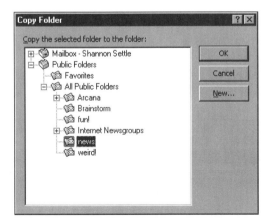

Figure 8.25   Copying a new folder to a set of public folders.

eight

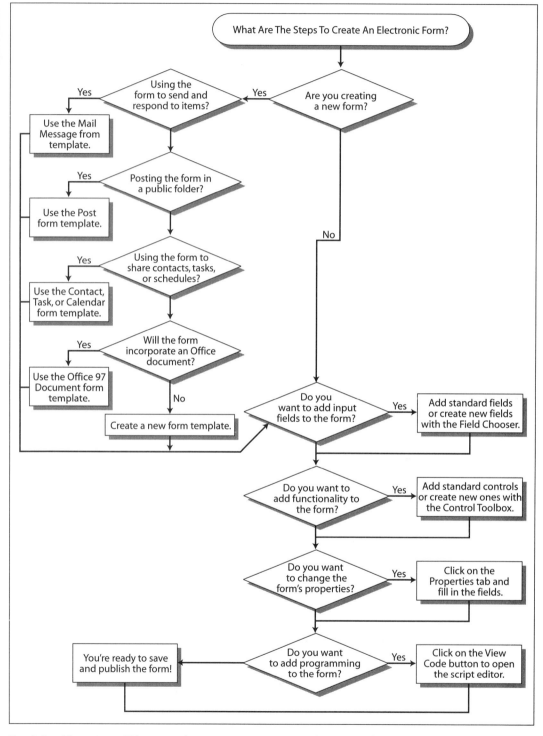

Decision Tree 8.2 What are the steps to create an electronic form?

Electronic forms serve many purposes on the Exchange Server system. As you've already learned, electronic forms can be installed in public folders to provide customized functionality for the public folder application. These kinds of forms are used to post information to the public folder for sharing among a workgroup. Forms can also be stored in Exchange Server's forms libraries and made available for general use or exchange via email, making it easy to distribute and collect information electronically. Finally, you can create forms for your own personal use that are not available to other Exchange Server users, such as expense report or mileage tracking forms.

Outlook's *Forms Designer* tool makes it simple to create custom electronic forms. Forms Designer provides a visual tool and many layout features for quickly creating professional-looking forms. You use Forms Designer to modify a standard form without programming to suit your application's purposes. For example, you can add and remove fields, controls, options, and tabs to change the behavior and look of the form in any way you like. You can even incorporate the functionality of another Office program into the form. Then, the form is saved as a file for use as a template or is installed in one of Exchange Server's forms libraries for access by other members of the organization or for installation in a public folder application.

Standard Forms

When using Forms Designer to build a new form, you start with one of the standard Outlook forms and all of that form's built-in functionality. All you have to do is modify the form to suit your purposes, rather than trying to design a new form from scratch. The standard Outlook forms include the following:

➤ **Mail Message.** Using the *Mail Message form,* users can send and respond to items, either via email or via a public folder.

➤ **Post.** The *Post form* is used to post and respond to items in a public folder and serves as the foundation for electronic bulletin board applications.

➤ **Contact, Task, and Calendar.** By showing additional pages on these standard Outlook forms, you can customize them to meet your application's specific needs.

➤ **Office 97 Document.** The *Office 97 Document form* is wrapped around an Excel, Word, or PowerPoint document so the document can be sent as a mail message or shared in a public folder.

Opening A Standard Form

We would like to create a telephone message form based on the Mail Message form. This type of form is used to record telephone messages and is then sent to the recipient via email. Let's go through the steps of opening, modifying, saving, and distributing the form.

eight

Mail Message Form Ideas

Using the Mail Message form as the foundation, you can build many different kinds of electronic form applications for collecting information from coworkers and customers. The following are some ideas for modifying the Mail Message form to create powerful business solutions:

- Create a product feedback form that is sent to customers through the Internet. By specifying a public folder as the return address, the filled-out form is automatically returned to the folder, allowing members of a department to view the feedback. (This type of form could even be linked to the company's Web page.)

- Create a request form that automates request processes in the organization, such as purchase order, vacation time, or travel service requests, which is automatically returned to the appropriate supervisor when filled out; the supervisor can then approve or deny the request and return it to the sender.

- Create a report form that is used to structure and distribute information, such as status reports, time sheets, or mileage reports. The forms are then automatically routed to the appropriate supervisor for approval.

To open the Forms Designer for modifying any of the standard Mail Message, Post, Contact, Task, or Calendar forms, follow these steps:

1. Open the item that you want to base the form on in Outlook; in this case choose New Mail Message from the File menu.

2. Select Design Outlook Form from the item's Tools menu (Figure 8.26).

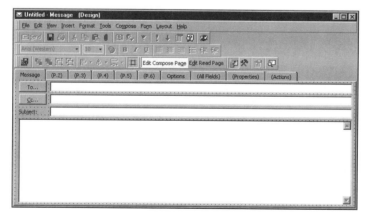

Figure 8.26   Modifying the standard Mail Message form with the Forms Designer.

Post Form Ideas

Post forms are also known as discussion forms because, when used in a public folder, they create online discussion forums. These forums can be especially useful for workgroups separated by geography or who work different hours to enable discussion about a group project. The following are some ideas for modifying the Post form to create powerful discussion applications:

- Create a technical users group where users can submit problems and respond with solutions to those problems.

- Create a job candidate application where human resources personnel can submit hiring recommendations to a public folder for review by supervisors.

- Create a product wish list application where designers can submit new product ideas to the public folder and others can review the ideas and respond with suggestions.

Opening An Office 97 Document Form

If you are creating a form from an Office 97 document, follow these steps:

1. Open an Outlook module or a public folder (not a file folder).

2. Select New from the File menu.

3. Select Office Document.

4. Double-click on the icon for the type of Office document you want to base the form on.

Office 97 Document Form Ideas

Office 97 Document forms let you build forms based on existing templates, adding the Office program's functionality to the form. For example, if you have already created Word templates like contract agreements or job estimates, you can wrap these templates in an Outlook form to use the template's properties in the form application. Using Office templates, you can easily create a library of forms that can be used over again for a variety of purposes, such as contracts, product specifications, job estimates, expense reports, status reports, Excel worksheets, or PowerPoint presentations.

5. To create a form for posting to a public or private folder that contains only a Document page, click on Post The Document In This Folder. To create a form for sending via email that contains the Document, Message, and Options pages, click on Send The Document To Someone.

6. Select Design Outlook Form from the Tools menu (see Figure 8.27).

Customizing Form Pages

Each standard Outlook form is made up of several pages that differ depending on the type of form you are customizing. When customizing a form's page, you add new fields and controls to the page. You can also hide or show the pages or change their order.

Generally, you can customize up to five pages on the form to create your mission-specific applications. Mail Message forms and Post forms contain a sixth page that you can customize: the Message page, which displays the standard functionality of an Outlook email message. Other named pages incorporate the functionality of that tab of the Outlook item; for example, the Options page of a Mail Message form displays the email message's options. Additional blank pages are not identified by name and include only a grid where you can place fields and controls.

To start customizing a form's page, simply click on that page's tab in the bottom toolbar of the Forms Designer. We're going to modify the Message page, so click on the Message tab (see Figure 8.28).

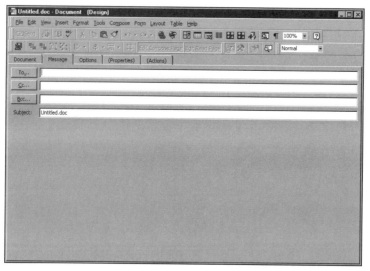

Figure 8.27   Modifying a form based on a Word document to send to someone via email.

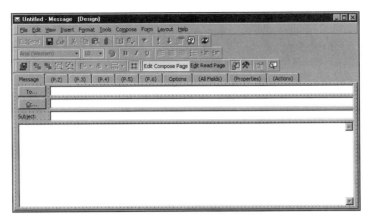

Figure 8.28   The Message page of the Mail Message form.

Adding Fields To The Page

Fields support calculated expressions, validation formulas, and formatting. For example, you can place a calculated expression field on a time card form to automatically calculate the total number of hours worked in a week. Field validation ensures that a specific value is entered into the field; for example, you can add a validation formula to a purchase order form that, when the value of the Total box exceeds a certain amount, opens a dialog box requesting that the user send the purchase order to a supervisor for approval.

Use the *Field Chooser* tool of the Forms Designer to add new fields to the page (see Figure 8.29). The Field Chooser displays a list of standard fields for the form and also allows you to create new fields, if needed. It opens automatically beside the form when you choose Design Outlook Form from the Tools menu. If the Field Chooser is not shown, click on the Field Chooser toolbar button or select Field Chooser from the Form menu.

To add a field to the page, simply drag the field from the Field Chooser to the page. For example, we're going to drag the From field to our telephone message form to create a field where the user can type in who the message is from or select the name from the Address Book by clicking on the From button. If you don't see the field you want, choose a new set of fields from the menu at the top of the Field Chooser. Outlook's *AutoLayout* feature automatically positions the field on the form in the best possible location and sizes the field for you.

Tip

To turn on and off the AutoLayout feature, select it from the Layout menu.

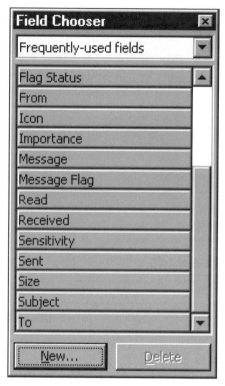

Figure 8.29   The Field Chooser.

Now, you can align, size, and set properties for the field. The Forms Designer is a visual editor, so if you want to move a field or resize it, you only have to select it and drag the handles. The background grid helps you place fields in relation to each other. You can also select fields and cut, copy, or paste them using the Edit menu; for example, we do not need the Cc field, so select it and choose Cut from the Edit menu to delete it. Then select the From field and drag the right handle until it is the same size as the To field (see Figure 8.30).

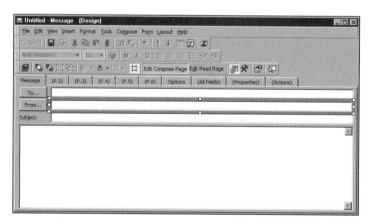

Figure 8.30   Adding the From field to the Mail Message form and resizing it.

The Layout menu provides many options for changing the layout of fields (many of these options are also available from the toolbar and from the right-click shortcut menu). For example, you can use the options on the Layout menu to align the field on the grid, size the field to the grid, make fields the same size, change spacing around the field, center the field, and group, arrange, or order fields. Try experimenting with these options to get used to their functions.

To set the properties of the field, follow these steps:

1. Select the field.

2. Click on the Properties toolbar button to display the Properties dialog box (see Figure 8.31).

3. Click on the Display tab.

4. Type a name for the field in the Name box: **FromButton**.

5. Type the caption that displays on the field in the Caption box: **Who Called**.

6. Set other display settings, such as the position of the field, caption font, and color of the field; we're going to leave these settings as the defaults.

Tip

To set additional, more advanced display properties for a field, right-click on the field and select Advanced Properties from the shortcut menu.

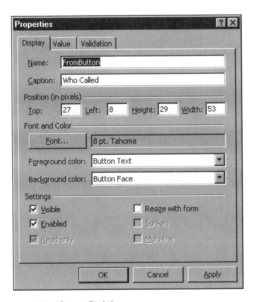

Figure 8.31   Setting properties for a field.

7. Click on the Value tab to set calculated expressions for the field or to bind a field to a control.

8. Click on the Validation tab to set validation settings and formulas for the field.

9. Click on OK when you're done to apply the new properties.

Now we're going to create a new field to show the time and date of the call. Follow these steps:

1. Click on New in the Field Chooser (see Figure 8.32).

2. Type the name of the field in the Name box: **Time**.

3. Select the field type from the Type list; in this case, choose the Date/Time type to automatically show the date and time of the call.

4. Select the field format from the Format list to show the format of the date and time; in this case, choose the DD/MM/YY 0:00 PM format.

5. Click on OK; the new field is added to the Field Chooser in the User-defined Fields set.

6. Drag the field to the form and set its alignment, size, and properties.

Let's add one more predefined field, the Importance field, to show the urgency of the call. Let's also create another new field where the phone number of the caller can be recorded. Finally, adjust the alignment, size, and properties of all the fields until the form looks like the one shown in Figure 8.33.

Adding Controls To The Page

You can insert controls in the form to add functionality and intelligence. Click on the *Controls Toolbox* toolbar button to open a toolbox of available controls (see Figure 8.34). Standard controls include Select Objects, Label, TextBox, ComboBox, ListBox, CheckBox, OptionButton, ToggleButton, Frame, CommandButton, TabStrip, MultiPage, ScrollBar, SpinButton, and Image. You can also right-click on the Controls Toolbox and select Custom Controls to find additional controls which can be added to your form, including ActiveX controls and multimedia controls.

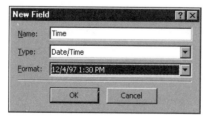

Figure 8.32   Creating a new field.

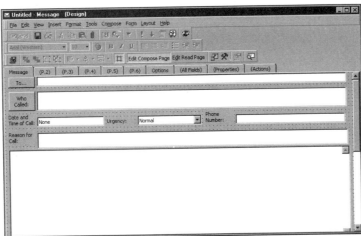

Figure 8.33   The completed form with added and modified fields.

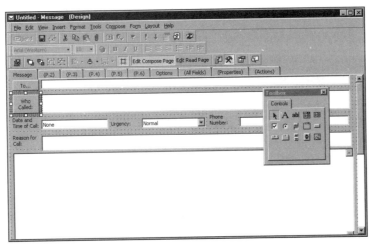

Figure 8.34   The Controls Toolbox.

As with fields, simply drag the control you want to the form. The AutoLayout feature automatically places the control in the best position and aligns the control on the page. Then, you can align, size, and set the control's properties in the same way you did for the fields. For example, you can combine multiple CheckBox and Label controls to add check boxes to the forms describing the reason for the call, such as "Personal," "Returning Your Call," and "Call Back ASAP" check boxes. Again, you should experiment with the available controls to customize the look and functionality of your form.

To remove a control from a form's page, right-click on the control and select Delete from the shortcut menu.

On Site

Manipulating Form Pages

To hide a form's page, click on the page and select Display This Page from the Form menu. For instance, we're going to hide the Options page because it is not needed for our form, so click on the Options tab and select Display This Page from the Form menu. Parentheses appear around the page's name on its tab to indicate that it is hidden.

Repeat the process to show the page again. Also, if you drag a new field or control to a hidden page, the page will automatically be shown. (You cannot show the All Fields, Properties, or Actions pages.) You can rename a page by choosing Rename Page from the Form menu and typing the new name in the Page Name box.

● ● *Tip* ● ● ●

To change what appears on the first page, hide the first page and create a new version on one of the blank pages.

Customizing The Properties Page

The Properties page lets you set the properties of the entire form. Much of the information you enter on this page appears in the About Form dialog box when it is selected from the Help menu and in the Properties dialog box for the form. Follow these steps to set properties for a form:

1. Click on the (Properties) tab (see Figure 8.35).

2. Type the name of the form that you want to appear on the title bar in the Form Caption box: **While You Were Out**.

3. If desired, type a category the Category box; this enables you to group similar forms. We're going to give our form a category of **Telephone Message**.

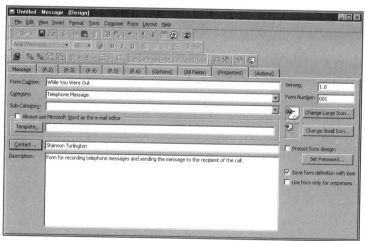

Figure 8.35   The Properties page.

4. If desired, type a subcategory for the form in the Sub-Category box; this enables you to further organize categories of forms.

5. Enter a number or text in the Version box that identifies the version of the form.

6. Enter a number for the form in the Form Number box.

7. Select the Always Use Microsoft Word As The Email Editor check box if you want to use Word to compose the form; the form will only be available to those who use Word as their email editor.

8. If you want to base the body of the form on a Word template, click on the Template button and select the template file.

9. If you want to change the icon of the form as displayed in icons view, click on the Change Large Icon and Change Small Icon buttons and select the new icon files.

10. Click on the Contact button and select the name of the person who should be contacted with problems about the form.

11. Type a short description of the form in the Description box.

12. If you want to protect your form with a password, select the Protect Form Design check box, click on Set Password, and type the password into the Password and Confirm boxes.

13. If you plan to send the form through email, select the Save Form Definition With Item check box.

14. If you want the form to show only for replies to messages, select the Use Form Only For Responses check box.

Customizing The Actions Page

The Actions page lists all the actions available for the form (see Figure 8.36). For instance, a Mail Message form includes the Reply, Reply To All, Forward, and Reply To Folder actions. The page tells you whether each action is enabled, the action's name, what form the action creates, and other properties of the action.

You can change any standard action's properties by selecting that action and clicking on the Properties button. For example, to disable a standard action, clear the Enabled check box. To change the form that is opened by the action, select the new form from the Form Name menu. You can also specify whether you want the action to appear as a command on both the form's item menu and the toolbar or just on the item menu. Click on OK when you're done modifying the properties of the action to save your changes.

You can also create custom actions that define how the form handles responses on the Actions page. Custom actions might be used to open other forms, including forms of different types; for example, you might create a Mail Message form with an action item

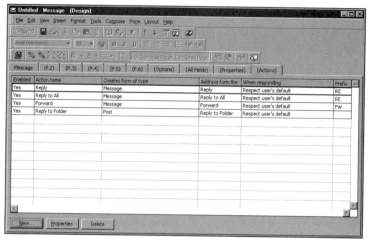

Figure 8.36   The Actions page for the Mail Message form.

that opens a Contact form. Actions can also be used to create new items; for example, an action item on a Mail Message form can create a new contact. To create a new action, click on New, and select the properties of the action (see Figure 8.37). Click on OK when you're done to add your new action to the list of actions for the form.

Testing The Form

Before distributing your new form or publishing it in a public folder, you should thoroughly test it to make sure it works the way you envisioned. The Forms Designer lets you easily switch between *design view,* or the view used when creating the form, and *read view,* a view of the form as it appears to the user. Just select Design Outlook Form from

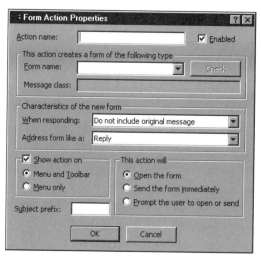

Figure 8.37   Creating a new action for a form.

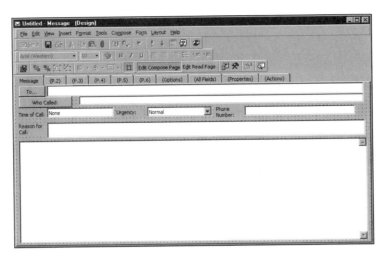

Figure 8.38   The form in design view.

the Tools menu (see Figure 8.38) to switch between the two views. While in read view, make sure that all elements of the form appear correctly. If necessary, you can select Design Outlook Form again to switch back to design view and make corrections.

Saving And Distributing The Form

You have three options for saving your electronic form:

➤ **Save the form to a personal folder.** Use this option when you want to send the form to others via email or when you do not plan to share the form. (Forms exchanged via email are called *send forms.*) Simply open the personal folder where you want to save the form and select Save from the File menu.

➤ **Save the form as a file.** This option enables you to work with the form in another program or save the form as a template; use it if you do not plan to share the form with others or if you plan to send the form via email. Select Save As from the File menu and click on a file type in the Save As Type box; for example, select Outlook Template and save the form to the Templates folder to create a new Outlook template.

Extending Forms

Visual Basic Scripting Edition (VBScript) is built into Forms Designer to provide another choice for customizing Outlook forms. Using VBScript, you can add even more functionality to forms, automatically create items and set their properties, automatically update fields, and add intelligence. You can directly view and modify the code of the form by clicking on the View Code toolbar button; this opens a script editor showing the code.

➤ **Save the form in a forms library.** Use this option if you want to save the form in a location on Exchange Server for easy access by others or to install the form in a public folder. See the following section for more information.

For more information on how to save an electronic form, see Decision Tree 8.3.

Forms Libraries

Forms libraries are storage areas on Exchange Server for saving forms. There are three forms libraries where you can save your electronic form:

➤ The *Personal Forms library* is where you save forms that are accessible only to you. Use it when you have created a form for your own personal use. These forms are stored in your Exchange Server mailbox.

➤ The *Folder Forms library* allows forms to be accessible to all users of a public folder. Use it when you're creating a form for installation in a public folder application.

➤ The *Organization Forms library* stores forms on Exchange Server so that they are accessible to everyone and provides an easy way to distribute the form throughout the organization.

To save the form to a forms library, follow these steps:

1. Select Publish Form As from the File menu.

2. Type the name of the form in the Form Name box.

3. Click on Publish In.

4. If you are saving the form to the Personal Forms library or the Organization Forms library, click on the Forms Library button and select the library where you want to save the form. If you are saving the form to a Folder Forms library, click on the Folder Forms Library button and select the folder where you want to save the form.

5. Click on OK.

6. Click on Publish.

Opening A Saved Form File

To open an electronic form saved as a file, select Find Items from the Tools menu. In the Look For box, click on Files and type the name of the file in the Named box. To open a form saved as an Outlook template, select Choose Template from the item menu, and click on the name of the template.

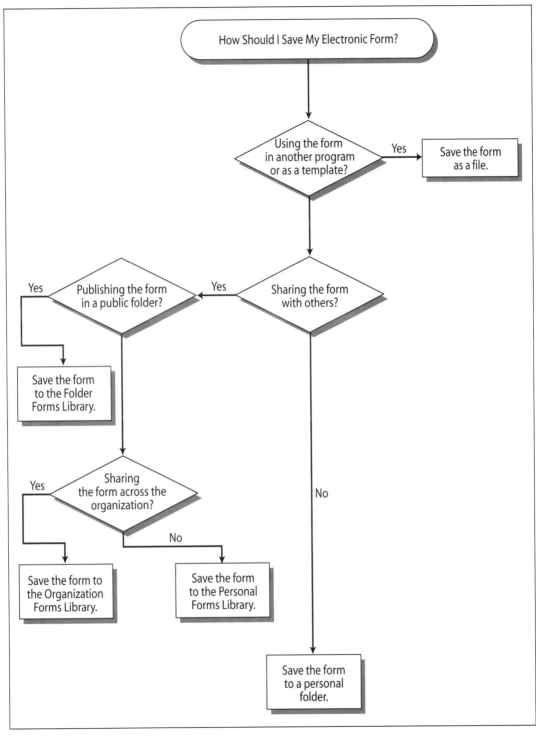

Decision Tree 8.3   How should I save my electronic form?

Managing The Organization Forms Library

The Organization Forms library is a *hidden public folder* that stores electronic forms available to every Exchange Server user but which is not displayed in the public folder hierarchy. Users can access the Organization Forms library through Outlook to use the forms in public folders and to send them via email. Use the *Forms Administrator* tool of the Administrator program to create the Organization Forms library and to set permissions for which users can create items and subfolders in the Organization Forms library.

Follow these steps to create the Organization Forms library:

1. From the Administrator program's Tools menu, select Forms Administrator (see Figure 8.39).

2. Click on New.

3. Type the name of the library in the Library Folder Name box.

4. Select a language for the library in the Language box.

●● *Tip* ●●●

You only need to assign a language to the Organization Forms library if foreign language clients will be logged on to Exchange Server. These clients search for forms that match their language. You need to create a separate Organization Forms library for each foreign language that you want to support. You cannot change the language once it is set.

5. Click on OK.

6. Click on Permissions to set permissions for accessing the Organization Forms library.

7. Click on Add, select the names of the users or groups to whom you want to grant permission, and click on OK.

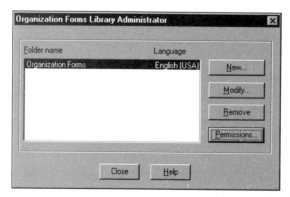

Figure 8.39   The Forms Administrator.

Opening The Form From A Forms Library

To open a form from any library, select Choose Form from the item menu. If you are opening a form in the Folder Forms library, the public folder where the form is installed must also be open. To group forms by categories in order to easily find the form you are looking for, select the Show Categories check box. Then, select the library where the form is saved, and click on the name of the form you want to open.

8. Select each user or group you added in the large window.

9. In the Roles menu, select either the Owner or None role for that user or group.

Tip

Although other roles are visible in the Roles menu, only the Owner or None roles can be selected.

10. Repeat steps 8 through 9 for each user or group you added.

11. Click on OK.

12. Click on Close when you're done to close the Forms Administrator.

Tip

If an Organization Forms library is no longer needed, select Forms Administrator from the Tools menu, select the library, and click on Remove to delete it. This removes all forms saved in the library as well.

Distributing The Form Via Email

If you saved the form to a personal folder or as a file, you can distribute the form via email by following these steps:

1. If you have not already done so, save and close the form.

Tip

Make sure the Save Form Definition With Item check box is selected on the Properties page of the form.

2. Open a new mail message and address it to the recipients to whom you want to send the form.

3. Select Item from the Insert menu.

4. Select the form that you want to send.

5. Click on OK.

6. Click on Send.

● ● *Tip* ● ● ●

You can only send a form to recipients outside the Exchange Server organization if the connector or gateway through which you are sending the form supports attachments in Microsoft Exchange *Rich Text Format (RTF)*.

Installing A Form To A Public Folder

You can easily install a form to a public folder from any forms library using Outlook's *Forms Manager* tool. Follow these steps to install a form to a public folder:

1. Right-click on the public folder where you want to install the form in the Folder List.

2. Select Properties from the shortcut menu.

3. Click on the Forms tab.

4. Click on Manage to open the Forms Manager (see Figure 8.40).

5. Select the form you want to install in the Allow These Forms In This Folder box.

● ● *Tip* ● ● ●

The Allow These Forms In This Folder box displays the contents of the Organization Forms library by default. To install forms located in a different forms library, click on Set and choose the library.

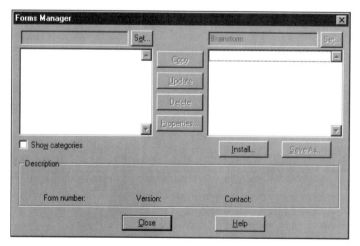

Figure 8.40   The Forms Manager.

6. Click on Copy.

7. To make the form the default form for the folder, select the form in the When Posting To This Folder, Use box.

8. Click on Close.

9. Click on an option to limit the forms you want to be available for others who use the folder under Allow These Forms In This Folder. You can choose only the forms you assigned to the folder, the forms you assigned to the folder plus all standard forms, or all forms in the Organization Forms library (see Figure 8.41).

10. Click on OK.

Publishing Directory Information

The Exchange Server *directory* collects and displays detailed up-to-date information about the members and resources of your organization. Every user who has a mailbox on the Exchange Server system is represented in the directory through the *Global Address List*. Users outside the organization are also represented if they have been added to the Global Address List as *custom recipients*. Each entry in the Global Address List has a set of properties that provide information about the user.

Users can connect to the directory and request information about other users listed in the Global Address List or search the Global Address List for particular users. For

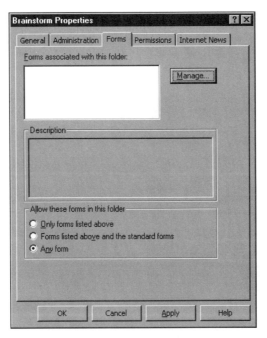

Figure 8.41   Assigning available forms to the folder.

example, users of Outlook and the Exchange Client can connect to the organization-wide directory by clicking on the Address Book toolbar button and selecting Global Address List in the Show Names From The menu (see Figure 8.42). Users can then select names in the Global Address List and click on the Properties button to find more information about other users listed in the directory.

Tip

You can view the Global Address List directly from the Administrator program by double-clicking on Global Address List in the Administrator window. You can then view and edit users' properties by selecting the user and clicking on the Properties toolbar button.

Using the Global Address List, you can create and manage a white pages listing of every member of your organization. Corporate white pages include an organization-wide listing of names, email addresses, and phone numbers. They can be viewed by anyone, including those outside the organization, using a wide variety of clients.

Customizing The Global Address List

When users access the Global Address List with Outlook, the Exchange Client, an LDAP client, or a Web browser, they can view address and telephone number information for every Exchange Server user or custom recipient. This is the information you entered when you created the user's or custom recipient's mailbox. Each field, such as the telephone number field or email address field, is called an *attribute,* or a predefined characteristic associated with the recipient object.

There are three ways you can customize how a recipient's attributes appear in the Global Address List. One way is to configure which predefined attributes display, depending on

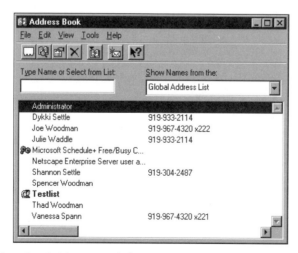

Figure 8.42   Viewing the Address Book from Outlook.

how the directory is accessed. For example, you can display different information when the Global Address List is accessed by an authenticated Exchange Server user than when it is accessed by an anonymous user connecting from outside the organization.

Another way is to add even more information using custom attributes. *Custom attributes* are recipient characteristics that you define to provide additional information specific to your organization. For example, you may define a custom attribute to display recipients' employee ID numbers, office numbers, or other characteristics not represented by the standard attributes.

You can also modify *details templates* to customize the way information about recipients appears in the Global Address List. Details templates let you limit which attributes and custom attributes can appear in the Global Address List. For example, if you do not want to publish a user's home address or home phone number for everyone to access, you can remove these attributes from the Global Address List by changing the details templates.

Configuring Attribute Settings

Follow these steps to determine what predefined information is available to different users of the Global Address List:

1. Click on the Configuration button in the Administrator window.

2. Double-click on DS Site Configuration.

3. Select the Attributes tab (see Figure 8.43).

Figure 8.43   Configuring settings for predefined recipient attributes.

4. In the Configure window, select one of the following: Anonymous Requests to set the attributes visible to anonymous accesses of the directory; Authenticated Requests to set the attributes visible to authenticated accesses of the directory; or Inter-site Replication to set the attributes included in directory replication and thus available to users in other sites.

5. In the Show Attributes For menu, select the type of recipient for which you want to configure attributes, or select All Mail Recipients to configure attributes for every recipient in the Global Address List.

6. In the large window, clear the check boxes by the predefined attributes that you do not want displayed for the selected request type.

7. Repeat steps 4 through 6 until you have completely defined how you want attributes to appear in the directory for each type of access and each type of recipient.

8. Click on OK when you're done to apply all of the new directory settings.

Creating Custom Attributes

Follow these steps to define custom attributes for recipient objects in the directory:

1. Click on the Configuration button in the Administrator window.

2. Double-click on DS Site Configuration.

3. Select the Custom Attributes tab (see Figure 8.44).

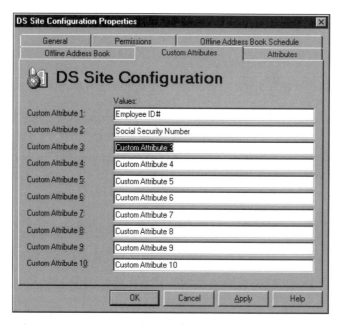

Figure 8.44   Creating new custom attributes fields.

4. Type the new custom attributes in the corresponding boxes under Values; you can specify up to 10 custom attribute fields.

5. Click on OK when you're done.

Then, you can fill out the custom attribute fields for individual recipients by following these steps:

1. Click on the Recipients button in the Administrator window.

2. Double-click on the recipient for whom you want to assign custom attributes.

3. Select the Custom Attributes tab (see Figure 8.45).

4. Fill out all the custom attribute fields you previously configured with the appropriate information.

5. Click on OK when you're done.

Creating Details Templates

Follow these steps to modify details templates:

1. Click on the Configuration button in the Administrator window.

2. Double-click on Addressing.

3. Double-click on Details Templates.

Figure 8.45 Filling out custom attributes fields for a mailbox.

4. Select one of the language containers.

5. Double-click on the template you want to modify.

6. Select the General tab (see Figure 8.46).

7. In the Display Name box, type the name of the details template.

8. Under Template Help, click on Import 16 Bit Help File or Import 32 Bit Help File to select the Help files that will be displayed with the details template.

Tip

Importing a new Help file permanently overwrites previously defined Help files. To save the old Help files, access all templates from a client computer and save the Help files from the Temp directory of that computer.

9. Select the Templates or MS-DOS Templates tab to view all the fields and controls that make up an existing dialog box.

10. Click on New to create a new template control and add a function to the details template.

11. Select a control in the window and click on either Remove to delete it or Edit to edit its properties.

12. Select a control in the window and click on either Move Up or Move Down to change its place in the list.

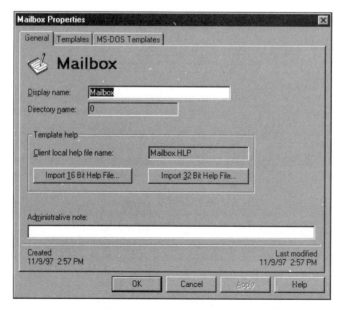

Figure 8.46   Modifying the details template for the mailbox object.

13. After modifying a template, click on Test to test its new appearance.

14. Click on OK when you're done to save your new template.

• • • *Tip* • • • •

You can revert to the original settings of the template, permanently overwriting any changes, by double-clicking on the template in the Administrator window, selecting the Templates tab, and clicking on Original.

Organizing The Global Address List

Using Exchange Server's *Address Book views* feature, you can group Exchange Server mailboxes, custom recipients, public folders, and distribution lists in the Global Address List by a common attribute, such as by city or by department. Grouping users in categories customizes the look of the Global Address List for your organization and makes it easier to find directory information in large corporate white pages. Address Book views are displayed in the Administrator program and as address lists in the Show Names From The menu in the Address Book in Exchange Client and Outlook (see Figure 8.47).

Each Address Book view contains one or more groupings that correspond to a particular attribute. Address Book view groups can be defined by company name, city, country, department, or any custom attributes, which give you the flexibility to define your own groupings. Any user with associated attributes that match the grouping in an Address Book view appears in that view under the appropriate grouping. You can then group the groupings by larger containers. For example, you can group cities by state or by country within the Address Book view.

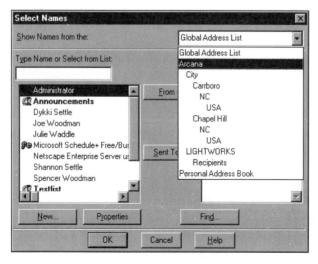

Figure 8.47   An Address Book view displayed in the Outlook Address Book.

Suppose your organization has offices in many different cities and you want to group users in the Global Address List by the cities where their offices are located. You would create an Address Book view container for each city where your company has an office. All users listed in the Global Address List who are located in that city are automatically sorted into the appropriate container for their city.

Creating An Address Book View

To create a new Address Book view, follow these steps:

1. In the Administrator window, select New Other from the File menu.

2. Select Address Book View.

3. Select the General tab (see Figure 8.48).

4. In the Display Name box, type a display name for the Address Book view.

5. In the Directory Name box, type a directory name for the Address Book view.

Defining Groupings

Next, you must define the groupings for the Address Book view. You can group users by any of the predefined attributes that appear on the Group By property page, or you can create custom attributes which allow you to further refine the Address Book view with information particular to your company. Once you have defined a custom attribute, it becomes available for grouping. For example, you might create a custom attribute called Office Building and then group recipients by their office building.

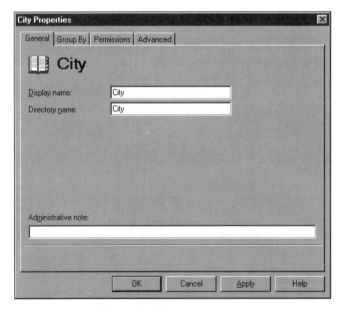

Figure 8.48   Creating a new Address Book view.

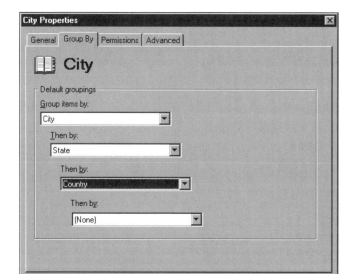

Figure 8.49   Defining groupings for an Address Book view.

Follow these steps to select groupings of an Address Book view:

1. With the Address Book View dialog box still open, select the Group By tab (see Figure 8.49).

2. In the Group Items By menu, select an attribute you want to use to group users by first.

3. If you would like to group users by additional attributes, select the attribute in the next available Then By menu.

4. Click on OK when you're finished.

Setting Advanced Grouping Options

You can further refine the groupings using advanced grouping options. For example, you can determine whether users should appear in one or more groupings and which groupings you want to display in the client's Address Book. You can also delete empty groupings.

Suppose you set up groupings of users by country, state, and city. You must determine whether to include the user only under the city grouping or in all the groupings. You only have the options of showing users in all the groupings or in the lowest level grouping.

Follow these steps to set the advanced options:

1. In the Administrator window, select Address Book Views.

2. Select the Address Book view for which you'd like to set advanced options.

3. Select Properties from the File menu.

4. Select the Advanced tab (see Figure 8.50).

5. Select the Promote Entries To Parent Containers check box to show users in all groupings that match their attributes; leave this check box deselected to show users in only the lowest level grouping that matches their attributes.

6. Select the Show This View In The Client Address Book check box to show the Address Book view and all the groupings in the Address Books of Exchange Client and Outlook.

7. Click on the Remove Empty Containers button to remove any empty groupings from the Address Book view.

8. Click on OK.

Modifying User Attributes In The Address Book View

Now that you have set up the Address Book view, you can easily modify the view. For example, you can move blocks of users between groupings or change the attributes of individual users to move them to a new grouping.

When you move users between groupings, the attribute that defined the user in the original grouping is automatically changed to the attribute of the new grouping. For example, five users are transferred from the New York office to the Los Angeles office. When you move the users from the New York grouping to the Los Angeles grouping, the users' associated city attribute is automatically changed to Los Angeles as well.

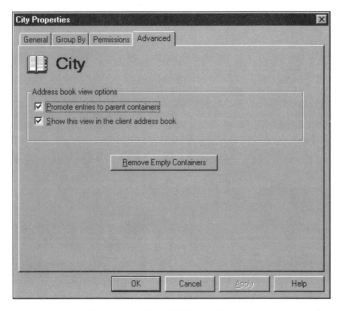

Figure 8.50   Setting advanced options for Address Book view groupings.

Follow these steps to move users between groupings:

1. In the Administrator window, click on the Recipients button.

2. Select one or more users that you want to move.

3. Select Add to Address Book View from the Tools menu (see Figure 8.51).

4. Select the grouping where you want to move the recipient object; if the container you want isn't displayed, click on New Container to create it.

5. Click on OK.

If you would like to add a new user to an existing Address Book view grouping, you only need to change the attribute value for that user. For example, if you would like to add a user to the City grouping of Washington, you simply need to change the City attribute for the user to Washington. The user will automatically be sorted into the new grouping based on the attribute you changed. Follow these steps:

1. Click on the Recipients button in the Administrator window.

2. Double-click on the user whose attribute value you'd like to change.

3. Select the General tab.

4. Edit the appropriate attribute.

5. Click on OK.

Modifying Groupings

Sometimes you'll want to delete a grouping of attributes from the Address Book view. For example, if the view is grouped by country, state, and city, you might want to delete the state grouping for countries that do not have states. Deleting a grouping removes

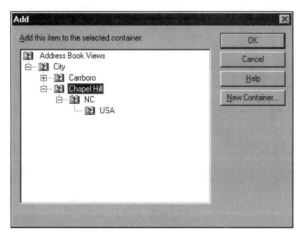

Figure 8.51   Moving a user to a new grouping.

only the grouping, not the users in the grouping. You can also change particular group-ings to show different attributes under different containers. Follow these steps:

1. In the Administrator window, click on the plus (+) button beside Address Book View to expand the groupings.

2. Select a grouping that contains a subcontainer you'd like to delete or change.

3. Select Properties from the File menu.

4. Select the Group By tab.

5. Select the None attribute in the Sub-containers menu to delete the subcontainer from that grouping (see Figure 8.52).

6. Select an alternative attribute in the Sub-containers menu to change the subcontainer for that grouping.

7. Click on OK.

Tip

If you would like to delete an entire Address Book view, click on the view name in the Administrator window and select Delete from the Edit menu. Doing so deletes only the view, not the users that appear in the view's groupings.

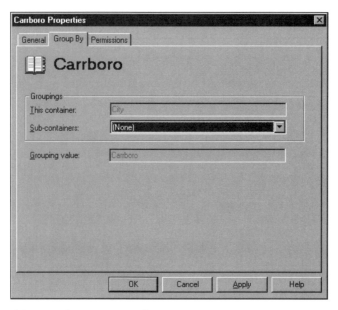

Figure 8.52 Modifying sub-containers for a grouping.

Setting Up LDAP Access To The Directory

The *Lightweight Directory Access Protocol (LDAP)* enables users with any standard LDAP client to search for names, phone numbers, and email addresses in the Exchange Server directory. LDAP clients enable people all over the world to access published corporate white pages anonymously via the Internet. The Exchange Server directory fully integrates the LDAP protocol, so that LDAP clients inside and outside of a firewall, such as Microsoft Proxy Server 2.0, can email, browse, read, and search Global Address List listings. For example, a user can search for specific information about members of the organization, such as phone numbers and office locations.

You must have established a connection to the Internet via the Internet Mail Service for LDAP clients to connect to the Exchange Server directory. Before allowing access to the directory with LDAP clients, you need to set up the directory for LDAP access. You can choose to set properties for LDAP access to the directory at either the site or server level. You can also configure anonymous connections to the directory. Perform these tasks with the Administrator program. See Decision Tree 8.4 for information on configuring the LDAP protocol.

Setting General LDAP Properties

Follow these steps to set up LDAP access to the Global Address List:

1. Select a site or server where you want to configure LDAP properties in the Administrator window.

2. Click on Configuration.

3. Double-click on Protocols.

4. Double-click on LDAP (Directory) Site Defaults if you are configuring site properties, or double-click on LDAP (Directory) Server Settings if you are configuring settings for a single server.

5. Select the General tab (see Figure 8.53).

6. Type a display name for the LDAP settings object in the Display Name box.

7. Select or clear the Enable Protocol check box to turn on or off LDAP access to the directory; it can take several minutes to make this change.

8. Click on OK.

Setting LDAP Authentication

Authentication determines whether to grant a particular user permission to connect to the directory with an LDAP client. One of the authentication methods the LDAP client supports must be enabled on the server before the client can connect to the directory.

eight

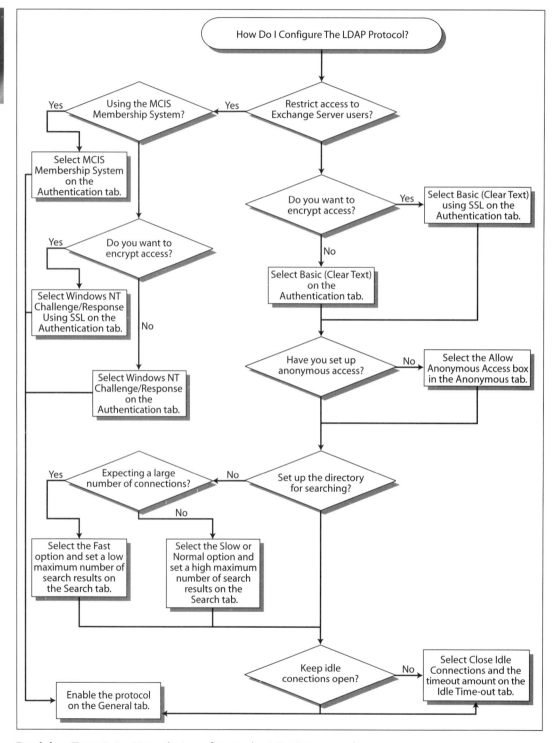

Decision Tree 8.4 How do I configure the LDAP protocol?

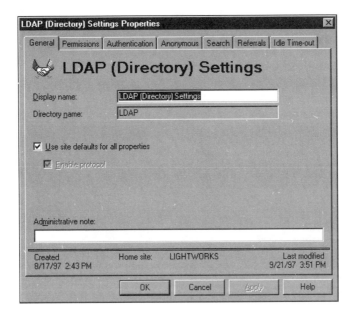

Figure 8.53 Setting general LDAP properties.

Follow these steps to set an authentication type:

1. Select the site or server in the Administrator window where you enabled the LDAP protocol.

2. Double-click on Configuration.

3. Double-click on Protocols.

4. Double-click on LDAP (Directory) Site Defaults if you are configuring authentication for an entire site, or double-click on LDAP (Directory) Settings if you are configuring settings for one server.

5. Select the Authentication tab (see Figure 8.54).

6. Select an authentication type of Basic (Clear Text); Windows NT Challenge/ Response, to enable authentication through an unencrypted username and password; Basic (Clear Text) Using SSL or Windows NT Challenge/Response Using SSL, to enable authentication through a SSL-encrypted channel (the *Secure Sockets Layer (SSL)* protocol provides secure data communication using data encryption and decryption); and/or MCIS Membership System.

 Tip ● ● ● ●

To use Secure Sockets Layer (SSL) encryption, Internet Information Server (IIS) must be installed on the Exchange Server computer.

7. Click on OK.

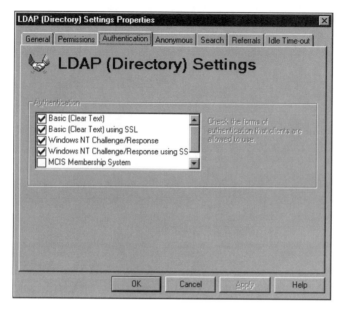

Figure 8.54   Setting authentication for LDAP access to the directory.

Setting Anonymous Access To The Directory

You might choose to specify that LDAP users can connect to the directory anonymously using Exchange Server's *anonymous access* feature. If you don't allow anonymous connections, only those Exchange Server users who have a valid Windows NT Server user account can connect to the directory. Anonymous access allows users outside the organization to connect to the directory. To set up anonymous access, follow these steps:

1. Select the site or server where you enabled the LDAP protocol in the Administrator window.

2. Double-click on Configuration.

3. Double-click on Protocols.

4. Double-click on LDAP (Directory) Site Default if you are configuring defaults for an entire site, or double-click on LDAP (Directory) Settings if you are configuring settings for a single server.

5. Select the Anonymous tab (see Figure 8.55).

6. Select the Allow Anonymous Access check box to enable anonymous access to the directory.

7. Click on OK.

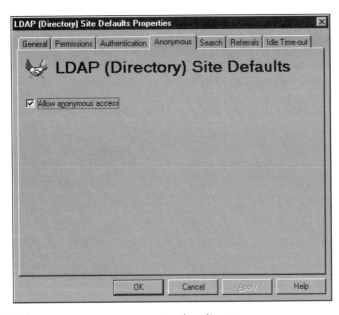

Figure 8.55 Enabling anonymous access to the directory.

Setting Search Properties

Follow these steps to specify how LDAP clients will perform searches of the Exchange Server directory:

1. Select the site or server where you enabled the LDAP protocol in the Administrator window.

2. Double-click on Configuration.

3. Double-click on Protocols.

4. Double-click on LDAP (Directory) Site Defaults if you are configuring defaults for the site, or double-click on LDAP (Directory) Settings if you are configuring settings for a single server.

5. Click on the Search tab (see Figure 8.56).

6. Under Substring Searches, click on one of the following options: The Treat "Any" Substring Searches As "Initial" Substring Searches (Fast) option specifies that only initial substring searches will be performed and any substring searches will be converted to initial substring searches; the Allow Only "Initial" Substring Searches (Fast) option specifies that only initial substring searches will be performed; the Allow All Substring Searches (Slow) option specifies that all substring searches will be performed.

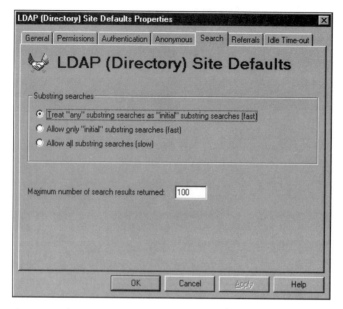

Figure 8.56   Setting search options.

7. Specify the maximum number of search results that will be returned for all searches (setting a high number will decrease server performance).

8. Click on OK.

Setting Idle Time-Out

You will probably want to automatically close LDAP connections after a period of inactivity. Follow these steps to set the *idle time-out* for LDAP connections:

1. Select the site or server where you enabled the LDAP protocol in the Administrator window.

2. Double-click on Configuration.

3. Double-click on Protocols.

4. Double-click on LDAP (Directory) Site Defaults if you are configuring settings for an entire site, or double-click on LDAP (Directory) Settings if you are configuring settings for a single server.

5. Select the Idle Time-out tab (see Figure 8.57).

6. Select the Close Idle Connections button.

7. Specify the amount of time in minutes that a connection can remain idle before being closed in the Time-out (Minutes) box.

8. Click on OK.

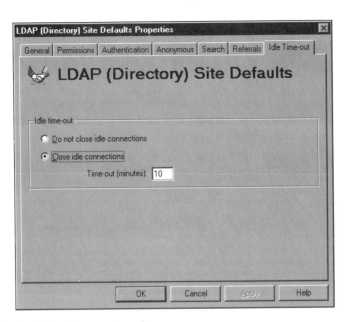

Figure 8.57   Setting idle time-out options.

Sharing Information Through Mailing Lists

Using Exchange Server, you can create and manage mailing lists of individuals numbering into the millions. You can then use the lists to automate mass mailings, sharing important information and building an ongoing relationship with your customers. You can also create mailing lists of members of a workgroup, department, or organization to facilitate sharing information quickly with members of your organization.

To create mailing lists, use Exchange Server's distribution lists feature. A *distribution list* is a group of users that can be addressed with one email address. Distribution lists facilitate the mass mailings of company-related messages and other information. Distribution lists are made up of members of the Global Address List, which can include users of the Exchange Server, custom recipients located outside the organization, public folders, and other distribution lists. When a message is addressed to a distribution list, all members of the list receive a copy of the message, saving you the trouble of addressing the message to each member of the list separately.

Distribution lists are initially created through the Administrator program, using the same commands as for creating mailboxes. Exchange Server then automates the management of distribution lists, helping to reduce costs and increase communication, and enabling Exchange Server to offer a wider range of options for distribution lists.

Once a distribution list is created, it is added to the Global Address List, so that users of the Exchange Server can send mail to the list with either Outlook or the Exchange Client (see Figure 8.58). By clicking on the Address Book toolbar button, users can search for distribution list criteria, display distribution list properties, and address messages to distribution lists, as with any other user in the Address Book. In every other way, a distribution list behaves like an individual's email address. For example, mail can be forwarded to the list or carbon copied to the list.

Creating A New Distribution List

To create a new distribution list, follow these steps:

1. Click on the Recipients button in the Administrator window.

2. Select New Distribution List from the File menu (see Figure 8.59).

3. Type the name of the distribution list in the Display Name box; this is the name of the list as it will appear in the Address Book.

4. Type the alias of the distribution list in the Alias Name box; this name is used to generate email addresses for the distribution list.

5. Under Expansion Server, select a server in your site where the distribution list will always be expanded; this is the server that will expand the list, resolve the names of all recipients, and determine the most efficient message routing, which can be processor intensive for large lists.

6. To add members to the list, click on the Modify button underneath the Members box, select recipients, and click on Add.

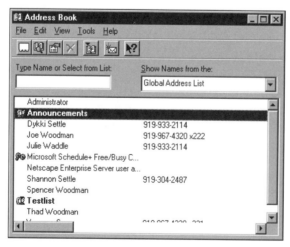

Figure 8.58   A distribution list displayed in the Address Book.

Figure 8.59   Creating a new distribution list.

7. Click on OK to show the list members in the Members box.

8. To assign an owner or primary contact person for the list, click on the Modify button underneath the Owner box, select a name, and click on OK (the owner can edit the list and remove members in the client).

9. Click on OK to create the list.

Setting Advanced Distribution List Properties

You might want to set advanced properties for the distribution list. For example, setting a message transfer limit ensures that large messages will not be distributed to the list, cutting down on bandwidth usage. You can also set options for how messages are sent, hide the list from the Address Book, and allow out-of-office messages. Follow these steps:

1. Select Recipients in the Administrator window.

2. Double-click on the distribution list for which you want to configure advanced properties.

3. Select the Advanced tab (see Figure 8.60).

4. Type a name in the Simple Display Name box that will be used by systems that cannot interpret the characters in the normal display name.

Figure 8.60 Setting advanced distribution list properties.

5. To set a message size limit, click on the Max (K) button and type the amount in kilobytes of the largest message the list can send or receive.

6. Under Distribution List Options, select the Report To Distribution List Owner option to automatically send a message to the list owner when there is a problem sending a message to the list.

7. Under Distribution List Options, select the Report To Message Originator option to copy the message to its originator when it is delivered to the list.

8. Under Distribution List Options, select the Allow Out Of Office Messages To Originator option to allow out-of-office messages to be sent to the list.

9. Under Distribution List Options, select the Hide From Address Book option to keep the list from appearing in the Address Book; mail can still be sent to the distribution list if the email address of the list is explicitly entered in the To box of a message.

10. Under Distribution List Options, select the Hide Membership From Address Book option to keep the list of distribution list members from appearing in the Address Book.

11. In the Trust Level menu, select a trust level for directory synchronization from 0 to 100.

12. Click on OK to set the advanced options.

Moving On

In this chapter, you've learned how to publish and share information stored on the Exchange Server in a variety of ways, including through public folders, electronic forms, the Global Address List, and distribution lists. In the next chapter, you'll explore the integration of Exchange Server with the Internet. You'll find out how Exchange Server's support for Internet standards enables Internet email, newsgroup, and Web access to Exchange Server users, extending Exchange Server's information-sharing capabilities even more.

Building An Online Community

In the previous chapter, you learned how to use Exchange Server's capabilities for organizing and publishing information to enable Exchange Server users to share important data with each other and with others outside the organization through public folders, corporate white pages, and mailing lists. In this chapter, you'll learn how to extend Exchange Server's communications and information-publishing capabilities to the worldwide community of the Internet.

With access to the Internet, Exchange Server users can communicate and share information with anyone around the world, including business partners and key customers. By embracing Internet standards, Exchange Server makes it easy for users to access the Internet in a variety of ways, such as through email, Usenet newsgroups, and the World Wide Web. Conversely, by making the Exchange Server a part of the Internet, your users can access their Exchange Server information through the Internet using a variety of clients and desktop operating systems, no matter whether they are working at home, from the road, or around the globe. By extending Exchange Server to the Internet, the server becomes more than just a company network for exchanging messages and files; it is transformed into a complete Internet solution, enabling your users to do more than ever before from one interface and using one server.

In this chapter, you'll learn how to set up and administer Exchange Server's support of standard Internet protocols to join your Exchange Server system with the Internet. You'll find out how to enable Internet email clients to access Exchange Server mailboxes and public folders. You'll discover how to turn your Exchange Server computer into a Usenet news server and how to publish your own Internet newsgroups. Finally, you'll learn how to make Exchange Server information available through the Web using the Outlook Web Access feature.

nine

Internet Standards Support

When developing a networking solution, no business can afford to leave the Internet out of the equation. Internet technologies have proved equally effective for facilitating communication internally among employees and externally with partners, customers, and potential customers. Exchange Server's native support of Internet standards has made it easy to meet those communication needs, enabling you to build an Internet collaboration solution with Exchange Server as the key component. You can use Exchange Server's Internet support to create many different kinds of collaboration solutions, from virtual teams of employees to virtual organizations with your business partners to widespread communities with your customers, using the Internet as a backbone.

Exchange Server supports most popularly used *Internet protocols* so that you have a choice when building a messaging and collaboration solution for your company. Rather than being locked into an environment that supports only one or two Internet protocols, you can choose the protocols and clients that work best for your company and start using them immediately. You can even mix and match protocols and clients as needed by your users for access to Internet email and discussion groups, without having to install and configure additional components each time you want to support a new Internet protocol. To help you choose which Internet protocols to support, see Decision Tree 9.1.

Internet protocols are part of the core architecture of the Exchange Server, which maintains the server's high performance. Because these standards are implemented natively on the Exchange Server, no protocol translation or overhead is involved in accessing the Exchange Server using any of the protocols. Exchange Server retains its scalability and high performance no matter which protocol is being used to access the server. For example, both Exchange clients and NNTP clients can access newsgroups on the Exchange Sever simultaneously, without impacting performance or scalability.

Exchange Server natively supports the following Internet protocols:

➤ *Simple Mail Transfer Protocol (SMTP)* for sending email to the Internet.

➤ *Post Office Protocol 3 (POP3)* for Internet email access.

➤ *Internet Message Access Protocol 4 (IMAP4)* for Internet email and private and public folder access.

➤ *Network News Transfer Protocol (NNTP)* for Usenet newsgroup access.

➤ *HyperText Transfer Protocol (HTTP)* for World Wide Web access.

➤ *Lightweight Directory Access Protocol (LDAP)* for access to the Exchange Server directory.

Refer to Chapter 8 for information on configuring Exchange Server's support of the LDAP protocol.

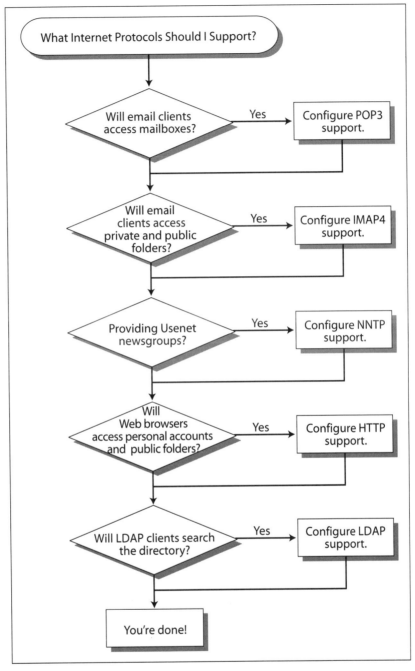

Decision Tree 9.1   What Internet protocols should I support?

Why The Internet?

You are probably already very familiar with the *Internet*, the global network that connects millions of smaller computer networks using *Transport Control Protocol/Internet Protocol (TCP/IP)*, enabling every connected network to exchange information as email, newsgroup postings, and multimedia publications on the Web. By connecting your Exchange Server to that global network, your organization becomes a part of the Internet and the worldwide community it serves.

Additionally, the Internet can be used to create a Virtual Private Network using the Point to Point Tunneling Protocol (PPTP). Using PPTP on the Internet allows for easy access and the privacy required for specific applications, such as collaborating with a worldwide sales staff. This is a highly cost-effective solution when compared with dedicated data lines.

Building A Complete Internet Solution

Previously, if your organization wanted to support Internet technologies, you had to set up and administer multiple servers to support each technology. For example, you needed a POP3 server for sending email across the Internet, an NNTP server for providing access to USENET newsgroups, and a Web server for publishing information on the Web, in addition to the company's internal email server. By providing native support for all key Internet standards, Exchange Server enables you to perform all these important tasks from one server, creating a complete Internet solution that you can configure and administer from the same interface with which you control all Exchange Server functions. Furthermore, Exchange Server is extendable to future Internet standards, so it can continue to grow and evolve as Internet technologies do. No matter what technologies become important, you will still be able to access data on the server using your choice of tools, even those that have not yet been developed.

Through its support for Internet standards, your Exchange Server becomes a part of the global Internet, enabling your users to perform two useful functions. When working on the Exchange Server with the Exchange Client or Outlook, your users not only have access to all the Exchange Server information and communications capabilities, but also gain access to important Internet functions. For example, users can send and receive email across the Internet and read and post messages to Usenet newsgroups seamlessly, from the same interface they use to send email to other Exchange Server users; manage their schedules and to-do lists; and access public folders.

Just as importantly, users can access their Exchange Server mailboxes, private folders, public folders, and address books on the Exchange Server through the Internet, using any POP3 email client, IMAP4 email client, NNTP client, or Web browser on any desktop operating system, including UNIX and Macintosh platforms. This enables users to access information stored on Exchange Server, such as their private email messages, from any computer connected to the Internet—whether they are working at home, on the road, or from a public terminal at a conference or hotel. Users have the freedom to switch between clients and desktops as needed, while retaining constant access to important information on the Exchange Server.

Finally, Exchange Server's support of Internet standards opens up your organization to non-Exchange Server users all over the world. Through Internet email, Exchange Server users can communicate one-on-one with anyone, including business partners, vendors, consultants, experts, existing customers, and potential customers. By providing access to existing Usenet newsgroups, users can enter into discussions on any topic imaginable with groups of Internet users, providing needed access to current information and experts on computing technologies, Web technologies, business news, and just-for-fun discussions. You can even publish and distribute your own Usenet newsgroups, an easy way to publish information about your organization. For example, you might publish newsgroups to provide technical support for your products, customer support for your services, or key business information for your partners. Finally, you can extend Exchange Server information and applications to the graphical *World Wide Web*, creating an easy-to-access information resource for anyone on the Internet with an interest in your organization's products, services, or company information.

Exchange Server's support of Internet standards helps your server and your organization to grow, rather than limiting it. By implementing Internet protocols on the Exchange Server, you open the server to access by a wide variety of clients and desktop operating systems, and you extend the reach of your server's information and users to the world-wide network, an essential part of any business's information-sharing solution.

Configuring Internet Protocols

Before setting up Internet email, Usenet, and Web access on your Exchange Server, you will find it useful to enable and configure properties for all Internet protocols that you want your Exchange Server system to support. You can configure Internet protocols from the Administrator program, the same interface you use to manage all other aspects of the Exchange Server.

Each site and server in your Exchange Server organization has a Protocols container that stores configuration objects for each Internet protocol. Using the site's Protocols container, you can configure default settings that apply to all Internet protocols in the site, rather than making the settings for each protocol and each server individually. When you configure default settings for protocols at the site level, those settings apply to all servers in the site. You can also change the protocol settings for individual servers to have the settings apply to only one server in the site. And you can change settings at the

mailbox level; for example, you might not want temporary employees to be able to download email using a POP3 client, so you can disable POP3 access for those employees only.

Tip

HTTP protocol settings can be configured at the site level and mailbox level only, not at the server level.

Follow these steps to configure the default Internet protocol settings:

1. Select the site or server for which you want to configure protocol settings in the Administrator window.

2. Click on the Configuration button.

3. Select Protocols.

4. Select Properties from the File menu.

5. Select the General tab (see Figure 9.1).

6. Type a name for the Protocols container in the Display Name box.

7. If you are configuring settings on a server, select the Use Site Defaults For All Properties check box to apply the site-level settings to that server.

8. Click on OK.

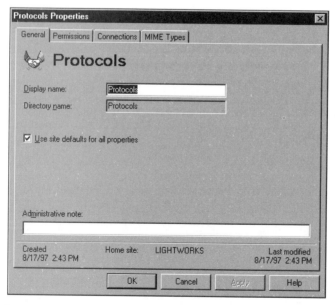

Figure 9.1   Configuring general Internet protocol settings for a server.

On Site

Configuring Connections

You can configure connection rules for POP3, IMAP4, NNTP, and LDAP access to the Exchange Server, which allow you to accept or reject access based on the Internet Protocol (IP) address or mask of the client attempting to access the server. (The *mask* is the value used with the IP address that identifies the network location of the client.) Creating a rule enables the server to match the IP addresses of hosts connecting to the server against the rule and accept or reject the connection accordingly. Otherwise, the connection is accepted by default.

Follow these steps to configure connection rules for the site-wide or server-wide defaults:

1. Select the site or server for which you'd like to configure defaults in the Administrator window.

2. Click on the Configuration button.

3. Select Protocols.

4. Select Properties from the File menu.

5. Select the Connections tab (see Figure 9.2).

6. Select the Accept/Reject Specified Connections option.

7. Click on New to add a rule that accepts or rejects connections based on IP address and mask (see Figure 9.3).

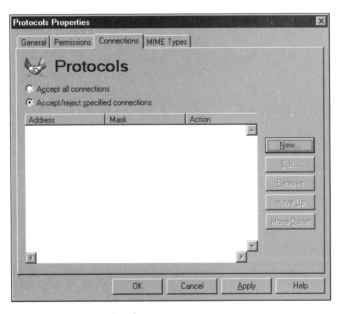

Figure 9.2   Setting connection rules for a server.

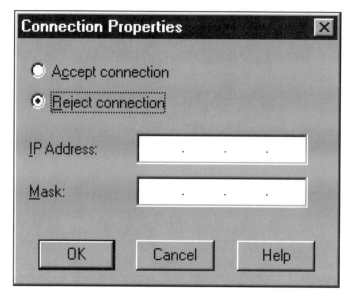

Figure 9.3   Creating a new rule for processing connections from a specific IP address.

8. Select the Accept Connection check box to specify an IP address whose connection will always be accepted, or select the Reject Connection check box to specify an IP address whose connection will always be rejected.

9. In the IP Address box, type the numeric IP address of the SMTP host whose connection will be accepted or rejected.

10. In the Mask box, type a numeric mask that identifies the network location of the client computer.

11. Click on OK; the new rule is displayed in the large window on the Connections property page.

12. Repeat steps 7 through 11 for every new rule you would like to add.

13. Click on OK when you're finished.

●● *Tip* ●●●●

After creating a new IP address to reject or accept, that rule is added to the list of connections rules on the Connections property page. You can change the order of rules in the list, and thus the order in which they are processed, by selecting the rule and clicking on Move Up or Move Down. Generally, the most specific rules should fall at the top of the list. You can also remove a rule from the list by selecting it and clicking on Remove.

Understanding MIME Types

The *MIME type* describes the contents of a particular type of data, so that the receiving system can display the data properly. For example, an email message might include an attached audio file in the WAVE format. When the message is sent, the audio file is tagged with the MIME type audio/x-wav. When it is received, the server uses the MIME type to launch the correct application to play the audio file.

MIME types are made up of two parts: the *primary type*, which describes the general content of a file, and the *subtype*, which describes the specific data of a file. For example, the MIME type *text/html*, which is applied to all HTML pages, has a primary type of *text* and a subtype of *html*, meaning that it is a text file containing HTML-formatted data.

Configuring MIME Types

Exchange Server's support of the *Multipurpose Internet Mail Extension (MIME)* protocol allows multimedia messages to be exchanged on the Internet as attachments to email messages and newsgroup postings. The MIME protocol permits a greater variety of files to be exchanged across the Internet, including graphics, audio, video, word processing documents, spreadsheets, and more. Exchange Server clients use the MIME protocol to launch the correct application for displaying these attached files automatically. They also tag outgoing attachments with the correct MIME type, based on the attachments' file extensions, for sending them across the Internet.

Exchange Server is already configured to recognize many standard MIME types in use on the Internet today. However, you can also configure the server to recognize non-standard MIME types to allow even more types of attachments to be transferred. For example, the server recognizes that an attached file with the MIME type of application/msword and the extension .DOC is a Microsoft Word document, and launches Word to display the document. Yet, it will not recognize an attached file with the MIME type of application/binary and extension .DOC. You can configure the server to recognize these nonstandard MIME types and assign them to the appropriate file extensions, so that the server will accept them and launch the correct applications when it encounters them. To do so, follow these steps:

1. Select the site or server for which you'd like to configure MIME types in the Administrator window.

2. Click on the Configuration button.

3. Select Protocols.

4. Select Properties from the File menu.

5. Select the MIME Types tab (see Figure 9.4).

6. Click on New to create a new MIME type.

7. In the MIME Content Type box, enter the MIME type for which you will associate a new file extension.

8. In the Associated Extension box, enter the extension you want to associate with the MIME type; do not use a period (.) when typing the extension.

9. Click on OK. The new MIME type is then added to the list.

10. Repeat steps 6 through 8 for every new MIME type you want to add.

11. Click on OK when you're done to close the MIME Types property page.

Tip

The MIME types in the list are processed in order from first to last, which becomes important if the same file extension maps to multiple MIME types, such as the extension .DOC for the application/msword and application/binary MIME types. You can select a MIME type in the list and click on Move Up or Move Down to change the order of the MIME types, or click on Remove to delete a MIME type from the list.

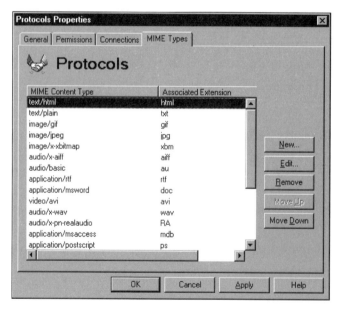

Figure 9.4 The MIME Types property page, showing the list of recognized MIME types.

Internet Email And POP3 Support

Exchange Server's native support for the POP3 email standard extends the reach of email capabilities beyond the server to encompass the entire Internet. Using the POP3 standard, any email client that supports POP3 can retrieve messages from an Exchange Server mailbox, including Internet Explorer Mail, Netscape Navigator Mail, and Eudora. POP3 email clients can only retrieve messages from the Exchange Server Universal Inbox; they do not have access to public folders, private folders, or encrypted messages. POP3 clients can also submit messages for delivery over the Internet using the Exchange Server Internet Mail Service, which provides a standard SMTP server. The Internet Mail Service routes messages from POP3 clients inbound to the Exchange Server or outbound to other SMTP hosts across the Internet.

With its support for the POP3 standard, Exchange Server allows users to access their Exchange Server email from clients other than the Exchange Client and Outlook and from any operating system that supports POP3 clients. Exchange Server users can switch between the Exchange Client or Outlook and POP3 clients as their needs dictate. As with other email messages, POP3 messages are stored in the Exchange Server's single-instance message store, saving disk space and cutting down on administration duties. Exchange Server's security, rich-text formatting, and multimedia attachment capabilities can also be applied to Internet email, in the same way that these features are used on email messages sent between Exchange Server users.

POP3 support is enabled by default when you install Exchange Server, allowing POP3 clients to begin retrieving mail as soon as the server is set up. However, you must perform the following tasks to set up POP3 access to the Exchange Server and to enable POP3 clients to send mail from Exchange Server:

➤ Configure site and server properties to customize the way POP3 clients receive messages.

➤ Configure the Internet Mail Service so POP3 clients can send messages out to the Internet.

➤ Configure POP3 clients so they can connect to the Exchange Server.

Configuring POP3 Site And Server Settings

You can configure POP3 settings at the site, server, or mailbox level. The site-level settings are default settings that can be passed on to the servers in the site, or options for each server can be configured individually. Individual mailboxes can inherit the server settings, or settings can be configured on a mailbox-by-mailbox basis. However, if POP3 is disabled at the server level, it is also disabled for each mailbox on that server, regardless of the individual mailbox settings. For more information on how to configure the POP3 protocol, see Decision Tree 9.2.

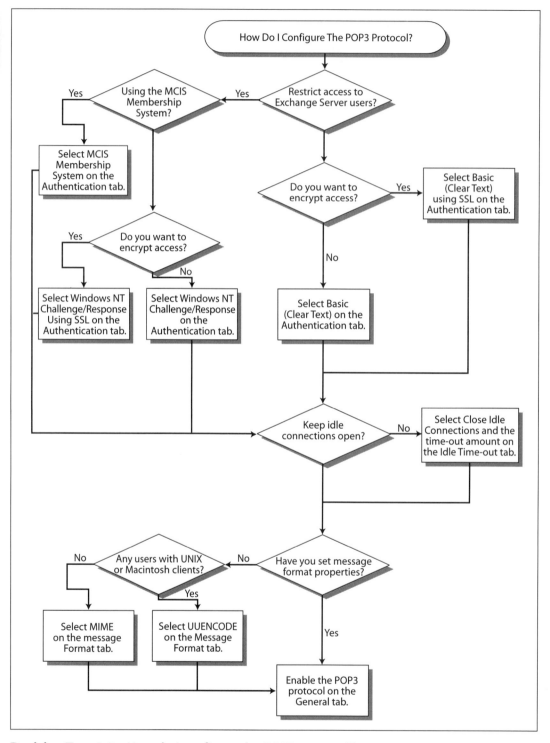

Decision Tree 9.2 How do I configure the POP3 protocol?

Follow these steps to configure site-level or server-level default settings for POP3 support:

1. Select the site or server for which you'd like to configure POP3 support in the Administrator window.

2. Click on the Configuration button.

3. Select Protocols.

4. Double-click on POP3 (Mail) Site Defaults to configure defaults for a site, or double-click on POP3 (Mail) Settings to configure defaults for a server.

5. Select the General tab (see Figure 9.5).

6. Type a name for the POP3 protocol in the Display Name box.

7. If you are configuring a server and would like to pass the site-level settings on to the server, click on the Use Site Defaults For All Properties check box.

8. Select the Enable Protocol check box to enable POP3 support on the site or server.

9. Click on OK.

Setting Authentication Methods

Keeping the data that travels over the Internet secure becomes of concern when implementing Exchange Server's support for Internet protocols. POP3 clients (and other Internet clients) use authentication when connecting to Exchange Server. *Authentication*

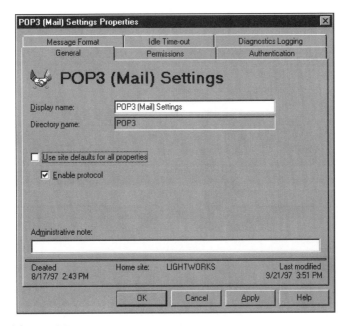

Figure 9.5   Enabling POP3 support on a server.

is the process the server uses to determine whether to grant permission to the POP3 client to connect to the server. The POP3 client must also support the specified authentication method to log on. For example, one method of authentication you can use is *Secure Sockets Layer (SSL)* encryption, which encrypts all data sent between clients and servers.

Tip

Before using SSL encryption, you will have to install Internet Information Server (IIS) and set up the KM server component.

Table 9.1 describes the available authentication methods.

Follow these steps to set authentication methods for POP3 clients:

1. Select the site or server for which you enabled POP3 access in the Administrator window.

2. Click on the Configuration button.

3. Select Protocols.

4. Double-click on POP3 (Mail) Site Defaults for a site, or double-click on POP3 (Mail) Settings for a server.

5. Click on the Authentication tab (see Figure 9.6).

Table 9.1   Supported authentication methods.

Authentication Method	Description	Level of Security
Basic (Clear Text)	Clients log on using an unencrypted username and password; supported by most clients.	Low
Windows NT Challenge/Response	Clients log on using a Windows NT account name and password; Exchange Server automatically accesses the mailbox associated with the Windows NT account name.	Medium
Secure Sockets Layer (SSL)	Clients log on using an encrypted username and password; all data sent is encrypted (IIS and KM server required).	High
MCIS Membership System	Clients log on using Windows NT network security occurring through the Microsoft Commercial Internet Server (MCIS) Membership System (you must purchase the MCIS Membership System separately).	High

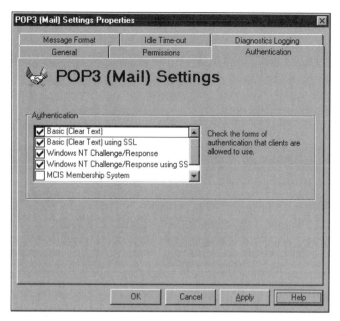

Figure 9.6 Setting POP3 authentication methods for a site.

6. Select one or more of the provided authentication methods: Basic (Clear Text); Basic (Clear Text) Using SSL; Windows NT Challenge/Response; Windows NT Challenge/Response Using SSL; MCIS Membership System; MCIS Membership System Using SSL.

7. Click on OK.

Setting Message Format Properties

Message formats establish the Internet mail format that Exchange Server messages are converted to when retrieved by a POP3 client. The *message format* determines how the message is displayed in the POP3 client. Messages sent by an Internet user to an Exchange Server client remain in their original message formats.

For example, you can enable support of Exchange Server's *Rich Text Format (RTF)*. If enabled, messages received by the POP3 client contain Exchange Server RTF information as attachments to the message. POP3 clients that understand RTF can use the information to display a rich-text version of the message, which retains special character formatting like bold, italics, and color.

To set site-level and server-level message format properties, follow these steps:

1. Select the site or server for which you've enabled POP3 support in the Administrator window.

2. Click on the Configuration button.

3. Select Protocols.

4. Double-click on POP3 (Mail) Site Defaults to configure site-level settings, or double-click on POP3 (Mail) Settings to configure settings for a single server.

5. Select the Message Format tab (see Figure 9.7).

6. Under Message Encoding, select the MIME option to specify that messages and attachments are encoded using the MIME standard, or select the UUENCODE option to render the message body as text with attachments encoded by the UUENCODE method, primarily used on UNIX operating systems.

7. If you selected the MIME option, select the Provide Message Body As Plain Text check box to specify that a plain-text MIME body part is generated for the message.

8. If you selected the MIME option, select the Provide Message Body As HTML check box to specify that an HTML MIME body part is generated for the message, enabling rich-text formatting like bold, italics, and color to appear in the message if supported by the POP3 client.

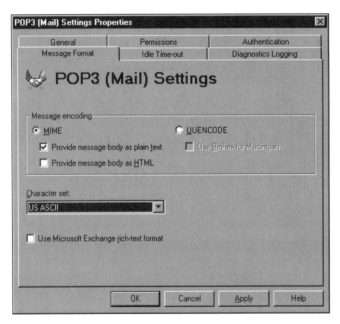

Figure 9.7 Setting POP3 message format properties.

• • **Tip** • • • •

Remember that not all POP3 clients understand HTML. In those clients, the HTML MIME body part is transmitted as an attachment, which uses more bandwidth than transmitting the MIME body part as plain text. Therefore, you should leave the Provide Message Body As HTML option unselected unless you're sure a majority of your users' POP3 clients support HTML.

9. If you selected the UUENCODE option, select the Use Binhex For Macintosh check box to render the message body as text with any attachments encoded by the BinHex method, commonly used on Macintosh operating systems.

10. In the Character Set list, select the character set used when generating messages that originate from Exchange Server if your Exchange Server system employs a foreign language character set.

11. Select the Use Microsoft Exchange Rich-Text Format check box to enable support of Exchange Server RTF in email messages.

12. Click on OK.

Setting Idle Timeout

Idle timeout specifies how long a POP3 client can remain connected to the server without performing any actions before the server automatically closes the connection. Each connection uses up some of the Exchange Server computer's hardware resources, even if the connection is idle. If only a few of your users are connecting to the Exchange Server computer with POP3 clients, you do not need to force idle connections to close. However, if several hundred users are connecting to the Exchange Server computer or if the server is performing many other tasks besides handling POP3 clients, you will want to close idle connections to better conserve server resources.

Follow these steps to change the idle time-out interval:

1. Select the site or server for which you've enabled POP3 support in the Administrator window.

2. Click on the Configuration button.

3. Select Protocols.

4. Double-click on POP3 (Mail) Site Defaults to configure site-level settings, or double-click on POP3 (Mail) Settings to configure a server's settings.

5. Select the Idle Time-out tab (see Figure 9.8).

6. Select the Close Idle Connections option to enable idle timeout.

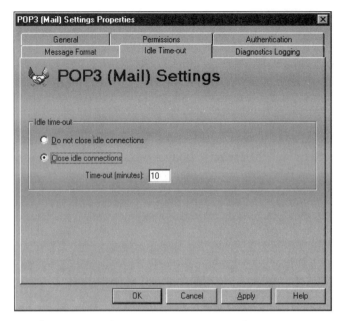

Figure 9.8   Setting idle time-out for POP3 connections for a site.

7. Enter the amount of time in minutes a connection can remain idle before being closed in the Time-out (Minutes) box.

8. Click on OK.

Configuring POP3 Mailbox Settings

You can also enable or disable POP3 support and customize message format settings on a per-mailbox basis. For example, you can choose to enable POP3 on the server but disable it for individual mailboxes. In many cases, the message format settings you can configure for individual mailboxes are the same as the settings you previously configured for the site or server.

Follow these steps to enable or disable POP3 support for a mailbox and change message format settings for the mailbox:

1. Double-click on the Recipients container in the Administrator window.

2. Double-click on the mailbox for which you want to configure POP3 settings.

3. Select the Protocols tab (see Figure 9.9).

4. Select POP3 (Mail).

5. Click on Settings (see Figure 9.10).

6. Select the Enable POP3 For This Recipient check box to enable POP3 support for the mailbox, or deselect the check box to disable POP3 support.

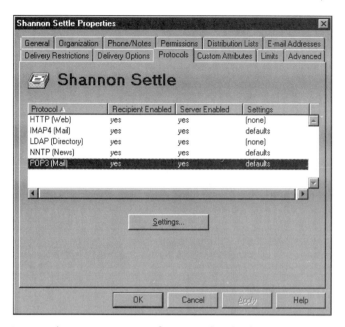

Figure 9.9   The Protocols property page for an individual mailbox.

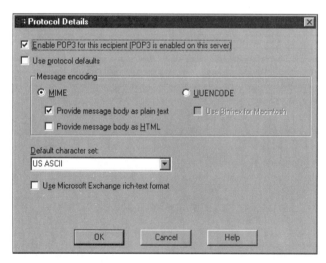

Figure 9.10   Configuring POP3 support for an Exchange Server mailbox.

7. Select the Use Protocol Defaults check box to have the mailbox use the message format defaults you set at the server level. If you leave this check box deselected, you can then customize the message format settings for the individual user as you did at the server level by selecting from the choices provided.

8. Click on OK twice to close all dialog boxes.

Configuring The Internet Mail Service

By configuring POP3 support on the server, you enable POP3 clients to receive Internet email. In order for those clients to send email to the Internet, you must also configure the SMTP server to reroute mail to other SMTP hosts on the Internet, using the Internet Mail Service. Otherwise, the SMTP server will not be able to reroute any messages submitted by POP3 clients to recipients outside the organization.

Follow these steps to configure the Internet Mail Service so POP3 clients can send email to the Internet:

1. Select the site where the Internet Mail Service is installed in the Administrator window.

2. Click on the Configuration button.

3. Select Connections.

4. Double-click on Internet Mail Service.

5. Select the Routing tab (see Figure 9.11).

6. Click on the Reroute Incoming SMTP Mail option.

7. Click on Add to open the Edit Routing Table Entry dialog box (see Figure 9.12).

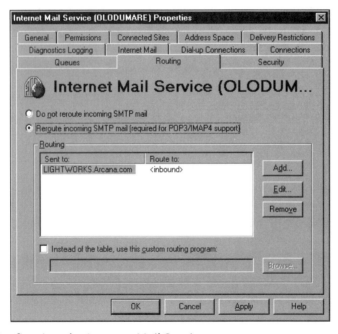

Figure 9.11   Configuring the Internet Mail Service.

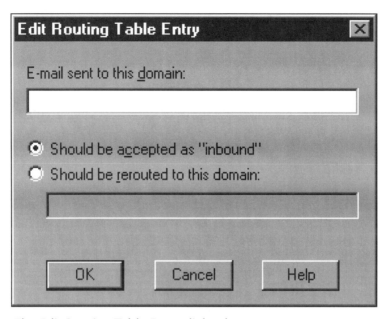

Figure 9.12   The Edit Routing Table Entry dialog box.

8. Type the SMTP domain name of your organization in the Email Sent To This Domain box.

9. Select the Should Be Accepted As "Inbound" button.

10. Click on OK twice to close all dialog boxes.

11. Stop and restart the Internet Mail Service in the Services control panel.

Configuring POP3 Clients

Before a POP3 client can connect to the Exchange Server, the following information must be specified for the client:

➤ **POP3 account name.** The alias name of an Exchange Server mailbox that supports POP3; it might be necessary to specify the Windows NT domain and user account as well in this format: **<Windows NT domain name>\<user account name>\ <mailbox alias name>**

The Internet Mail Service

The Internet Mail Service provides access and message exchange with any system that supports the SMTP protocol. You should have installed the Internet Mail Service and set up the connection to the Internet when installing Exchange Server.

➤ **POP3 password.** The Windows NT user account password associated with the Exchange Server mailbox specified as the POP3 account name.

➤ **POP3 email address.** The SMTP email address configured for the Exchange Server mailbox specified as the POP3 account name.

➤ **POP3 server name.** The name of the Exchange Server computer that hosts the Exchange Server mailbox specified as the POP3 account name.

➤ **SMTP server name.** The name of the Exchange Server computer running the Internet Mail Service.

For example, George Jackson is an Exchange Server user at the company Jackson & Jackson with an Internet domain name of jj.com. You previously created an Exchange Server mailbox for him with the alias name, GeorgeJ, on the computer, Exchange1. The Internet Mail Service is also running on the Exchange1 computer. Therefore, George Jackson would provide the following information when configuring a POP3 client to retrieve email from his Exchange Server mailbox:

➤ POP3 account name: GeorgeJ

➤ POP3 password: Windows NT password associated with the account name GeorgeJ

➤ POP3 email address: GeorgeJ@jj.com

➤ POP3 server name: Exchange1

➤ SMTP server name: Exchange1

• • • *Tip* • • • •

The steps for configuring different POP3 clients varies from client to client. Consult the client's documentation for more help.

Internet Email And IMAP4 Support

A new feature of Exchange Server version 5.5 is its support for the IMAP4 protocol, strengthening Exchange Server's integration with the Internet. By enabling IMAP4 support on the Exchange Server, any IMAP4 client can send and receive email via Exchange Server in much the same way that POP3 clients can. (IMAP4 clients include Outlook Express, Netscape Communicator, Pine, and Simeon.)

The IMAP4 protocol allows users to take advantage of even more email management features than the POP3 protocol. Users can maintain a server-based message store and download copies of messages to the client. Users can also preview message headers before downloading the complete messages, so they do not have to take the time to download unimportant messages when connecting to the server over a slow link. Also, users can employ IMAP4 clients to access and manipulate messages stored in their private and public folders and thus participate in discussion groups on the Exchange Server system. Users can even access other users' mailboxes on the Exchange Server with the IMAP4 client if they have been granted the appropriate access.

IMAP4 works similarly to POP3 for the sending and receiving of email messages. To access messages, the IMAP4 client submits requests to the Exchange Server computer and downloads messages from the server's information store. The Internet Mail Service routes messages that the IMAP4 client sends to the appropriate Exchange Server user or out to the Internet via the SMTP protocol.

When you set up IMAP4 support, you must perform the following tasks:

➤ Configure IMAP4 site and server properties to customize the way IMAP4 clients receive messages.

➤ Configure the Internet Mail Service so IMAP4 clients can send messages to the Internet.

➤ Configure IMAP4 clients to connect to Exchange Server.

Configuring IMAP4 Site And Server Settings

As with POP3, IMAP4 settings can be configured at the site level, the server level, and the mailbox level. Site-level settings are default values that can be inherited by individual Exchange Server computers in the site. Then, to customize the settings on different servers, you can configure options for each server individually. Those settings are inherited by mailboxes on the server. You can also customize IMAP4 access for individual users by setting options for their Exchange Server mailboxes; however, if IMAP4 support is disabled at the server level, it is also disabled for all mailboxes on that server. For more information on how to configure the IMAP4 protocol, see Decision Tree 9.3.

Follow these steps to configure IMAP4 site- and server-level defaults:

1. Select the site or server where you want to configure IMAP4 settings in the Administrator window.

2. Click on the Configuration button.

3. Select Protocols.

4. Double-click on IMAP4 (Mail) Site Defaults to configure settings for an entire site, or double-click on IMAP4 (Mail) Settings to configure settings for an individual server.

5. Select the General tab (see Figure 9.13).

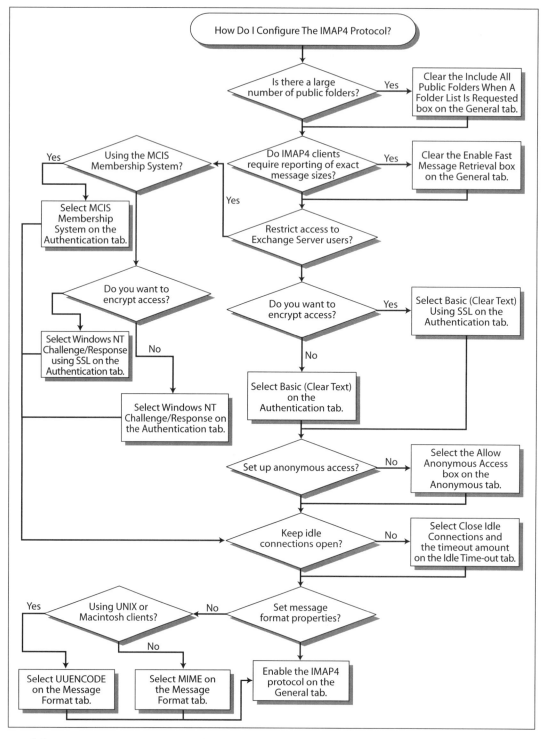

Decision Tree 9.3 How do I configure the IMAP4 protocol?

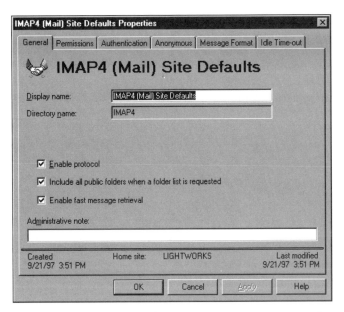

Figure 9.13   Setting general properties for IMAP4 support on an Exchange Server site.

6. Type a display name for the IMAP4 protocol in the Display Name box.

7. If you are configuring settings for a server, select the Use Site Defaults For All Properties check box to pass the site-level settings down to the server.

8. Select the Enable Protocol check box to enable IMAP4 support.

9. Clear the Include All Public Folders When A Folder List Is Requested check box if you want to disable the listing of all public folders by the IMAP4 client and improve performance for clients that have problems listing a large number of public folders.

10. Clear the Enable Fast Message Retrieval check box to disable fast message retrieval for IMAP4 clients that require reporting of exact message sizes.

11. Click on OK.

Tip

Leaving the Enable Fast Message Retrieval check box selected approximates message sizes and thus increases the speed of message retrieval. However, the fast-message retrieval feature is not supported by all IMAP4 clients, so you should clear this check box unless you are sure all connecting clients support fast-message retrieval.

Setting Authentication Methods

As with the POP3 protocol, you must specify the methods of authentication that IMAP4 clients can use when connecting to the Exchange Server, so that the server can determine whether to grant the IMAP4 client permission to access the system. The IMAP4 client must support one of the enabled authentication methods to log on to the server. Follow these steps to set the IMAP4 authentication methods:

1. Select the site or server where you enabled IMAP4 support in the Administrator window.

2. Click on the Configuration button.

3. Select Protocols.

4. Double-click on IMAP4 (Mail) Site Defaults for a site, or double-click on IMAP4 (Mail) Settings for a server.

5. Select the Authentication tab.

6. Select an authentication type in the Authentication menu; to review the available authentication methods, see the section on configuring authentication methods for POP3 clients earlier in this chapter.

7. Click on OK.

Setting Up Anonymous Access

You can enable *anonymous access* connections for IMAP4 users to allow them access to certain areas of the Exchange Server system without needing a Windows NT user account. For example, to make specific public folders available to users outside the organization, you can enable anonymous IMAP4 connections. IMAP4 clients logging in anonymously will only be able to access public folders for which anonymous user permissions have been granted. The IMAP4 client will be unable to send and receive email when connecting anonymously, because it will not have access to any Exchange Server mailbox.

Follow these steps to configure anonymous IMAP4 access:

1. Select the site or server for which you enabled IMAP4 support in the Administrator window.

2. Click on the Configuration button.

3. Select Protocols.

4. Double-click on IMAP4 (Mail) Site Defaults for a site, or double-click on IMAP4 (Mail) Settings for a server.

5. Select the Anonymous tab (see Figure 9.14).

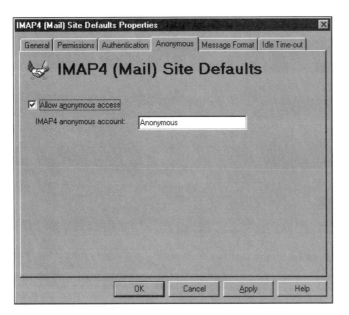

Figure 9.14 Configuring anonymous access for IMAP4 clients.

6. Select the Allow Anonymous Access check box.

7. To specify a name for the anonymous login account other than the default of Anonymous, type the new name in the IMAP4 Anonymous Account box.

8. Click on OK.

Tip

By setting a different anonymous login account name than Anonymous, you can limit anonymous connections to only those non-Exchange Server users to whom you have provided the anonymous login account information. Otherwise, any Internet user with an IMAP4 client can connect to the Exchange Server computer and open the public folders designated for anonymous access.

Setting Message Format Properties

As with POP3 clients, message format properties specify the format that Exchange Server messages are converted to when retrieved by IMAP4 clients and are based on the message formats that the IMAP4 clients support when connecting to the server. Messages sent by Internet users are not converted, but are instead retrieved in their original formats. Follow these steps to set message format properties:

1. Select the site or server for which you enabled IMAP4 support in the Administrator window.

2. Click on the Configuration button.

3. Select Protocols.

4. Double-click on IMAP4 (Mail) Site Defaults for a site, or double-click on IMAP4 (Mail) Settings for a server.

5. Select the Message Format tab.

6. Under MIME Encoding, select the Provide Message Body As Plain Text check box to specify that a plain-text body part for the message is generated.

7. Under MIME Encoding, select the Provide Message Body As HTML check box to specify that an HTML body part for the message is generated, enabling the display of rich-text formatting like bold, italics, and color.

● ● *Tip* ● ● ●

Not all IMAP4 clients understand HTML. In those clients, the HTML MIME body part is transmitted as an attachment, which uses more bandwidth than transmitting the MIME body part as plain text. Therefore, you should leave the Provide Message Body As HTML option unselected unless you're sure a majority of connecting IMAP4 clients support HTML.

8. In the Character Set list, select the default character set used when generating messages if your Exchange Server system employs a foreign language character set.

9. Click on OK.

Setting Idle Timeout

You can specify how long IMAP4 connections to the Exchange Server remain idle before they are automatically closed by the server. Each connection uses up some of the Exchange Server computer's hardware resources, even if the connection is idle. If only a few of your users are connecting to the Exchange Server computer with IMAP4 clients, you do not need to force idle connections to close. However, if several hundred users are connecting to the Exchange Server computer or if the server is performing many other tasks besides handling IMAP4 connections, you will want to close idle connections to better conserve server resources.

Follow these steps to set the idle timeout:

1. Select the site or server for which you enabled IMAP4 support in the Administrator window.

2. Click on the Configuration button.

3. Select Protocols.

4. Double-click on IMAP4 (Mail) Site Defaults for a site, or double-click on IMAP4 (Mail) Settings for a server.

5. Select the Idle Time-out tab.

6. Select the Close Idle Connections option to enable idle timeout.

7. Enter the amount of time in minutes a connection can remain idle before being closed in the Time-out (Minutes) box.

8. Click on OK.

Configuring IMAP4 Mailbox Settings

To customize IMAP4 access on a user-by-user basis, you might wish to make individual mailbox settings for the IMAP4 protocol. For example, you can disable IMAP4 support for some users, or you can customize the message format settings for messages retrieved by IMAP4 clients for some users. (The message format settings you can configure for individual mailboxes are the same as the settings you previously configured for the site or server.) You can also enable an IMAP4 user to have delegate access to another user's mailbox and all private folders in that mailbox. (*Delegate access* is an Exchange Server feature that enables one user to give permission to another user to manage his or her private mailbox and folders.)

Follow these steps to configure IMAP4 options for an individual mailbox:

1. Double-click on the Recipients container in the Administrator window.

2. Double-click on the mailbox for which you want to customize IMAP4 settings.

3. Select the Protocols tab.

4. Select IMAP4 (Mail).

5. Click on Settings (see Figure 9.15).

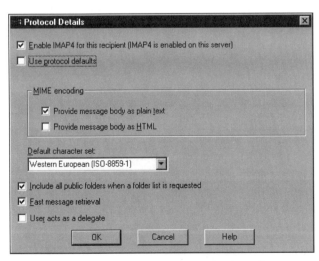

Figure 9.15 Configuring IMAP4 access for an individual mailbox.

6. Select the Enable IMAP4 For This Recipient check box to enable IMAP4 access for that user, or deselect the check box to disable IMAP4 access for that user.

7. To use the options that you enabled at the server level, select the Use Protocol Defaults check box; otherwise, choose from the message format options.

8. Clear the Include All Public Folders When A Folder List Is Requested check box to disable listing of all public folders for that user.

9. Clear the Fast Message Retrieval check box to disable fast message retrieval for IMAP4 clients that require reporting of exact message sizes.

10. Select the User Acts As A Delegate check box to grant that user delegate access to the mailbox.

11. Click on OK twice when you're finished to close all dialog boxes.

Configuring The Internet Mail Service

As with the POP3 protocol, IMAP4 is enabled on the Exchange Server site by default, so IMAP4 clients can begin receiving email as soon as the Exchange Server is set up. However, IMAP4 clients cannot send mail out to the Internet until the Internet Mail Service is configured for rerouting mail to the SMTP server. Follow these steps to configure the Internet Mail Service so IMAP4 clients can send email:

1. Select the site where you installed the Internet Mail Service in the Administrator window.

2. Click on the Configuration button.

3. Select Connections.

4. Double-click on the Internet Mail Service you want to configure.

5. Select the Routing tab.

6. Select the Reroute Incoming SMTP Mail option.

7. Click on Add.

8. Type the SMTP domain name of your organization in the Email Sent To This Domain box.

9. Select the Should Be Accepted As "Inbound" option.

10. Click on OK twice to close all dialog boxes.

11. Stop and restart the Internet Mail Service in the Services control panel.

Configuring IMAP4 Clients

Before an IMAP4 client can connect to the Exchange Server, the following information must be configured on the client:

➤ **IMAP4 account name.** The alias name of an Exchange Server mailbox that supports IMAP4; it might be necessary to specify the Windows NT domain and user account as well in this format: **<Windows NT domain name>\<user account name>\<mailbox alias name>**.

➤ **IMAP4 password.** The Windows NT user account password associated with the mailbox specified in the IMAP4 account name.

➤ **IMAP4 email address.** The SMTP email address configured for the mailbox specified in the IMAP4 account name.

➤ **IMAP4 server name.** The name of the Exchange Server computer that houses the mailbox specified in the IMAP4 account name.

➤ **SMTP server name.** The name of the Exchange Server computer running the Internet Mail Service providing the SMTP server for the IMAP4 client.

Tip

IMAP4 clients vary, so the steps for configuring different clients will likewise vary. Be sure to consult the client's documentation for configuration information for that client.

Internet Newsgroups

You've previously learned how Exchange Server's public folders provide many different options for organizing and sharing information with others across the enterprise. With Exchange Server's native support for the NNTP standard, you can reach out to the Internet community by transforming public folders into Usenet newsgroups. Any Exchange Server public folder can be published as a newsgroup and then accessed by an NNTP client or replicated with outside NNTP servers, easily extending your ability to publish important information and internal discussions on the Internet for access by Exchange Server users, customers, business partners, or anyone else.

You can also use the NNTP protocol to bring the thousands of existing Usenet newsgroups to your organization, so Exchange Server users can participate in ongoing discussions across the Internet. You can configure the Exchange Server to receive all or some of the thousands of available newsgroups and then make them available to Exchange Server users through newsgroup public folders. Because all Usenet newsgroups are stored in the

What Is Usenet?

Usenet is a network of computers that exchange messages organized by topic into groups called *Usenet newsgroups*. Users share information by posting messages to the appropriate newsgroup. Over 18,000 global and regional newsgroups are currently available through Usenet. They are organized into broad subject hierarchies, which are further organized into subcategories and sub-subcategories, covering every conceivable topic of discussion. The following are the most popular of the broad newsgroup hierarchies (although hundreds more are available for regional or special interest forums):

- alt   Discussion of alternative or controversial topics.
- comp   Discussion of computer topics.
- misc   Discussion of miscellaneous topics not included under other categories.
- news   Discussion of information about Usenet.
- rec   Discussion of art, hobbies, and other recreational activities.
- sci   Discussion of the sciences and scientific research.
- soc   Discussion of social issues and socializing newsgroups.
- talk   Discussion of politics, religion, and similar topics.

public information store as public folders, the Exchange Client and Outlook can easily access the newsgroups through the hierarchy of public folders, while NNTP clients can access the newsgroups by connecting to the Exchange Server and requesting them.

Because of Exchange Server's native support for HTML and MIME standards, it's possible to add more information to newsgroup posts, such as hypertext, rich-text formatting, and even multimedia attachments. And newsgroups can take advantage of Exchange Server's wide range of advanced security capabilities, including anonymous access, authentication, secure logons, and SSL encryption.

There are many benefits to including Usenet newsgroups on the Exchange Server. You can use newsgroups to communicate with other professionals in your industry and find the latest in industry-related news. Computing and Web publishing professionals in your company can use newsgroups to ask technical questions and stay abreast of the latest technological developments. Members of the marketing team can access newsgroups to conduct topic-specific market research, keep in touch with industry news, and post marketing-related announcements. And individual users can communicate with others across the Internet on almost every imaginable subject, from the latest features of Microsoft Word to the latest episodes of *The X-files*, and everything in between.

The Internet News Service

The *Internet News Service* is the Exchange Server tool that makes it possible to receive Usenet newsgroups and newsgroup postings from the Internet and replicate Exchange Server public folders as worldwide Usenet newsgroups. The Internet News Service provides bidirectional newsfeeds that allow Exchange Server users to send and receive messages to and from the Internet.

The Internet News Service regularly connects to other Usenet hosts using either a dedicated connection or a dial-up connection to send push feeds or perform pull feeds. With a *push feed,* the newsfeed provider's computer initiates newsfeeds to Exchange Server. With a *pull feed,* Exchange Server initiates a connection and delivers messages to the newsfeed provider's computers; pull feeds also check for new messages and retrieve them. Push feeds are better for handling large newsfeeds, but require more interaction between Exchange Server and the newsfeed provider, because the provider controls the newsgroups you receive. Pull feeds work better for small newsfeeds and over dial-up connections than push feeds, and they are easier to configure because you have direct control over the newsgroups in the newsfeed.

The Internet News Service works with the Exchange Server information store to provide newsgroups. The public information store handles incoming connections from NNTP clients and accepts push feeds from other host computers. NNTP clients do not need to access the Exchange Server computer because NNTP client support is provided by the public information store.

When an Exchange Server user posts an item to a newsgroup public folder, the Internet News Service sends the item to an Internet newsfeed provider or another organization that has servers running NNTP. It also receives newsfeeds from these hosts, so Exchange Server users can read messages posted to the newsgroups by others all over the Internet.

Multiple newsfeeds from multiple hosts can be configured on the Exchange Server. For example, you might receive a newsfeed for all newsgroups in the *alt* hierarchy from one provider and receive a newsfeed for all newsgroups in the *rec* hierarchy from another

Newsfeeds

A *newsfeed* is the flow of messages from one Usenet site to another, replicating newsgroup messages between computers that host newsgroups. A *Usenet site* is a group of server computers that run NNTP to host Usenet newsgroups. Each Usenet site can be configured to accept and to generate an NNTP connection and newsfeed. The host computer receiving your newsfeed is configured as the *outbound host,* while the host computers providing your newsfeed are configured as the *inbound hosts.*

provider. You should never receive overlapping newsfeeds for the same newsgroups from different providers, however, as this will cause redundant messages to be replicated across your organization and increase network traffic. Instead, if you want users in different sites to access the same newsgroups, you should replicate the newsgroup public folders to the additional sites rather than setting up different newsfeeds for the same newsgroups on each site.

When you configure a newsfeed on your Exchange Server, you must complete the following tasks:

➤ Plan the type of newsfeed you want.

➤ Create the newsfeed by running the Newsfeed Configuration Wizard.

➤ Configure properties for the newsfeed.

➤ Enable NNTP support by configuring NNTP properties.

➤ Configure NNTP clients to access newsgroups.

Planning The Internet News Service

Before installing the Internet News Service, you should plan it carefully. You will need to decide how much disk space to allocate to the newsgroups you want to support and whether to use push feeds or pull feeds. Newsgroups can erode your free disk space rapidly, so choose newsgroups wisely. Finally, you will need to contact a newsfeed provider and subscribe to a Usenet service.

Planning Newsgroup Disk Space

When deciding how much disk space you will need for the newsgroups you want to make available to your organization, consider the following:

➤ **Network throughput.** Make sure that your Internet connection has the bandwidth to support a newsfeed without disrupting the traffic that shares the network, such as email. Keep in mind that a newsfeed can send hundreds of megabytes of data across your network.

➤ **Storage space.** The Exchange Server computer must have enough disk space to support the newsfeed. Keep in mind that the daily volume of a full Usenet newsfeed is 1.7GB or more. You can control this volume by limiting the number of newsgroups you receive and setting age limits on newsgroup public folders.

➤ **Load balancing.** The Exchange Server computer must support the number of users who will be accessing the newsgroup public folders. You can control this number by replicating newsgroup public folders to other servers. However, unlike with Exchange Client or Outlook, you will have to configure NNTP clients to connect directly to the server with the newsgroup replica that the user wants to access.

Subscribing To A Newsfeed

Before running the Internet News Service, you will need to contact an Internet newsfeed provider and subscribe to a Usenet newsfeed. Your local Internet Service Provider should also provide Usenet newsfeed subscriptions or, if not, should be able to recommend a newsfeed provider.

Tip

Yahoo! provides a list of newsfeed providers at http://www.yahoo.com/ Business_and_Economy/Companies/Internet_Services/Usenet_Servers/Commercial/.

You will have to provide the following information to the newsfeed provider:

➤ The domain name or Internet Protocol (IP) address of the Exchange Server computer running the Internet News Service.

➤ Whether you plan to use a push feed or pull feeds for inbound messages and for outbound messages. Generally, use push feeds if you plan to receive large newsfeeds over a LAN connection, and use pull feeds if you plan to receive smaller newsfeeds over a dial-up connection.

➤ The inbound host account and password. This is not required, but will make your system more secure by requiring the newsfeed provider's host computer to log on to the Exchange Server computer.

You should also receive the following information from the newsfeed provider:

➤ The host computer's fully qualified domain name or IP address.

➤ How to access the newsfeed provider's active file (the *active file* contains a list of all the newsgroups you can subscribe to through the provider and is generally sent via email, transferred via FTP, or downloaded directly from the host computer).

➤ The outbound host account and password if the newsfeed provider requires the use of secure connections; this allows the Exchange Server computer to log on to the provider's host computer.

Running The Newsfeed Configuration Wizard

The *Newsfeed Configuration Wizard* takes you step by step through the process of creating one or more newsfeeds on your Exchange Server computer. To run the Newsfeed Configuration Wizard, follow these steps:

1. Select the site where you are configuring the Internet News Service in the Administrator window.

2. Click on the Configuration button.

3. Select Connections.

4. Select New Other from the File menu.

5. Select Newsfeed (see Figure 9.16).

6. Follow the instructions in the Newsfeed Configuration Wizard.

After you have started the Newsfeed Configuration Wizard, you will be asked to provide the following information:

➤ The Usenet site name of your newsfeed provider (typically the fully qualified domain name of the host computer sending the newsfeed).

➤ The mailbox name of the newsgroup public folder administrator, or the person who can add and remove newsgroup public folders.

➤ The name and location of the active file if it will not be downloaded from the newsfeed provider's host computer.

Configuring Newsfeed Properties

After using the Newsfeed Configuration Wizard to set up a newsfeed, you must enable the newsfeed. Then, you can edit any of the newsfeed properties originally set through the Newsfeed Configuration Wizard by opening the newsfeed's property pages with the Administrator program. See Decision Tree 9.4 for more information on adjusting your newsfeed configuration. To enable the newsfeed, follow these steps:

1. Select the site where you created the newsfeed in the Administrator window.

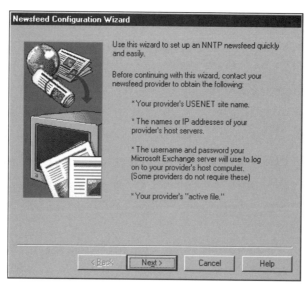

Figure 9.16 The Newsfeed Configuration Wizard.

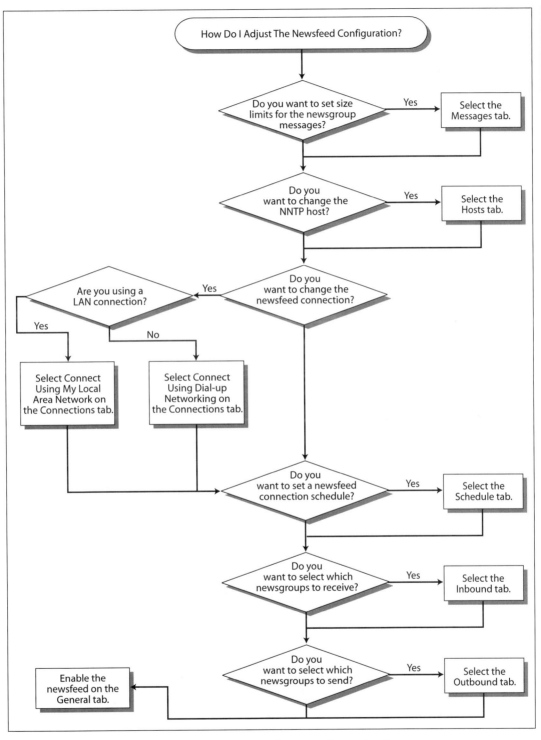

Decision Tree 9.4   How do I adjust the newsfeed configuration?

2. Click on the Configuration button.

3. Select Connections.

4. Double-click on the newsfeed you created.

5. Select the General tab (see Figure 9.17).

6. Type a display name for the newsfeed in the Display Name box.

7. Select the Enable Newsfeed check box.

8. To change the administrator of the newsgroup public folders, click on the Change button and select a new user from the Global Address List.

9. Click on OK.

Setting Message Size Limits

You can set a maximum size for incoming and outgoing newsgroup messages. These limits enable you to control the size of newsgroup messages sent and received via Exchange Server and to reduce the bandwidth used by newsgroup messages. For example, setting a message size limit prevents newsgroup postings with large attachments, which can greatly increase network traffic. The message size limits for the Internet News Service should correspond with your policies for the maximum sizes of email messages sent through connectors and gateways on the Exchange Server system.

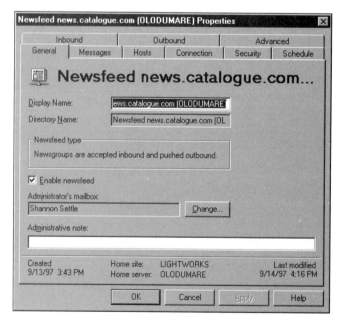

Figure 9.17 Setting general properties for the newsfeed.

Follow these steps to set message size limits for newsgroup postings:

1. Select the site where you created the newsfeed in the Administrator window.

2. Click on the Configuration button.

3. Select Connections.

4. Double-click on the newsfeed.

5. Select the Messages tab (see Figure 9.18).

6. Select the Maximum (K) option under Outgoing Message Size.

7. Type a number that represents the largest message in kilobytes that can be sent out.

8. Select the Maximum (K) option under Incoming Message Size.

9. Type a number that represents the largest message in kilobytes that can be received.

10. Click on OK.

Setting Up Hosts

Hosts are the NNTP computers supplied by your newsfeed provider. Typically, you receive newsfeeds from an inbound host computer and send newsgroup postings to an outbound host computer. The inbound and outbound host computers can also be the same.

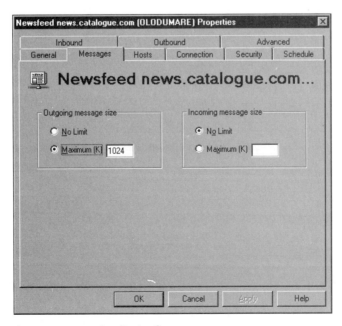

Figure 9.18   Setting message size limits for newsgroup messages.

Follow these steps to change the NNTP hosts:

1. Select the site where you created the newsfeed in the Administrator window.

2. Click on the Configuration button.

3. Select Connections.

4. Double-click on the newsfeed.

5. Select the Hosts tab (see Figure 9.19).

6. If the Exchange Server initiates connections through a push feed, you must connect your newsfeed to the remote Usenet site by specifying its domain name in the Remote Usenet Site Name box.

7. In the Remote Usenet Host Name box, type the fully qualified domain name or IP address of the remote Usenet host providing your newsfeed.

8. If you want to accept push feeds from a provider that uses multiple hosts, you must set up additional host names by typing the domain names or IP addresses of the additional hosts into the Remote Host Name box under Additional Inbound Hosts and clicking on Add.

9. Click on OK when you're finished.

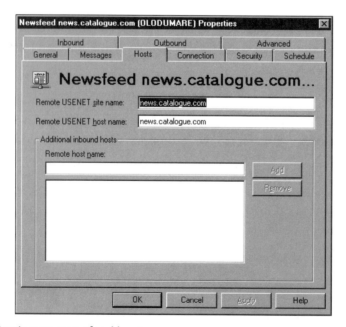

Figure 9.19   Setting up newsfeed hosts.

Tip

If you no longer want to receive newsgroups from a particular host computer, you can remove the host by selecting its name in the Remote Host Name window under Additional Inbound Hosts and clicking on Remove.

Setting Up Connections

You can change the type of Internet connection you use to connect to the remote Usenet host. Follow these steps:

1. Select the site where you created the newsfeed in the Administrator window.

2. Click on the Configuration button.

3. Select Connections.

4. Double-click on the newsfeed.

5. Select the Connection tab (see Figure 9.20).

6. To use a LAN connection to connect to your newsfeed provider's host computer, select the Connect Using My Local Area Network (LAN) option.

7. To connect to the newsfeed provider's host computer using a dial-up connection, select the Connect Using Dial-up Networking option and select the dial-up connection you want to use from the Connection menu.

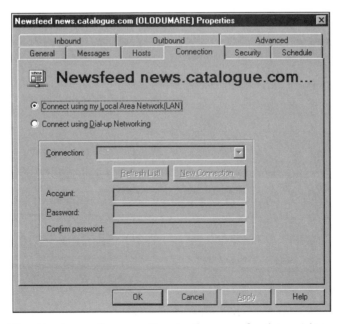

Figure 9.20   Setting the type of connection to the newsfeed provider.

nine

••• *Tip* •••

If the dial-up connection you want to use is not displayed in the list, click on New Connection to add the connection, and click on Refresh List to show the new connection in the list. You might also have to enter your dial-up connection's account name and password.

8. Click on OK when you're finished.

Setting Up Security

Although it is not required to support Usenet newsgroups, you can make your Exchange Server more secure by specifying an account and password the server uses to log on to remote newsfeed hosts and the account and password that the remote hosts use to log on to the server. Check with your newsfeed provider first to make sure that the security method you choose is supported by the newsfeed hosts.

Follow these steps to set up security:

1. Select the site where you created the newsfeed in the Administrator window.

2. Click on the Configuration button.

3. Select Connections.

4. Double-click on the newsfeed.

5. Select the Security tab (see Figure 9.21).

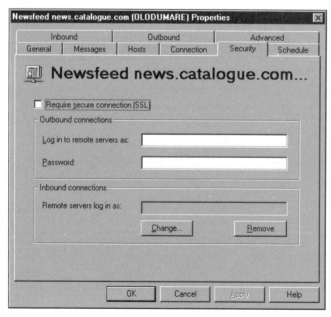

Figure 9.21   Setting security options for outbound and inbound newsfeed connections.

6. Under Outbound Connections, type the account name for all outbound host connections supplied by the newsfeed provider in the Log In To Remote Servers As box.

7. Under Outbound Connections, type the password for all outbound host connections supplied by the newsfeed provider in the Password box.

8. Under Inbound Connections, click on Change.

9. Select the Exchange Server mailbox or custom recipient you want to use to authenticate remote servers that log on to the Exchange Server; remote computers will have to provide this mailbox's account name and password to log on.

10. Click on OK; the mailbox you chose is displayed in the Remote Servers Log In As window.

11. Click on OK again to close the Security property page.

Setting A Newsfeed Connection Schedule

You should specify when the Exchange Server will connect to the remote Usenet site to send and retrieve newsgroup information. Select a schedule that best fits your users' needs to view current information in newsgroups. For example, if it is critical that users access the latest information, set up a schedule that makes connections several times a day. But if users do not need to access updated information as soon as it is available, set up a schedule of less frequent connections—such as once a day—to decrease the network traffic caused by transferring newsgroup messages. You should also try to set the connection schedule during off-peak times, such as in the middle of the night, to keep the increased traffic from interfering with your users' other activities on the server.

Follow these steps to set the newsfeed connection schedule:

1. Select the site where you created the newsfeed in the Administrator window.

2. Click on the Configuration button.

3. Select Connections.

4. Double-click on the newsfeed.

5. Select the Schedule tab (see Figure 9.22).

6. Select from one of the following options: Never, to disable newsfeed connections; Always, to enable connections at the default of every 15 minutes; or Selected times, to select the times for connections in the Schedule grid.

7. Click on OK.

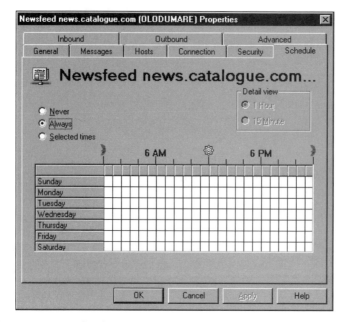

Figure 9.22   Setting a newsfeed connection schedule.

Selecting Inbound Newsgroups

Depending on the type of inbound newsfeed you configured with the Newsfeed Con-figuration Wizard, you will either select newsgroups from the property page for inbound pull feeds or from the property page for inbound push feeds. Either page displays the list of all available newsgroups in the active file. From this list, you can choose which newsgroups to include or exclude in the newsfeed, with the default being to include all available newsgroups.

Be warned—thousands of Usenet newsgroups are currently available, and the majority of them will be of no interest to your company or your users. Each of these newsgroups can receive hundreds of messages a day, including messages with large binary and mul-timedia attachments. Unwanted newsgroups will only drain your server's resources unnecessarily. Therefore, it is well worth your time to go through the list of newsgroups that your newsfeed provider has made available and exclude the large majority of them. You can even set up an administrative policy determining which newsgroups will be unavailable to your organization's users. For example, you could choose to exclude the following types of newsgroups:

➤ Entertainment newsgroups, particularly those found in the alt, rec, soc, and talk hierarchies.

➤ Newsgroup hierarchies of no relation to your business; for example, if your business has nothing to do with education, you will probably want to exclude the k12 hierarchy.

➤ Newsgroups that violate company-wide policies, such as those with sexual, violent, or discriminatory content.

➤ Newsgroups whose names include the word "binaries," which contain large binary attachments that require a large amount of bandwidth and server storage space.

➤ Regional newsgroup hierarchies that are not of local interest.

Follow these steps to modify the available newsgroups:

1. Select the site where you created the newsfeed in the Administrator window.

2. Click on the Configuration button.

3. Select Connections.

4. Double-click on the newsfeed.

5. Select the Inbound tab (see Figure 9.23).

6. If you configured an inbound pull feed and want to add additional newsgroups to the list, select the newsgroups you want to add from the large window and click on Include. If you configured an inbound push feed and want to add additional newsgroups, select the newsgroups from the large window and click on Accept.

7. If you configured an inbound pull feed and want to remove newsgroups from the list, select the newsgroups you want to remove from the large window and click on

Figure 9.23   Selecting inbound newsgroups for a push feed.

Exclude. If you configured an inbound push feed and want to remove newsgroups from the list, select the newsgroups from the window and click on Reject.

8. To create new newsgroup folders for an inbound push feed, click on Create Newsgroup Folders, select the newsgroups for the new folders, and click on Include; click on OK when you're finished.

9. To select a new active file for the inbound pull feed, click on New Active List and select the Download From The Newsfeed Provider Via NNTP option to import the new active file from your newsfeed provider, or select the Import From A File option to import a new active file. To select a new active file for an inbound push feed, click on Create Newsgroup Folders, click on New Active List, and select from the same options. Click on OK when you're finished.

10. Click on OK when you're finished adding and removing newsgroups.

Selecting Outbound Newsgroups

If you configured the Internet News Service to send outbound newsfeeds to the newsfeed provider, you can change the newsgroups that you send at the Outbound property page. Follow these steps:

1. Select the site where you created the newsfeed in the Administrator window.

2. Click on the Configuration button.

3. Select Connections.

4. Double-click on the newsfeed.

5. Select the Outbound tab.

6. To add a newsgroup to an outbound feed, select the public folder containing the newsgroup in the large window and click on Include.

7. To remove a newsgroup from an outbound feed, select the public folder containing the newsgroup in the large window and click on Exclude.

8. Click on OK when you're finished.

Configuring NNTP Properties

You must configure NNTP properties as well to send and receive USENET newsfeeds. You can choose to set NNTP properties for an entire site of servers or for an individual Exchange Server. See Decision Tree 9.5 for more information on how to configure your NNTP protocol.

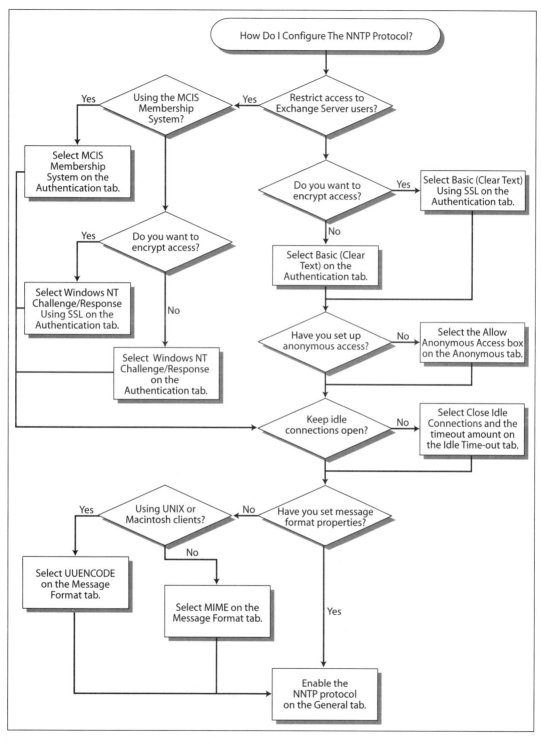

How Do I Configure The NNTP Protocol?

Restrict access to Exchange Server users? — Yes → Using the MCIS Membership System? — Yes → Select MCIS Membership System on the Authentication tab.

Using the MCIS Membership System? — No → Do you want to encrypt access? — Yes → Select Windows NT Challenge/Response Using SSL on the Authentication tab.

Do you want to encrypt access? — No → Select Windows NT Challenge/Response on the Authentication tab.

Restrict access to Exchange Server users? — No → Do you want to encrypt access? — Yes → Select Basic (Clear Text) Using SSL on the Authentication tab.

Do you want to encrypt access? — No → Select Basic (Clear Text) on the Authentication tab.

Have you set up anonymous access? — No → Select the Allow Anonymous Access box on the Anonymous tab.

Keep idle connections open? — No → Select Close Idle Connections and the timeout amount on the Idle Time-out tab.

Have you set message format properties? — No → Using UNIX or Macintosh clients? — Yes → Select UUENCODE on the Message Format tab.

Using UNIX or Macintosh clients? — No → Select MIME on the Message Format tab.

Have you set message format properties? — Yes → Enable the NNTP protocol on the General tab.

Decision Tree 9.5   How do I configure the NNTP protocol?

Follow these steps to set general NNTP properties:

1. Select the site or server where you installed the newsfeed in the Administrator window.

2. Click on the Configuration button.

3. Select Protocols.

4. Double-click on NNTP (News) Site Defaults if you are setting properties for an entire site, or double-click on NNTP (News) Settings if you are setting properties for a single server.

5. Select the General tab (see Figure 9.24).

6. Type a display name for the NNTP protocol in the Display Name box.

7. Click on the Enable Protocol check box to enable the NNTP protocol.

8. Click on the Enable Client Access check box to enable email clients to access newsgroup public folders.

9. If you are setting values for a server and would like to use the site defaults, select the Use Site Defaults For All Properties check box.

10. Click on OK.

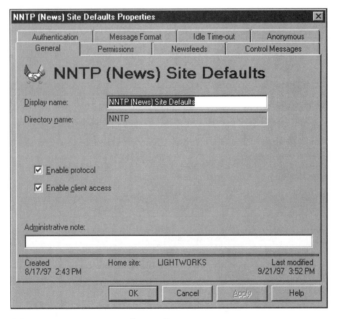

Figure 9.24 Enabling NNTP support for a site.

Configuring Newsfeed Properties

Using the site or server NNTP object, you can view the properties of the newsfeed you previously set up. You can also change certain newsfeed properties, including the name of the Usenet site (the name stamped on each NNTP message so servers can identify messages they receive that they have already processed). Or you can create an active file of newsgroup public folders that other Usenet hosts and NNTP clients can subscribe to and download. Follow these steps to view and edit newsfeed properties:

1. Select the site or server for which you enabled the NNTP protocol in the Administrator window.

2. Click on the Configuration button.

3. Select Protocols.

4. Double-click on NNTP (News) Site Defaults for a site, or double-click on NNTP (News) Settings for a server.

5. Select the Newsfeeds tab (see Figure 9.25).

6. Select the newsfeed whose properties you would like to view in the Newsfeeds window and click on Properties.

7. To change the Usenet site name, type the new name in the Usenet Site Name box (you can only make this setting at the server level).

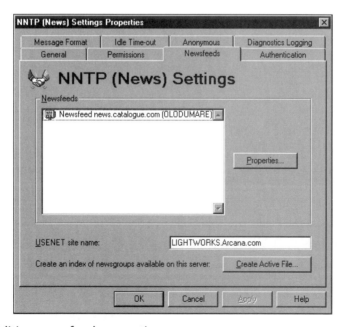

Figure 9.25   Editing newsfeed properties.

8. To create an active file of newsgroup public folders for other hosts and clients to subscribe to, click on Create Active File and specify the newsgroup public folders you want to add to the active file.

9. Click on OK when you're done.

Setting Authentication Methods

You should use the Authentication property page to specify the method of authentication NNTP clients use when connecting to the Exchange Server. The server uses the authentication method to determine whether to grant the connecting NNTP client permission to connect to the system. The NNTP client must support the enabled authentication method before it can log on to the system. (To review the supported authentication methods, see the "Setting Authentication Methods" section under "Internet Email And POP3 Support" section earlier in this chapter.)

Follow these steps to set the authentication method:

1. Select the site or server where you enabled NNTP support in the Administrator window.

2. Click on the Configuration button.

3. Select Protocols.

4. Double-click on NNTP (News) Site Defaults for a site, or double-click on NNTP (News) Settings for a server.

5. Select the Authentication tab.

6. Under Authentication, select one or more of the supported authentication methods.

7. Click on OK.

Setting Message Format Properties

Message format properties specify how both incoming and outgoing newsgroup items are encoded. They determine the format Exchange Server messages are converted to when retrieved by an NNTP client. Messages sent by Internet users are retrieved by the NNTP client in the original format and are not affected by these settings. Follow these steps to set message format properties:

1. Select the site or server where you enabled NNTP support in the Administrator window.

2. Click on the Configuration button.

3. Select Protocols.

4. Double-click on NNTP (News) Site Defaults for a site, or double-click on NNTP (News) Settings for a server.

5. Select the Message Format tab (see Figure 9.26).

6. Under Message Encoding, select the MIME option to encode text and attachments of newsgroup items using the MIME standard, or select the UUENCODE option to render the message body as text and encode any attachments with the UUENCODE method, commonly used by the UNIX operating system.

7. If you selected the MIME option, select the Provide Message Body As Plain Text option to generate a plain text MIME body for the message.

8. If you selected the MIME option, select the Provide Message Body As HTML option to generate an HTML MIME body part for the message, enabling rich-text formatting to appear in messages in NNTP clients that support them.

Tip

Not all NNTP clients understand HTML. In those clients, the HTML MIME body part is transmitted as an attachment, which uses more bandwidth than transmitting the MIME body part as plain text. Therefore, you should leave the Provide Message Body As HTML option unselected unless you're sure a majority of connecting NNTP clients support HTML.

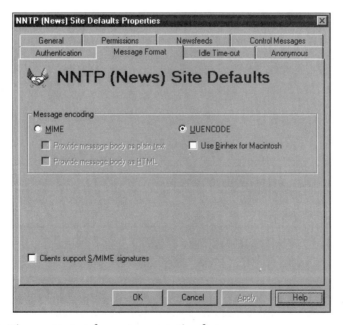

Figure 9.26   Setting message format properties for newsgroup messages.

9. If you selected the UUENCODE option, select the Use BinHex For Macintosh option to render the message body as text and encode any attachments with the BinHex method, commonly used by the Macintosh operating system.

10. Select the Clients Support S/MIME Signatures check box to enable support for newsgroups containing encrypted S/MIME messages.

11. Click on OK.

Setting Idle Time-Out

Setting idle time-out properties specifies how long NNTP connections to the server can remain idle before they are automatically closed. Each connection uses up some of the Exchange Server computer's hardware resources, even if the connection is idle. If you enable anonymous connections, anyone on the Internet with an NNTP client can connect to your Exchange Server computer to access Usenet newsgroups. In that case, it is possible that the server will be hosting several hundred connections at once. Therefore, you will want to force idle connections to close to better conserve server resources.

Follow these steps to set the idle timeout for NNTP clients:

1. Select the site or server where you enabled NNTP support in the Administrator window.

2. Click on the Configuration button.

3. Select Protocols.

4. Double-click on NNTP (News) Site Defaults for a site, or double-click on NNTP (News) Settings for a server.

5. Select the Idle Time-out tab.

6. Select the Close Idle Connections option to specify that idle connections will be automatically closed.

7. In the Time-out (Minutes) box, specify the amount of time in minutes that the idle connection can remain open before it is automatically closed.

8. Click on OK.

Setting Up Anonymous Connections

By setting up anonymous NNTP connections, you allow non-Exchange Server users to connect to the server to access Usenet newsgroups. You might wish to provide anonymous NNTP access to the newsgroups available on the Exchange Server as a public service or to give customers and business partners easy access to public folders configured as newsgroups. If you do not choose to allow anonymous connections, only users with a valid Windows NT account can connect to the Exchange Server and access the Usenet newsgroups.

Follow these steps to set up anonymous NNTP connections:

1. Select the site or server where you enabled NNTP support in the Administrator window.

2. Click on the Configuration button.

3. Select Protocols.

4. Double-click on NNTP (News) Site Defaults for a site, or double-click on NNTP (News) Settings for a server.

5. Select the Anonymous tab.

6. Select the Allow Anonymous Access check box to enable anonymous access to newsgroup public folders.

7. Click on OK.

Configuring NNTP For Mailboxes And Custom Recipients

You can specify whether an NNTP client can use any Exchange Server mailbox or custom recipient's Windows NT authentication credentials to connect to the server. Disabling NNTP access on a mailbox or custom recipient means that an NNTP client using that account name cannot connect to newsgroups on the server. For NNTP access to be enabled for a particular mailbox or custom recipient, it must also be enabled for the entire Exchange Server computer; otherwise, none of the mailboxes and custom recipients on the server will have NNTP access to the server.

Follow these steps:

1. Double-click on the Recipients container in the Administrator window.

2. Double-click on the mailbox or custom recipient for which you want to enable or disable NNTP access.

3. Select the Protocols tab.

4. Select NNTP (News).

5. Click on Settings (see Figure 9.27).

6. To enable NNTP access, select the Enable NNTP For This Recipient check box, or clear the check box to disable NNTP access for that user.

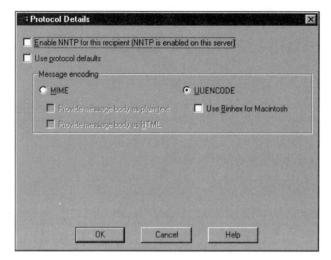

Figure 9.27 Setting up NNTP access for an individual mailbox.

7. To configure that the mailbox or custom recipient uses the message format properties you previously set at the server level, select the Use Protocol Defaults check box. Otherwise, you can customize the message format properties for that user in the same way you set them at the site or server level.

8. Click on OK twice to close both dialog boxes.

Testing The Newsfeed Connection

Once you have set up the newsfeed and edited all of its properties, you should test it to make sure that it works properly. You test a newsfeed by posting a message and verifying that the other server received it. Post the message in a test newsgroup public folder, such as alt.test. Then, if you have access to the remote server, connect to it and make sure that your message was posted to the newsgroup. Otherwise, ask the remote site administrator to confirm that the message was posted. Some systems automatically send a response when a message posted to a test newsgroup is received.

Configuring NNTP Clients

Before an NNTP client can connect to the newsgroups on the Exchange Server, it must be configured to access the server. This process will differ depending on the client that is being used to connect to the server. No matter which client is being used, you will need to know the following to configure the client:

➤ **NNTP account name.** The alias name of the Exchange Server mailbox or custom recipient that supports NNTP (not necessary if anonymous connections are allowed); it might be necessary to specify the Windows NT domain and user account in this format: **<Windows NT domain name>\<user account name>\<mailbox alias name>**.

➤ **NNTP password.** The Windows NT user account password associated with the Exchange Server mailbox specified by the NNTP account name (not necessary if anonymous connections are allowed).

➤ **NNTP server name.** The name of the Exchange Server computer that contains the newsgroups being accessed.

For example, suppose an Exchange Server user named Janet King with a mailbox alias name of JanetK is configuring her NNTP client to access newsgroups on her company's Exchange Server, which is named Exchange1. She will need to provide the following information:

➤ NNTP account name: JanetK

➤ NNTP password: Windows NT password for account JanetK

➤ NNTP server name: Exchange1

Administering The Internet News Service

Because NNTP administration is fully integrated with Exchange Server administration through the Administrator program, you can administer Internet newsgroups from the same interface through which you perform all your server administration duties. The Administrator program lets you manage newsgroup public folders, process NNTP control messages, and catch up to current newsfeeds if the server falls behind.

Managing Newsgroup Public Folders

When you created the newsfeed, a hierarchy of newsgroup public folders was automatically created in the main public folder hierarchy. The parent folder for this *newsgroup hierarchy* is named Internet Newsgroups. The Internet Newsgroups folder is created automatically on each server and cannot be deleted. However, it can be configured as a hidden folder and thus made invisible in the Folder List, the display name can be changed, and the folder and all the newsgroup subfolders it contains can be moved within the public folder hierarchy.

Because the names of newsgroups are dependent on their places in the newsgroup public folder hierarchy, the hierarchy is automatically structured to retain the correct names of newsgroups (see Figure 9.28). The top levels of the hierarchy contain the most general newsgroup hierarchies, such as *comp* and *misc*. As you move down through the newsgroup subfolders, you move through increasingly narrow topics. For example, the business subfolder of the misc hierarchy contains newsgroups pertaining to general discussions about business. Within that subfolder, you'll find more subfolders that contain the actual newsgroups, each relating to a specific business topic, such as consulting, credit, and records management.

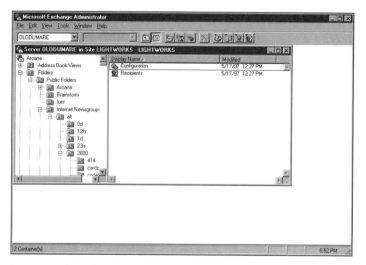

Figure 9.28 The hierarchy of Usenet newsgroups, displayed in the Administrator window.

You cannot move individual newsgroup public folders in the hierarchy because that would alter the newsgroups' names. However, you can choose to move an entire branch of newsgroup public folders, including the parent folder and all subfolders, to another part of the hierarchy without affecting the names of the newsgroup public folders. For example, if you move the branch of comp newsgroup folders underneath a public folder called activities, the comp newsgroups will retain their proper names.

This hierarchy structure can be used to control and manage the newsgroup public folders on the server. For example, you can change an existing branch of the public folder hierarchy into newsgroup public folders simply by making the parent folder of the branch a newsgroup. All subfolders contained underneath the parent folder also become newsgroup public folders. To do so, follow these steps:

1. In the Administrator window, choose Newsgroup Hierarchies from the Tools menu (see Figure 9.29).

2. Click on Add.

3. Select the public folder you want to designate as a hierarchy parent newsgroup public folder.

4. Click on OK twice to close both dialog boxes.

To remove a public folder from the newsgroup hierarchy, click on the folder in the Newsgroup Hierarchies dialog box, select Remove, and click on OK.

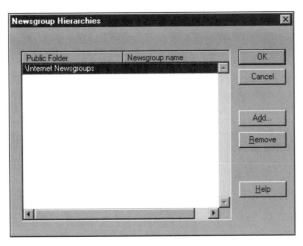

Figure 9.29   The Newsgroup Hierarchies dialog box.

Managing NNTP Control Messages

Control messages are the way NNTP host computers communicate with each other. They contain commands that are used to create and remove newsgroups or cancel posted messages. When a new newsgroup is created, for example, the newsfeed host sends a control message to all hosts receiving the newsfeed, indicating that the newsgroup has been created. This kind of control message is called a NEWGROUP message. The Internet News Service processes the control message and uses the information to determine whether to add a new newsgroup public folder to the hierarchy. Other types of control messages the Internet News Service understands include the RMGROUP message, which indicates that a newsgroup has been removed from the newsfeed, and the Cancel message, which requests that a single item posted to a newsgroup be deleted.

When the Exchange Server receives control messages of the NEWGROUP and RMGROUP types, they are queued so that you can decide whether to accept them. You should check the queue on a regular basis for these control messages (once a week should be adequate unless your organization relies heavily on updated newsgroup information). You can then choose to delete the control messages without accepting the changes if you do not trust the Usenet host that sent them. If you accept the control messages, the Internet News Service automatically creates public folders for new newsgroups and deletes the public folders for removed newsgroups.

Follow these steps to check the control message queue and accept or reject NEWGROUP and RMGROUP control messages:

1. Select the site or server where you enabled NNTP support in the Administrator window.

2. Click on the Configuration button.

3. Select Protocols.

4. Double-click on NNTP (News) Site Defaults for a site, or double-click on NNTP (News) Settings for a server.

5. Select the Control Messages tab (see Figure 9.30).

6. Select the queued control message you want to process from the Control Message Queue window.

Tip

To update the list of queued control messages, click on Refresh.

7. Click on Accept to accept the control message in the queue and perform the action, or click on Delete to delete the control message from the queue and not perform the action.

8. Click on OK when you've finished processing control messages.

Cancel control messages are processed transparently by the Internet News Service. The Internet News Service only accepts Cancel control messages after it has verified that the user deleting the item is in the Exchange Server's Global Address List and that the

Figure 9.30 Managing control messages.

control message originated from the organization. When an item is deleted from a newsgroup public folder, Exchange Server generates and sends out its own Cancel control messages.

Catching Up To Newsfeeds

The volume of items transmitted daily in newsfeeds is considerable, and Usenet hosts must be able to keep up with a constant flow of data. Sometimes, the host cannot process new newsgroup items quickly enough and falls behind the newsfeed. The longer items are backed up waiting for the host to process them, the harder it is for the host to catch up with the current flow of newsgroup items.

Using the Internet News Service, you can mark all items posted to newsgroups as delivered, so that the host can catch up to the most current newsfeed. This enables the hosts to flush their queues of newsgroup items waiting to be sent to other hosts, which effectively deletes the posted items before they are delivered. You can perform this catching up on either push or pull feeds. For example, if Exchange Server is configured for a push feed and the host computer that receives your newsfeeds has not processed them for several days, you can flush the queue of postings waiting to be sent to the host, enabling the host to ignore old postings and process only the most recent postings.

When Exchange Server performs a pull feed, it retrieves only the newsgroup items that were posted since the last time it connected to the host and saves the time of that connection. The next time it connects, it retrieves messages posted since the saved time. When you catch up to a pull feed, you flush the queue of messages and reset the baseline time for future connection, which is useful if the server falls behind in processing newsfeeds received from other hosts. Instead of requesting items posted since the last saved time, the Internet News Service requests items posted since the current time, resulting in no items being sent. The current time is then saved as the last time of connection. The next time the Internet News Service connects, it requests items posted since the new saved time, allowing it to bypass several hours' worth of posted messages and catch up to the newsfeed.

Follow these steps to flush the queue of waiting newsgroup items and catch up to the current newsfeed:

1. Select the site where you created the newsfeed in the Administrator window.

2. Click on the Configuration button.

3. Select Connections.

4. Double-click on the newsfeed.

5. Select the Advanced tab (see Figure 9.31).

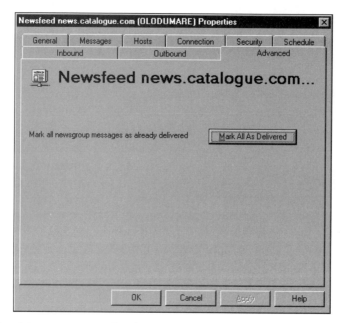

Figure 9.31   Catching up to newsfeeds.

6. Click on Mark All As Delivered.

7. Click on OK.

Setting Newsgroup Age Limits

The daily volume of a Usenet newsfeed can be considerable, quickly eating up the Exchange Server's hard disk space; for example, a full Usenet newsfeed can exceed 200,000 messages daily. To control the number of messages being stored on the server, you should set a default age limit for all public folders on the public information store. Setting an age limit flushes out old items and frees storage space for incoming messages.

You can also choose to set age limits on individual newsgroup public folders, depending on the types and number of messages frequently posted to those newsgroups. For example, binary newsgroups often contain large messages with multimedia and graphical attachments, so you should set short age limits for these public folders to flush them out sooner. Many alt newsgroups are very popular, receiving hundreds or even thousands of messages per day, so you might also want to set short age limits to flush out old alt messages often. But you can set longer age limits on folders that contain short messages or that do not receive postings as frequently, particularly folders where you might want to store important information for longer periods of time for research or archival purposes. To review how to set age limits for the public information store and public folders, see Chapter 5.

Publishing Public Folders As Newsgroups

If you have owner permission, you can create newsgroup public folders using Outlook. For example, you might create a newsgroup on the Internet to provide customer support or a public discussion forum about company products. By publishing a public folder as a newsgroup, you open the public folder to access by any NNTP client, such as Microsoft Internet News or FreeAgent, which can also be used to view and submit information to the folder. Items in the newsgroup will be sent along the newsfeed and replicated to other Usenet hosts, making the newsgroup available on the Internet. At the same time, Exchange Server users can read and post items in the newsgroup with Outlook, exchanging information with other Exchange Server users and with Internet users all over the world.

Since newsgroup public folders are just like any other Exchange Server public folders, you can leverage all the features of public folder publishing that you've already learned about, including threaded discussions, customized views, and more. Newsgroup public folders can also be replicated anywhere in the organization, just like any other public folder, and this replication can be managed with the same tools you already use to manage replication of other public folders on the server. Replicated newsgroup public folders retain their newsgroup properties. If a newsfeed is set upon the server that the folder is replicated to, then the replicated newsgroup is included in the newsfeed. See Chapter 8 to review how to create public folders.

Creating A Newsgroup Public Folder

Before a public folder can be made an Internet newsgroup, the folder must be added to the newsgroup hierarchy. The Internet Newsgroups public folder is the default location for the hierarchy of newsgroup public folders.

To create a new Usenet newsgroup in Outlook, follow these steps:

1. Create a new public folder and copy it to the appropriate level of the newsgroup hierarchy. For example, your company makes a new kind of roller skate called SpeedSkate, and you want to create a newsgroup where SpeedSkate enthusiasts can discuss the sport with employees of the company. You would create a new public folder called "speedskate" and copy it to the appropriate newsgroup subfolders: rec/sport/skating (see Figure 9.32).

2. Select the public folder you just created (speedskate) in the Folder List.

3. Select Folder Properties from the File menu.

4. Select the Internet News tab; the Internet newsgroup name for the newsgroup public folder will be displayed automatically (see Figure 9.33).

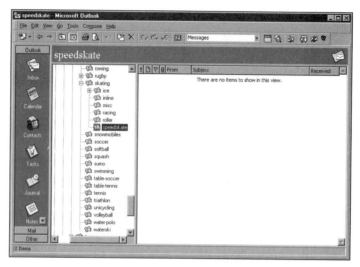

Figure 9.32   Creating a public folder in the newsgroup hierarchy.

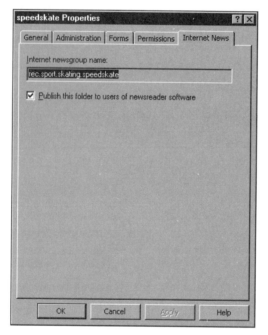

Figure 9.33   Making a public folder into a newsgroup.

5. Select the Publish This Folder To Users Of Newsreader Software check box to make the folder a newsgroup.

6. Click on OK.

The newsgroup public folder is assigned a name based on its location within the hierarchy of newsgroups. This enables NNTP clients to access the newsgroup public folder. The newsgroup public folder inherits a part of its name from its parent folder, which must also be a newsgroup hierarchy. Therefore, the full Usenet name of the folder is a combination of the folder's name and the name of each parent folder, separated by a period (.). For example, you just created a folder called "speedskate" in the rec.sport.skating newsgroup hierarchy, so the name of the newsgroup you created becomes "rec. sport.skating.speedskate". Names are assigned automatically, so you do not have to worry about this step when creating a new newsgroup public folder.

After creating the new newsgroup in the hierarchy of newsgroup public folders, you need to add the newsgroup to the list of outbound newsgroups to send it to your newsfeed provider and thus replicate it across the Internet. See the section, "Selecting Outbound Newsgroups," earlier in this chapter to review how to do this.

Creating Moderated Newsgroups

After creating a newsgroup public folder, the folder owner can then use Outlook to set properties for the folder. For example, you can make the newsgroup moderated. This means that all items posted to the newsgroup are first routed to the newsgroup's moderator by the Internet News Service for approval or rejection before being made public, allowing the moderator to tightly control the content of the newsgroup public folder. You might decide to moderate the postings in your new rec.sport.skating.speedskate newsgroup in order to keep the discussion focused on aspects of the sport, weeding out advertisements posted by competitors for their own brands of SpeedSkates or for SpeedSkate accessories.

Follow these steps to create a moderated newsgroup public folder using Outlook:

1. Select the newsgroup public folder (rec/sport/skating/speedskate) in the Folder List.

2. Select Folder Properties from the File menu.

3. Select the Administration tab.

4. Click on Moderated Folder (see Figure 9.34).

5. Select the Set Folder Up As A Moderated Folder check box.

6. Under Forward New Items To, click on To.

7. Select the name of the newsgroup's moderator.

8. Click on OK until you've closed all open dialog boxes.

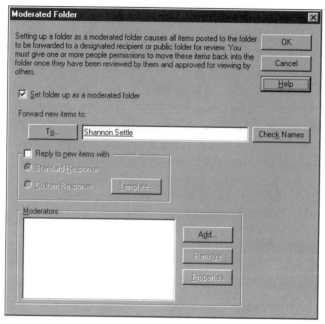

Figure 9.34   Creating a moderated newsgroup public folder.

Outlook Web Access

Outlook Web Access is an Exchange Server component that enables Exchange Server users to access data on the server using a *Web browser,* such as Internet Explorer or Netscape Communicator. Exchange Server's native support of the HTTP standard enables data on the server to be sent to the browser and translated into *HyperText Markup Language (HTML),* to be displayed as Web pages in the browser. In this way, Outlook Web Access extends Exchange Server's infrastructure to the Web.

Outlook Web Access enables Exchange Server users to log on to their personal accounts and access and manage their email, calendars, public folders, and the Global Address List using a Web browser on any UNIX, Macintosh, or Windows computer. Outlook Web Access also provides support for anonymous, non-Exchange Server users to access public Exchange Server information from the Web, such as public folders and the directory. Using Web-based public folder access, for example, you can build public knowledge bases and discussion forums on the Internet in which your customers and business partners can participate, expanding your Exchange Server community.

Outlook Web Access communicates through Internet Information Server (IIS) to provide a client interface to an Exchange Server mailbox. IIS must be installed on the same Windows NT Server computer as the Exchange Server computer or on a Windows NT Server computer that can be accessed by the Exchange Server computer before Outlook Web Access will work. If your organization is small, it might make more sense to

Active Server Platform And Outlook Web Access

The *Active Server Platform* aspect of IIS is instrumental in the support of Outlook Web Access. Active Server Platform acts as a liaison between the Outlook Web Access component of Exchange Server and the Web browser. By combining HTML, server-executed scripts, and Remote Procedure Calls (RPCs), Active Server Platform can generate HTML pages dynamically. These dynamic Web pages are called *Active Server Pages (ASP)*, and they provide the functionality and user interface for Outlook Web Access. They can also be customized for your organization. For example, you can add company information to a title, change graphics, or otherwise modify the operation of Outlook Web Access.

combine your Exchange Server and IIS on the same computer; if your organization is large, however, you can choose to separate the Exchange Server computer from the IIS computer or connect multiple IIS computers to one computer running Exchange Server. You should have installed IIS before installing Exchange Server, so that the Outlook Web Access component is installed automatically during Exchange Server Setup.

Configuring Outlook Web Access

Outlook Web Access is configured using the Administrator program. To allow Outlook Web Access to work, you must enable the HTTP protocol for a site and set options for the HTTP protocol. You must also determine whether you will allow anonymous access through the Web and set up public folders and the directory accordingly.

Configuring HTTP Settings For A Site

HTTP protocol settings can only be specified at the site level. Follow these steps to enable the HTTP protocol and set options for the HTTP protocol on your Exchange Server site:

1. Select a site where you want to allow Web access in the Administrator window.

2. Click on the Configuration button.

3. Double-click on Protocols.

4. Double-click on HTTP (Web) Site Settings.

5. Select the General tab (see Figure 9.35).

6. Type a name that identifies the HTTP (Web) Site Settings object in the Display Name box.

7. Select the Enable Protocol check box to enable the HTTP protocol, allowing users to connect to Exchange Server with a Web browser.

Figure 9.35   Enabling HTTP access and setting general HTTP options for a site.

8. To enable anonymous access of public folders on Exchange Server with a Web browser, select the Allow Anonymous Users To Access The Anonymous Public Folders check box.

9. To enable anonymous access of the directory with a Web browser, select the Allow Anonymous Users To Browse The Global Address List check box.

10. Click on OK.

Configuring HTTP For A Mailbox

After setting up the HTTP protocol on your Exchange Server site, you can enable or disable HTTP access for individual users. If you disable HTTP access for a mailbox, the user associated with that mailbox will be unable to use Outlook Web Access to view his or her email, calendar data, public folders, and the Global Address List with a Web browser.

Follow these steps to configure HTTP options for an individual mailbox:

1. Double-click on the Recipients container in the Administrator window.

2. Double-click on the user for whom you would like to configure HTTP settings.

3. Select the Protocols tab.

4. Select HTTP (Web).

5. Click on Settings.

6. Select the Enable HTTP For This Recipient to turn on the HTTP protocol for that mailbox, or clear the check box to turn off the HTTP protocol for that mailbox.

7. Click on OK twice to close all dialog boxes.

Setting Up Published Public Folders

If you allow anonymous access to Exchange Server public folders through a Web browser, you must designate *published public folders*—the folders that can be viewed with Outlook Web Access—and give anonymous users permission to access those folders. You do this by setting up *folder shortcuts*, or links to the published public folders on Exchange Server. Setting up folder shortcuts creates the list of public folders that anonymous users see when they log on to Exchange Server with their Web browsers.

Follow these steps to set up folder shortcuts:

1. Select the site where you enabled HTTP support in the Administrator window.

2. Click on the Configuration button.

3. Select Protocols.

4. Double-click on HTTP (Web) Site Settings.

5. Select the Folder Shortcuts tab (see Figure 9.36).

6. Click on New to display a list of all public folders.

Figure 9.36   Setting up folder shortcuts.

7. Select a public folder in the New Folder Shortcut box.

8. Click on OK; this creates a folder shortcut to the selected folder and shows it in the Public Folder Shortcuts window.

9. Click on Properties to display the properties for the selected public folder.

10. Click on Client Permissions.

11. In the window at the top of the Client Permissions dialog box, select Anonymous (see Figure 9.37).

12. Choose the appropriate access level for anonymous users from the Roles menu or customize the access level by selecting from the options provided.

13. Click on OK twice to close the Client Permissions dialog box and the Properties page.

14. Repeat steps 6 through 13 for each folder shortcut you want to create.

15. When you've finished creating folder shortcuts, click on OK.

● ● ● *Tip* ● ● ● ●

If you ever want to remove a public folder from the Public Folder Shortcuts window and thus keep it from being accessed anonymously from the Web, simply select it and click on Remove.

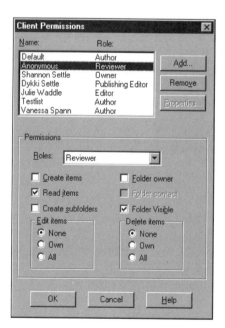

Figure 9.37 Assigning anonymous users permission to access the published public folder.

Setting Up Anonymous Access To The Directory

When you allow anonymous access to the Exchange Server directory through the Web, you allow users outside the organization to log on to Exchange Server and search the Global Address List for information about members of your organization. You might wish to limit the number of search results returned to prevent the entire directory from being displayed, which is not desirable for large directories. If a search result returns a larger number of entries than the maximum value, a message informs the user to refine the search. Follow these steps:

1. Select the site where you enabled HTTP support in the Administrator window.

2. Click on the Configuration button.

3. Select Protocols.

4. Double-click on HTTP (Web) Site Settings.

5. Select the Advanced tab (see Figure 9.38).

6. Select the Maximum Number Of Entries option to limit the number of Address Book entries returned to the user.

7. Type a number into the Maximum Number Of Entries box that represents the maximum number of entries that can be returned; the default is 50.

8. Click on OK.

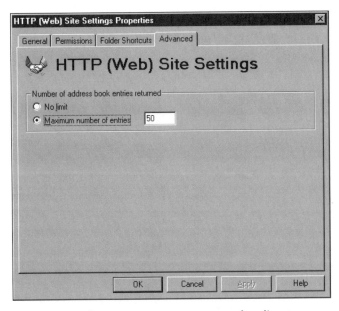

Figure 9.38   Setting options for anonymous access to the directory.

Using Outlook Web Access

When connecting to Exchange Server using Outlook Web Access, Exchange Server users can perform a number of important tasks, all from within their preferred Web browsers. When viewing their Universal Inboxes, users can create, send, and reply to email messages and otherwise manage their mailboxes. They can access and edit their individual calendars and keep up with group scheduling. Users can also read and participate in discussions in public folders and search the global directory.

Outlook Web Access opens up many of the most important communication and information-sharing functions of Exchange Server to otherwise unsupported computing platforms through the Web browser. For example, users can access the resources of Exchange Server from the UNIX, OS/2, and Macintosh platforms, extending Exchange Server capabilities to every platform.

Outlook Web Access also enables users to work more easily from a remote location. Using their dial-up Internet connections, preferred Web browsers, and home PCs or laptops, users can access important data like email, calendars, public folder postings, and the Address Book from home or from the road. They can even use public Web terminals at other corporations, convention halls, hotels, and airports to read and send email, schedule appointments, or participate in public folder discussions. Outlook Web Access provides an easy way to keep users in touch with what is going on at the office without actually being at the office.

Users who have an Exchange Server account start using Outlook Web Access by connecting to the Internet with their preferred Web browsers and specifying the *Uniform Resource Locator (URL)* of their Internet Information Server. The Web browser must support JavaScript and frames; for example, users can employ either Microsoft Internet Explorer, version 3.0 or later, or Netscape Communicator, version 3.0 or later, to use Outlook Web Access. The URL users should open with the Web browser is in this format: **http://<IIS server name>/exchange/**.

Opening this URL displays the logon page for the Exchange Server computer, which prompts users to log on by entering their Exchange Server mailbox alias and pressing the Enter key. The Enter Network Password dialog box then appears, prompting users for a Windows NT username and password associated with that Exchange Server mailbox alias. For example, the user would enter a domain name and Windows NT user account alias name in the User Name box in this format: **<domain name>\<Windows NT user account alias>**. The user would then enter the Windows NT user account password in the Password box (remember that the password is case-sensitive).

The IIS computer uses the Windows NT Server account information to log the user on to the Exchange Server computer. The password is validated before permission is granted to use Outlook Web Access and access Exchange Server data. Logging on in this manner establishes an authenticated, encrypted session between the Web browser and the IIS computer. After logging on, users can access data in their private Exchange Server mailboxes and calendars, as well as information in public folders and the directory on the server. They have the same permissions as when they log on to a computer that is connected directly to the network.

Users without Exchange Server mailboxes can also log on to the Exchange Server through their Web browsers using anonymous access. Anonymous users cannot access private mailboxes, but they can view published public folders and the directory, as specified in the Administrator program.

Moving On

In this chapter, you discovered how Exchange Server's native support of the POP3, IMAP4, SMTP, NNTP, and HTTP Internet protocols enable you to build a complete Internet solution using Exchange Server. By supporting these Internet protocols natively, Exchange Server becomes part of the global Internet, allowing your users to communicate with others around the world through email, Usenet newsgroups, and the Web and building an online community of your organization and its business partners, customers, potential customers, and other key people. Chapter 10 describes ways to extend Exchange Server to do even more for your company. You will learn how to implement Microsoft and third-party solutions to extend Exchange Server's administration, information publishing, communication, and collaboration capabilities and to work Exchange Server even harder for your company.

Extending Exchange Server

The previous chapters described everything that Exchange Server can do for your business. However, Exchange Server's usefulness does not stop there. There are many ways to extend the Exchange Server system and make it work harder to provide the solutions to your business's needs. One way is to extend Exchange Server with *third-party products* and add-ins designed to address specific needs. These software solutions, developed by independent software vendors, greatly extend the powerful capabilities of Exchange Server for working with email, managing information, creating collaborative groupware, communicating with others, and more. Another way is to use Microsoft technologies and products to extend Exchange Server's capabilities. Exchange Server is part of the BackOffice family of servers and so works well with all of those products. Exchange Server also integrates with many other Microsoft technologies, such as *Visual Basic Scripting Edition (VBScript)* and ActiveX, to extend your publishing and application development efforts.

This chapter will discuss some of the best third-party and Microsoft products for extending Exchange Server. It will introduce you to methods for enhancing Exchange Server's powerful features even further with software solutions. You will learn how these products can help with all your tasks, including administrative duties, information management, remote access, and communicating and collaborating with others. Many third-party developers have provided demonstration, scaled-down, or even full-fledged versions of their products for downloading from the Internet, so you can try before you buy. (Also, some of these products are included on the CD-ROM with this book—see the inside front cover of the book for more information.) Many of the Microsoft products and technologies you can use with Exchange Server are included with the server software, are open to all developers, or are provided in evaluation versions online. So it will not require a large financial investment to begin extending your Exchange Server system and making it work harder for you.

ten

Administering Exchange Server

When learning how to administer your Exchange Server system, you discovered how important it is to protect your data from harm through virus protection, regular backups, and *advanced security* measures. Windows NT Server utilities like the *Backup program* and Exchange Server components like the *Key Management (KM) server* go a long way toward accomplishing these goals. However, they might not fully meet the data protection needs of your business. This section will introduce you to some of the best third-party products available for further protecting your system.

Virus Protection

Your organization relies on the Exchange Server system as the principal mechanism for sharing and storing important information through email, public folders, and document databases on multiple servers. Because your Exchange Server system also acts as a repository for critical business data, you must use robust anti-virus tools to protect the availability, integrity, and security of your data. Otherwise, one virus could wipe out critical information needed to do business.

When you connect your messaging system to the Internet, the need to protect your system's data from viruses hidden in email file attachments becomes paramount. Because information on Exchange Server is shared and stored primarily through email, undetected viruses have the potential to spread rapidly, reach all users, and infect every part of the system. Tried-and-true virus protection software is your best defense. Fortunately, many such products are available for Exchange Server. These products work at the *Simple Mail Transport Protocol (SMTP)* gateway, server, and client levels. When considering a virus protection product, remember that any virus scanner is only as good as its most recent update, so the ability to acquire virus pattern updates cheaply and easily is just as important for maintaining the security of your Exchange Server system as is the original product itself.

AntiVirus For Internet Email Gateways

If you have set up an email gateway to the Internet using the *Internet Mail Service,* then the possible infection of your system by computer viruses should be of concern to you. Virus protection products like Symantec Norton AntiVirus for Internet Email Gateways go to work at your SMTP gateway to intercept and destroy viruses hidden in email attachments before they spread through your system. AntiVirus automatically scans all attachments and removes viruses with minimal impact on network or firewall performance.

AntiVirus for Internet Email Gateways scans a wide variety of file extensions, including the most popular compression and encoding formats. Even when new file types are developed, your network is still protected. You can set up custom protection with options for quarantining or repairing infected files. You can also configure separate scanning policies for incoming and outgoing files. And you can block potentially dangerous objects, such as Java applets, from entering the network. Detailed logs give you easy access to important information, and email alerts ensure fast response to contain infections. AntiVirus can be configured and administered from any location on the network through your *Web browser* with a convenient *HyperText Markup Language (HTML)* interface.

A dedicated team of virus experts at the Symantec Anti-virus Research Center backs AntiVirus for Internet Email Gateways. Get free virus definition updates online with LiveUpdate software to keep your virus protection up-to-date without interrupting network activities. For more information, see their Web site at http://www.symantec.com/nav/fs_navieg.html.

ScanMail

Virus infections, especially macro viruses, can be difficult to eradicate from the system because the viruses can hide in old message attachments and public folders. Products like ScanMail stop macro viruses from spreading through documents, folders, and email messages on the Exchange Server system. ScanMail scans all email traffic, shared documents, and shared folders for viruses, including encoded and compressed attachments. ScanMail also enables you to scan old files manually to ensure your system is clean. Infected attachments are isolated at the server while email notifications are sent to the message's sender, the message's recipients, and the system administrator. Because ScanMail works at the server, it is transparent to your users and prevents viruses from spreading through the system.

ScanMail includes a macro virus scanning engine to find and remove known and unknown macro viruses. When new viruses are found, built-in ActiveX controls send the infected file to the Virtual Virus Hospital for 24-hour diagnosis and repair. ActiveX controls also deliver virus alerts and updates. Virus updates are downloaded from the Web and distributed throughout the system automatically. For more information, see their Web site at http://www.antivirus.com/products/smex/index.htm.

Thunderbyte Anti-Virus Services For Microsoft Exchange

Using Exchange client applications with traditional anti-virus software will not protect your system against email messages that have contaminated file attachments. ThunderBYTE Anti-Virus, however, works at the client level to provide a transparent virus protection envelope. It works with Outlook and other Windows Messaging clients. All mail messages the client receives are scanned for file attachments and the presence of known and unknown viruses, including polymorphic and macro viruses. ThunderBYTE Anti-Virus also prevents users from inadvertently sending file attachments that contain viruses.

You can configure ThunderBYTE Anti-Virus through a convenient icon on the Exchange Server toolbar. When a virus is found, the sender and recipients are alerted, and you have the option of either deleting or quarantining the file. Updates are offered via an email subscription service. The Exchange Server system is automatically updated with the latest software as soon as it arrives and is authenticated. For more information, see their Web site at http://www.authentex.com/antivirus/tbavmx.html.

Backup

Your users will quickly come to depend on the information stored on Exchange Server. Backing up Exchange Server data, particularly the data in the information stores and directory, is critical for protecting your business's information in case of hardware failure, software corruption, or another emergency. You have already learned how to use the Backup program to protect data through multiple backup strategies and to restore data in case of a server failure. However, the Backup program might not provide all the flexibility, ease of use, or features you need to carry on your company's backup and information maintenance policies. Many other backup programs have integrated Exchange Server data protection into their operations. These programs work with the Backup program or alone to provide the features you need, including support for multiple backup strategies, different devices, unattended backups, further security, and more.

Seagate Agent For Exchange Server

The Seagate Agent for Exchange Server complements Seagate Backup Exec to integrate automated, unattended backups of your Exchange Server data into your routine network backup operations. (Seagate Backup Exec provides high performance, reliable, Windows NT data protection and is fully compatible with all BackOffice products.) The Seagate Agent supports online backups that protect the entire information store, directory, Message Transfer Agent (MTA), and system attendant without interrupting users—the ideal backup solution for Exchange Server. It helps optimize system performance by minimizing network traffic and backup time. Such features as drive pooling, dynamic load balancing, drive cascading, fault-tolerant processing, and media overwrite protection maximize backup performance as well. Network-wide administration, monitoring, and management are made easier with at-a-glance, user-defined, and predefined reports. Streamlined data recovery includes the ability to direct the information store to any Exchange Server computer. Backup Exec and the Seagate Agent for Exchange Server also support data interchange with the Backup program, providing additional reliability. For more information, visit their Web site at http://www.smg.seagatesoftware.com/.

Exchange Agent For Ultrabac

The Exchange Agent for UltraBac supports unattended, online backup of the public and private information stores with your choice of full, incremental, and differential backup strategies and support for a wide number of tape and disk devices. It works with

UltraBac, a Windows NT backup solution. A software compression feature maximizes backup storage space on disk, magneto optical, and tape drives that do not support hardware compression. UltraBac reroutes backups to alternate devices if the primary device fails and cascades backups in sequence to the next designated device when a device becomes full for added security during unattended backups. Strategic files, directories, and disks are backed up in prioritized order to ensure that critical files are protected first. Media verification can be performed on a backup at any time to verify the media's integrity and confirm the ability to restore files. And a host of other features makes backing up your Exchange Server data more automated, more secure, and easier to manage and restore than using the Backup program. For more information, visit their Web site at http://www.ultrabac.com/.

Security

Connecting your Exchange Server system to the Internet has become a necessity for doing business, because it increases productivity, enables collaboration with others around the world, and provides customer service solutions. Exchange Server makes Internet integration easy with the Internet Mail Service and with support for all standard Internet protocols. However, once your system is connected to the Internet, security becomes an important issue. You must protect your network from unauthorized access and protect your users and data from the problems that arise once the internal network becomes part of the global Internet. Exchange Server's built-in advanced security features go a long way toward protecting data sent through email messages with *encryption* and *digital signatures*. However, your company might need additional security measures for more complete protection, such as firewalls and content security programs.

Microsoft Proxy Server

Microsoft Proxy Server 2.0, a BackOffice product, integrates well with Exchange Server to provide additional security through firewalls, content caching, and management tools. Proxy Server is a *firewall* and Web cache server in a single product. It provides Internet security while improving network response time and efficiency. For a complete guide to using Proxy Server 2.0, see *Microsoft Proxy Server 2 On Site* by Kevin Schuler (The Coriolis Group).

Proxy Server is a scalable caching solution to meet your business's unique performance needs, ranging from small or home offices to large enterprises. It is also an extensible firewall, providing many security features for protecting your Exchange Server system when it becomes a part of the Internet. Its extensible foundation allows it to work with other security products, including virus scanners, content filters, and traditional firewalls. Built on the same Windows NT Server foundation as Exchange Server, Proxy Server is just as simple to administer and manage from any location in the network. For more information, visit http://www.microsoft.com/proxy/default.asp.

MIMEsweeper

MIMEsweeper is implemented on your SMTP gateway to monitor and control the content of email, Web, and File Transfer Protocol (FTP) communications. Unlike firewalls, which provide access security, MIMEsweeper provides content security. It looks into the content of your communications to ensure that you do not receive or send viruses, and it quarantines large attachments that could clog your network, blocks Java applets, sanitizes cookies, and protects confidential or sensitive information from being exported. MIMEsweeper can also be configured in accordance with your company's policies to limit inappropriate material, add legal disclaimers to outbound messages, manage junk mail, and block access to certain kinds of Web sites. And because MIMEsweeper is server based, it works transparently and automatically to control all possible threats before they enter your Exchange Server network. For more information, visit http://www.us.integralis.com/.

Working With Exchange Server

In this book, you have learned how easy it is to perform a wide range of tasks on the Exchange Server system, including sending email, managing and publishing information, and working in groups. The addition of third-party products makes completing these tasks on Exchange Server more efficient and easier for your users. This section describes some of the many products available for enhancing Exchange Server's capabilities and making working with Exchange Server easier and more robust. These products include tools for accessing the Exchange Server system remotely, publishing real-time news and information, managing documents and searching information stored on Exchange Server, and enhancing Outlook with a variety of utilities and add-ins.

Remote Access

In today's business world, many users are constantly on the go, traveling to conferences, seminars, sales meetings, and more. Being on the road separates users from the important information they need on the Exchange Server system, including email, the Address Book, schedules, and contacts. To keep in touch with recent developments, users need access to the same information while traveling that they have while in the office. They need to maintain a constant connection with colleagues to remain a part of information flow and decision making. Keeping up with email while traveling ensures that important messages are not left unanswered and that the user does not return to a backlog of messages. And finally, if users can continue to work even during plane delays, traffic jams, and other off-times, productivity during travel is increased.

Exchange Server's built-in support for *remote access* enables users to stay in touch while on the road. When they combine Exchange Server's remote access capabilities with the wide range of hardware, software, and connection choices available, users will find that their abilities to work remotely have expanded exponentially. Whether they use laptops or Handheld PCs, connect through phone lines or over wireless networks, work with Outlook or with software clients designed specifically for remote access, users will be able to perform the same tasks as in the office, from anywhere and at any time.

Windows CE Devices

The Handheld PC, Microsoft Windows CE, Outlook, and Exchange Server make an effective combination, allowing mobile users to access their calendars, email, and the Address Book while away from the office. The Handheld PC puts the desktop computer in the palm of your hand, helping you become more productive while on the go and keeping vital data at your fingertips. Windows CE is the familiar Windows interface that runs on the Handheld PC. Windows CE supports the Handheld PC version of Outlook, which is fully compatible with the desktop version, supporting information exchange and automatic synchronization of email messages and attachments, contacts, calendar, tasks, Office documents, and *group scheduling* requests. These tools work over a variety of remote connections.

Using the Handheld PC version of Outlook, you can perform all the following tasks:

➤ Send and receive email messages and attachments.

➤ Open email messages.

➤ Read and receive *Post Office Protocol 3 (POP3)* email over the Internet.

➤ Maintain your individual schedule.

➤ Schedule and confirm group meetings.

➤ Maintain and manage your contacts.

➤ Quickly visit a contact's Web page.

➤ Address email messages using the Contacts module.

➤ Keep to-do lists and prioritize projects.

➤ Work with additional messaging services, such as paging and faxing.

For more information, visit http://www.microsoft.com/windowsce/default.asp.

AT&T Wireless Services

Using AT&T Wireless Services, you can remotely access the Exchange Server system without a phone line. AT&T Wireless Services let you access important information anywhere and at any time, including your personal schedule, Address Book, and email. In addition, you can access all the information stored on the Exchange Server system with the added security of the latest encryption and *authentication* technologies. So you can continue to work whether you are at home, in a hotel, or even stuck in rush-hour traffic in a cab. For more information, visit http://www.attws.com/.

Mail On The Run!

Mail on the Run! provides access to the most popular local area network (LAN)-based email systems, including Exchange Server, so you can access your company email from anywhere. You can also send, store, filter, forward, and reply to messages and review message headers to retrieve only the mail you need to read. Mail on the Run! even provides the ability to access your Internet email through Exchange Server's Internet gateway. It also supports downloading of offline Address Books and sending and receiving of document attachments. Mail on the Run! is integrated into the Windows CE platform and supports a wide variety of communications options. For more information, visit http://www.riverrun.com/motr.htm.

Wireless Extension For Microsoft Exchange

Using Wynd's Wireless Extension for Microsoft Exchange, mobile users can remain in touch with important corporate communications and information resources. The Wireless Extension enables easy, secure access to Exchange Server over the leading wireless data networks and supports the Windows 95, Windows NT Workstation, and Windows CE platforms. Because the Wireless Extension is fully *Message Application Programming Interface (MAPI)*-compliant, it works with Outlook and any other MAPI application, as well as with standard *HyperText Transfer Protocol (HTTP)*, POP3, SMTP, and *Network News Transport Protocol (NNTP)* applications to provide access to Internet services. The Wireless Extension leverages the built-in security features of Exchange Server, including encryption and Windows NT authentication, while adding additional encryption capabilities to protect your data while in transfer. For more information, visit http://www.wynd.com/.

Realtime News

Exchange Server is an invaluable tool for publishing and disseminating information. From public folders to Internet newsgroups to Web access, Exchange Server offers many choices for accessing the information that is important to your users and your business. Third-party products and subscription services give you even more choices for disseminating information through the Exchange Server system, and one of the most exciting of these is the ability to access news and information in real time. Realtime news services enable your company to keep up-to-date on the latest business news and integrate seamlessly into Exchange Server to personalize information and make it easy to access.

topicNEWSCAST

Using Verity's topicNEWSCAST, your Exchange Server system can deliver news and information in real time to the desktops of your users. topicNEWSCAST works with the WavePhone NEWSCAST data broadcasting network to gather and transmit personalized business information from leading information providers about the market, customers, competitors, and anything else of interest to your organization. The news is captured in your SQL database, filtered and customized according to the profiles you set up, and forwarded to a public folder, where it can be easily accessed by any user or replicated throughout the organization. Exchange Server users then employ their client software programs to view the up-to-the-minute news and information on their desktops. The process is seamlessly integrated into the Exchange Server system to provide yet another valuable information access tool to your users. For more information, visit their Web site at http://www.newscast.com/.

NewsEDGE

NewsEDGE enables Exchange Server users to view real-time news items from multiple, leading-edge business sources and set up customized searches of that information. News is continuously delivered to the Exchange Server system and filtered based on individual user interest profiles. Current news can even be seamlessly integrated into Exchange Server applications and databases. For example, you could integrate breaking news about your customers into a customer tracking public folder application. A story database maintained on the NewsEDGE server is also accessible to Exchange Server users for unlimited searching. For more information, visit http://www.desktopdata.com/neexchng.htm.

Information Management

You have already discovered the wide variety of methods Exchange Server offers for publishing information. However, when you work with large volumes of information published across the enterprise, information management can become a time-consuming and labor-intensive task. Document management tools like the ones described in this section streamline administrative tasks and make workgroup collaboration efforts more efficient by supporting automated methods for publishing, organizing, and updating information published on the Exchange Server network.

FrontOffice For Microsoft Exchange

FrontOffice for Microsoft Exchange is a powerful tool for information organization, management, and publishing. Unlike other document management systems, FrontOffice for Microsoft Exchange can be deployed across the entire enterprise and is scalable from small workgroups to thousands of users. It enables workgroups to collaborate on document creation, publish documents to the corporate intranet or to the Internet, and share information across the enterprise using email and public folders. Because FrontOffice for Microsoft Exchange is fully integrated with BackOffice, Office, and Windows NT, it can take advantage of the administrative tools, security features, and functionality of your existing Exchange Server system and Windows NT domains to extend your document management capabilities.

In FrontOffice for Microsoft Exchange, information is organized in a familiar, useful, customized way and is presented in a unified view that makes sense to your users. FrontOffice for Microsoft Exchange provides a complete suite of features for document management, including version control, access control, extensive searching, and comprehensive document histories. It streamlines processing between the client and server and can implement services on multiple servers or take advantage of high-end features to support large numbers of users or volumes of documents. Multiple servers can even be linked together to form an enterprise-wide network of workgroups with the ability to search and retrieve documents from all linked servers. And FrontOffice's integration with the Exchange Server system enables information to be replicated easily among multiple sites and to be delivered through *connectors*. For more information, visit their Web site at http://www.frontofficetech.com/.

DOCS Interchange For Microsoft Exchange

DOCS Interchange for Microsoft Exchange acts as an add-on to DOCS Open to facilitate electronic document publishing and information access within the Exchange Server organization. It provides a set of tools that enables publishing of documents and document profiles created with DOCS Open in Exchange Server public folders. (DOCS Open is a client-server document management solution that offers a secure infrastructure for storing, locating, and managing corporate information.) Information is automatically distributed to public folders and previously published documents are automatically updated using the DOCS Interchange agent. By integrating with Exchange Server's *replication* capabilities, DOCS Interchange allows documents to be efficiently distributed throughout the enterprise. DOCS Interchange also enhances collaboration through its support of discussion threads and group revision of published documents. For more information, visit their Web site at http://www.pcdocs.com/.

Full-Text Retrieval

The knowledge base of your corporate information resides in many different repositories on the Exchange Server system, including public folders, mailboxes, private folders, file systems, databases, document management systems, and more. While this enables information to be published and organized in many different ways, it makes it much more difficult to locate needed information quickly. Full-text retrieval products go beyond Outlook's Find function to allow multiple, diverse information stores to be accessed, searched, and processed seamlessly, and they return a unified result list, regardless of where information was gathered. As your Exchange Server organization grows, you might find that full-text retrieval products such as the ones described in this section are the best solution to managing vast stores of information in diverse formats and keeping that information easily accessible to your users.

Fulcrum Knowledge Network

Once a large volume of information is available on the Exchange Server system, it becomes more and more difficult for users to locate just the information they need. The Fulcrum Knowledge Network enables users to employ Outlook and other Exchange clients to search for and retrieve the information they need from anywhere in the enterprise, with a single, unified interface. The Fulcrum Knowledge Network supports simultaneous searching of multiple information resources, including mailboxes, public folders, shared file systems, databases, legacy applications, and even Web sites. Users can search files, email messages, attachments, discussion items, and form data for the resources they need. Retrieved information is delivered to users' desktops via email or the Web browser, and information can be shared with others via email, just like any other Outlook item.

The Fulcrum Knowledge Network works by automatically gathering and maintaining indexes of mailboxes and public folders stored on multiple Exchange Server computers. These indexes are kept up-to-date through a synchronization feature. Because the Fulcrum Knowledge Network integrates seamlessly with Exchange Server, it can be administered from any computer in the network using the *Administrator program* and works with the *Event Viewer,* the *Performance Monitor,* and Windows NT security methods by transferring access permissions automatically. The Fulcrum Knowledge Network makes the entire Exchange Server knowledge base easily available from your users' client applications and lets your users concentrate on information that is relevant to their projects. For more information, visit http://www.fulcrum.com/english/products/fknhome.htm.

SEARCH'97 Personal For Microsoft Exchange

SEARCH'97 provides a comprehensive way of organizing and navigating information resources on the enterprise. SEARCH'97 Personal for Microsoft Exchange enables users to manage indexing and retrieval of mailbox and public folder information, as well as information on the local hard drive and in private folders, without the need for a server or centralized administration. SEARCH'97 Personal is tightly integrated with the Outlook or Exchange Client interface, providing seamless functionality. All information resources can be searched with SEARCH'97 Personal, including Office documents, email, folders, network file systems, and Web pages. Search results are organized into categories on-the-fly and displayed in the way that best meets user needs, including lists, trees, graphs, information maps, and file folders.

Also available is the SEARCH'97 Information Server for Microsoft Exchange, an enterprise search-and-indexing server. It enables you to organize, build, and maintain central indexes of information in public folders throughout the enterprise from one Windows NT application. It also provides connectivity to external Web and PC document indexes and processes user searches. The SEARCH'97 Information Server includes two groupware applications, which enable workgroups to share, categorize, organize, and track Web sites and to track and share information through moderated and threaded discussions. For more information, visit http://www.verity.com/products/prd.html.

ten

Outlook Add-Ins

Microsoft Outlook '97 is the best client for accessing and working with information on Exchange Server and for sending email across the Exchange Server system. Many third-party add-ins, wizards, patches, extensions, utilities, drivers, and templates are currently available that extend Outlook's features and make it even easier to use, most of them free for the downloading. The following are just a few examples of the ways Outlook can be extended using third-party solutions:

➤ **Calendar Access for Schedule+ 7.x.** This driver enables access to Outlook calendars from within Schedule+ 7.x.

➤ **Crystal Reports Designer.** Organize all the information you have collected in Outlook in the way that works best for you, with added support for graphics and column totals and even for publishing Outlook data as simple HTML pages.

➤ **Crystal Reports Viewer/Analyzer.** View and analyze reports created with the Crystal Reports Designer for Outlook.

➤ **Data Access Control.** This ActiveX control enables developers to create Outlook forms for accessing databases like SQL Server and Microsoft Access, without the need for coding or scripting.

➤ **Email Forms Fix Utility.** Configure your email client to switch between Outlook and the Exchange Client on demand with this utility.

➤ **Export Wizard for Timex Data Link Watch.** This wizard enables you to export appointments, phone numbers, and other daily reminders from Outlook to your Timex Data Link Watch.

➤ **Import/Export Converters.** Find converters for importing and exporting information between Outlook and a wide variety of programs, including Starfish Sidekick, Symantec ACT!, and NetManage Ecco Pro.

➤ **Inbox Icon.** Replace the Exchange Inbox icon on your desktop with an Outlook icon.

➤ **Internet Mail Enhancement Patch.** Improve Outlook's Internet mail feature with this patch, making it even easier to send and receive Internet email.

➤ **Microsoft Draw 97.** Draw 97, an OLE-compliant drawing application, lets you access the OfficeArt drawing tools inside Outlook.

➤ **Print Schedule+ Calendars.** These files enable you to print a Schedule+ 7.0 calendar directly from Outlook.

➤ **Rules Wizard.** Create and edit *rules* for managing incoming and outgoing email messages with an intuitive wizard.

➤ **Sample Groupware Applications.** Extend your choices for developing Outlook applications and forms and for creating groupware solutions.

➤ **Support for Lotus cc:Mail.** If you have a Lotus cc:Mail post office, install this *information service* to get all the power of Outlook with a cc:Mail email account.

➤ **Switch Forms Utility for Email.** This utility enables you to switch between the Exchange Client and Outlook on the same system.

➤ **Three-Pane Extension.** This extension displays an entire email message at the bottom of a view without opening the message, enabling even faster reading and processing of email.

➤ **vCards Copier.** With this add-in, you can click on vCards you find on the Web to transform them into Outlook contacts.

For more information, visit http://www.microsoft.com/officefreestuff/outlook/.

Communication

Exchange Server provides a complete email solution, establishing email transfer throughout the enterprise, to and from the Internet, and to and from a wide variety of other messaging systems. Exchange Server also fosters communication in other ways, including through public folder discussions and *Usenet newsgroups.* You can continue to extend Exchange Server's communication abilities with third-party connectors and gateways. These products can add a fax server, a paging gateway, a voice mail system, and even a chat server to your Exchange Server system, fostering enhanced communication among users and between your company and customers, partners, and vendors out in the wider world.

Fax Connectors

Faxing remains an important part of any business's communication strategy, yet it can also be one of the most trying forms of communication technologically. With Exchange Server's support for connector components and a wide choice of fax connectors, you can integrate your fax communications with your Exchange Server email infrastructure. Faxing is as easy as sending email, and faxes are sent and received directly from the *Universal Inbox.* Because fax connectors function as connector components to Exchange Server, they can be configured from the Administrator program and support all the features of any other connector, including least-cost routing and load balancing. Faxing becomes easier than ever when integrated with Exchange Server.

Alcom LanFax NT

Alcom LanFax NT is fax server software that is fully integrated with Exchange Server to enable the sending and receiving of faxes from within email clients like Outlook. It gives users a unified messaging approach to faxing by integrating faxing with other messaging activities, making it as easy to send a fax as it is to send an email message. Incoming faxes are automatically delivered to your Inbox and can be manipulated like any other email item. Alcom LanFax NT is fully integrated with the Address Book and your contacts list to enable point-and-click sending of faxes and also supports document attachments to faxes, just like email. Alcom LanFax NT provides helpful additional features, such as customized cover sheets, confirmations of the fax transmission, a queue manager for all outgoing and incoming faxes, and detailed reports on faxing activity. For more information, visit their Web site at http://www.alcom.com/products/50/lfnt50.htm.

FACSys Fax Connector For Microsoft Exchange

The FACSys Fax Connector for Microsoft Exchange operates as a core component of the Exchange Server architecture, enabling faxing capabilities while taking advantage of the message routing, management, authentication, administrator notification, and monitoring features of Exchange Server. It is configured and operates like any other Exchange Server connector, with least-cost routing and load balancing capabilities configured through the Administrator program. The FACSys Fax Connector's property pages also provide the ability to design cover pages, control message processing, get reports on fax deliveries, and enable or disable remote fax devices. Users create fax messages just like email messages in the client and can even include *Rich Text Format (RTF)* in their faxes. For more information, visit http://www.facsys.com/prodffc.htm.

Fax Resource Integral Fax Connector For Exchange Server

The Fax Resource Integral Fax Connector runs as a native Exchange Server application to provide fax services for any Exchange client application, putting faxes right on the recipient's desktop. Users send faxes from within the client, with support for features like multiple cover pages, mixed fax and email recipient lists, personal queue status, Address Book integration, document attachments, delayed transmissions, and transmission reports. Incoming faxes are automatically forwarded to a mailbox or public folder. The Fax Resource Integral Fax Connector can even be transformed into a full-fledged groupware application, with support for workflow, message follow-up, and an out-of-office manager. Administrative features include access rights, performance statistics, cost optimization, and fax performance alarms, which can all be configured through the Administrator program. For more information, visit http://faxresource.com/fxmlgtwy.html.

msXfax Connector

msXfax is integrated into Exchange Server as a connector component and works as part of the email system, using the Universal Inbox to send and receive faxes from Outlook and other Exchange client applications so that no special client software is needed. Like any other connector, msXfax supports Exchange Server's least-cost routing feature to send the fax from the preferred fax server. It also streamlines the distribution of inbound faxes with a number of options and can route faxes directly to the recipient's Exchange Server mailbox. For more information, visit their Web site at http://www.msxfax.com/.

Pager Gateways

Pager gateways function like gateways to foreign mail systems to enable you to send pages from Outlook as easily as sending email and to extend Exchange Server beyond the walls of your enterprise. Using pager gateways, users do not have to be out of touch just because they are out of the office. Information is automatically rerouted from the Universal Inbox to any pager or other wireless device. Important Exchange Server and Internet email is delivered immediately, which can be especially critical with timely business communications or network alerts. And because the pager gateway is integrated with the rest of the system, the gateway is as easy to configure and administer as any other Exchange Server component.

MobileCHOICE Wireless Messaging For Exchange Server

Using MobileCHOICE Wireless Messaging for Exchange Server, you can send messages from Exchange Server to any pager. Information is rerouted from the Universal Inbox directly to a pager or other wireless device so that users can receive important information and emails immediately, wherever they are. Sending a message to a pager using an Exchange client application is as easy as sending an email message. Users can even create rules to forward email messages that meet specific criteria directly to their pagers when they are not at their desktops. By configuring MobileCHOICE Wireless Messaging to work in conjunction with the Internet Mail Service, users can send pager messages via the Internet from anywhere in the world. And all administration of MobileCHOICE Wireless Messaging is done through the Administrator program, just like any other Exchange Server component. For more information, visit http://www.ikon.net/wms/default.asp.

PageMaster/ex

PageMaster/ex works as a paging gateway for Exchange Server, enabling users throughout the organization to send pages just like email messages and to forward important email and Schedule+ reminders to their pagers based on mail filters. Pager recipients, like email recipients, appear in the Global Address List and in *Personal Address Books*, enabling pages to be addressed as easily as email messages. PageMaster/ex automatically sends error reports and transmission confirmations to the sender of the page. It even supports a mix of numeric and alphanumeric pages simultaneously. Designed to handle the paging needs of even the largest organizations, PageMaster/ex batch-processes pages whenever possible, sending multiple pages in a single phone call and saving costs. The paging gateway is configured and administered through the Administrator program, without the need for additional software. For more information, visit http://www.omnitrend.com/pmex.html.

ten

Voice Mail

As your organization's communication needs grow, you will find that managing different applications, servers, and operating systems for voice messaging, faxing, and email is a daunting task. With Exchange Server, you can standardize all your communications systems on a single server and operating system to streamline management and administrative tasks. Exchange Server also gives your users the ability to access all of their messages—including voice mail, faxes, and email—from one place, their Universal Inbox. This feature not only simplifies management of different kinds of messages, but also provides quick and easy access to critical voice mail. And it gives users the choice of many different media for responding to messages, so the entire communication process is made more efficient and effective.

ActiveVoice ViewMail For Microsoft Messaging

By giving access to voice, fax, and email messages from the Universal Inbox, ActiveVoice ViewMail provides true unified messaging. Users get access to voice mail as email attachments along with their email and faxes in Outlook or another Exchange client application. Data from voice mail messages can even be used to facilitate managing tasks, creating appointments, and sharing information. Onscreen access to voice mail adds additional flexibility. For example, users can view a list of voice messages with detailed sender information and play them in any order and at any time using multimedia sound devices. Users can also check voice mail messages either from their computer or from their telephone, whichever is more convenient. Finally, users can send new voice mail messages or redirect messages from their client applications, using an onscreen list of all voice mail subscribers. For more information, visit http://www.activevoice.com/pr_vmm.html.

CallXpress

CallXpress is a computer telephony server that leverages the power of Exchange Server and Windows NT Server. It provides voice and call processing, unified messaging, fax processing, and customer service applications, all seamlessly integrated with the Exchange Server environment. A Desktop Message Manager lets users see all their voice and fax messages at a glance in the same client interface as their email messages, along with sender details, so they can easily identify the most important messages and manage all their messages using the same tools. An Email Access feature lets users access their email, fax, and voice messages; forward email messages to a fax machine or to a co-worker; send faxes; and reply to email with a voice message—all from the telephone. CallXpress is one of the only communications services to provide a unified interface both from the desktop and from the telephone to all fax, voice, and email communications. For more information, visit http://www.appliedvoice.com/site-pgs/showroom/products/cxnt/cxnt.htm.

Octel Unified Messenger

Octel Unified Messenger is an add-on to Exchange Server that brings together voice and email messaging in one mailbox, which can be accessed using either a telephone or a computer. Unified Messenger stores voice messages in the Exchange Server mailbox. Users have the choice of responding to all messages with either voice or email and can even listen to their email over the telephone and include voice mail in their email messages. Using the Exchange Server directory, which manages addressing for the Unified Messenger, and the Administrator program, the Unified Messenger simplifies administration by eliminating the need for separate messaging systems. For more information, visit http://www.octel.com/unified.messenger/index.html.

Chat

You learned earlier in this book how Exchange Server fosters bulletin board discussion over the Internet through its support of Usenet newsgroups. Suppose you want to host realtime discussion groups over the Internet as a way to conduct online meetings and collaborate on documents and projects with others all over the world. With *Internet Relay Chat (IRC),* realtime discussion over the Internet becomes possible. By hosting a chat server on your Exchange Server system, you enable any user with a standard IRC client to participate in realtime discussion and foster collaboration, communication, and customer service efforts.

Microsoft Exchange Chat Service

To facilitate realtime Internet discussion, Exchange Server includes the *Microsoft Exchange Chat Service.* The Chat Service is an IRC server that can host up to 10,000 simultaneous users in realtime chats. It enables one-to-one, one-to-many, and many-to-many conversations. Using the Chat Service, you can build online communities that include employees, customers, business partners, vendors, and others from all over the world. Use the Chat Service to host product information forums, technical support discussions, lectures with guest speakers, conferences with business partners, workgroup collaboration discussions, online games, and other value-added services. The Chat Service can also be added to an Active Server Pages (ASP) application, incorporating real-time chat into your Web-based applications. For more information, visit http://backoffice.microsoft.com/product/chat/.

Microsoft Internet Locator Service

The *Microsoft Internet Locator Service (ILS)* works with the Chat Service to track who is online and ready to enter into realtime discussion. It maintains a dynamic database of users who are currently online to help you quickly find the person you are looking for, and it is continuously updated as users connect and disconnect from the chat server. ILS also works with Microsoft NetMeeting in the same fashion. ILS is integrated with Exchange Server, enabling a user to select a name from the directory and initiate a NetMeeting without having to maintain or consult a separate Address Book. ILS also works with ASP technology to create customized Web pages that display the names of users who are currently online and initiate real-time chat sessions with those users. For more information, visit http://backoffice.microsoft.com/product/ils/.

Collaboration

Fostering collaboration and information sharing among virtual teams is an important function of Exchange Server. Exchange Server includes many powerful features for improving workgroup collaboration, including group scheduling and group tasks through Outlook and group discussion and applications through public folders, Usenet newsgroups, and realtime chat. Building on these features and using a common set of tools and development environments, you can increase Exchange Server's collaboration functions by creating customized applications. For example, you can integrate third-party groupware, electronic forms, and workflow applications into your Exchange Server system to meet your business's specific needs. Or you can develop your own collaboration applications and electronic forms by using such technologies as VBScript, ActiveX, and the Microsoft Exchange Scripting Agent. No matter which methods you choose, you will soon find that Exchange Server is flexible and extensible enough to provide a solution to any workgroup collaboration need your company develops.

Groupware

Groupware is any application that fosters collaboration and communication among a group of users. In this book, you have learned how Exchange Server enables group collaboration through its support of *public folders* and *instant groupware*. But Exchange Server's groupware capabilities do not end there. In addition to developing your own groupware applications by using the *sample applications* provided with Exchange Server, you can also purchase a number of third-party groupware applications to use as-is or to customize to meet the needs of your own business. The following are just a few examples of the many groupware products available for use with Exchange Server.

C2C Systems NewsBoard

NewsBoard is a groupware application that supports posting and viewing of notices on a community bulletin board inside a public folder. Notices are organized by topic, and a New Items topic enables users to access new notices right away. NewsBoard is a self-managing system, organizing items and deleting old items automatically. It is also flexible enough to meet the requirements of small, single-site organizations as well as complex, multisite organizations that have thousands of user groups and a wide range of security levels. Finally, NewsBoard for Exchange Server supports replication of Microsoft Mail- and Lotus cc:Mail-based NewsBoard systems to enable consistency among all connected messaging systems. Notices can even be viewed from the Web. For more information, visit http://www.c2c.co.uk/products/nb.htm.

TeamTalk

TeamTalk is an easy-to-use group discussion application for Exchange Server that enables information sharing and collaboration among workgroup members or among all members of an organization. It provides a graphical forum for workgroups to share information and ideas about ongoing projects and tasks across the network. Conversations in TeamTalk are organized into a hierarchical structure of topics, so that each conversation appears as one document instead of as a list of messages, providing continuity not possible in *electronic bulletin boards*. Users can review and add to topics by typing comments and embedding objects created in other applications directly into the document. Users can also create new topics as needed, making them public or private and building member lists for the topics. TeamTalk can be combined with other products from Microsoft and third parties or even with your own in-house applications to create powerful groupware. For example, you can integrate TeamTalk with your inventory or accounting applications to add group discussion and information-sharing capabilities to those applications. For more information, visit their Web site at http://www.traxsoft.com/teamtalk.html.

Electronic Forms

By replacing paper forms with *electronic forms,* you can streamline business processes, such as expense reports, loan applications, and more. Because electronic forms are available on the network, are easily updateable and can be adapted to different purposes, are context-sensitive, and can be distributed via email, they greatly improve productivity and reduce costs when used in place of paper forms. You have already learned how electronic forms can be designed in Outlook for use in public folder applications and as stand-alone forms. You can further extend these electronic forms by using third-party products and by customizing forms with scripting languages, such as VBScript.

InTempo

Using InTempo electronic forms software with Exchange Server, you can leverage existing technology investments to automate business processes, such as expense reports and purchase requisitions. InTempo is a fully scalable electronic forms solution that enables users to work with data from multiple sources. InTempo forms can be integrated into public folder applications, accessed from Outlook's Compose menu, and distributed to multiple servers by using Exchange Server's replication feature. For more information, visit http://www.jetform.com/p&s/eforms.html.

Electronic Forms And VBScript

Sometimes the standard Outlook forms do not meet all your business's needs for collaboration solutions. For example, some solutions require connectivity to other data sources, like the SQL Server or Microsoft Access, or they might need customized functionality. To provide the flexibility and extensibility you need, Outlook and Exchange Server support the hosting of VBScript in Outlook forms. VBScript is built directly into *Forms Designer* to add functionality, such as intelligent fields, automation, and customized items, to your forms. For more information, see the Outlook documentation or http://www.microsoft.com/vbscript/.

Workflow

Workflow is an enabling technology for streamlining and automating business processes using groupware. Workflow applications include the following: document and message routing, such as resume review and voting; administrative forms, such as expense reports; queue-based applications, such as electronic help desks; collaborative applications, such as loan processing; and production workflow applications, such as insurance claims processing. Exchange Server's public folders, directory, electronic forms, and application coding tools make it the ideal infrastructure for deploying workflow applications. Microsoft is working with leading independent software vendors to create robust workflow solutions, like the ones described in this section.

JetForm Workflow

JetForm Workflow transforms manual, paper-based form processes into electronic form workflow applications. It combines a powerful workflow system with the electronic forms feature and messaging infrastructure of Exchange Server to automate underlying business processes, including company policies, business rules, and organizational roles. With JetForm Workflow, you can develop applications for interdepartmental processes and collaborative work. Examples of applications you can develop include policy reviews and distribution, expense requisitions, budget reviews, project costing, document reviews, purchase requests, vacation requests, and human resource surveys. These applications can be implemented by a central department and distributed throughout the enterprise. All processing is centralized on the server, simplifying management of the workflow applications. For more information, visit http://www.jetform.com/p&s/adminwf.html.

Motiva

Motiva is a collaborative document management and workflow solution for automating processes, streamlining operations, and enhancing communications among workgroups on Exchange Server. Motiva's object-oriented design incorporates ActiveX technologies to provide document management, process automation, and publishing services across the enterprise. You can use Motiva to reduce cycle times in developing applications, improve vendor and customer communications, and ensure that key processes are implemented correctly. Using Motiva's Solution Builder feature, you can also develop customized interfaces to document management, workflow, and information structure services that adhere to your company's implementation requirements. For more information, visit their Web site at http://www.motiva.com/.

ActiveX

Exchange Server and Outlook fully support Microsoft ActiveX technologies to create full-fledged business applications for deployment on the Web and to bring Exchange Server's collaboration capabilities to those Web applications. Using tools like Visual InterDev (included with Exchange Server), developers can combine HTML with core Exchange Server technologies like messaging, calendaring, and groupware to create customized applications accessible through a Web browser. You build the Web application and then use Exchange Server to deliver specific aspects of the application's functionality. These applications are based on *Active Server Pages (ASP),* a combination of HTML, Dynamic HTML (DHTML), ActiveX scripts, and ActiveX controls, allowing applications to be designed and modified easily and providing dynamic access to data stored on Exchange Server.

With ActiveX technologies, businesses of all sizes can easily create a line of customized Web-based applications that seamlessly integrate Exchange Server messaging and groupware services into Web sites with little or no coding. Existing Exchange Server applications can also be extended to the Web and enriched with additional interactivity and functionality using ActiveX. ActiveX supports the development tools and platforms you are already familiar with, so you can start creating applications right away. And because Exchange Server is integrated with the Active Server development platform, you can leverage Microsoft and third-party ActiveX controls in developing your Web-based groupware applications. For more information, visit http://www.microsoft.com/msdn/ and http://www.microsoft.com/activex/.

Collaboration Data Objects

Collaboration Data Objects are the object library used for building powerful, Exchange Server-based, ASP applications. Collaboration Data Objects can be programmed using Outlook or any standard Web programming tool or language, like JavaScript and VBScript. They enable HTML to be combined with core Exchange Server technologies—such as personal calendaring, group scheduling, data storage, the directory, the Universal Inbox, public folders, and messaging capabilities—to create interactive applications for deployment on the Web. You can also build groupware applications that combine Exchange Server features with the features of other BackOffice servers, such as the SQL Server for database access.

Applications that use Collaboration Data Objects make your Web pages more interactive and compelling. For example, you can add threaded discussions to your Web site; all the HTML for the discussion is generated automatically by Exchange Server, reducing the need to program complex HTML. You can also give Web users anonymous access to Exchange Server public folders so they can participate in open discussions; create an online helpdesk for your customers; publish information like FAQs, reports, and press releases to the Web directly from Exchange Server; enable users to send, receive, delete, and move email messages; access and create schedules; or look up directory information directly from your Web site. You can even extend the functionality of Outlook to the Web, including such features as grouping, sorting, filtering, custom views, and conversation threading, without having to program complex HTML. Because Collaboration Data Objects are extensible and provide rich functionality, you can use them to create custom solutions to almost any business need.

Internet Control Pack

The *Internet Control Pack* is a set of ActiveX controls that enable you to integrate Internet functionality into your Outlook applications. For example, you might create a research application by placing an HTML ActiveX control on a Mail Message form, enabling users to browse the Web from within the form. You can then add VBScript to the form to save the Web page address to a form field. Researchers use the application to browse the Web, save the addresses of relevant Web pages, and send the form to other users in their workgroups. The recipients of the message can then view the relevant Web pages by clicking on the saved *Uniform Resource Locators (URLs)* in the form. This is just one example of how ActiveX controls in the Internet Control Pack can be integrated with Outlook collaboration applications.

Microsoft Exchange Scripting Agent

Using the *Microsoft Exchange Scripting Agent*, you can create simple workflow and other collaboration applications that implement custom events based on user actions, enabling you to further automate common business processes. The Scripting Agent runs a VBScript or JavaScript script on the server when a specific event occurs in a public folder, such as posting a new item, changing an item, or deleting an item. The *Microsoft Exchange Event Service* component, which is included with Exchange Server and installed during Setup, detects the event and automatically runs an agent in response. It can also run an agent when a scheduled event or a timer event occurs within the public folder.

The Scripting Agent can be used to design applications that perform automatic error validation or route purchase requisitions to the appropriate recipients, among other automated processes. An example of an application developed with the Scripting Agent is a customized electronic form for ordering office supplies. When the form is submitted to a public folder, a script is invoked that checks the total amount field of the form. If the

10

total amount is less than a set amount, the form is automatically sent on for processing, whereas if it is more than the set amount, the form is routed to a manager for approval.

Outlook automatically loads the Scripting Agent for creating, editing, and saving scripts when you are designing public folders. All you have to do is open the public folder, select Properties from the File menu, click on the Agents tab, and choose New. Then, create the agent and click on Edit Script to write the script. For more information, see the Exchange Server documentation or http://www.microsoft.com/exchange/default.asp.

Moving On

You are now ready to put your new Exchange Server system to work for your business. The appendices and glossary following this chapter provide valuable information that you will find helpful when implementing and administering the Exchange Server system, including the following: a glossary of Exchanger Server terms, troubleshooting tips and tricks in Appendix A, and additional online resources in Appendix B. As your business and your Exchange Server organization grow, you will want to keep developing and extending your Exchange Server system to take advantage of the latest technologies and to keep providing the solutions your business needs.

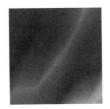

Glossary

Access control list   List of Windows NT user accounts and groups that have been granted access to view or modify the properties of a directory object; list of recipients who have been granted access to view, edit, create, or delete items in a public folder.

Active file   List of all Usenet newsgroups available for subscription from a newsfeed provider.

Active Server Components   Technology for integrating Exchange Server functionality with HTML pages.

Active Server Pages (ASP)   Technology that combines ActiveX scripts and HTML to integrate ActiveX components with Web pages.

Active Server Platform   Development platform for building applications by integrating Internet and PC technologies.

Address Book   How the directory displays in Outlook.

Address Book view   Exchange Server feature for grouping recipients in the Global Address List by a common attribute.

Address space   Addressing information that identifies a message and its route.

Administrator program   Software program that gives a single-seat view of the entire Exchange Server organization and enables administrators to manage and configure objects in the directory.

Advanced security   Exchange Server's collection of security features for protecting and verifying messages and other data.

Age limit   The maximum number of days that deleted messages are retained in the information store for possible recovery before they are permanently erased.

Alert log   Performance Monitor configuration that monitors several counters simultaneously, tracks events, and sends alerts if there are problems.

Alert state   State of a connector or site indicating that there is a serious problem.

Alias name   Shortened version of the name of a mailbox owner used to address messages to the mailbox.

Anonymous access   Exchange Server feature that enables non-validated users without a Windows NT user account to access specified areas of the Exchange Server organization, such as public folders and the directory, using Internet clients.

APDU log   Binary representation of communication among Message Transfer Agents (MTA) in different sites and between the MTA and clients within a site used for troubleshooting problems with the MTA.

ASP   See *Active Server Pages*.

Association   Path that is contained within a connection and is opened to another system in order to transfer messages to that system.

Attribute   Predefined characteristic associated with a recipient.

Auditing   The ability to detect and record important security events.

Authentication   Validation of an Exchange Server user's Windows NT Server logon username and password.

AutoArchive   Outlook feature that automatically files or deletes old items according to user-defined criteria.

AutoCreate   Outlook feature that automatically creates one type of item based on another when the item is dragged to a different module.

AutoLayout   Forms designer feature that automatically places and sizes fields on an electronic form.

AutoPick   Outlook feature that automatically chooses the next available time for a group meeting based on the invitees' schedules.

AutoPreview   Outlook feature that displays the first three lines of an unread message in the Inbox.

Backup Domain Controller (BDC)   Computer that stores copies of the security database and authenticates user logons when the Primary Domain Controller is unavailable.

Backup program   Enhanced version of the Windows NT Server Backup application included with Exchange Server that includes the capability for online backup and restoration of the information store and directory.

Bounce duration   The longest acceptable time for a ping message to travel between the Link Monitor and another server or foreign system.

BDC   See *Backup Domain Controller.*

CA   See *Certification Authority.*

Certification Authority (CA)   Computer that certifies public signing and encryption keys and maintains the Certification Revocation List.

Certification Revocation List (CRL)   List of all users whose advanced security has been revoked.

Circular logging   Process of writing over transaction log files after the data they contain has been written to the database.

Client   Software program that accesses services on a network by making requests of a server computer.

Client installation point   Shared directory on a file server to which users can connect to install a client application to the local disk.

Client/server architecture   The basis of the Exchange Server system, in which a client program sends requests to a server computer, and the server carries out the client's instructions.

Collaboration Data Objects   Object library used to build Exchange Server-based, Active Server Pages applications.

Complete trust model   Domain model in which every domain on the network trusts every other domain, and every domain has complete control over its own user accounts and resources.

Connector   Exchange Server component that routes messages between sites or between the Exchange Server system and foreign messaging systems.

Container   Directory object that contains related objects.

Container area   Area of the Administrator program interface that displays all the containers in the directory.

Contents area   Area of the Administrator program interface that displays the objects in a selected container.

Control message   Command used by Usenet host computers to create and remove newsgroups or cancel posted messages.

Control Toolbox   Forms Designer tool for adding controls to an electronic form.

Copy backup   Full backup created without disturbing ongoing differential or incremental backups.

Cost   Number assigned to a message route that represents the desirability of using that route when compared to other possible routes.

Critical site   Site that is in a warning or alert state.

CRL   See *Certification Revocation List.*

Custom attribute   Administrator-defined attribute associated with recipients to provide additional information.

Custom recipient   Recipient in a foreign messaging system whose address is in the Exchange Server directory.

Dedicated recovery system   One or more Exchange Server computers that are connected to the network but are not configured as part of the site until they are needed to replace a failed server.

Delegate Access   The ability to give permission to one user to access and manage another user's mailbox, Outlook modules, or private folders.

Delivery restriction   Setting that prevents specified recipients from sending email messages through certain connectors or to individual mailboxes.

Design view   Forms Designer view used when creating an electronic form.

Details template   Localized template that defines how object details are displayed in the Address Book.

Diagnostics logging   Process of regulating the level of detail of information written to the event log.

Differential backup   Backup of information that has changed since the last full backup but that does not delete the transaction log files.

Digital signature   Advanced security feature that enables message recipients to verify the sources of messages and that messages have not been modified during transit.

Directory   Exchange Server component that stores all the information about the organization's resources and users; other components use the directory to address and route messages.

Directory import   Process of importing user account information into the directory.

Directory name   Name used to permanently identify an object in the directory.

Directory object   A record, such as a server, mailbox, or distribution list, in the directory that has properties that can be defined.

Directory replication   Process of updating the directories of all servers in and between Exchange Server sites.

Directory replication bridgehead server   Exchange Server computer that is configured with a directory replication connector and establishes directory replication between two sites.

Directory replication connector   Exchange Server component that sends directory replication messages between two sites.

Directory synchronization   Process of synchronizing the Exchange Server directory with the Microsoft Mail directory.

Dirsync requestor   Directory synchronization component that sends directory update messages to the Microsoft Mail directory server postoffice.

Dirsync server   Directory synchronization component that processes incoming update messages from Microsoft Mail directory requestors.

Disaster recovery kit   Kit that contains all materials needed to recover from a server failure.

Discretionary access control   Feature that enables the owner of a resource to determine who can access the resource and what actions they can perform.

Disk striping   Process of creating a virtual disk over two or more physical disks to provide high capacity and high performance.

Display name   Name used to identify a directory object in the Administrator window.

Distribution list   Group of recipients addressed as a single recipient and available in the Address Book.

Domain   Group of computers running Windows NT Server that share common security policies and user account databases.

Domain controller   Windows NT Server computer that maintains the security database for a domain and authenticates logons.

Domain model   Group of one or more domains arranged for best management of users and resources.

Dynamic RAS Connector   Exchange Server component that routes messages between sites on the same local area network using Windows NT Remote Access Service.

Electronic bulletin board   Online discussion public folder.

Electronic form   Structure for posting and viewing information.

Email address   Address by which a recipient is known to a foreign system.

Email address generator   Exchange Server tool that automatically generates email addresses for installed connectors.

Encryption   Advanced security feature that encodes data as it resides on disk and travels over a network.

Error event   Event that indicates a significant problem.

Escalation actions   Automatic processes that occur when an Exchange Server service stops.

Escalation path   Prioritized list of people to notify when a site or connector enters a warning or alert state.

Event   Any significant occurrence in a system or application.

Event Viewer   Windows NT Server tool that displays application, security, and system event logs.

Exchange Client   Simple information management tool that acts as a client application to Exchange Server.

Exchange Server   Microsoft's client/server messaging system; a Windows NT Server computer running Exchange Server software.

Exchange Server organization   Collection of Exchange Server sites; a company's entire Exchange Server system.

Exchange Server site   One or more Exchange Server computers connected by a high-bandwidth, permanent network that communicate with each other via synchronous Remote Procedure Call connections to share directory information, which is automatically updated and replicated to all computers.

Failure audit event   Audited, unsuccessful security access event.

Fault tolerance   A system's ability to respond to an event like a power failure so that information is not lost and operations continue uninterrupted.

Field Chooser   Forms Designer tool for adding fields to an electronic form.

Firewall   Security system that prevents unauthorized access to an internal network from any foreign source.

Folder Assistant   Outlook tool for creating rules for a public folder.

Folder Contact   Contact for reporting problems with or requesting changes to a public folder.

Folder Forms library   Electronic forms library that resides within a public folder and contains all the forms used in that public folder.

Folder List   Hierarchy of public and private folders displayed in Outlook.

Folder set   Container used to store and organize Exchange Server folders.

Folder shortcut   Link to a published public folder.

Foreign system   Messaging system other than Exchange Server.

Form   See *electronic form.*

Forms Administrator   Tool for creating the Organization Forms library and for setting permissions for which users can create items and subfolders in the Organization Forms library.

Forms Designer   Exchange Server tool for creating customized electronic forms.

Forms Manager   Outlook tool used to install electronic forms in a public folder.

Full backup   Complete backup of the information store and directory.

Gateway   Connector that delivers messages between the Exchange Server system and a foreign system.

Gateway Routing Table (GWART)   Table of all possible message routes in the Exchange Server organization.

Geographic profile   Assessment of where a company's offices and other facilities are located.

Global Address List   Listing of all mail recipients and information about those recipients contained in the directory.

Group scheduling   The ability of groups of Exchange Server users to manage tasks and set up meetings across the network.

GWART   See *Gateway Routing Table.*

Hidden public folder   Public folder that is not displayed in the public folder hierarchy.

Home server   Exchange Server computer that contains a user's mailbox.

HTML   See *HyperText Markup Language.*

HTTP   See *HyperText Transfer Protocol.*

Hunt system   System that enables a call to a single phone number to be switched to an available modem, rather than requiring a separate phone number for each modem.

HyperText Markup Language (HTML)   Mark-up language for creating documents displayed on the Web.

HyperText Transfer Protocol (HTTP)   Internet protocol used by Web servers to transfer HTML pages for display in Web browsers.

Idle timeout   Amount of time a client can be connected to a server without performing any actions before the server automatically closes the connection.

ILS   See *Microsoft Internet Locator Service.*

IMAP4   See *Internet Message Access Protocol 4.*

Inbound host   Usenet host computer providing a newsfeed.

Inbox Assistant   Outlook tool for automatically processing and organizing incoming email messages.

Incremental backup   Backup of information that has changed since the last full backup, including the deletion of transaction log files that have had all transactions written to the database.

Information event   Infrequent, significant event indicating the successful operation of a major service.

Information flow   Exchange of information stored on different Exchange Server computers among the sites in an organization.

Information service   Tool that enables Exchange Server clients and foreign systems to exchange email.

Information store Exchange Server component that stores users' mailboxes and public folders.

Information Store Integrity Checker (ISINTEG) Exchange Server utility for finding and eliminating common errors from the information store database.

Information Viewer Area of the Outlook interface that displays the items or files in the open folder.

Instant groupware Groupware created without programming by combining an Outlook module with a public folder.

Internet Worldwide system of networked computers that use TCP/IP to transfer data and convert messages.

Internet Control Pack Set of ActiveX components that enables Internet functionality to be integrated into Outlook applications.

Internet Mail Service Exchange Server component that enables users to send messages to the Internet and connects Exchange Server sites over the SMTP backbone.

Internet Message Access Protocol 4 (IMAP4) Internet protocol that enables client programs to retrieve and manipulate email messages, private folders, and public folders from the Exchange Server computer.

Internet News Service Exchange Server component that enables an Exchange Server computer to host Usenet newsgroups.

Internet protocol Set of communication rules that enables different types of computers to seamlessly exchange information over the Internet.

Internet Relay Chat (IRC) Internet protocol that enables realtime discussion over the Internet.

Internetwork Packet Exchange/Sequenced Packet Exchange (IPX/SPX) Network protocol built into Windows NT Server and compatible with Exchange Server.

Interoperability log Log consisting of the binary contents of X.400 protocol messages transported by the Message Transfer Agent used to troubleshoot MTA configuration problems.

IPX/SPX See *Internetwork Packet Exchange/Sequenced Packet Exchange.*

IRC See *Internet Relay Chat.*

ISINTEG See *Information Store Integrity Checker.*

Key Management (KM) server   Exchange Server component that provides advanced security features.

KM server   See *Key Management (KM) server.*

Knowledge base   Store of publicly available information.

LDAP   See *Lightweight Directory Access Protocol.*

Lightweight Directory Access Protocol (LDAP)   Internet protocol that enables clients to access and search the Exchange Server directory.

Link Monitor   Exchange Server tool that monitors the status of connections between sites and foreign systems and alerts administrators to any problems.

Load Simulator   Exchange Server tool that shows a realistic load on the server by simulating the behavior of Outlook clients.

Local delivery   The sending of email messages between users that share the same home server.

Location   Small group of servers within a site that are generally located on the same network segment.

Logging level   Used in diagnostics logging to determine which Exchange Server events are written to the event log.

Lotus cc:Mail Connector   See *Microsoft Exchange Connector for Lotus cc:Mail.*

Macintosh-accessible volume   Directory on the Exchange Server computer containing the Microsoft Mail Connector postoffice that enables Microsoft Mail (AppleTalk) postoffices to exchange mail with the Microsoft Mail Connector for AppleTalk Networks.

Mailbox   Delivery location for electronic mail messages to an Exchange Server user.

Mailbox agent   Messaging-enabled server application written to operate from data sent to a specific mailbox.

Mailbox template   Mailbox object whose configuration is copied to other mailboxes as they are created.

Mail Message form   Electronic form that enables users to send and respond to items through email or inside a public folder.

MAPI   See *Message Application Programming Interface.*

Mask   Value used with an IP address to identify the network location of the client.

Master domain model   Domain model in which user accounts are defined only on the first-tier domain and each organizational group manages its own resources on second-tier domains.

Max open retries setting   Setting that specifies the number of times a connector can attempt to transfer an email message before returning the message as a non-delivery report.

Meeting Planner   Built-in tool of Outlook's Calendar module that enables users to schedule group meetings.

Memory protection   Prevents anyone from reading information directly from memory after a data structure has been released back to the operating system.

Message Application Programming Interface (MAPI)   Standard interface used by Exchange Server and Outlook components to communicate with each other.

Message archive   Archive of the entire text of each message sent or received by the Internet Mail Service; used for troubleshooting problems with Internet mail.

Message Flag   Outlook feature that enables email messages to be marked up with due dates or follow-up actions.

Message format   Determination of how an email message is displayed in the client.

Message queue   Collection of messages waiting to be transferred by the Message Transfer Agent; there are different queues for messages going to other servers, other sites, and connectors to foreign systems.

Message Recall   Outlook feature that enables sent email messages to be recalled by the sender before they are opened.

Message routing   Process of transferring and delivering email messages.

Message tracking   Exchange Server feature that enables sent email messages to be located anywhere in the system.

Message Transfer Agent (MTA)   Exchange Server component that routes messages to other servers, connectors, and third-party gateways.

Messaging bridgehead server   Exchange Server computer that provides a connection between two sites and routes messages through the connection.

Microsoft Certificate Server   Software that enables the server to act as a Certification Authority for certifying public keys.

Microsoft Cluster Server   Software that enables Exchange Server to be installed on a pair of clustered servers, providing greater reliability in the event of hardware failure.

Microsoft Exchange Chat Service   Internet Relay Chat server included with Exchange Server to enable the hosting of realtime discussion over the Internet.

Microsoft Exchange Connector for Lotus cc:Mail   Exchange Server component that provides email exchange and directory synchronization between the Exchange Server system and a Lotus cc:Mail system.

Microsoft Exchange Event Service   Exchange Server component that detects an event in a public folder and runs an agent in response.

Microsoft Exchange Scripting Agent   Exchange Server tool for creating applications that implement custom events based on user actions.

Microsoft Internet Locator Service (ILS)   Software that works with the Microsoft Exchange Chat Service to maintain a dynamic database of the names and IP addresses of users who are online.

Microsoft Mail Connector for AppleTalk Networks   Exchange Server component that provides connectivity to Microsoft Mail (AppleTalk) systems.

Microsoft Mail Connector for PC Networks   Exchange Server component that provides connectivity to Microsoft Mail (PC) systems.

Microsoft Mail Connector Interchange   Windows NT Server service that routes messages between the Exchange Server system and the Microsoft Mail Connector postoffice.

Microsoft Outlook 97   See *Outlook*.

Microsoft Team Manager 97   See *Team Manager*.

Migration   The process of moving information on an existing mail system to the Exchange Server system.

Migration Wizard   Exchange Server tool for importing migration files into the Exchange Server system; also acts as a source extractor for some kinds of mail systems.

MIME   See *Multipurpose Internet Mail Extension*.

MIME type   Description of the contents of a particular type of data that enables the data to be displayed properly.

Modular architecture   System composed of separate components that can be connected together.

Module Exchange Server component; Outlook folder that enables different tasks to be performed, such as calendaring or managing email.

MS Mail (AppleTalk) Connector See *Microsoft Mail Connector for AppleTalk Networks.*

MS Mail (PC) Connector See *Microsoft Mail Connector for PC Networks.*

MTA See *Message Transfer Agent.*

MTACHECK Exchange Server utility for finding objects that are interfering with Message Transfer Agent message queue processing, for routine checks of the integrity of MTA message queues, and to restart the MTA if it cannot be started from the Services control panel.

MTA transport stack Networking software that contains the configuration information required to support server-to-server message transport over an X.400 connection.

Multiple master domain model Two-tier domain model in which the first tier contains two or more single master domains that encompass all user accounts and the second tier contains all resources.

Multipurpose Internet Mail Extension (MIME) Internet protocol that enables binary data to be published and read on the Internet.

NDR See *non-delivery report.*

Net available bandwidth Network bandwidth available after consumption by other applications.

NetBIOS Extended User Interface (NetBEUI) Network protocol built into Windows NT Server and compatible with Exchange Server.

NetBEUI See *NetBIOS Extended User Interface.*

Network alert Alert message sent to a specific computer or person logged on to the network.

Network bandwidth The data transmission capacity of a network link.

Network News Transport Protocol (NNTP) Internet protocol that enables clients to read and post information to Usenet newsgroups.

Network protocol Set of rules that enables computers to connect to each other and exchange information.

Network segment Part of a network that connects to a router or bridge.

Network share   Directory on a file server to which users can connect to install and run an Exchange client application from the network server.

Network traffic   Amount of data that travels through a network link.

Newsfeed   Flow of items from one Usenet site to another.

Newsfeed Configuration Wizard   Exchange Server tool for creating Usenet newsfeeds.

Newsgroup hierarchy   Hierarchy of Usenet newsgroup public folders displayed in the Administrator window and Outlook.

NNTP   See *Network News Transport Protocol.*

Non-delivery report (NDR)   Notice that a message was not delivered to its recipient.

Normal backup   See *full backup.*

Normal site   Exchange Server site that is not in a warning or alert state.

Object   See *directory object.*

Office 97 Document form   Electronic form that is wrapped around an Office 97 document so the document can be sent as an email message or shared in a public folder.

Offline Address Book   Version of the Address Book that remote users download for working offline.

Offline Address Book server   Exchange Server computer that generates offline Address Book files where remote users can connect to download the offline Address Book.

One-off address template   Localized template used to determine the specific information needed when creating a new email address for Outlook.

Open retry count   Number of times the Message Transfer Agent has tried to transfer a message through a connector and failed.

Organization   See *Exchange Server organization.*

Organization Forms library   Library of electronic forms that are available to all Exchange Server users.

Out of Office Assistant   Outlook tool that automatically replies to all email messages with an out-of-office message.

Outbound host   Usenet host computer that receives a newsfeed.

Outlook   Workgroup and individual desktop information-management tool that acts as a full-featured client application to Exchange Server.

Outlook Address Book   Address Book that is automatically created by Outlook from all contacts that have an email or fax listing.

Outlook Bar   Area of the Outlook window that contains Shortcuts to frequently used folders, organized in groups.

Outlook item   Predefined electronic form that is organized with other forms of the same type and is used to interact with Outlook modules.

Outlook Web Access   Exchange Server component that interacts with the Active Server function of the Internet Information Server to enable Web browsers to view mailboxes and public folders stored on Exchange Server.

Pass-through traffic   Network traffic that originates in one Exchange Server site and passes through a second site while destined for a third site or foreign system.

PDC   See *Primary Domain Controller.*

Performance Monitor   Windows NT Server tool that tracks statistics on system characteristics, including characteristics relating to the Exchange Server system.

Performance Optimizer   Exchange Server tool used to optimize disk access and server performance.

Permission   Authorization to access a directory object in the Administrator program or to perform an action in a public folder.

Personal Address Book   Customizable Outlook Address Book used to store personal distribution lists.

Personal distribution list   Distribution list created and stored in a user's Personal Address Book.

Personal Forms library   Private library of electronic forms residing either on Exchange Server or on the hard drive.

Personal user profile   Group of settings that provides information about a user's configuration of Outlook.

Ping message   Round-trip test message sent by the Link Monitor to test the performance and availability of connectors.

Polling interval   How often the Server Monitor checks Exchange Server services or the Link Monitor checks Exchange Server connections.

POP3   See *Post Office Protocol 3*.

Post form   Electronic form used to post and view information in a public folder.

Post Office Protocol 3 (POP3)   Internet protocol that enables clients to retrieve email from an Exchange Server mailbox.

Primary Domain Controller (PDC)   See *domain controller*.

Private information store   Area of the information store that maintains information stored in users' mailboxes.

Private key   Advanced security key, known only to its owner, that is used to verify or decrypt data.

Property pages   Logical groupings of a directory object's properties in the Administrator window that enable properties for that object to be configured.

Public folder   Folder where a group of Exchange Server users can share information, such as email messages, spreadsheets, graphics, and voice mail.

Public folder affinity   Exchange Server feature that enables users in one site to access public folders on servers in other sites.

Public folder content   Information contained inside a public folder.

Public folder hierarchy   Structure of public folders as they appear in the client and in the Administrator program.

Public folder replication   Process of updating identical copies of a public folder on multiple Exchange Server computers.

Public folder server   Exchange Server computer dedicated to storing public folders.

Public information store   Area of the information store that maintains the information contained in public folders.

Public key   Publicly known advanced security key used to sign or encrypt data.

Published public folder   Public folder that can be viewed anonymously via the Web.

Pull feed   Newsfeed initiated by the receiving system.

Push feed   Newsfeed initiated by the newsfeed provider.

RAS   See *Remote Access Service*.

Read view   View of an electronic form in Forms Designer as it would appear to the user.

Recipient   Directory object that can receive email and information and is displayed in the Address Book; recipients include mailboxes, distribution lists, custom recipients, and public folders.

Remote access   Consistent method for users to dial into the Exchange Server system and operate remotely, using the built-in Remote Access Service of Windows NT Server.

Remote Access Service (RAS)   Windows NT Server protocol for remote connectivity.

Remote dirsync requestor   Internal representation of a Microsoft Mail directory requestor that uses an Exchange Server computer as its directory synchronization server.

Remote distribution list   Distribution list of recipients on another site.

Remote Procedure Call (RPC)   Protocol for client/server communications used by the Exchange Server system.

Replication   Process of copying new and updated information in the directory and in the public information store to other servers.

Revocation   Process of invalidating a user's advanced security certificate.

Rich Text Format (RTF)   Allows mail messages to be formatted with fonts, character formatting, paragraph alignment, and bullets.

Role   Group of permissions.

Routing table   Contains information about connectors and gateways needed by the Message Transfer Agent for routing messages.

RPC   See *Remote Procedure Call.*

RTF   See *Rich Text Format.*

Rule   User-specified criteria for automatically routing and storing incoming messages in Outlook or for processing incoming information to a public folder.

Sample application   Public folder application included with Exchange Server that can be used as-is or modified.

Schedule+   Group scheduling and tasks application that acts as a client to Exchange Server.

Schedule+ Free/Busy Connector   Exchange Server component that enables Exchange Server users to share scheduling information with Microsoft Mail for PC Networks systems.

Schedule+ Free Busy Information public folder   Hidden public folder that stores the

Schedule+ free and busy information for all users in a site and is accessed by the Outlook and Schedule+ clients for group scheduling functions.

Secure logon   Windows NT Server logon process that requires users to enter a unique username and password before they are allowed access to the system.

Secure/Multipurpose Internet Mail Extension (S/MIME)   Internet protocol that enables the exchange of encrypted email by S/MIME-aware clients via the Exchange Server system.

Secure Sockets Layer (SSL)   Internet protocol that enables secure communications between Internet clients and the Exchange Server system.

Secured queue   Message queue that does not appear in the Message Transfer Agent queue list unless the connector has sent or received a message to or from the MTA.

Send form   Electronic form used to exchange information with other users.

Send-on-behalf-of permission   Authority of one user to send messages on behalf of another mailbox.

Server   Software program that receives and fulfills client requests.

Server Monitor   Exchange Server tool that enables monitoring of key Exchange Server services and implements an automatic escalation process if a service is stopped.

Service account   Windows NT user account used to run Exchange Server services.

Shared private folder   Private folder to which other users have been granted access.

Simple Mail Transport Protocol (SMTP)   Internet protocol used to transfer messages between Exchange Server and the Internet.

Single domain model   Domain model that has only one domain where all user accounts are created.

Single-instance message storage   Exchange Server feature that enables a message addressed to multiple recipients on the same server to be stored as a single copy in the server's information store.

Site   See *Exchange Server site.*

Site Connector   Exchange Server component that enables messages to be sent between sites on the same local area network.

Site layout   Map of an Exchange Server site that shows the underlying network, the placement of servers and user groups, and other factors that affect the site design.

S/MIME See *Secure/Multipurpose Internet Mail Extension.*

SMTP   See *Simple Mail Transport Protocol.*

SMTP protocol log Log of SMTP information used to troubleshoot problems with Internet mail.

Source extractor   Tool that creates migration files from an existing mail system for import into the Exchange Server system.

SSL   See *Secure Sockets Layer.*

Storage limit   The maximum amount of space a mailbox or public folder can occupy in the information store.

Success audit event   Audited, successful security access event.

System attendant   Exchange Server component that provides core maintenance services.

Target server   Exchange Server computer that acts as the endpoint of a site connection.

TaskPad Tool in Outlook's Calendar module that displays the task list so that time to work on tasks can be scheduled.

TCP/IP   See *Transport Control Protocol/Internet Protocol.*

Team Manager   Group tasks application that works with Outlook to enhance its workgroup capabilities.

Temporary key   Random character string used once to establish the connection between the Key Management server and the client, enabling advanced security on the client.

Third-party product   Software solution developed by an independent software vendor for extending the capabilities of Exchange Server and Outlook.

Thrashing   Excessive paging between physical memory and virtual memory, which often degrades server performance.

Tombstone   Marker in the directory indicating that an object has been deleted from a server.

Top-level folder   Public folder that is in the highest tier of the public folder hierarchy and contains related subfolders.

Total available bandwidth   Bandwidth provided by a network connection.

Tracking application   Public folder application that enables constantly updated information to be recorded and tracked.

Traffic pattern   Trend of data flow through a network link over a period of time.

Transaction log file   File that provides fault tolerance in case data needs to be restored to the information store or directory databases.

Transport Control Protocol/Internet Protocol (TCP/IP)   Network protocol built into Windows NT Server and compatible with Exchange Server; protocol that enables computers to exchange data over the Internet.

Trust level   Number assigned to an Exchange Server mailbox to determine if the mailbox is sent to a Microsoft Mail system during directory synchronization.

Trust relationship   Relationship between two domains that enables a user in one domain to access resources in the other.

Uniform Resource Locator (URL)   Internet addressing system that contains information about the Internet protocol, the server computer to be accessed, and the pathname of the file to be accessed.

Universal Inbox   Exchange Server feature that provides access to information resources through the MAPI and PPP protocols.

Unsecured queue   Message queue that appears in the queue list whenever the receiving service is running.

URL   See *Uniform Resource Locator.*

Usenet   Collection of host computers and networks that exchange articles organized by subject into newsgroups.

Usenet newsgroup   Internet discussion group focusing on a specific topic.

Usenet site   Collection of one or more Usenet host computers.

User account   Windows NT Server account that contains information about the username, password, group membership, and permissions for each user of the server.

VBScript   See *Visual Basic Scripting Edition.*

View   Predefined format for displaying items in an Outlook folder or public folder.

View type   Basic view structure that determines how information in the view is arranged and formatted.

Visual Basic Scripting Edition (VBScript)   Scripting language built into Forms Designer to add more functionality and customization to electronic forms.

Visual InterDev   Visual development tool used to create HTML forms and collaborative Active Server Pages applications within Outlook.

Voting   Outlook feature that enables opinions to be gathered, tallied, and tracked through email.

Warning event   Event that indicates possible problems in the system.

Warning state   State of a site or connector indicating a possible problem.

Web browser   Client application that displays HTML files on the Web.

Windows NT domain   See *domain*.

Windows NT Server   Network operating system required to run Exchange Server.

Workflow   Technology for streamlining and automating business processes using groupware.

World Wide Web   System of HTML pages connected by hyperlinks that can be displayed and navigated with a Web browser; also called the Web.

X.400 Connector   Exchange Server component that connects sites or routes messages to foreign X.400 systems.

Appendix A
Troubleshooting
Tips And Tricks

Your Exchange Server system is not static, but is instead constantly changing and growing, which can sometimes lead to problems. Troubleshooting the Exchange Server system involves using the tools and resources available to you to narrow down the cause of a system problem to a particular component, service, computer, or network connection. This appendix describes Exchange Server tools you can employ in the troubleshooting process, as well as tips and tricks for troubleshooting major problems with the system and minor problems often experienced by users and administrators. The information in this appendix is intended to complement the information provided in the earlier chapters of this book.

Troubleshooting Message Transfer

Problems with message transfer on Exchange Server are not uncommon. Because message transfer can involve multiple servers, sites, mail systems, and components, tracking down the root of a problem can be very difficult. Exchange Server includes several features to help with troubleshooting message transfer problems. Two of the most useful of these are message tracking and message queues. This section briefly describes how to use these tools to diagnose problems with message transfer.

Message Tracking

Using the *message tracking* feature, you can track any email message sent to and from the Exchange Server system. Message tracking is a good way to troubleshoot message transfer problems. Use it to locate slow or stopped connections, find lost mail, remove unauthorized messages, determine where routing delays are occurring, and trace *ping messages* and replication messages. Just keep tracking different messages until you find the source of the problem. You can enable message tracking on the Message Transfer Agent (MTA), information store, and many connectors.

Tip

Message tracking should only be enabled when you suspect a problem, because it creates large logs that can degrade the performance of your servers.

Enabling Message Tracking

Turning on message tracking for the MTA or information store enables message tracking on all MTAs or information stores in the site. However, you must enable message tracking for each connector in the site separately, even connectors of the same type. Table A.1 describes the directory object and property page used to enable message tracking on different Exchange Server components.

Tip

After turning on message tracking, you must stop and restart the affected services in the Services control panel.

Each server component where message tracking is enabled records its mail-handling activities in a message tracking log maintained by the system attendant on each server. The message tracking log traces all mail-handling *events* as messages are received, processed, and delivered to the next component. You must first turn on message tracking on all Exchange Server computers for a message to be traced through to the point of delivery.

Tracking A Message

The process of tracking a message searches the daily message tracking logs for events generated when server components processed the message. The message's route is followed through the logs of all servers on the same network. The tracking process is complete when the message is delivered or when it leaves the system. Follow these steps to track a message:

1. Select Track Message from the Tools menu in the Administrator program.

2. Connect to the server that has either the sender or the recipient of the message you want to track in its Global Address List.

Table A.1   Directory objects and property pages used to enable message tracking on different Exchange Server components.

Component	Directory Object	Property Page
MTA	MTA Site Configuration	General
Information store	Information Store Site Configuration	General
MS Mail Connector	MS Mail Connector	Interchange
Internet Mail Service	Internet Mail Service	Internet Mail
Lotus cc:Mail Connector	Lotus cc:Mail Connector	Post Office

Tip ● ● ●

If the sender and recipient of the message are located only in a *Personal Address Book* or are Exchange Server components, then you can connect to any server in the site.

3. Specify the message to track.

4. Select the sender of the message in the From box.

5. Select the recipient(s) of the message in the Sent To box.

Tip ● ● ●

If the Sent To box is left blank, all messages sent by the sender are tracked.

6. To search for a message sent by an Exchange Server component or sent from outside the system, click on Advanced Search.

7. Select Sent By Microsoft Exchange Server to search for a message sent by an Exchange Server component; click on Browse to find the server, and select the component in the From box.

8. Select Transferred Into This Site to search for a message that originated outside the system; type the email address of the sender in the Select Inbound Message To Track box, select the recipient(s) in the Sent To box, and select the connector that transported the message in the Transferred From box.

9. To specify how many daily tracking logs to search, enter a number in the Look Back box; enter 0 to search only the current day's log.

10. Click on Find Now to start tracking the message.

After a message is found, the Message Tracking Center displays general details about the message, including its ID number, its originator, the server where the message was sent from or where it entered the network, and the date the message was sent or entered the network. Mail-handling events that relate to the message are shown in the Tracking History window; each level in the hierarchy represents a branch in the path of the message. To get more detailed information about the message at the time an event was generated, select the event in the hierarchy and click on Properties. Table A.2 describes the properties of a mail-handling event.

Tip ● ● ●

To find events involving a recipient of the tracked message in the Tracking History window, click on Find Recipient In Tracking History and specify the recipient.

Table A.2	Mail-handling event properties.
Property	**Description**
Event Type	A description of the mail-handling event.
From	The directory name of the message's originator.
Time	The time the message was sent or received.
Transferred To	The component that generated the event.
Size	The message size in bytes.
Priority	The importance level assigned to the message.
Recipients List	A list of all addresses to which the message was sent.

Any of the following methods are effective for following up a problem message:

➤ Consult the message queues of affected components.

➤ Raise the *logging levels* of affected components or services.

➤ Change the configuration of affected components.

Message Queues

Consulting the *message queues* for the MTA and different connectors can be very helpful in diagnosing problems with message transfer. In Chapter 5, you learned how to manipulate the MTA message queue to troubleshoot problems with transferring mail inside the Exchange Server system. If you are experiencing problems with Internet mail or with mail to a Microsoft Mail system, you can consult the message queues for those connectors as well.

Internet Mail Service Queues

Consult the *Internet Mail Service* message queues when you suspect problems with Internet mail. The Queues property page for the Internet Mail Service displays important details about messages sent to and received from the Internet. You can also use this property page to delete problem messages. To open the Queues property page, double-click on the Internet Mail Service and select the Queues tab. The Internet Mail Service has four message queues, as described in Table A.3.

Select a queue name and message in the Queues property page to view additional information about the message that can help you isolate the cause of a problem. The following message details are helpful in diagnosing problems with the transfer of messages to and from the Internet:

➤ The Retries option shows the number of times the Internet Mail Service attempted to deliver the message and failed; focus on messages that have failed at least one delivery.

Queue	Queues Property Page Option	Queue Description
Table A.3	**Internet Mail Service queues.**	
MTS-OUT	Outbound Messages Awaiting Conversion	Outgoing messages received from the MTA and waiting to be converted by the Internet Mail Service.
Out	Outbound Messages Awaiting Delivery	Converted outgoing messages waiting for delivery to the Internet.
In	Inbound Messages Awaiting Conversion	Messages received from the Internet and waiting to be converted by the Internet Mail Service.
MTS-IN	Inbound Messages Awaiting Delivery	Converted incoming messages waiting for delivery to the MTA or to the message recipient.

➤ Look for common characteristics of messages that have failed delivery attempts, such as a common destination host or recipient, to isolate the cause of the failed deliveries.

➤ If messages are accumulating in the queue, check the configuration of the destination host server for the first few messages in the queue.

➤ Check the delivery status and information about failed attempts to detect corrupt messages.

➤ The message transfer system ID (MTS-ID) and message ID are helpful for searching for the message in the tracking log or event log.

➤ Compare the Submit Time box, which displays the time the message arrived in the queue, with the time the message was sent to determine where delays might be happening.

➤ Create an *SMTP protocol log* for the Internet Mail Service to log *Simple Mail Transport Protocol (SMTP)* events that might be causing problems with message transfer.

➤ Delete undeliverable messages to keep them from blocking the message queues.

Microsoft Mail Connector Queues

Each *Microsoft Mail Connector* maintains a queue of pending outbound messages, which can be useful in diagnosing message transfer problems to the connected MS Mail system. View the queue by double-clicking on an MS Mail Connector, selecting Connections, and clicking on Queue. Each line under Queued Messages represents one outbound message waiting for delivery. Select a message and take a look at it to detect problems with the message or with the connector. You can also return or delete messages that might be causing message transfer problems.

Check the following message details when troubleshooting problems with message delivery through the MS Mail Connector:

➤ Messages normally stay in the queue for only a brief time, so investigate any lingering messages as they are likely to be the sources of problems.

➤ The Message ID enables you to trace the message in the tracking log, event log, and MTA queues.

➤ Compare the time displayed in the Submit Time box, which is the time the message arrived in the queue, to the time the message was sent to determine at which point delays are occurring.

➤ If a message appears to be blocking the queue, return it to its sender by selecting the message and clicking on Return.

➤ To test the path of a message, return it to its sender and then use the message ID to follow the returned message in the tracking log.

➤ If a message appears to be delaying the processing of a queue and you do not want to return it because you suspect it might cause further problems, select the message and click on Delete to erase it from the disk; select the Send Non-Delivery Reports When Messages Deleted check box to return a *non-delivery report (NDR)* to the message's originator.

➤ If sent messages are not appearing in the MS Mail Connector queue, check the MTA queue to the MS Mail Connector to verify that messages are being submitted to the connector.

➤ Check the integrity of the connected postoffice to ensure that the MS Mail server is not the source of message transfer problems.

Troubleshooting Tools

Many Exchange Server tools, Windows NT utilities, and third-party and shareware products are available to help with troubleshooting problems with the Exchange Server system. Two of the most useful of these—the MTACHECK utility and the Information Store Integrity Checker—are included with the Exchange Server software and are used to fix problems with the MTA and the information store. Following the brief descriptions of these utilities is a list of additional tools you can employ when troubleshooting problems.

MTACHECK

Use the *MTACHECK* utility to find objects that are interfering with MTA message queue processing, for routine checks of the integrity of MTA message queues, and to get the MTA running if it stops and cannot be restarted from the Services control panel.

MTACHECK scans the internal database of the MTA and places objects that are in error in Db*.dat files, located in the path Exchsrvr\Mtadata\Mtacheck.out\, so you can examine the defective objects at a later time. It also rebuilds message queues so that the MTA can resume processing messages when it is restarted. While MTACHECK is running, it creates a report of any errors it finds, specifying the queue where the error was found, the type of error, the object ID of any removed objects, the message ID of any corrupted messages, and the number of messages returned to the rebuilt queue.

Stop the Microsoft Exchange Message Transfer Agent Service and empty the Mtacheck.out subdirectory before running MTACHECK. Type **mtacheck** at the command prompt of the server that is experiencing MTA problems to run MTACHECK. Table A.4 describes options that can be used with the **mtacheck** command.

Information Store Integrity Checker

Use the *Information Store Integrity Checker (ISINTEG)* utility to find and eliminate common errors from the information store database. You should run ISINTEG when the information store is stopped and you cannot restart it from the Services control panel and when users are experiencing problems logging on and receiving, opening, or deleting mail.

ISINTEG has three modes: check mode, check and fix mode, and patch mode. Running ISINTEG in check mode searches the information store database for table errors, incorrect reference counts, and unreferenced objects; the results are simultaneously displayed and written to a log file (Isinteg.pri for the private information store or Isinteg.pub for the public information store). Running ISINTEG in check and fix mode corrects all found errors; this mode should only be used at the advice of Microsoft Technical Support and after performing a full backup. Running ISINTEG in patch mode repairs an information store that will not start after being restored from an offline backup.

ISINTEG must be run separately on the public and private information stores. Before running ISINTEG, stop the Microsoft Exchange Information Store service in the Services control panel. (Note that you do not have to stop all Exchange Server services, just the Information Store; stopping all Exchange Server services will create an error condition.) Type **isinteg** at the command prompt of the server that is experiencing information store problems, followed by any of the options described in Table A.5.

Table A.4 MTACHECK command options.	
Option	**Description**
mtacheck /v	Increases the frequency and detail of progress messages created by MTACHECK.
mtacheck /f \<filename\>	Displays progress messages and sends them to the specified *file name*.

Table A.5 ISINTEG command options.

Option	Description
isinteg -?	Displays the option list without running ISINTEG.
isinteg -pri	Runs ISINTEG in check mode on the private information store.
isinteg -pub	Runs ISINTEG in check mode on the public information store.
isinteg -fix	Runs ISINTEG in check and fix mode.
isinteg -patch	Runs ISINTEG in patch mode.
isinteg -verbose	Verifies and reports all activity by ISINTEG.
isinteg -l <filename>	Changes the default name of the ISINTEG log file to *file name*.

Additional Troubleshooting Tools

In addition to the *Server Monitor, Link Monitor, Performance Monitor,* MTACHECK, and ISINTEG, consider using any of the tools shown in Table A.6 to troubleshoot and monitor your Exchange Server system.

Table A.6 Tools that can be used to troubleshoot the Exchange Server system.

Tool	Description
Dr. Watson	Creates reports on application errors.
Inbox Repair Tool	Repairs defective PST files by scanning the selected PST file for errors and prompting the user to make the necessary change.
Netstat	Shows network protocol statistics and current TCP/IP network connections.
Network Analyzer	Monitors network traffic on a LAN or WAN, including the available bandwidth and collision errors.
Network Topology Maps and Routing Maps	Usually prepared when planning the network, these maps show the locations of servers, third-party gateways, site boundaries, client installation points, monitors, and user connections to the network; they have keys that describe bandwidth, supported protocols, file servers, routers, and bridges to help interpret the data you collect from monitors and to find outage patterns.
Ping	Tests the connectivity between hosts that use IP addresses, such as SMTP servers.
Ping-1	Measures the travel time of a ping message from one IP address to another.
Pview	Displays the memory and resources in use by each process on a Windows NT Server computer.
RPC Ping	Similar to Ping, this is a very handy tool that is often used to troubleshoot RPC connectivity problems between clients and servers.
Telnet to Port 25	Tests communication connections to SMTP networks.
Windows NT Diagnostics	Displays system information.
Windows NT Server Manager	Configures services and server shares remotely on Windows NT Server computers.

On Site

Troubleshooting Major Processes

This section outlines methods for troubleshooting problems with major Exchange Server services and functions using the tools described in this appendix and in earlier chapters. By combining different methods to isolate problem components, servers, and areas of the network, you can effectively locate the cause of any major problem in the system and take steps to fix the problem.

Troubleshooting Message Routing

Problems with sending mail, or *message routing,* can usually be traced to a particular client, server, connector, or recipient. Diagnosing the cause of the problem is generally a process of eliminating components along the message route that are working properly, thereby isolating the problem components. For example, if many different clients are having problems sending mail to the same recipient, then you can be sure that the problem is either with the destination server or the recipient, not with the clients. If you suspect a problem with message routing, try the following methods to track down the problem:

➤ Verify that the originator of the problem message can send mail to other mailboxes to make sure the problem is not with the client or the originating server.

➤ Rebuild the *routing table* by clicking on Recalculate Routing in the General property page of the MTA.

➤ Trace the problem message using message tracking to find the server along the message's route that is causing delays.

➤ Check the message queues of MTAs along the route; if a message queue to another MTA is growing, it indicates that the destination MTA service is down or that there is a problem with the destination MTA or server.

➤ Use the Server Monitor to make sure that all MTA services along the route are up and running.

➤ Use the Server Monitor to make sure that all information stores along the message route are up and running.

➤ If message tracking is enabled, check to see if one of the message tracking logs on servers along the route has run out of disk space (this is a common problem).

➤ Check that all servers and connections between servers along the route are available and working properly; pay particular attention to network traffic, which might be slowing down message transfer.

➤ Check for problems with any connectors along the message route (see the following section).

Troubleshooting Connectors

If you are experiencing problems with sending mail messages through a *connector* to another site or to a *foreign system,* try these methods to find the cause of the problem (see the sections "Problems With The Internet Mail Service," "Problems With The MS Mail Connector," and "Problems With The X.400 Connector" later in this appendix for solutions to problems with specific connectors):

➤ Make sure that *address spaces* are configured correctly; removing old routes before adding new ones often causes address space problems.

➤ Trace the problem message to the connector using message tracking.

➤ Check the MTA message queue to the connector; a long message queue indicates a problem with the connector, such as an incorrect configuration.

➤ Check the message queues of the connector to find out if a message is blocking the queues or if delivery attempts of a message have failed; remove or return any stalled messages.

➤ Use the Link Monitor to check the status of the connector and determine when the connector was last working.

➤ Use the Server Monitor to make sure the connector's service is up and running.

➤ Check the Windows NT application event log for errors related to the connector.

➤ If the problem is with a message sent to the Internet, increase the logging level to Maximum on all Internet Mail Service categories except Message Archival, restart the Internet Mail Service, re-create the error, and check the application event log and SMTP protocol logs for error messages.

Troubleshooting Directory Replication

Directory replication problems are usually caused by a problem with the connection between two sites, by a problem with the connection between two servers, or by the incorrect configuration of directory replication. If you suspect a problem with directory replication, try these methods to help track down the cause of the problem:

➤ Check the directory replication schedule in the Administrator program to make sure directory replication is proceeding as scheduled; click on the Update Now button to initiate directory replication manually.

➤ Use the Link Monitor to test the connection between the two sites.

➤ Use the Server Monitor and Performance Monitor to make sure that the *directory replication bridgehead servers* in both sites are functioning correctly.

➤ Track replication messages using message tracking to find the point where messages are getting delayed.

➤ Increase the logging level for the Directory Replication Events and/or for the Replication Updates categories, and check the event log for errors in directory replication.

➤ Because changes to the directory are automatically replicated to all servers within a site, a problem with directory replication between servers in the same site indicates that a server is not functioning correctly or that there is a network connection problem between servers.

Troubleshooting Directory Synchronization

Directory synchronization is the process of exchanging directories between the Exchange Server system and an MS Mail (PC) system or an MS Mail (AppleTalk) system. This process relies on the proper configuration and functioning of the *Microsoft Mail Connector Interchange,* the MS Mail Connector MTA, the Exchange Server MTA, and the Exchange Server directory. Problems with directory synchronization can be caused by improper planning, problems with the connection between the systems, or configuration problems at either the Exchange Server end or the MS Mail end. Try the following methods to diagnose problems with directory synchronization:

➤ Verify that the directory synchronization server and requestor information is configured correctly on both systems, including postoffice names, network names, passwords, and address types.

➤ Send a message to the directory synchronization postoffice from an Exchange Server user and reply when it is delivered to check for message connectivity to the MS Mail directory synchronization server.

➤ Check the message queues on the MS Mail Connector to make sure that mail is being processed through the connector.

➤ Check the message queues on the connecting MS Mail postoffice to make sure that messages are being processed on that side of the connection.

➤ Check the dispatch logs on the postoffices for reported failures and to make sure that dispatch is running.

➤ If the problem is with an MS Mail (AppleTalk) computer, the directory exchange requestor might not be running correctly; try replacing the MSMail GW file in the System Extension folder.

➤ If the problem on an MS Mail (AppleTalk) computer persists, the directory exchange requestor might not have enough memory or it might be corrupted.

Troubleshooting Public Folder Replication

Often, users cannot access public folders because of a problem with *public folder replication,* which can be caused by configuration, message routing, or network connectivity problems. Try the following methods to diagnose problems with public folder replication:

➤ Check the public folder replication schedule to make sure that replication is proceeding as scheduled.

➤ Trace public folder replication messages using message tracking to find the point where messages are being delayed.

➤ If public folder replication is occurring between two sites, use the Link Monitor to check the connection between the sites.

➤ Use the Server Monitor to check that the MTA and public information store services on the destination server are up and running.

➤ Use the Performance Monitor to check the performance of the public information store on the destination server.

➤ Increase the logging level of the Replication category group and check the event log for public folder replication errors.

Troubleshooting Connections Between Servers

Exchange Server computers within the same site communicate using *Remote Procedure Calls (RPCs).* Problems with the connections between servers are usually related to the configuration of the servers or to network problems. If you are experiencing problems with a server connection, try the following methods to track down the source of the problem:

➤ Use the Server Monitor and Performance Monitor to make sure that the MTA and information store services on the destination server are running and that mail is being processed. If a service is down, check the event log for the cause of the problem before trying to restart the service.

➤ Check the MTA message queues; a long message queue can indicate a problem with the physical connection between servers or a configuration error with a server or the MTA service.

➤ Use a network analyzer to check network usage and make sure there is enough bandwidth to support the traffic between servers.

➤ Use the Ping command from one server to the other to make sure they can communicate with each other.

➤ Use the Net View \\<server name> command at the command prompt to make sure that the network connection between the servers is not down.

➤ If the servers are in different sites, use network tools to test the connectivity and transport network protocol between the *messaging bridgehead servers* in the two sites.

➤ If message transfer stopped working after a change in network configuration, this indicates a problem with network connectivity due to the reconfiguration; use network tools to test the network connectivity.

Solving Common Problems

This section describes solutions to problems often experienced by Exchange Server users and administrators. Try each of the suggested solutions in the order listed to fix the problem that you are having. If none of the suggested solutions takes care of the problem, then begin looking for larger problems in the Exchange Server system, such as problems with message routing, connectors, replication, or the underlying network.

Problems With Setup

There is an error copying files:

➤ Other applications might be using the files; close all applications before running Setup.

➤ If the error persists, remove all programs from the StartUp group, restart the computer, and run Setup again.

You cannot connect to an existing server when installing a new server in the site:

➤ The Windows NT *user account* running Setup might not have permission for the existing server; log on with the user account used to install the existing server.

➤ This might indicate a connection problem between the two servers.

Exchange Server services do not start automatically when Setup is complete:

➤ There might not be enough memory to run the Exchange Server services; increase virtual memory or add more physical memory.

Other errors during Setup:

➤ Setup problems are commonly caused by incorrect configuration of the *service account*.

➤ Setup problems can also be caused by incorrect configuration of the server or inadequate hardware resources on the server.

Problems With Using The Administrator Program

You cannot open a server in the *Administrator program:*

➤ If you are using the Browse button to open the server, the server might not be in the same local area network (LAN) segment; try typing the server's name in the Connect To Server box instead.

➤ You might not have permission to access the server. Consult the site administrator; if the site administrator is unavailable, log on as the service account and start the Administrator program.

➤ Use the Server Monitor on another server in the same site to check the status of the directory and make sure it is running.

➤ Make sure the server is running.

➤ Check for a network connection to the server (this might indicate a problem with the connection between the servers).

➤ If the server is located in another site and has never been visible in the Administrator program, this might indicate that there is a problem with directory replication or that directory replication was never configured.

Another site is not visible in the Administrator program:

➤ This might indicate that directory replication was never configured or that it is not working properly.

➤ The directory might be corrupted and might need to be restored from tape backup.

You cannot modify a directory object:

➤ You might not have permission to modify the object; check with the site administrator.

➤ The object might be located in a different site in the same physical network; connect to a server in the site where the object is located.

Problems With Using Clients

The client cannot connect to an Exchange Server computer:

➤ Check that the server and mailbox name are configured correctly in the Exchange Server information service in the client.

➤ Check that the Windows NT user account you logged on as has User permissions for the mailbox.

➤ Make sure the server is running.

➤ Make sure the network connection to the server is available.

➤ Make sure the server and the client are using the same *network protocol.*

➤ If the server and client are using the same network protocol, it might not be routed between LAN segments; either move the client and server computers to the same LAN segment, or modify the router or bridge to route the network protocol.

➤ If you are using a Novell NetWare client, use the Network control panel to check that the server is running the Gateway Services for NetWare and that the NWLink *Internetwork Packet Exchange/Sequenced Packet Exchange (IPX/SPX)* transport is configured correctly. Also, make sure that the internal network number is unique and that Auto Frame Type Detection is not selected.

➤ Keep in mind that problems with connecting email clients to the server are usually related to client configuration errors, Windows NT permissions, or the network.

● ● *Tip* ● ● ●

Most often, *client* problems are caused by the incorrect configuration of the client, rather than the server. Check first if other clients are experiencing the same problem. If not, the problem is probably with the client.

Problems With Sending Mail

You cannot find a recipient in the *Global Address List:*

➤ The recipient might be hidden from the *Address Book;* choose Hidden Recipients from the View menu in the Administrator program.

➤ Check the Administrator program to make sure the recipient was not removed from the directory.

➤ If the recipient is in a different site or in a foreign system, the directory might not have been replicated yet; check the directory replication schedule for the next replication time or force replication manually. (Problems with directory replication may be indicated.)

The Personal Address Book entry for a recipient is invalid:

➤ Check the entry against the recipient's entry in the Global Address List to make sure it is correct.

➤ Check the Global Address List to make sure the recipient was not moved to another recipients container.

➤ If the recipient is not present in the Global Address List, check if the recipient was removed from the directory.

➤ Check the connector's Address Space property page to make sure the recipient's address space was mapped correctly.

You cannot send mail to another Exchange Server recipient:

➤ Check the Global Address List to make sure the recipient still exists in the directory and was not moved to another recipients container.

➤ If the recipient is located in another site, this might indicate a directory replication or site connector problem.

➤ Check for a message routing problem or a problem with the connection between servers.

You receive a non-delivery report (NDR):

➤ Check the NDR for details about why the message was returned.

➤ Make sure that the recipient's address is correct, is unique, and exists in the network or in the domain of the gateway host.

➤ Make sure that the recipient's address is listed correctly in the Global Address List or Personal Address Book.

➤ If the recipient was removed from another site or foreign system, the directory might not yet have been replicated or synchronized; check the Global Address List again after the next replication or synchronization cycle. (This could indicate a directory replication problem.)

➤ The size of your message might have been larger than allowed by the information store or by the recipient's mailbox; if the message is too large, try resending it without an attachment or breaking it down into multiple messages.

➤ Check for a message routing or connector problem.

Sent mail arrives late or never arrives:

➤ If the recipient is located in another site or on a foreign system, the connector's schedule might not be set to transfer mail at this time; check the connector's Schedule property page.

➤ Make sure that network traffic is not slowing down mail delivery.

➤ Check for a message routing problem.

➤ If the user is in another site or on a foreign system, this could indicate a problem with the connector.

You cannot send or receive mail using an Internet Message Access Protocol 4 (IMAP4) or Post Office Protocol 3 (POP3) client:

➤ Make sure that the user information in the IMAP4 or POP3 client was configured properly.

➤ Make sure that rerouting is correctly configured to route mail outbound to the Internet or intranet.

➤ Make sure that the Internet Mail Service is running.

➤ Make sure that the Internet Mail Service is installed and is configured properly.

Problems With The Internet Mail Service

You cannot start the Internet Mail Service:

➤ Make sure that you installed and configured the Internet Mail Service.

➤ Make sure that *Transport Control Protocol/Internet Protocol (TCP/IP)* is installed.

➤ Make sure that the domain name of the Internet Mail Service host is added to the DNS Configuration dialog box in the Network control panel.

➤ This problem could indicate that the delivery route of an email domain cannot be resolved; review the list in the Email Domain box in the Connections property page, and verify that all domain names appear in the DNS or local Hosts file.

➤ Try stopping and restarting all Exchange Server services.

➤ If the error cannot be resolved, remove and reinstall the Internet Mail Service.

Changes made to the Internet Mail Service in the Administrator program are not taking effect:

➤ You must stop and restart the Internet Mail Service for any changes to take effect.

➤ If the system is slow, the directory might not have updated the changes before you restarted the Internet Mail Service; wait a minute and then restart it again.

You cannot send mail to or receive mail from the Internet:

➤ Make sure that the Internet Mail Service is running.

➤ Make sure that the MTA on the server where the Internet Mail Service is installed is running.

➤ Check that the delivery restrictions configured for the Internet Mail Service do not exclude the sender from sending mail to the Internet.

➤ Make sure that the address space for the Internet Mail Service is configured correctly; to send all SMTP mail to the Internet Mail Service, type an asterisk (*) in the Address column.

➤ On the Connections property page, type an asterisk (*) in the Email Domain box so that all SMTP traffic is routed through the Internet Mail Service.

➤ The Internet Mail Service might be configured for Flush Queue mode; change the Transfer Mode setting in the Connections property page.

➤ If you can receive messages but cannot send them or vice versa, the Transfer Mode might be configured for Inbound Only or Outbound Only; change the Transfer Mode setting in the Connections property page.

➤ If you cannot receive messages from a particular host, check the Accept Or Reject By Host box of the Connections property page to make sure that the Internet Mail Service is not configured to reject connections from that host.

➤ The receiving host might not have responded before the time delay for retries exceeded the Internet Mail Service's threshold set in the Connections property page.

➤ Check the Routing property page to make sure that the domain is set for inbound message transfer.

➤ Make sure that the domain address for Exchange Server users is valid by verifying the SMTP site address in the Site Addressing property pages.

➤ Make sure that the DNS server address is correct in the Network control panel.

➤ If you are using DNS, check for an MX record for the Exchange Server SMTP address.

➤ Make sure that the TCP/IP address on the Internet Mail Service matches the values in the DNS, Hosts file, or Windows Internet Name Server list.

➤ Make sure that the connection to the Internet Mail Service is operating.

➤ Make sure that external SMTP hosts have the correct IP address for the Internet Mail Service server.

➤ Check that the receiving host exists and is operating.

➤ Check for a message routing or connector problem.

Mail sent from Exchange Server to the Internet is received with garbled text or extra attachments:

➤ The message was formatted with *Rich Text Format (RTF)*, which could not be resolved by the receiving system. Double-click on the recipient's name in the Personal Address Book, select the Address tab, and clear the Always Send To This Recipient In Microsoft Exchange Rich-Text Format check box.

➤ If the recipient is a *custom recipient*, clear the Allow Rich Text In Messages check box in the custom recipient's Advanced property page.

➤ Turn off RTF on all messages sent to the Internet by opening the Internet Mail Service's Internet Mail property page, choosing Interoperability, and clearing the Send Microsoft Exchange Rich Text Formatting check box.

Problems With The MS Mail Connector

You cannot create an instance of the MS Mail Connector MTA:

➤ You might not have the appropriate permissions; check with the site administrator.

➤ An instance with the same name that previously existed on the system might have been removed improperly; use a different instance name or click on Apply three times and ignore the error messages.

Different instances of the MS Mail (PC) Connector MTA are trying to use the same modem:

➤ Both instances might be using a modem script that specifies use of the same communications port; edit the modem script source file to change or remove the communications port setting.

➤ Both instances might be configured to use the same communications port; combine instances or configure them to use different communications ports.

You cannot initialize a modem in the MS Mail (PC) Connector MTA:

➤ Check for a problem with the modem script.

➤ Make sure that the modem cable supports Request To Send (RTS) or Clear To Send (CTS) flow control.

You cannot send or receive mail through the MS Mail Connector:

➤ Make sure the MS Mail Connector Interchange service has been started.

➤ Make sure the MS Mail Connector MTA service has been started.

➤ A custom MS Mail (PC) Connector MTA called PCMTA Performance Monitor is created at installation for performance monitoring, which might be interfering with the MS Mail Connector MTA; stop the PCMTA Performance Monitor service in the Services control panel.

➤ Make sure the address space for the MS Mail Connector is configured properly.

➤ Make sure you have permission for the postoffice shares or volumes; consult the MS Mail system administrator.

➤ Check that the correct network protocol is installed on Exchange Server.

➤ Check for network connectivity to MS Mail postoffices.

➤ Check that all connector postoffice directories exist and that their contents are intact.

➤ Check that all target postoffice directories exist and that their contents are intact.

➤ The MS Mail (AppleTalk) Connector MTA might be spawning a 16-bit application; comment out the nw16 line in the Autoexec.nt file to disable the 16-bit NetWare redirector.

➤ Check for a message routing or connector problem.

Mail sent to the MS Mail (PC) system arrives without OLE attachments:

➤ The MS Mail Connector Interchange might have been configured improperly; try selecting the Maximize MS Mail (PC) Compatibility check box in the Interchange property page.

Files sent from the Macintosh arrive without an extension:

➤ Edit the Mappings.txt file to map the file's creator and type to an extension.

Problems With The X.400 Connector

The Exchange Server MTA cannot connect to the X.400 MTA:

➤ Make sure that the MTA name and password are correct and that they match the name and password used in the configuration of the connector.

➤ Make sure that each MTA is using a common transport stack.

➤ Check for a problem with the network connection.

You cannot send or receive mail through the *X.400 Connector:*

➤ Because configuration of the X.400 connection depends on the system you are connecting to and the method you use for connecting, it is very easy to make configuration mistakes, which is a common cause of problems with sending mail through the connector; double-click the configuration carefully to make sure it is correct.

➤ Make sure the address space for the connector is defined correctly.

➤ Make sure that custom recipients on the X.400 system have the correct email addresses in Exchange Server.

Messaging fails when changing the MTA conformance:

➤ Make sure that the MTA conformance option on the X.400 Connector's Advanced property page matches the conformance used by the X.400 system at the other end of the connection.

➤ Restart all services on both servers after making any changes.

Messages sent across the X.400 backbone lose RTF:

➤ The Exchange Server MTA is not configured to pass Transport-Neutral Encapsulation Format (TNEF) information; change the MTA configuration in the X.400 Connector's General property page.

Unwanted binary attachments are being sent to the X.400 MTA:

➤ The Exchange Server MTA is configured to pass TNEF information; change the MTA configuration in the X.400 Connector's General property page.

Problems With Using Public Folders

You cannot access a *public folder* or the public folder is not visible in the *public folder hierarchy:*

➤ Make sure you have permission to access the folder.

➤ The connection to the server might have been lost; try restarting the client.

➤ Check that the server hosting the public folder is running.

➤ If the public folder is on a server in another site, make sure that either the public folder was replicated to the local site or that *public folder affinity* was set up between the sites.

➤ If the public folder is on a server in another site and public folder affinity was set up, make sure the client's network protocol is able to reach the site.

➤ Check for a problem with public folder replication.

You cannot send mail to a public folder:

➤ The public folder might be hidden from the Address Book; clear the Hide From Address Book check box in the public folder's Advanced property page.

➤ You might not have permission to send mail to the public folder; check the public folder's Delivery Restrictions property page.

➤ The public folder might not have permission to create messages; select Create Items under Client Permissions in the public folder's General property page.

Problems With The Internet News Service

One or more newsgroups was not replicated to the *newsgroup hierarchy:*

➤ Make sure that the connection to the *newsfeed* host is configured properly.

➤ Make sure that the server has sufficient disk space to store all replicated *Usenet newsgroups* (newsgroups use an enormous amount of disk space).

➤ Check for a problem with Internet or network connectivity.

Appendix B
Related Internet Resources

If you're craving additional information about Exchange Server and Outlook, you won't find a larger free resource than the Internet. You'll discover software updates, official information, discussion groups, free utilities and add-ins, commercial products, and the latest news about Exchange Server online—as long as you know where to look. This appendix will point you toward some of the best Exchange Server and Outlook resources on the Net, so start up Internet Explorer to supplement your Exchange Server know-how!

Official Information Sources

Table B.1 shows the official resources for information about Exchange Server and Outlook, provided by Microsoft.

Other Information Sources

A host of companies, user groups, and individuals other than Microsoft have also made information about Outlook and Exchange Server available on the Web. Table B.2 shows information sources that include tips, tricks, white papers, case studies, link collections, reviews, and more.

Table B.1   Official information resources.

Resource	URL
Exchange Server Home Page	http://www.microsoft.com/exchange/default.asp
Exchange Server 5.5 Developer Forum	http://www.microsoft.com/msdn/news/feature/120197/exchange/default.htm
Microsoft Outlook	http://www.microsoft.com/outlook/default.asp
Outlook Developer Forum	http://www.microsoft.com/OutlookDev/

Table B.2   Unofficial information resources.

Resource	URL
Exchange Groupware Collateral	http://ourworld.compuserve.com/homepages/marcse/groupwar.htm
Exchange Main Page	http://www.ncgroup.com/abu/exchange/exchange.htm
Exchange Page	http://www.donadams.com/exchange.htm
Exchange Resource Center	http://www.amrein.com/eworld.htm
Exchange Server FAQ	http://www.i405.com/ExchFAQ/
Introduction to Microsoft Exchange	http://home.istar.ca/~anthony/intro.html
Microsoft Exchange Forum Web Page	http://www.msexchange.org/exchlist/new_default.htm
Microsoft Exchange Solutions Page	http://www.exchangestuff.com/
Microsoft Mail and Exchange	http://www.mysite.com/hall/msmail.htm
Outlook Resource Site	http://www.outlook.useast.com/
Slipstick Systems Exchange Center	http://www.slipstick.com/exchange/

Discussion Groups

Feel like talking to some other Exchange Server or Outlook users to get help with a problem or find out how they're creating business solutions? Try the Usenet newsgroups and mailing lists in Table B.3.

Table B.3   Discussion resources.

Resource	URL
Advanced Exchange Administrators Mailing List	listserv@sice.oas.org
MSExchange Mailing List	msexchange-request@insite.co.uk
MS-EXCHANGE-L Mailing List	MANAGER@LISTS.LANSOFT.COM
Exchange Administration Newsgroup	microsoft.public.exchange.admin
Exchange Applications Newsgroup	microsoft.public.exchange.applications
Exchange Clients Newsgroup	microsoft.public.exchange.clients
Exchange Connectivity Newsgroup	microsoft.public.exchange.connectivity
Exchange General Newsgroup	microsoft.public.exchange.misc
Exchange Setup Newsgroup	microsoft.public.exchange.setup
Outlook 97 Newsgroup	microsoft.public.outlook97

Continued

Table B.3   Discussion resources (Continued).

Resource	URL
Outlook 97 Add-ins Newsgroup	microsoft.public.outlook97.addin_utility
Outlook 97 Forms and Application Development Newsgroup	microsoft.public.outlook97.program_forms
Outlook 97 Installation Newsgroup	microsoft.public.outlook97.installation
Outlook 97 Usage Newsgroup	microsoft.public.outlook97.usage

Freeware And Shareware

When you're looking for ways to enhance Exchange Server and Outlook, there is no better source for free and almost-free stuff than the Web. The sites shown in Table B.4 provide freeware and shareware utilities, add-ins, sample applications, demos, and more.

Commercial Products

Looking to spend some more money on your Exchange Server system? You'll find commercial software and hardware products at the sites shown in Table B.5.

Table B.4   Software resources.

Resource	URL
Cool Add-ins for Microsoft Exchange and Outlook	http://www.slipstick.com/exchange/add-ins.htm
DataEnter's Utilities for Microsoft Mail and Exchange	http://www.dataenter.co.at/
Exchange Templates	http://www.nsoftware.com/et.htm
Microsoft Exchange Application Farm	http://backoffice.microsoft.com/downtrial/moreinfo/appfarm.asp
Optimize Your Outlook	http://www.microsoft.com/Outlook/Optimize/
Outlook Enhancements Library	http://www.microsoft.com/outlook/outenharch.asp
Widgets for Microsoft Exchange and Outlook	http://www.angrygraycat.com/goetter/widgets.htm

Table B.5   Commercial product resources.

Resource	URL
ActivExchange	http://www.ActivExchange.com/home.html
Nemx Software	http://www.nemx.com/
Outlook Third-party Add-ons	http://www.microsoft.com/Outlook/documents/thirdparty_addons.htm
Third-party Solutions for Microsoft Exchange	http://www.microsoft.com/exchange/partners/default.asp

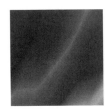

Index

D

E

F

M

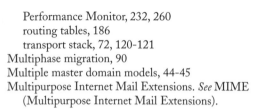

P-Q

T

Task form, 371
TaskPad, 21
Tasks management with Delegate Access, 324
Tasks module, 21-22, 297, 310-315
   assignment progress tracking, 314-315
   Send Status Report option, 311
   task assignments, 312-314
TCP/IP (Transport Control Protocol/Internet Protocol), 41, 71, 416
Team Manager 97, 31
   integrating task list with Outlook 97 tasks, 329-332
   task progress tracking in Outlook 97, 332-333
   Task view, 333
   workgroup tool, 329-330
TeamTalk, 503
Temporary key, 173-174
Thrashing, 269
ThunderBYTE Anti-Virus, 487-488
Tombstones, 100
Tools
   Administrator, 4-6
   Backup program, 5
   Event Viewer, 5
   Field Chooser, 375
   Folder Assistant, 360-362
   Form Manager, 388
   Forms Administrator, 386
   Forms Designer, 15, 23, 30, 371
   Internet News Service, 445-447
   Load Simulator, 59
   Meeting Planner, 315-318
   Migration Wizard, 89
   Performance Monitor, 5
   Performance Optimizer, 5-7, 78-79
   Team Manager, 329-330
Top-level public folders, 337-338
TopicNEWSCAST, 492-493
Topology
   checklist, 52
   customizable, 270
Total available bandwidth, 39
TP0/x.25 connections, 71
TP4 connections, 71
Traffic patterns, 80
Transaction log files, 78, 242-243, 260
Transport Control Protocol/Internet Protocol. See TCP/IP (Transport Control Protocol/Internet Protocol).
Trust relationships, 43-45

U

Uninterruptible power supplies. See UPS (Uninterruptible power supplies).
Universal Inbox, 12, 20
   AutoPreview feature, 20
   Message Flag feature, 20
   Message Recall feature, 20
   message tracking feature, 20
   voting feature, 20
Universal Inbox module, 297
Unsecured message queues, 188
UPS (uninterruptible power supplies), 85
Usenet newsgroups, 13, 32, 443-444
   host connection setup, 453
   message size limitations, 450-451
   newsfeed subscriptions, 447
User actions, 59
User groups, 55, 94-96. See also Mailboxes.
   assigning to servers, 57
   creating, 34
   group scheduling, 9-10
   groupware, 10
   instant groupware, 32
   logon authentication, 43
   needs assessments, 33-35
   remote, 80
   server limits for, 59
User interface, 9
   Administrator program, 177-178
   platform independence of, 9

V

VBScript (Visual Basic Scripting Edition), 383, 504
View types, 298
Views
   Address Book views feature, 395-396
   By Conversation Topic, 364
   column additions, 348-349
   creating for public folder, 347-348
   filters for, 351-352
   public folder, 343
   row additions, 348-349
   sorting items in, 350
   testing, 353-354
Virtual memory, 269
Virtual Private Networks, 416
Virus protection
   AntiVirus for Internet Email Gateways, 486-487